THE NEW INSTITUTIONAL ECONOMICS AND THIRD WORLD DEVELOPMENT

T   ly of
th   the
si   tical
a   lop-
m

b   NIE
cl   Two
a   ates
a   s on
es   ent,
th   with
ra   vide

pl   itive
b   s on
ec   s of
st   t its

ec   ics,
th   l to
ti   oar-

J   ent
St   nce
(L   and
Sc   atin
A   sti-
tu

THE NEW INSTITUTIONAL ECONOMICS AND THIRD WORLD DEVELOPMENT

Edited by John Harriss, Janet Hunter and Colin M. Lewis

London and New York

First published 1995
by Routledge
11 New Fetter Lane, London EC4P 4EE

Simultaneously published in the USA and Canada
by Routledge
29 West 35th Street, New York, NY 10001

First published in paperback 1997

Typeset in Garamond by Michael Mepham, Frome, Somerset
Printed and bound in Great Britain by
T.J. International Ltd, Padstow, Cornwall

British Library Cataloguing in Publication Data
A catalogue record for this book is available
from the British Library

Library of Congress Cataloguing in Publication Data
The new institutional economics and Third World
development/edited by John Harriss, Janet Hunter
and Colin M. Lewis.
p. cm.
Includes bibliographical references and index.
1. Institutional economics. 2. Economic development. 3.
Developing countries–Economic policy. I. Harriss, John. II
Hunter, Janet. III. Lewis, Colin M. HB99. 5.N493 1995
338.9′009172′4–dc20
95–1523

ISBN 0–415–15791–9

CONTENTS

CONTENTS

ILLUSTRATIONS

FIGURES

TABLES

CONTRIBUTORS

Jeremy Adelman is Associate Professor in the Department of History, Princeton University.

Beatriz Armendariz de Aghion lectures in Economics at the London School of Economics and Political Science, University of London.

Robert H. Bates is Professor in the Department of Government at Harvard University.

Anne Booth is Professor in the Department of Economics, School of Oriental and African Studies, University of London.

E.A. Brett is Programme Director in the Development Studies Institute, London School of Economics and Political Science.

W.G. Clarence-Smith is Reader in the Department of History, School of Oriental and African Studies.

Francisco Ferreira works for the World Bank, Washington, DC.

Robert G. Greenhill is Principal Lecturer in the Department of Business Studies at the Guildhall University of London.

E. Gyimah-Boadi teaches in the Department of Political and Administration Studies, University of Swaziland.

Stephen Haber is Professor in the Department of History at Stanford University.

John Harriss is Senior Lecturer in Anthropology in the Development Studies Institute, London School of Economics and Political Science.

CONTRIBUTORS

Barbara Harriss-White is based at the International Development Centre of the University of Oxford.

Heba Handoussa is Professor in the Department of Economics at The American University of Cairo.

Janet Hunter is Saji Senior Lecturer in Japanese Economic and Social History at the London School of Economics and Political Science.

Mushtaq Khan is Assistant Director of Development Studies in the Department of Land Economy and a Fellow in Economics at Sidney Sussex College, University of Cambridge.

Colin M. Lewis is Senior Lecturer in Latin American Economic History at the London School of Economics and Political Science and Associate Fellow at the Institute of Latin American Studies, University of London.

Ioanna Pepelasis Minoglou teaches Economic History in the Department of International Relations, Panteion University, Athens.

Douglass C. North is Professor in the Department of Economics, Washington University, Saint Louis, and winner of the 1993 Nobel Prize for Economics.

Howard Stein is Professor in the Department of Economics, Roosevelt University, Chicago.

B.R. Tomlinson is Professor in the Department of History, Strathclyde University.

John Toye is Professor and Director at the Institute of Development Studies, University of Sussex.

PREFACE AND ACKNOWLEDGEMENTS

The conference from which this collection originates was organised under the auspices of the Third World Economic History and Development Group and hosted by the Department of Economic History and Institute of Development Studies at the London School of Economics and Political Science in September, 1993. Financial support was obtained from the Overseas Development Administration, the Suntory/Toyota International Centre for Economics and Related Disciplines and the British Academy. Their assistance is gratefully acknowledged.

The conference demonstrated with great clarity the congruence of interest amongst development theorists, policy-makers and historians of economic change. It is to be hoped that this volume reinforces the existence of common interests between those concerned with the present and the past, not just because they may happen to study the same geographical areas but because there are valid topics of intellectual debate and disciplinary approach which are common to both sides. The tone and content of debate at the conference illustrated the benefits to be derived from such an exchange.

The integrity of this volume – and indeed the success of the conference – owes much to the willingness of contributors to engage in a dialogue with each another. A particular debt is owed to Douglass C. North, Robert Bates and John Toye, who presented keynote papers at the conference, for their enthusiasm and encouragement, but we would like to extend our thanks to all those who participated in the event, including those who presented papers not included in this volume. The success of any conference rests on the willingness of all participants to engage in debate. We would also like to thank other staff in the Department of Economic History and the Development Studies Institute who helped with the organisation of the conference and the production of this manuscript.

J.H., J.H., C.M.L.

1

INTRODUCTION
Development and significance of NIE

John Harriss, Janet Hunter and Colin M. Lewis

The importance of the new institutional economics (NIE) has been confirmed by the award of the Nobel Prize for Economics first in 1991 to Ronald Coase, whose seminal papers on 'The Nature of the Firm' (1937) and on 'The Problem of Social Cost' (1960) are widely referred to here, and then in 1993 to Douglass C. North, who contributes the following chapter in this book. The 'new institutionalism' is important for perhaps three reasons above all. First, it is an emerging body of theory which starts out within the frame of neo-classical economics, but offers answers to what have otherwise remained as puzzles in neo-classical theory. One of these puzzles, which, as Toye explains in his chapter, 'acted as a catalyst of the NIE', is the problem of the existence of the firm as an administrative and financial organisation – to which Coase offered an answer in his essay of 1937. So the NIE is important as a major development within the dominant paradigm of modern economics. Second, it is important in the context of economic policy in the 1990s because it has challenged the dominant role ascribed to the market by the orthodoxies of the last ten years or so. Thus, as Bates puts it in his chapter in this book, '[Those] who had emphasised the importance of market failure in development economics find in the new institutionalism new justification for their interventionist beliefs.' However, the NIE does not simply reintroduce the state and revive the sterile confrontation between 'state' and 'market'. Rather – as Toye explains – it shows that neither state nor market is invariably the best way in which to organise the provision of goods and services. Also, it offers 'a set of tools to inform institutional design'. Herein lies much of the importance of the new institutionalism for the study of development. Third, its significance for development studies relates to another factor which underlies the contemporary prominence of NIE. In a period in which 'grand theory' in the social sciences has generally been on the retreat, it claims to offer just such a grand theory of social and economic change – a theory of development in terms of appropriate institutional change (which fosters further economic growth).

The NIE is, moreover, a body of economic theory which ascribes an important role to ideas and ideologies, and one which is accessible to other social scientists, seeming to open up the terrain of genuinely inter- (not just

1

'multi-') disciplinary enquiry. This aspect is reflected in the fact that contributions to this book have been written by political scientists and historians as well as by economists. Among other things, the NIE provides scholars with a means of dealing rather more rigorously with the issue of distinguishing between the real world and individuals' and groups' perceptions of it. The question of 'mental models' plays a prominent part in the historical chapters, and suggests the possibility that the NIE can go a considerable way toward bridging a very real gulf between the perfectly rational actors of neo-classical theory and the often seemingly irrational decisions of economic actors in history – a problem which scholars such as Scott attempted to address through the concept of the moral economy of the peasant (Scott 1976). Mental models, however, offer another perspective on how to deal with market interaction and transaction costs. Phrases such as 'market failure' and 'market imperfections' dominate the study of late-developing economies. They also feature largely in – and are fundamental to – the NIE, given the focus on production externalities, public goods, imperfect information and the free-rider problem. Institutions, for economic historians such as North, are the way in which economies cope with 'market failure'. Thus, by attempting to incorporate the concepts of public/rational choice into economic decision-making, NIE not only tries to suggest something about the relationship between the individual and the collective in rational decision-making, but also appears to offer an explanation as to why the evolutions of individual countries differ from each other. And this, perhaps, is the fundamental dilemma of the scholar of economic change – to find a position on the spectrum which at one end argues that the development of every economy is unique, and at the other argues, like Marx or Rostow, that there is a universality about economic development, from which economies are incapable of deviating.

WHAT IS THE 'NIE' AND WHY IS IT SIGNIFICANT IN MODERN ECONOMICS?

North (Ch. 2, this volume) tells us that NIE

> builds on, modifies, and extends neo-classical theory to permit it to come to grips and deal with an entire range of issues heretofore beyond its ken. What it retains and builds on is the fundamental assumption of scarcity and hence competition – the basis of the choice theoretic approach that underlies micro-economics.

Thus the NIE retains the neo-classical axioms of methodological individualism but rejects certain very restrictive assumptions in the notion of 'the market' that is central to neo-classical economics: namely, the conception of the market:

> as an abstract realm of impersonal economic exchange of homogeneous

goods by means of voluntary transactions on an equal basis between large numbers of autonomous, fully-informed entities with profit-maximising behavioural motivations and able to enter and leave freely.

(Harriss-White, Ch. 6 this volume)

The NIE starts from the reality that information is rarely complete, and that individuals have different ideas (or mental models) of the way in which the world about them works. Transactions thus have costs associated with them which are assumed not to exist in the neo-classical model: these are the costs of finding out what the relevant prices are, of negotiating and of concluding contracts, and then of monitoring and enforcing them. Institutions are broadly defined as means of reducing these information and transaction costs.

North also argues that institutions are formed precisely to reduce uncertainty in human exchange. Institutions – notably property rights in the North view – are thus crucial determinants of the efficiency of markets. He attributes this basic insight to Coase, who argued that the existence of 'real-world' firms' actual administrative organisations – as opposed to the abstraction of 'the firm' as an economic actor in general equilibrium theory – stems from the fact that they allow for the reduction of information and transaction costs. This leads to the recognition, uncomfortable for some economists, that markets are only one type of social device for settling the terms of transactions, and that the performance of markets may be judged against that of other devices. To summmarise, the NIE is a development of neo-classical economics to include the role of transaction costs in exchange and so to take account of institutions as critical constraints on economic performance.

North adds yet another aspect that is of central importance. This is that the NIE modifies the 'rationality postulate' of neo-classical economics which maintains that values are given and constant and that individual economic agents select the most efficient means of maximising rationally chosen ends. North, however, argues here that individuals make choices on the basis of their mental models. Drawing on Boyd and Richerson (1985), North has shown that these are in part culturally derived, differ widely, are not easily changed and give rise not to the one determinate position of general equilibrium theory but potentially to multiple equilibria (North 1990a: 37). As the chapters by Clarence-Smith and Greenhill – on cocoa production and the Brazilian coffee trade respectively – show, mental models can sustain systems that are anything but efficient.

A further perspective on the origins and significance of the NIE is suggested by Bates. He, possibly echoing Toye, who refers to the over-arching concern in classical economics with the problem of the reconciliation of private passions and public interests, maintains that the key argument of the new institutionalism is the claim 'that institutions provide the mechanisms whereby rational individuals can transcend social dilemmas'. By 'social dilemmas' he refers to those kinds of problems which arise when choices made by rational individuals yield outcomes that are socially irrational. This is a real-world problem quite beyond the definitional framework of the abstract world of general equilibrium theory. Bates also alludes to ways in which institutions such as property rights resolve problems of market failure (for example, those arising from production externalities), how non-market institutions resolve problems that undermine the creation or the maintenance of public goods, and how information costs give rise to different types of contracts. For Bates, then, the 'core logic' of the new institutionalism is that 'Rational individuals, confronted with the limitations of individually rational behaviour, create institutions that, by creating new incentives or by imposing new constraints, enable them to transcend these limitations' (Ch. 3, this volume).

WHAT IS 'NEW' ABOUT NIE?

The NIE is 'new' because there is an older school of institutionalism in economics. Rutherford argues that the old institutionalism was largely rooted in North American traditions associated with, amongst others, the work of Thorstein Veblen, John R. Commons, Clarence Wendell and Allan Grunchy. This approach pointed to a dichotomy between business and industry and between institutional and technical aspects of an economy. It sought to analyse societal and organisational constraints on, or reactions to, innovation and the diffusion of new technology. As implied above, questioning assumptions of equilibrium embedded in orthodox theory, the old institutional economics (OIE) maintained that economics systems evolved as a result of adjustments to existing institutions provoked by technical change (Rutherford 1994: 1–3). In his chapter in this book, Stein provides a direct account of the origins of NIE. He shows that older institutionalists like Commons and Veblen 'reject the emphasis on rational-maximising self-seeking behaviour of individuals which is at the heart of both neo-classical economics and new institutionalism'. More controversially, Stein asserts that institutions are less instrumental and should be envisaged more as settled habits of thought common to the generality of man. As indicated, North inclines to these ideas in his chapter when he refers to the enduring qualities of the different mental maps with which individuals confront the world, and argues (problematically for Stein) that the NIE refutes the postulate of instrumental rationality. Although Toye refers in his note 4 to the emphasis in this older school on descriptive 'realism', and is critical of its lack of a theoretical framework, Stein finds more insight in the OIE than the NIE in his critique of structural adjustment policies in Africa. He argues that the latter is flawed because of its 'capture' by neo-classical theory, and that this '... limits its understanding of how capitalism operates and by implication how to design institutions to build markets in African countries'. Stein is critical of the NIE focus on firms as transaction-costs minimisers, and the failure to provide an adequate explanation of firm-level innovation. On the other hand, he argues that a differentiation between types of capitalism based on the organisation of firms, in part founded on an attempt to take account of response to innovation, constitutes the strength of the OIE. This, of course, may be disputed and it remains unclear whether the OIE offers a convincing theoretical explanation for the occurrence of innovation. Moreover, as manifest in the implicit tension between chapters by Handoussa and Stein in this volume, the specifics of the links between NIE and OIE are a subject of continuing debate.

In sum, the OIE may be presented as descriptive, holistic and behaviourist and the NIE as formalist and reductionist. In ideological terms, the former can be depicted as collectivist and lacking technical rigour, the latter as anti-interventionist and excessively devoted to highly mathematical rational choice modelling. Nevertheless, institutionalists – old and new – are concerned with the determinants of change over time. In neo-Schumpeterian fashion, NIE presents change as evolutionary while attaching greater importance to the role of the individual, thereby acknowledging a larger debt to classical economics. This accounts for its emphasis on legal systems, property rights and organisations. Hence, too, the importance attached to public choice theory and the empowerment of the individual agent, and to rent-seeking behaviour and distributive coalitions, processes that reduce or increase transaction costs and positively or adversely affect income distribution and therefore impact on economic efficiency. Thus, as indicated above, whereas classical theory seeks to analyse an economy at a particular moment and takes little cognizance of peculiarities of time and place, institutionalists examine process and seek to explain why some economies have advanced and others have not. This is an aspect of the approach that has always commended institutionalism to historians. Moreover, it is an explicit incorporation of the political and the social into analyses of the formation of institutions that has generated interest in institutional economics amongst social scientists. These characteristics, given the multi-disciplinarity of a large part of the existing literature, also point to the relevance of NIE for future research on Third World development.

THIRD WORLD DEVELOPMENT

Proponents of both OIE and NIE have drawn on the development experience of areas of the Third World. James Street has attempted to establish parallels between old-school US institutionalism and Latin American structuralism associated with the writing of Raúl Prebisch, approaches which, according to Street, are particularly appropriate to the study of sub-Saharan Africa and Latin America (Street and James 1982). Though the technological process was paramount for old institutionalists, while structuralism centred on the mechanics of exchange, both were concerned with the impact of these conditions on the frameworks within which development occurred. Post-Second World War Africa and Latin America were presented as 'frontier' regions of rapid population growth and physical space, where imported technology would interact with existing cultures to produce growth-oriented institutions. In less optimistic vein, for North Third World countries provide examples of anti-development frameworks. Statist regulation, ill-defined property rights and other constraints restrict rather than stimulate economic activity. These conditions result in rent-seeking and redistribution, not rising productivity. Organisations that operate within Third World institutional frameworks are not inefficient; they are efficient at making a society more unproductive (North 1990a: 9).

Arguably, it is the focus upon the interaction between institutions and organisations in some of the most recent NIE writing that makes the NIE approach especially relevant for students of long-run Third World development. If some exponents of the 'old' institutionalism were particularly exercised by the impact of technical change on institutions (defined as regulatory systems of formal laws, informal conventions and norms of behaviour) and early 'new' institutionalists were primarily interested in the behaviour of organisations (that is, individual agents, groups, firms, businesses, collective bodies and so forth), recent contributors have stressed the inter-dynamics between institutions and organisations. In quite different ways Haber and Khan show how distinct institutional arrangements can shape organisational behaviour and how alternative sets of organisational responses may impact on institutions. Consequently, while it may be argued that to a large extent growth is institutionally path determined, agents being conditioned by prevailing cultural norms and possibly deflected from behaviour that is optimal or maximising, this does not preclude individual organisations acting as agents for institutional change. Similarly, novel productivity-enhancing institutions can emerge almost spontaneously, triggered by minimal individual initiatives, and are not invariably rooted in collective behavioural change. This implies a greater recognition of cultural – institutional – diversity and the prospect of positive institutional change resulting from a range of individual actions, presuming that action to be largely driven by optimising rationality. This points to the need for further research on market formation (or failure) – in particular the creation of a framework for individual maximisation, the role of the state in setting and policing the game rules and the influence of interest groups – organisations – in shaping institutions in the Third World. Two of the chapters in this book examine a particular organisation – the plantation – in terms of the interplay between organisations and institutions. Clarence-Smith demonstrates that the survival of cocoa plantations was largely due to the existence of dominant interests able to exert political influence, rather than to economic rationality in a sector of agriculture where the economics of production might well have dictated sharecropper rather than estate operation. Similarly, in Brazil, planter power ensured that the response to market failure was official action in support of rent-seeking rather than measures 'to improve the working of the markets' (Greenhill). This analysis is extended by Haber in his analysis of regulatory regimes and the provision of industrial finance.

Many chapters in this book illustrate the contribution of NIE to the understanding of development. Booth and Brett offer particular insights into the role of institutions in shaping patterns of economic activity in the long-run in Africa and Asia. They confirm Bates's general argument that the new institutionalism offers ways of understanding the economic significance of features of Third World societies and cultures that market-based reasoning might misunderstand or ignore, for example different forms of contracts, aspects of which are also described in the Toye chapter. The NIE also expands the menu of policy alternatives, offering positive guidelines for policy interventions overlooked by orthodox economists. Here the NIE merges with a wider body of thought, which includes public choice theories, to which Gyimah-Boadi refers in his review of explanations for the success of the Rawlings regime in Ghana. This literature has given rise to a new vein of thinking about the design of institutions and organisations for development. As North writes below, 'We simply don't know how to transform ailing economies into successful ones but some fundamental characteristics of institutions suggest some clues.' The ones which he draws out imply that the panaceas prescribed for the economies of Eastern Europe or Sub-Saharan Africa are unlikely to succeed. The problem of collective action has emerged as a major theme in the growing body of literature on institutional design, notably Wade (1988), Ostrom (1990), and more recently Ostrom *et al.* (1993). The last pays particular attention to the design of institutions 'that motivate all actors in infrastructure development to keep transformation, coordination, and information costs down' (Ostrom *et al.* 1993: 220). Nevertheless, as Beatriz Armendariz and Francisco Ferreira argue, 'institutions may ... adapt sluggishly', a process which in turn constrains the crisis-response capacity of organisations.

Yet it is possible, while arguing forcefully for the value of institutional analysis, to point to some problems with NIE as a means of analysing the micro-foundations of economies. Harriss-White demonstrates that the NIE is a relatively blunt instrument for the empirical analysis of 'real institutionalised markets' (as opposed to the theoretical abstraction of neo-classical theory). By comparison with other approaches to empirical analysis she concludes, with Khan, that NIE suffers from problems both with theoretical consistency and with the derivation of an empirical methodology. The former include the tendency of NIE, also considered by Toye and by Bates, to tautology; 'existing institutions minimise transaction costs because transaction cost minimisation is their function'. More than one of the chapters in this volume conclude that some of the propositions derived from the NIE approach to the analysis of markets, including property rights, are too indeterminate to bear empirical investigation, and express concern that insufficient effort has been put into the actual measurement of transaction costs.

While the use of the conventional de-institutionalised conception of 'the market' as a basis for policy advocacy can result in unintended outcomes, it is also important, as Bates argues, to be aware of the ways in which NIE approaches may provide misleading or biased analyses for policy purposes. Bates takes as an example the case which, under the NIE approach, can be made for the benefits of marketing boards in Africa. However, as he points out, policy advocacy based on these arguments alone would reflect only a partial view – one which ignores the costs of the boards – and so would promote a systematic bias. The NIE does not cost out alternative options, and Bates concludes that the proper role of the new institutionalism might be to provide diagnoses rather than to prescribe cures. This view is generally supported throughout the book.

INSTITUTIONS AND THE STATE IN HISTORY

From the perspective of an economic historian, commented North (1981), the neo-classical formulation of economic activity appears to beg all the interesting questions. 'The world with which it is concerned is a frictionless one in which institutions do not exist and all change occurs through perfectly operating markets. In short, the costs of acquiring information, uncertainty and transaction costs do not exist (North 1981: 5). An attempt to incorporate these elements of friction into what remains a neo-classical based model is what lies behind the new institutional economics. As indicated above, even those who question its general value would accept that this makes the NIE particularly relevant to the study of developing economies, where non-market institutions and 'market failure' have been of particular importance.

In some respects NIE would seem to historians evidence that economists are at long last 'discovering' what historians have always known: namely that institutions play a significant role in the growth and change of economies. Those who study economic change in history have devoted much of their attention to the features highlighted by NIE, such as the role of the state, disparities between perceptions and actuality and the significance of, for example, transaction costs and property rights. Yet as Adelman observes in his chapter, public choice theorists assume that 'states exist to defend and uphold property rights' but rarely address the issue of how rules become encoded. States matter and can effect quite dramatic institutional changes as Booth, Haber, Khan and, indeed, Adelman indicate.

This is not to say, however, that the NIE is superfluous as far as economic historians are concerned. First, the value of economic and other theories to the historian of economic change is not as a series of models to which an economy may be expected to conform, but rather as a heuristic device, a means of suggesting what questions may be usefully asked of historical data, and of helping historians to make sense of the huge amount of disparate and often unreliable qualitative and quantitative data with which they are confronted. To that extent NIE is not, at least not yet, a new theory of economic history. Rather, as several chapters in this book demonstrate, it is a device that assists historians to reframe the questions they can ask of their material. It is not exclusive; it can usefully be employed in conjunction with other theories and concepts to sort information. However, insofar as it articulates in a more formal manner some of the concepts already familiar to economic historians, particularly those of late developing countries – for example the role of the state, already identified with the work of Alexander Gerschenkron on Russia (e.g. 1962) – it enhances the range of tools which can be applied with rigour to the study of economic change in the past.

There is a second reason why the NIE may be of particular value to historians. As a group of scholars concerned with economic change over time, economic historians are interested in what is essentially a dynamic process. Consequently, like other social scientists, historians have often found the economic theories associated with general equilibrium models and the neo-classical school less than helpful in understanding why economies change and develop as they do. For that reason in particular, historians of late developing or Third World countries, many of whose concerns lie in the presence or absence of a transformation from an agrarian to an industrial economy, have turned to the more dynamic concepts of development economics. The new institutional economics is a body of ideas which is essentially dynamic, or at least seeks to introduce an element of dynamism into the static stereotype of neo-classical theory. It would seem, therefore, to be particularly suited to the interests of those who study economies which have yet to reach the level of full industrialisation so often depicted as the ultimate goal, whether it is – as Ioanna Pepelasis Minoglou shows – nineteenth-century Greece, or sixteenth-century Western Europe, or twentieth-century Africa.

The more historically oriented papers in this book demonstrate both of these axioms, and between them they take up in greater detail some of the concepts introduced by North in his first chapter as integral to the whole NIE approach. The importance of these ideas has long been recognised by historians, but has not always resulted in their formal integration into any body of theory or concrete hypothesis. The one exception, perhaps, is consideration of the role of the state. For Gerschenkron, the state in late developing countries had a crucial role to play in compensating for the lack of prerequisites for industrialisation – it was what could enable such economies to 'catch up'. However, the mechanisms whereby the state could intervene were acknowledged to be diverse, and much of the formality of Gerschenkron's 'theory of relative backwardness' has been bestowed on his writings by subsequent scholars. Notwithstanding the accuracy or otherwise of his historical conclusions, his ideas have remained a potent source of inspiration up to the present (Sylla and Toniolo 1991). Under the NIE, the state has a particular importance in enacting or enforcing the rules of the game, the institutional framework in North's sense. The significance of this role is shown in Booth's chapter on the role of the state in Indonesian development, and, as Handoussa demonstrates, in the case of Egyptian economic growth. It becomes clear that, as Khan states, according to the circumstances, there are both pros and cons to the extent of intervention. Clarence-Smith is highly critical of official intervention which, often justified in terms of macroeconomic efficiency and welfare, resulted in support schemes skewed in favour of socially and politically important planters. Moreover, the state is invariably a reflection of the hold over power within a society, representative of the dominant economic interest groups. The institutions of a society – formal and informal – are created to serve those in possession of bargaining power, and the effort to uphold these institutions, even in the face of changes in transaction costs, information flows and their increasing disutility, leads to the formation of dominant interest groups. This is shown to be found not just in Indonesia, but in the case of China and India, where, as Tomlinson shows, the weak and often corrupted nature of market stimuli promoted the strength of social and political mechanisms for controlling land and the surplus, while these very mechanisms reinforced the absence of public institutions which might otherwise have filled this vacuum. This leads, in Bates's view, to the ultimate primacy of political activity and the need to ask whether NIE is less an economic theory than a theory of political economy. Adelman would probably agree. In the hurly burly of a free political market such as mid-nineteenth-century Argentina, no single agent wielded sufficient authority to impose a given set of rules. Of necessity, analyses of institution-building have to deal with the exercise of political power and manipulation of economic advantage.

Clearly, there are states and states. It is, therefore, valid to ask what the NIE has contributed to the classification of states old and new. One suggestion may be that institutional economics offers explanatory insights into the functioning of the predatory state, which features prominently in the literature on the Third World, and the 'weak' or 'lethargic' state featured in several chapters in this collection. A number of contributors – for example, Booth, Greenhill, Handoussa, Pepelasis Minoglou and Tomlinson – hint at path-dependent development associated with quite distinct institutions.

A 'GRAND THEORY' OF DEVELOPMENT

The broader claims of NIE, resting on the view that the past can only be made intelligible as a story of institutional evolution (North 1990a: vii), are that it provides a basis on which to develop 'a dynamic theory of social change' (North, Ch. 2, this volume). Economic development depends upon the existence of a favourable institutional environment. How does an 'appropriate' pattern of institutions and of institutional change come about?

The neo-classical answer, as Toye records, is based on implicit appeal to the biological analogy of natural selection: just as competition, working through the market, induces efficient outcomes in a static framework, the result over time will be an institutional framework conducive to growth and development. Only 'fit' institutions will survive. An instance of this kind of reasoning, applied to institutional innovation in the context of agricultural economies, is found in the work of Ruttan and Hayami (1984). But, as Toye maintains, 'the problem with the biological analogy is not that people cannot choose between institutions, but exactly the opposite one – that they can' and as a result undesirable institutions survive over long periods. A case in point may be that of the social institutions of rural Bengal explored by Boyce (1987), where an 'appropriate' path of institutional change has apparently not been induced in the way suggested by Ruttan and Hayami (1984).

It would appear from North's account in this book, that the NIE approach to the grand theory of institutional development ends up by emphasising the constraints upon change. It follows from the above analogy that 'once an economy is on an "inefficient" path that produces stagnation it can persist (and historically has persisted) because of the nature of path dependence' and because '... the individuals and organisations with bargaining power as a result of the institutional framework have a crucial stake in perpetuating the system'. Given its role in specifying and enforcing formal rules, the nature of the state is bound to play a central role in determining the path of development. So, for North, 'a dynamic model of economic change entails as an integral part of that model analysis of the polity'.

The short account of North's approach to the analysis of change over time which then follows is limited. He suggests little more than that change is a complex process which comes about as a consequence of 'choices that individuals and entrepreneurs of organisations are making every day' – subject to limited information, diverse mental models, and the influence of historically deeply rooted norms and conventions. This account seems amply to justify Toye's comment that the NIE, in spite of the aims of some of its exponents, is much less successful at a macro-theoretic level:

> The main weakness of the NIE as a grand theory of socio-economic development is that it is empty. As a critique of other theories which altogether ignore the role of institutions ... it is welcome. But when it comes to new general insights about how [institutional] determination works, the theory adds nothing to what we already have.

Nevertheless, North's account demonstrates the need to bring 'history' back into the explanation. But, again according to Toye, this is only the first step as 'history' means many different things. There are many possible historiographies.

NIE: A CRITICAL EVALUATION

The contributions to this book show that the 'discovery' of transaction costs and the demonstration of their significance in NIE is a major contribution, and likely to be of enduring significance in the social sciences. This has resolved some puzzles in neo-classical theory, has opened up new avenues of enquiry and has brought about a shift in the terms of the discourse about development. Accordingly, the NIE has encouraged renewed interest in the way in which economies actually work, but in a way that is theoretically much more rigorous than in the older tradition of institutionalism within economics. However, this book also highlights the limitations of the NIE. The power of the new institutionalism lies in the capacity to illuminate the micro-foundations of economies and the dynamics of institutions and organisations. As 'grand theory' its claims at present far out-run its achievements. Harriss-White correctly shows that even for the analysis of the micro-foundations of economies, the perspectives of the NIE essentially complement insights derived from other approaches; they do not constitute a comprehensive, new framework. Moreover, as Stein argues, for all its theoretical limitations the older institutionalism still offers perspectives, and raises questions, that illuminate contemporary problems. The significance of the OIE emphasis on understanding diversity in the organisation of firms, and differences in the way in which capitalism works in distinct contexts, is recognised in the emerging literature on East Asian industrial organisation.

Toye, Bates and some other contributors refer to the limitations which inhere in the NIE to tendencies to tautological, functionalist reasoning. The lack of effort which has been made thus far to measure transaction costs, the failure to 'cost out' alternative institutional solutions – and the practical difficulties of doing so – exacerbate this weakness. Bates points out that the theory does not discriminate among an infinite number of possible outcomes (as people create institutions); and both he and Khan show that the same economic institutions can have different consequences in distinct contexts. Bates's example is that of the very different outcomes of the establishment of coffee marketing boards in Kenya and Tanzania, Khan's of industrial policy in South Korea and Pakistan. These examples help to introduce the crucial argument developed independently by both authors: '... the necessity of embedding the new institutionalism within the study of politics' (Bates). The reasons for the different outcomes have to do with the political context, or what Khan refers to as 'the political settlement', meaning the balance of power between the classes and groups affected by an institution. This balance crucially influences the net effects of an institution. Thus, in the case discussed by Bates, the Kenya Coffee Marketing Board 'lay within a political setting that created incentives for its officials to employ their powers in ways that would promote the efficient operations of [the] industry', which was not the case in Tanzania. Similarly, Khan shows that the nature of the political settlement significantly influences the 'transition costs' – the costs involved in institutional change. In the end both Bates and Khan bring out the unresolved dilemma in NIE, which centres around the determinants of institutional forms. The new institutional economists suggest that, for example, the type of property rights which will prevail, depends upon the costs of transacting. As Bates points out in his discussion of Coase's Theorem there is, however, 'a second possible answer:

that it would depend upon the structure of politics'. The NIE emphasises choices, whereas the reality is often that outcomes are determined by constraints which have to do with the political settlement. In short, while the NIE has brought about an important shift in the discourse of development, it has to be encompassed within a more thoroughly *political* economy.

Thus, as several of the chapters in this volume suggest, not only is NIE immensely diverse and separate, it is in many ways flawed. At the macro-level many of the institutional operations on which the new framework focuses – for example, the role of the state – cannot be measured. Possibly, the main role of the NIE may be in setting future agendas for economic historians and students of development and in providing them with an additional tool to analyse the institutional features of economies. This would be an important contribution to the methodology. The approach has a further importance, however, which lies in Toye's observation that NIE can serve as a 'bridge' to mathematical neo-classicists from whom the path of economic historians and development specialists has shown a sustained tendency to diverge over recent years. If NIE seems to show that economists are rediscovering institutions, it is a valuable bridge indeed.

This book, therefore, offers a nuanced view of NIE. It concludes that the NIE is a significant theoretical contribution to development studies and confirms the vitality of the substantive study of history for analysts and policy-makers concerned with institutional change in the Third World. It is not, however, the philospher's stone.

Part I

NIE: HISTORY, POLITICS AND DEVELOPMENT

2

THE NEW INSTITUTIONAL ECONOMICS AND THIRD WORLD DEVELOPMENT

Douglass C. North

This chapter is intended briefly to summarise the essential characteristics of the new institutional economics, to describe how it differs from neo-classical theory, and then to apply its analytical framework to problems of development.

INSTITUTIONS AND ECONOMIC THEORY

The new institutional economics is an attempt to incorporate a theory of institutions into economics.[1] However, in contrast to the many earlier attempts to overturn or replace neo-classical theory, the new institutional economics builds on, modifies and extends neo-classical theory to permit it to come to grips and deal with an entire range of issues heretofore beyond its ken. What it retains and builds on is the fundamental assumption of scarcity and hence competition – the basis of the choice theoretic approach that underlies micro-economics. What it abandons is instrumental rationality – the assumption of neo-classical economics that has made it an institution-free theory.

Herbert Simon has accurately summarised the implications of this neo-classical assumption as follows. If values are accepted as given and constant, if an objective description of the world as it really is can be postulated, and if it is assumed that the decision-maker's computational powers are unlimited, then two important consequences follow. First, it is not necessary to distinguish between the real world and the decision-maker's perception of it: he or she perceives the world as it really is. Second, it is possible to predict the choices that will be made by a rational decision-maker entirely from a knowledge of the real world and without a knowledge of the decision-maker's perceptions or modes of calculation (of course, his or her utility function must be known) (Simon 1986: 210). In a world of instrumental rationality institutions are unnecessary; ideas and ideologies don't matter: and efficient markets – both economic and political – characterise economies.

In fact, information is incomplete and there is limited mental capacity by which to process information. Human beings, in consequence, impose

17

constraints on human interaction in order to structure exchange. There is no implication that the consequent institutions are efficient. In such a world ideas and ideologies play a major role in choices and transaction costs result in imperfect markets.

The place to begin a theory of institutions, therefore, is with a modification of the instrumental rationality assumption. Although a complete under-standing of how the mind processes information has not yet been achieved, cognitive science has made impressive strides in recent years. Individuals possess mental models to interpret the world around them. These are in part culturally derived – that is, produced by the intergenerational transfer of knowledge, values and norms which vary radically among different ethnic groups and societies. In part they are acquired through experience which is 'local' to the particular environment and therefore also varies widely with different environments. Consequently there is immense variation in mental models, and as a result different perceptions of the world and the way it 'works'. And even the formal learning that individuals acquire frequently consists of conflicting models with which to interpret the world. Individuals make choices on the basis of their mental models. Individuals do learn, and changes in mental models stem from outcomes inconsistent with expectations; but in Frank Hahn's words 'there is a continuum of theories that agents can hold and act upon without ever encountering events which lead them to change their theories' (Hahn 1987: 324). In consequence there is not one determinate equilibrium which will obtain; but multiple equilibria can occur.

The incomplete information and limited mental capacity by which to process information determines the cost of transacting which underlies the formation of institutions. At issue is not only the rationality postulate but the specific characteristics of transacting that prevent the actors from achieving the joint maximisation result of the zero transaction cost model. The costs of transacting arise because information is costly and asymmetrically held by the parties to exchange. The costs of measuring the multiple valuable dimensions of the goods or services exchanged or of the performance of agents, and the costs of enforcing agreements determine transaction costs.[2]

Institutions are formed to reduce uncertainty in human exchange. Together with the technology employed they determine the costs of transacting (and producing). It was Ronald Coase (1937, 1960) who made the crucial connection between institutions, transaction costs and neo-classical theory; a connection which even now has not been completely understood by the economics profession. Baldly stated, the neo-classical result of efficient markets only obtains when it is costless to transact. When it is costly to transact, institutions matter. And because a large part of national income is devoted to transacting, institutions and specifically property rights are crucial determinants of the efficiency of markets.[3] Coase was (and still is) concerned with the firm and resource allocation in the modern market economy; but his insight is the key to unravelling the tangled skein of the performance of economies over time, which is our primary concern here.

How does this new institutional approach fit in with neo-classical theory? It begins with the scarcity hence competition postulate; it views economics as a theory of choice subject to constraints; it employs price theory as an essential part of the analysis of institutions; and it sees changes in relative prices as a major force inducing change in institutions.

How does this approach modify or extend neo-classical theory? In addition to modifying the rationality postulate, it adds institutions as a critical constraint and analyses the role of transaction costs as the connection between institutions and costs of production. It extends economic theory by incorporating ideas and ideologies into the analysis, modelling the political process as a critical factor in the performance of economies, as the source of the diverse performance of economies, and as the explanation for 'inefficient' markets.

This last point – inefficient markets – requires further explanation because it highlights the major contribution that the new institutional economics can make to economics, economic history and economic development. Coase began his 1960 essay by arguing that when it is costless to transact, the efficient neo-classical competitive solution obtains. It does so because the competitive structure of efficient markets leads the parties to arrive costlessly at the solution that maximises aggregate income regardless of the institutional arrangements. Now to the extent that these conditions are mimicked in the real world, they are mimicked because competition is strong enough via arbitrage and efficient information feedback to approximate the Coase zero transaction cost conditions and the parties can realise the gains from trade inherent in the neo-classical argument.

But the informational and institutional requirements necessary to achieve that result are stringent. Players must not only have objectives but know the correct way to achieve them. But how do the players know the correct way to achieve their objectives? The instrumental rationality answer is that even though the actors may initially have diverse and erroneous models, the informational feedback process and arbitraging actors will correct initially incorrect models, punish deviant behaviour and lead surviving players to the correct models.

An even more stringent implicit requirement of the discipline-of-the-competitive-market model is that when there are significant transaction costs, the consequent institutions of the market will be designed to induce the actors to acquire the essential information that will lead them to correct models. The implication is not only that institutions are designed to achieve efficient outcomes, but that they can be ignored in economic analysis because they play no independent role in economic performance.

But these are stringent requirements that are realised only very exceptionally. Individuals typically act on incomplete information and with subjectively derived models that are frequently erroneous; the information feedback is typically insufficient to correct these subjective models. Institutions are not necessarily or even usually created to be socially efficient; rather they, or at least the formal rules, are created to serve the interests of those with the bargaining power to create new rules. In a zero transaction cost world, bargaining strength does not affect the efficiency of outcomes; but in a world of positive transaction costs it does – and it thus shapes the direction of long-run economic change.

It is exceptional to find economic markets that approximate the conditions necessary for efficiency. It is impossible to find political markets that do (North 1990b). Because it is the polity that defines and enforces property rights, it is not surprising that efficient economic markets are exceptional. Moreover, once an economy is on an 'inefficient' path that produces stagnation it can persist (and historically has persisted) because of the nature of path dependence.

Institutional path dependence exists because of the network externalities, economies of scope and complementarities that exist with a given institutional matrix. In everyday language the individuals and organisations with bargaining power as a result of the institutional framework have a crucial stake in perpetuating the system. Paths do get reversed (witness Argentina – from growth to stagnation in the past half century; or Spain – the reverse since the 1950s). But reversal is a difficult process about which we know all too little – as witness the ongoing fumbling efforts at such reversal in Central and Eastern Europe. The reason is that we still know all too little about the dynamics of institutional change and particularly the interplay between economic and political markets. What may be done with this analytical framework?

THE SOCIAL ENVIRONMENT OF ECONOMIC CHANGE

An institutional/cognitive story of long-run economic change begins by examining the changing initial conditions confronting diverse groups of individuals. As tribes evolved in different physical environments they developed different languages and, with different experiences, different mental models to explain the world around them. To the extent that experiences were common to different tribes the mental models provided common explanations. The language and mental models formed the informal constraints that defined the institutional framework of the tribe and were passed down intergenerationally as the customs, taboos, myths that provided the continuity of culture and forms part of the key to path dependence.

With growing specialisation and division of labour the tribes evolved into polities and economies: the diversity of experiences and learning produced increasingly different societies and civilisations with very different degrees of success in solving the fundamental economic problems of scarcity. The reason for differing success is straightforward. The complexity of the environment increased as human beings became increasingly interdependent, and more complex institutional structures were necessary to capture the potential gains from trade. Such evolution required that the society develop institutions that would permit anonymous, impersonal exchange across time and space. But to the extent that 'local experience' had produced diverse mental models and institutions with respect to the gains from such cooperation, the likelihood of creating the necessary institutions to capture the gains from trade of more complex contracting varied.[4] The key to this story is the kind of learning that organisations acquired to survive. If the institutional framework made the highest pay-offs for organisations' piracy, then organisational success and survival dictated that learning would take the form of being better pirates. If on the other hand productivity-raising activities had the highest pay-off, then the economy would grow.

There is no guarantee that the perceived pay-offs will favour the latter rather than the former, and indeed economic history bears abundant testimony to economic growth being the exception. The long evolution of the Western world from the relative backwardness of the tenth century to its growth, pre-eminence, and hegemony by the eighteenth century is striking, not only because of the relative failures in the rest of the world (China and Islamic countries for example), but equally for the diverse degrees of success in the West itself.[5] What went wrong with the failures and, more urgently, why is it so hard to make it right? An explanation entails some analysis of the institutional requirements necessary to capture the productivity implications of modern technology.

The second economic revolution which began in the second half of the nineteenth century was the systematic application of the modern scientific disciplines to technology and more broadly to the economic problems of scarcity.[6] For those economies that could realise their potential the productivity implications have resulted in standards of well-being simply unimagined by prior generations. But to realise the advantages of this technology has entailed a fundamental restructuring of economic activity, and, more than that, of the entire society. The economic restructuring involves realising the productive implications of world-wide specialisation and division of labour. While Chandler (1977) has captured some of the key elements of this transformation for individual firms, the overall costs of coordinating and integrating economies – transaction costs – entail economy-wide restructuring, including the development of a polity that will enact and enforce the rules of the game necessary to such integration.

Why is such a polity so difficult to accomplish? A simple parable derived from game theory highlights the dilemma. Cooperative solutions in game theory are most likely when the play is repeated, when the players have complete information about the other players' past performance, and when there are small numbers of players. To turn that story around, cooperation is difficult to achieve when the play is not repeated or there is an endgame, when the players do not possess information about the other players, and when there are large numbers of players. In those circumstances the gains from defection typically outweigh the gains from cooperation.

The second economic revolution created an economic world characterised by impersonal markets and all the attendant characteristics of the latter game theoretic conditions. To overcome them entails the creation of institutions that so structure the rules and their enforcement as to alter the pay-offs to induce cooperative solutions. This analysis is hardly new (although the terminology may be different). Karl Marx long ago pointed out that the tension between the organisational imperatives of a technology and the existing property rights was a fundamental source of conflict and change. Marx's error was that he thought that it was capitalism that was incompatible with the new technology. In fact it has been the flexibility of the political and economic institutions of the market economies that has enabled them to adjust to realise the productivity implications of the second economic revolution. And, ironically, it has been the inflexibility and rigidities of centrally planned economies that have led to their demise.

But there is still more to the issue of institutional adjustment to the second economic revolution. That adjustment entails a total societal transformation. Impersonal exchange, minute specialisation and division of labour, a radical reduction in information costs, and world-wide interdependence entail a complete transformation of every aspect of societal organisation. Urbanisation, ubiquitous externalities, the insecurity arising from interdependence, and radical alteration of the traditional functions of the most fundamental organisation of all prior societies – the family – have produced and continue to produce immense modern social problems. Again it has been the flexibility of the political and economic institutions of Western economies that have, very imperfectly, provided substitutes for the traditional role of the family: insured against the new insecurities affecting individuals; and dealt with the externalities, environmental as well as social, that accompany this economic transformation.

INSTITUTIONS AND ORGANISATIONS

It is precisely in this economic and social context that the modern problems of economic development must be considered. The fundamental issue can be stated succinctly. Successful development policy entails an understanding of the dynamics of economic change if the policies pursued are to have the desired consequences. And a dynamic model of economic change entails as an integral part of that model analysis of the polity, since it is the polity that specifies and enforces the formal rules.

Such a model has not yet been devised but the structure that is evolving in the new institutional economics, even though incomplete, suggests radically different development policies than those of either traditional development economists or orthodox neo-classical economists. Development economists have typically treated the state as either exogenous or as a benign actor in the development process. Neo-classical economists have implicitly assumed that institutions (economic as well as political) do not matter, and that the static analysis embodied in allocative-efficiency models should be the guide to policy; that is, 'getting the prices right' by eliminating exchange and price controls. In fact the state can never be treated as an exogenous actor in development policy, and getting the prices right only has the desired consequences when agents already have in place a set of property rights and enforcement that will then produce the competitive market conditions.

Before going further it is essential to distinguish clearly institutions from organisations. Institutions are the rules of the game of a society, or, more formally, are the humanly devised constraints that structure human interaction. They are composed of formal rules (statute law, common law, regulations), informal constraints (conventions, norms of behaviour and self-imposed codes of conduct), and the enforcement characteristics of both. Organisations are the players: groups of individuals bound by a common purpose to achieve objectives. They include political bodies (political parties, the senate, a city council, a regulatory agency): economic bodies (firms, trade unions, family farms, cooperatives); social bodies (churches, clubs, athletic associations); and educational bodies (schools, colleges, vocational training centres). These definitions undergird five propositions that define the essential characteristics of institutional change:

1 The continuous interaction of institutions and organisations in the economic setting of scarcity, and hence competition, is the key to institutional change.
2 Competition forces organisations continually to invest in skills and knowledge to survive. The kinds of skills and knowledge individuals and their organisations acquire will shape evolving perceptions about opportunities and hence choices that will incrementally alter institutions.
3 The institutional framework dictates the kinds of skills and knowledge perceived to have the maximum pay-off.
4 Perceptions are derived from the mental constructs of the players.
5 The economies of scope, complementarities and network externalities of an institutional matrix make institutional change overwhelmingly incremental and path dependent.

These propositions may be elaborated further. Economic change is a ubiquitous, ongoing, incremental process that is a consequence of the choices individuals and entrepreneurs of organisations are making every day. While the vast majority of these decisions are routine (Nelson and Winter 1982), some involve altering existing 'contracts' between individuals and organisations. Sometimes that recontracting can be accomplished within the existing structure of property rights and political rules; but sometimes new contracting forms require an alteration in the rules. Usually existing informal norms of

23

behaviour will guide exchanges, but sometime such norms will gradually be modified or wither away. In both instances institutions are gradually being modified. Modifications occur because individuals perceive that they could do better by restructuring exchanges (political or economic). The source of the changed perceptions may be exogenous to the economy – for instance a change in the price or quality of a competitive product in another economy that alters the perceptions of entrepreneurs in the given economy about profitable opportunities. But the fundamental source of change is learning by entrepreneurs of organisations.

While some learning is a result of idle curiosity, the rate of learning will reflect the intensity of competition amongst organisations. Competition is a ubiquitous consequence of scarcity and hence organisations in an economy will engage in learning to survive. But the degree can and does vary. If competition is muted as a result of monopoly power the incentive to learn will be reduced.

The rate of learning determines the speed of economic change, the kind of learning determines the direction of economic change. The kind of learning is a function of the expected pay-offs of different kinds of knowledge, and therefore will reflect the mental models of the players and most immediately at the margin, the incentive structure embodied in the institutional matrix. As noted earlier, if the institutional matrix rewards piracy (or more generally redistributive activities) more than productive activity, then learning will take the form of learning to be better pirates.

Change is typically incremental, reflecting ongoing ubiquitous evolving perceptions of the entrepreneurs of organisations in the context of an institutional matrix that is characterised by network externalities, complementarities and economies of scope among the existing organisations. Moreover since the organisations owe their existence to the institutional matrix, they will be an ongoing interest group to assure the perpetuation of that institutional structure – thus assuring path dependence. Revolutions do occur, however, when organisations with different interests emerge (typically as a result of dissatisfaction with the performance of existing organisations) and the fundamental conflict between organisations over institutional change cannot be mediated within the existing institutional framework.

POLITICAL ECONOMY, RULES AND ADAPTIVE EFFICIENCY

It is one thing to describe the characteristics of economic change; it is something else to prescribe the correct medicine to improve the performance of economies. It simply is not known how to transform ailing economies into successful ones, but some fundamental characteristics of institutions suggest some clues:

24

1 Institutions are made up of formal rules, informal norms and the enforcement characteristics of both, and it is the admixture of rules, norms and enforcement characteristics that determines economic performance. While the formal rules can be changed overnight, the informal norms change only gradually. Since it is the norms that provide the essential 'legitimacy' to any set of formal rules, revolutionary change is never as revolutionary as its supporters desire, and performance will be different than anticipated. More than that, societies that adopt the fomal rules of another society (for example, the adoption by Latin American countries of constitutions similar to the United States of America) will have very different performance characteristics than the original country because both the informal norms and the enforcement characteristics will be different. The implication is that transferring the formal political and economic rules of successful Western market economies to Third World and Eastern European economies is not a sufficient condition for good economic performance. Privatisation is not a panacea for solving poor economic performance.

2 It is polities that shape economic performance because they define and enforce the economic rules of the game. Therefore the heart of development policy must be the creation of polities that will create and enforce efficient property rights. Unfortunately, however, research in the new political economy (the new institutional economics applied to polities) has been largely focused on the USA and other developed countries. While a great deal is known about the characteristics of the polities of Third World countries there is very little theory about such polities.[7] Even less is known about the consequences of radically altering the institutional framework of Central and Eastern European societies. However, the characteristics of institutions described in the foregoing sections of this chapter suggest some implications:

   (a) Political institutions will be stable only if they are supported by organisations with an interest in their perpetuation. Therefore an essential part of political/economic reform is the creation of such organisations.
   (b) It is essential to change both the institutions and the belief systems for successful reform since it is the mental models of the actors that will shape choices.
   (c) Evolving norms of behaviour that will support and legitimise new rules is a lengthy process and in the absence of such reinforcing norms polities will tend to be unstable.
   (d) While economic growth can occur in the short run with autocratic regimes, long-run economic growth entails the development of the rule of law and the protection of civil and political freedoms.
   (e) Informal constraints – norms of behaviour, conventions, and codes of conduct – are a necessary (but not sufficient) condition for good

economic performance. Societies with norms favourable to economic growth can sometimes prosper even with unstable or adverse political rules. The key is the degree to which there is enforcement of the adverse political rules. Little is known about the evolution of belief systems and consequent informal constraints, although religions have clearly been a basic component of belief systems.

3 It is adaptive rather than allocative efficiency which should be the guide to policy. Allocative efficiency is a static concept with a given set of institutions; the key to continuing good economic performance is a flexible institutional matrix that will adjust in the context of evolving technological and demographic changes as well as shocks to the system. It is the creation of a stable polity with complementary norms that is the essential characteristic. Successful political/economic systems have evolved such characteristics over long periods of time. The critical issue is how to create such systems in the short run or, indeed, whether it is even possible to create them in short periods of time. However it is doubtful if the policies that will produce allocative efficiency are always the proper medicine for ailing economies. Efficient policies that are perceived to be inequitable will engender political reactions which can stall or reverse effective reforms.

There is no greater challenge facing today's social scientist than the development of a dynamic theory of social change that will fill in many of the gaps in the foregoing analysis and yield an understanding of adaptive efficiency.

NOTES

1 The first section of this chapter is drawn from the John R. Commons lecture given at the American Economic Association meetings in January 1992 and subsequently published in the *American Economist* (Spring 1992: 3–6) under the title 'Institutions and Economic Theory'.

2 The transaction cost approach is unified only in its agreement on the importance of transaction costs. The approach developed here might most appropriately be termed the University of Washington approach. Oliver Williamson has pioneered a somewhat different approach.

3 Wallis and North (1986) found that 45 per cent of national income was devoted to transacting in 1970.

4 Ronald Heiner (1983) in a pathbreaking article first articulated the connection between uncertainty and institutions, and suggested that institutional development could be arrested using an argument similar to that advanced here.

5 See Jones (1981, 1988), Rosenberg and Birdzell (1986) and North and Thomas (1973) for explanations of this evolution.

6 See North (1981: Ch. 13, 'The Second Economic Revolution') for an elaboration of this argument.

7 Interest in modelling the polities of Third World economies is still in its infancy. Robert Bates (1981, 1983, 1989) has been a pioneer in applying the new political economy to African economies.

3

SOCIAL DILEMMAS AND RATIONAL INDIVIDUALS

An assessment of the new institutionalism

Robert H. Bates

The new institutionalism represents an attempt to build a coherent account of institutions from micro-foundations. It seeks to apply to non-market institutions the same forms of reasoning that neo-classical economics has applied to the analysis of markets. Focusing on the law, property rights, bureaucracies, and other non-market structures, the new institutionalism seeks to demonstrate how rational individuals might employ non-market institutions to secure (in equilibrium) collective levels of welfare that they otherwise might not be able to attain, given their responses to market incentives. When applied to the study of development, the new institutionalism focuses on sources of growth hitherto ignored by market-oriented forms of economic reasoning: those arising from the institutional setting within which economic activity takes place.

By the 1980s neo-classical theories had become the new orthodoxy in the study of economic development. They stressed the central importance of markets and counselled against an activist role for government (Little 1982; Lal 1984). While development specialists made early, critical contributions to the new institutionalism,[1] the approach first conquered the field of economic history[2] before re-entering the field of development. There it has been welcomed as an antidote to the prescriptions flowing from the neo-classical orthodoxy (see, for example, Bates 1989; Klitgaard 1991). An older generation, who had emphasised the importance of market failure in development economics, finds in the new institutionalism new justification for their interventionist beliefs. And a new generation, seeking a middle ground between the champions of the market and the defenders of the state, finds in the new institutionalism a justification for basing development efforts on community action and civic engagement.

The new institutionalism has thus reinvigorated old debates and animated new departures in the field of development. It is therefore important to subject the approach to close scrutiny. This chapter attempts to do so by examining its origins, isolating its core arguments, and assessing their logic and significance for the study of development.

THE ORIGINS

Neo-classical economics seeks to explain collective outcomes in terms of the choices made by rational individuals. Radical individualism constitutes a defining premise for the field. It informs its methodology: market demand, for example, is built up from the choices of individuals who seek to maximise their utility, subject to the constraint of their budgets and in the face of market prices. It also provides its normative core. Because Pareto optimality respects the inviolability of the individual's judgement of his or her own welfare, it constitutes the sole ethical criterion that wins broad support among neo-classical economists.

A crisis of embarrassment

Given the centrality of radical individualism, it was profoundly embarrassing to modern economics that in its models market forces did not rest on the choices of individuals. On the side of demand, households made consumer choices; on the supply side, production decisions were made by firms. Neo-classical models analysed the choices of these entities as if they were made by individuals. But even Milton Friedman's (1953) spirited defence of 'as if' explanations served only to paper over the basic reality: that the social science most profoundly committed to radical individualism rested on 'collective' foundations.

Despite its unconventional assumptions, Gary Becker's (1981) theory of the family therefore won rapid and widespread recognition as a major contribution to neo-classical economics. The reason was obvious: it offered the possibility at last of resting the theory of demand upon the foundations of individual choice. Oliver Williamson (1985) also made notoriously idiosyncratic and unconventional assumptions. His work nonetheless rapidly won recognition as a contribution to knowledge, for it too promoted the completion of the neo-classical programme.[3] Through the work of Williamson and others, economists have begun to build up a theory of the firm, and thus of supply, from the rational choices of individuals.

Embarrassment may not be the mother of invention. But the fundamental embarrassment of neo-classical economics – that of having collectivities where individuals should be – does help to express why the contributions of Williamson, Coase, Becker and others so quickly became established within the discipline, despite what for mainstream economists were important limitations: their tendency to make unconventional assumptions and, in the cases of Coase and Williamson, their lack of rigorous mathematical foundations.

A crisis arising from triumph

A theoretical deficiency in the existing structure of economics thus provided one source for the new institutional economics. A theoretical triumph provided a second: the codification of the necessary and sufficient conditions for the existence of an equilibrium in a market economy.

The work of Arrow (1951), Debreu (1951) and others proved the conditions under which it would be feasible for prices in markets to shape the decisions of consumers and firms such that all consumers would maximise their utility and all firms would maximise their profits. As this allocation enables all agents simultaneously to maximise, it constitutes an equilibrium; no agent could make herself better off by unilaterally varying her consumption or production decisions. In addition, the allocation would be efficient, that is, Pareto optimal. Under the conditions that generate market equilibrium, it would be impossible to improve the utility of any consumer or the profits of any firms without reducing the welfare of another. Insofar as Pareto optimality constitutes a defensible criterion of the social welfare, the Arrow/Debreu conditions thus render the choices of rational individuals consistent with the social welfare.

On the one hand, the proof of the fundamental theorems represented a triumph; it represented the culmination of the quest to substantiate Adam Smith's claims about the properties of markets. On the other hand, it posed a powerful challenge; with the proof of the fundamental theorems, market economics no longer was interesting. Economists were compelled to turn from the study of perfect markets to other subjects, ones whose core properties had not yet been formalised and whose characteristics had not yet been explored using economic reasoning. The study of the conduct of rational individuals under various forms of market failure quickly became a major branch of economics. And the new institutional economics represents an outgrowth of this research.

The sections that follow focus on a series of market failures and trace the arguments that attribute to each impetus for the creation of new institutions. The sketches impart a sense of the structure of the reasoning deployed in this literature. In particular, they highlight the central role played by social dilemmas. A social dilemma arises when radical individualism becomes inconsistent with social welfare, namely when the choices made by rational individuals yield outcomes that are socially irrational. The core argument of the new institutionalism is that institutions provide the mechanisms whereby rational individuals can transcend social dilemmas. Non-market institutions enable individuals to escape the tensions between individual and social rationality created by the perverse incentives that produce the failure of markets. Market failures yield social dilemmas and thereby elicit the innovation of institutions.

SOURCES OF THE NEW INSTITUTIONALISM

Market failures arise when the necessary and sufficient conditions for market equilibrium fail to hold. These failures are discussed in the section below and related to the creation of institutions other than markets, such as property rights, contracts, revolutionary parties, and labour movements.

Production externalities

An externality represents a direct, physical link between the production functions of two or more agents. The activities of one may impose costs on another; the impact of water use by an upstream agent upon the production possibilities of one living downstream furnishes an example. Alternatively, the activities of one agent could confer benefits upon another; firms that provide generalised training increase the productivity of the labour force for all other firms in the industry. Such externalities constitute one source of market failure.

In the presence of production externalities, the private decisions of rationally maximising agents will fail to promote socially rational outcomes; the outcomes will be inefficient. Firms will engage to too great an extent in the activities that generate negative externalities; they will undertake to too little an extent the activities that generate positive ones. There will be too much water use by upstream users and too little job training, in terms of the above examples.

As analysed in the new institutional economics, the creation of property rights represents a response to the problem of external effects (see for example, Barzel 1989; Libecap 1989; Ostrom 1990). The assignment of property rights enables exchange to span the links created by the physical interdependence of production functions, thereby strengthening the role of economic incentives and making it in the private interests of maximising individuals to make socially appropriate production decisions.

When there are negative externalities, for example, the creation of property rights enables the agent incurring the damage to elicit compensation. The resultant economic costs to the producer of the externality provide an incentive for that agent to engage in less of the undesirable activity. In the case of positive externalities, when property rights exist, the beneficiary would have financially to reward the provider of external benefits; and those rewards would create an incentive for the latter to undertake more of the socially desirable activity. As a result of the creation of property rights, then, producers incur financial costs or reap financial benefit. The social effects of their behaviour are thereby internalised and the overlaying of exchange relationships on top of the physical relationships provides incentives for the agents to take into private account the external (or social) impact of their production decisions.[4]

Public goods

Public goods constitute a second source of market failure. In the case of public goods, interdependence exists not between the production functions of firms but rather between the utility functions of individuals. A good is a public good, as opposed to a commodity, if its consumption by one individual does not diminish the utility derived from its consumption by another: the consumption of the good is non-rivalrous and its provision non-excludable.

Behaving as rational individuals, consumers do not take into private account the benefits that their choices create for others; they fail to take into account the social benefit of their decisions. The private choices of individuals create allocations of resources between private and public goods that are inefficient because, in the presence of public goods, individuals, behaving rationally, will free ride. Rather than incurring the costs of contributing to the creation of a public good, individuals might instead seek to exploit its 'non-rivalrousness' and 'non-excludability'. They might seek to enjoy the benefits for free. When people behave this way, they fail to contribute to the costs of creating public goods. While they might place a high value on the public good, then, they might nonetheless fail to finance as much of it as they truly desire. The equilibrium generated by the private choices of rational individuals thus would be inefficient, given that all might feel better off were each to contribute more of their private wealth to the creation of greater amounts of the public good.

The dilemma created by the perverse incentives that undermine the creation of public goods promotes, theorists argue, a demand for the creation of non-market institutions. Confronted with unrealised collective gains, they assert, rational individuals create institutions that make it in the private interests of individuals to make socially correct decisions. Political leaders, or political entrepreneurs,[5] create organisations that provide selective incentives, rewarding with private benefits those who contribute to the provision of public goods and targeting with sanctions those who do not. The tax power of the state replaces decentralised exchange, as people voluntarily submit to the Leviathan in order to transcend the limits of individual rationality.

Imperfect information

Information constitutes a third source of market failure. The acquisition of information is costly; individuals might therefore rationally choose to be imperfectly informed. Several implications follow.

For the fundamental theorems to hold, all economic agents in a market must confront the same set of prices. Only in this way will utility and profit maximising choices lead to similar ratios of marginal utility across all consumers and similar ratios of marginal value products across all factors of production. Without these equalisations, Pareto optimality cannot hold. When agents are imperfectly informed, however, then their estimates of prices will differ. Poorly informed consumers will pay higher prices than will those with better information, for example. In the presence of higher prices, the poorly informed consumer may cease consumption at a point where the marginal valuation of his or her expenditure is higher than that of the better informed consumer. The result is a failure to achieve Pareto optimality.

31

Leadership, persuasion, influence: these phenomena represent social processes whose origins may lie in efforts by people to compensate for the imperfection of information. For given imperfect information, economic actors may not know their best choices. In seeking to determine where their interests lie, they may seek to acquire information from persons whose tastes could be presumed to resemble their own, but who for a variety of reasons could be expected to be more knowledgeable. The possession of (slightly) greater amounts of education,[6] superior exposure to specialised media and sources of information, or greater experience becomes sufficient, in environments of imperfect information, to render a person influential: an 'opinion leader', in the jargon of studies of the phenomenon.[7] Social processes thus replace individual maximisation in environments of costly information, as people seek to economise on the costs of searching.

Uncertainty about price is not the sole means whereby costly information generates the use of non-market mechanisms. So too is uncertainty about the choices or intentions of other actors and about future contingencies.

Hidden action

High information costs limit the ability of people to monitor the choices of others. An example is provided by someone with land and capital who seeks to secure labour services. Were the landowner able to monitor labour effort and output, then the landlord could simply pay the labourer the value of the marginal product of labour. However, when it is costly to gauge effort accurately or to monitor the relation between effort and output, then it is also difficult to reward labour in a way that maximises the returns to both parties. The result is the substitution of contracts for spot exchanges of money for effort. One contract might be a wages contract: paying the labourer a fixed wage, with the landlord securing all the surplus – but also absorbing all the risk. This form of contract provides weak incentives for altering the intensity of effort, however, as in response to changes in the weather or to the incursion of pests. A rental contract provides an alternative option: the labourer could pay the landlord a fixed amount for the use of the land and capital, and retain all the surplus – and accept all the risk. Where variability in output arises from the use of land and capital equipment, however, this form of contract will provide insufficient incentive; not being the residual claimant, the landlord possesses few incentives to increase the quality of land or to vary the use of capital so as to increase total profits. Under these circumstances, then, the best form of organisation – given the high costs of monitoring – might be one in which the landlord and the labourer reward themselves for their inputs of land, capital and labour by dividing the total output. Neither accepts a fixed payment. Nor does either become the sole residual claimant. Rather, they share the total output – and thus the risk – of rural production.

Incentives arising from the costs of information thus can lead to the substitution of contractual relationships for spot markets in rural societies, structuring institutional arrangements that combine land, capital and labour into productive arrangements (see Stiglitz 1986: 257–65 and the discussion in Barzel 1989).

Hidden type

Uncertainty about prices or choices is not the sole source of non-market organisation; so too is costly information and the resultant uncertainty about 'type': the quality of a good or the capabilities or intentions of another. This information is often asymmetrically held; an agent may know his or her own type, even when others cannot. The magnitude and structure of such uncertainty may make it costly for maximising agents to make valuable transactions. The resultant losses of welfare, it is argued, motivate the creation of non-market institutions.

Labour markets once again provide an example. Consider the problems of an employer facing a pool of potential employees. To secure the services of able workers, the employer could offer a high wage. But ability is difficult to measure. One response might be to offer a wage that represents the average ability of the pool of applicants. The job applicants know their own abilities, however, and those with above average abilities will find the wage too low while those with low abilities will find it attractive. The result then is a shift downward in the average quality of the applicant pool. And should the employer respond by revising downward his or her assessment of the average quality of the job applicants and adjust the wage offer accordingly, the process will simply repeat itself. In Akerloff's (1970: 488; see also 1984) famous phrase, the result is the creation of a 'market for lemons': a market in which workers of high quality fail to offer themselves, even though employers desire their services and would be willing to reward them for their superior skills.

In such a situation, people possess incentives to engage in 'non-market' activities. One way of transcending the dilemma is for employees to invest in signals that reveal their hidden type. If the cost of the signal is less for those who possess higher abilities,[8] then employers could select for ability by choosing those who emit strong signals. Education constitutes an obvious illustration. Insofar as ability lowers the costs of academic attainment, then employers, by paying a higher wage to those with more schooling, can transcend the dilemma generated by costly information, asymmetrically distributed in the labour market.

The problem of costly, asymmetric information concerning 'type' reappears in a wide variety of settings and the institutional responses to it assume varied forms. Employers can encourage employees to reveal their type by offering a spectrum of contracts, in which those with high ability (or high preference for risk) will select one form of contract and those with lower abilities (or lower preferences for risk) will select another. To prevent the degeneration of markets as a result of adverse selection, people may also find other ways of signalling. They may, for example, incur costs that would reveal their type. Those seeking to convince insurers that they are good risks may, for example, choose higher deductibles. Or, in inter-temporal settings, people may offer collateral or post bonds to signal their good faith. Offering 'hostages' provides evidence of one's intentions; it enables one to commit credibly to a course of behaviour.

Preferences are difficult to measure. Because opportunism often pays, verbal protestations provide unreliable evidence of true intentions. The consequence is that many desirable agreements cannot be arrived at. In such a world, people possess incentives to engage in behaviour that reveals private information. They possess incentives to engage in costly acts that reveal their type. By doing so, people provide the information needed for others to infer their type, such that they may take part in transactions that would otherwise be infeasible. People engage in these non-market forms of behaviour in order to escape the imperfections of markets.

Unforeseen contingencies

There is a third source of imperfect information: that arising from the inability of human beings to foresee future states of the world. This source of uncertainty also motivates the creation of institutions other than markets.

As noted by Arrow (1971a), were people able to foresee all possible states of the world, then they could use the market to insure themselves against risk. They could trade contracts in which they promised to exchange commodities or services whose prices, quantities or type varied according to specific circumstances. By buying or selling such contingent claims, they could optimally adjust their holdings so as to assure themselves of a level of utility that reflected their assessment of the probabilities and their preferences for risk.

In practice, of course, not all contingencies can be foreseen; it is prohibitively expensive to write contracts that completely specify actions to be undertaken under all possible states of the world. As a result, the insurance market is not complete and people therefore cannot use the market to maximise their welfare. In response, they employ other institutions.

The inability to foresee and 'contract around' future contingencies affects most directly capital markets. When investors invest, they put themselves at risk; they sacrifice present consumption out of a desire for future gains. Insofar as they cannot foresee the future and trade contracts that generate rewards or incur obligations, depending upon the contingencies, they are unable to insure against losses from their investments. As argued by Williamson (1985) and others (in Putterman 1986), the result is the creation of non-market institutions. Williamson calls these 'governance structures'. Given their inability to foresee all possible contingencies, the suppliers and demanders of investments may instead form long-term relationships through which to renegotiate and adjust their obligations in response to changing circumstances. In particular, they may withdraw investment decisions from the realm of the market and instead create firms.

THE CORE LOGIC

This series of sketches outlines the multiple sources of the new institutionalism: its theories of property rights, contracts and governance structures, for example. It also highlights the logic that underlies its reasoning. This is perhaps best summarised by Kenneth Arrow (1971b; quoted in Przeworski 1991: 109): 'When the market fails to arrive at an optimum state, society will, to some extent at least, recognize the gap, and non-market social institutions will arise attempting to bridge it.' In situations of market failure, people acting rationally generate social dilemmas. Their individually rational choices fail to elicit allocations of resources that maximise the social welfare. By providing forms of pre-commitment, altering individual incentives, generating governance structures and so forth, non-market institutions provide mechanisms that enable individuals to transcend these dilemmas and thereby attain higher levels of collective welfare.

This reasoning thus implies a kind of contractual behaviour. Rational individuals, confronted with the limitations of individually rational behaviour, create institutions that, by creating new incentives or by imposing new constraints, enable them to transcend these limitations. Institutions are demanded – and supplied – by rational agents who engineer solutions to social dilemmas.

THE NEW INSTITUTIONALISM AND THE STUDY OF DEVELOPMENT

The new institutionalism has entered the development field from the domain of its close cousin, economic history, where scholars, most notably North (1981), have sought to explain the growth of economies in terms of the property of their institutions and in particular their capacity to equate social and private returns at the margin, thereby structuring incentives so that rational individuals would make choices that would lead to the efficient use of scarce resources. Nonetheless, in an earlier period, research into Third World agriculture gave a strong impetus to this new approach. Thus Stiglitz's otherwise puzzling choice of title – 'The New Development Economics' (1986) – for his review of the literature on share-cropping. Not only has the study of development thus played a seminal role in the creation of the new institutionalism. The new institutionalism now also plays – and will continue to play – a major role in the study of development.

Market failures: micro-perspectives

The economies of the developing world are characterised by pervasive market failure. Recognition of this property enables those armed with the insights of the new institutionalism to attempt to account for a wide variety of social forms that otherwise might appear mysterious and to appreciate the economic significance of seemingly non-economic institutions.

One example is provided by institutions that offer 'generalised reciprocity': institutions in the developing world in which people invest resources, not in expectation of specific recompense, but rather in an effort to create a general fund of goodwill that can subsequently be tapped should a specific need arise. Families constitute the most striking example of such institutions. And, as argued by Posner (1980), Binswanger and others (Binswanger and Rosenzweig 1984, Bates 1989, 1990), the structure and organisation of families reflects the degree of risk, the structure of risk and the availability of other instruments for coping with it in economies in which market-based sources of insurance do not exist. Families become larger – blending virtually into lineages – the greater the level of risk. For the larger and more widely situated the family, the greater its ability to diversify risk by occupying diverse ecological niches.

The new institutionalism highlights the economic significance of other forms of non-market institutions in the developing world. In the absence of capital markets, for example, persons in developing nations devise 'social' means for pooling savings: they form credit rings or savings societies (see, for example, Montiel 1993). In the absence of secure property rights, they mobilise family ties, religious groups or ethnic associations in support of commerce and trade; the richness of information in such environments facilitates calculations of the appropriate level of trust and the density of social ties increases the costs of the loss of reputation, rendering probity of greater value than opportunism in economic transactions (see Cohen 1981). In the absence of effective states, capable of providing public goods, moreover, people are likely to join religious associations, fundamentalist groups or revolutionary parties in an effort to secure them. An example is provided by Popkin's (1979) classic study of Vietnam, in which he examines the role of churches and the Communist Party in providing property rights, public works and (ironically, perhaps) the simple decencies of life – freedom from political predation, corruption and the arbitrary use of force.

Research into the new institutionalism not only highlights the economic significance of non-market institutions; it suggests as well new policy alternatives. Like other branches of economics, the development field has been caught between advocates of two contrasting perspectives: those who underscore the role of the state and those who advocate the primacy of the market. Viewed from the perspective of the new institutionalism, this debate appears impoverished. For the new institutionalism highlights the role of institutions that are neither fully centralised, as is the state, or fully decentralised, as is the market.

36

In research that led to an award-winning doctoral dissertation, for example, Arun Agrawal studied the role of village-based institutions that provided safeguards for water, timber and land in village communities in India.[9] He examined the manner in which villages overcame the incentives to over-utilise such resources, not by creating private property rights and promoting markets, nor by invoking the bureaucratic power of the state, but rather by mobilising communal pressures and cultural institutions. As argued by others, most notably Ostrom (1990), the new institutionalism thus multiplies the range of policy interventions and forms of remedy by highlighting the role of agencies other than the market or the state. Such insights have strongly reinforced the claims of non-governmental organisations (NGOs) for a major role in the development programmes of Third World nations and for access to the development assistance budgets of the advanced industrial nations.

The new institutionalism thus offers ways of understanding the economic significance of features of Third World societies and cultures that market-based reasoning might misunderstand or ignore. And it expands the menu of policy alternatives, offering positive guidelines for policy interventions over-looked by orthodox economists.

Market imperfections: macro-perspectives

The discussion thus far has focused on micro-level institutions: ones that affect the behaviour of individuals or the performance of specific industries or markets. The new institutionalism also addresses behaviour at the level of the national economy.

Soskice et al. (1992), for example, focus on the role of institutions in providing credible commitments to safeguard investments. In the absence of international markets for the diversification of country risks, capital may fail to flow to some nations, they argue, because those who govern cannot provide credible promises to refrain from expropriating the fruits of such investments. In the absence of well-developed international markets for risk, investors may therefore turn elsewhere, investing their capital in regions where it may yield a lower marginal product but a higher expected return, given the lower level of policy risk. Soskice et al. construct 'rules for the political game' which provide conditions sufficient to make it in the interests of ambitious politicians, who desire power as well as wealth, to credibly commit to refrain from policies of predation. In doing so, they show how political institutions can enable policy-makers to increase the flow of capital to their underdeveloped regions, even in the absence of market mechanisms for spreading risks internationally.

Newbery and Stiglitz (1981) have shown that in the absence of complete contingent claims markets, risk averse agents would rationally prefer autarky to specialisation and trade. Theory and the lessons of recent history under-score, however, the costs of such a choice: over recent decades, the countries that have most successfully exploited their position of relative advantage in international markets have achieved the most rapid rates of growth. In another article, Bates *et al.* (1991) analyse the impact upon trade policy of institutions for coping with terms of trade risk. They explore the relationship between programmes of social insurance, levels of protectionism and terms of trade risk. Using measures of openness derived from studies by the World Bank, they find that increased levels of risk correlated with greater levels of protection; but they also find that, holding other variables constant, governments that invest more in programmes of social insurance achieve greater levels of openness. While plagued by possible measurement and sampling errors, their results suggest that government expenditures to socialise the risks of trade achieve greater levels of openness.

In interpreting these results, Bates *et al.* treat government investments in social insurance as costly signals to those being asked to invest in specific assets – signals of society's willingness to compensate for the assets' loss of value, should relative prices shift adversely. Economic agents that, behaving rationally, would not form capital in the face of terms of trade risk now might agree to invest even in an open trading environment, given the credible signalling of society's commitment to such compensation.

Students of the new institutionalism have focused as well on monetary institutions, attempting to comprehend the manner in which banking systems and monetary authorities can be constructed such that governments can credibly commit to stable monetary policies. Research into the developing countries of Africa encounters the level of variation necessary to support systematic research into this phenomenon. There is variation over time: colonial currency boards constrained local monetary polices but were replaced by national authorities which, being sovereign, possessed the capacity for discretion. There is also regional variation: in the post-independence period, nations in French West Africa limited their discretion by linking their currencies to the French franc, while those in British West Africa refused to tie their hands in this way. While still at too early a stage to yield definitive conclusions, the results of investigation into this variation suggest that agencies of restraint have been useful to governments. Governments that have been able to use external agencies of constraint to bind themselves have been better able to achieve the results they desire: fuller employment, greater price stability, and higher rates of growth (see Collier 1993).

Focusing on the macro-level, students of development have also concentrated on the impact of governmental structures. They have been joined in these investigations by their colleagues in economic history, themselves preoccupied with the relationship between the politics and economics of growth. While failing to find a general relationship between such macro-level variables as measures of democracy and economic performance (Barro 1993), the 'new institutionalists' nonetheless have secured interesting insights into the links between governmental institutions and the growth of economies. These insights suggest that more refined measures might find higher levels of confirmation in future empirical work. North and Weingast (1993), for example, explore the reconfiguration of political institutions in Britain following the Glorious Revolution; they find that by devolving power to Parliament, the monarch was better able to signal to the owners of financial assets his commitment to use his powers in ways that were consistent with their interests. As a result of the reorganisation of the structure of government, they argue, the Treasury was able to secure a far greater volume of loans, and at a *lower* rate of interest. Similar research by Root (1989), in his studies of Old Regime France, and Conklin (1993), in his studies of sixteenth-century Spain, underscore the way in which the structuring of political institutions promotes – or inhibits – the capacity of governments to mobilise public savings. Firmin (1992), working in Africa, compares economic growth in two sub-national states in Ghana. In one, Akim Abuakwa, the traditional authorities, by empowering commoners and giving them control over an effective Treasury, were able to secure higher levels of public revenues than in the other, the kingdom of the Ga, where the traditional authorities were unable to empower commoners or to construct stable public institutions.

As pioneered by Romer (1986) and others, the new development economics attempts to account for lasting divergence in the rates of growth of national economies. In doing so, it focuses on fundamental market failures: nonconvexities that make it impossible for rational individuals to allocate resources such that they yield the same rate of return at the margin in all uses. The new institutionalism focuses on the response of rational individuals to such market failures. As illustrated above, it therefore focuses on the ways in which they construct non-market solutions to the social dilemmas engendered by market failures, creating social organisations, political institutions and agencies of constraint that generate incentives that make it in the interests of individuals, choosing rationally, to make decisions that enhance the collective welfare.

A CRITIQUE

This section highlights the limitations of the new institutionalism as a form of policy analysis and points, also, to its theoretical limitations. On the one hand, it stresses errors of omission and, in particular, its failure to take political factors into account. On the other, it identifies errors of commission, namely the flawed attempt to build a theory of non-market institutions on neoclassical foundations. The section concludes by arguing that when fully developed, the new institutionalism will become a form of political economy.

To understand is to pardon

The new institutionalism seeks to reveal the way in which non-market institutions compensate for market failures. It can properly be criticised for failing to analyse the costs of these corrections or of advocating lower cost alternatives. As a result, it provides misleading, indeed biased, analyses for use by the makers of public policy.

One illustration comes from recent reappraisals of single-channel marketing systems in Africa. Marketing boards are frequently viewed as monopsonies designed to facilitate the shifting of relative prices against farmers. They have been criticised for promoting redistribution at the cost of efficiency. Recent treatments, drawing on the new institutionalism, view them in a different light, seeing their exclusive right to purchase crops as a way of underpinning markets for rural credit. Given poorly defined land rights, and the illegality of alienating rights over persons, rural borrowers of capital are unable to offer collateral for loans, it is argued. Farmers can only offer title to their crop. At the beginning of the crop year, the managers of the marketing boards advance seasonal loans, as well as credit for the purchase of farm implements, and receive in return exclusive rights to purchase the farmers' production at the end of the crop cycle. The creation of monopsonistic rights over the products of farmers provides the lenders of capital assurance of repayment of their loans. The right to the crop thus constitutes a form of collateral, enabling lenders to advance credit at rates that reflect lower levels of risk (this account draws on material reported in Bates 1989).

This reinterpretation of marketing boards views the creation of single-channel markets as a response to market imperfections. It analyses the behaviour of government marketing boards from the same perspective as has been applied to the study of tied factor and credit markets in village India, one of the original contributions to the literature on the new institutionalism (see the review in Basu 1990). In doing so, it highlights the danger of using the new institutionalism as the basis for policy prescriptions.

The new institutionalism underscores the benefits provided by single-channel marketing systems. Earlier research, based upon neo-classical, market-based reasoning, documented their costs: the low quality and high price of their services; the misallocation of resources over time and space resulting from the inflexibility of their prices; the promotion of corruption and rent-seeking; and so on.. The job of the policy analyst is to design and to choose forms of government intervention. Before the analyst can decide whether to retain or disband marketing boards, the benefits they provide must first be compared to their costs. Yet to point to the benefits, as the new institutionalists are inclined to do, is to fail to give a full appraisal. Policy advocates who draw on institutionalist arguments are basing their arguments on but one portion of the total equation, a portion that would promote a systematic bias in favour of keeping forms of intervention in place that might in fact be inefficient.

When used in the appraisal of institutions, the proper role of the new institutionalism might instead be to provided diagnoses rather than to prescribe cures. In economic settings, the existence of non-market institutions, the new institutionalism suggests, might signal underlying market imperfections. Viewed in this light, the proper role of the new institutionalism might be to discern and to analyse the economic problem to which the institution represents an attempted response. Put another way, the new institutionalism takes but the very first step in what must be a more extended process of institutional appraisal and design.

Errors of omission

The new institutionalism seeks to provide an economic theory of non-market institutions. But it fails to take account of several key problems, each of which highlights the necessity of focusing on the politics as well as the economics of the process of creating new institutions.

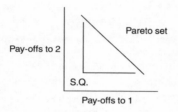

Figure 3.1 Pay-offs to two players and the Pareto set for the status quo point

Consider Figure 3.1, which portrays a space of pay-offs to two players, a status quo point and the Pareto region for that point. The new institutionalism highlights the ways in which the players could organise movements from the status quo to the Pareto frontier, even in the face of perverse incentives arising from externalities, asymmetric information and other market imperfections. But note that there are a (countably) infinite number of points on the Pareto frontier; that the frontier is sloped; that neither player will be indifferent among them; and that the two players will therefore disagree as to which point should be chosen. Note too that any movement from the status quo toward the frontier creates a public good: the benefits reaped by one player are not in rivalry with those enjoyed by the other.

The diagram highlights several weaknesses in the new institutionalists' account. The new institutionalists suggest that people create institutions in an effort to move toward the Pareto frontier. However, that argument is not very powerful: there is a countably infinite number of non-equivalent points in the Pareto set, and a theory that merely accounts for movements to that set therefore fails to discriminate among an infinite number of possible outcomes. The new institutionalism, in short, provides a very blunt theory.[10] That players cannot be indifferent to the points in the Pareto set and possess conflicting preferences over them underscores a second weakness: the failure to recognise the centrality of politics. Given the properties of the Pareto set, the players will have difficulty agreeing on a solution to the problem of market failure: different solutions impose different distributional outcomes. Combining the two insights emphasizes the factors omitted from new institutionalist accounts: the political power of the players and the nature of the political setting that enables one player to gain a preferred institutional solution and thus yields one outcome as opposed to another within the Pareto set.

The analysis thus far suggests the necessity of embedding the new institutionalism within the study of politics. Recognising that institutions promote movements toward the Pareto frontier, and that such moves constitute public goods, provides additional reasons for doing so. In the presence of public goods, people possess incentives to free ride; attempted movements toward the Pareto frontier will therefore be plagued by high transaction costs, as people attempt to reap the benefit of such movements for free. As stressed by Olson (1965), Frohlich and Oppenheimer (1978) and other students of collective action, people who seek to organise the supply of public goods must mobilise selective incentives, such as coercion, or exploit 'size effects', wherein large actors find it privately advantageous to incur the private costs of providing public benefits. The first implies the use of political power. The second implies the mobilisation of large interests. 'Political facts' thus lurk just beneath the surface of the new institutionalism.

As has less frequently been stressed by contributors to this field, the creation of economic institutions introduces coercion into economic life. The institutions that support the attainment of efficient outcomes create structures of power; to overcome incentive problems arising from market imperfections, they enable the offering of hostages, the utterance of credible threats, the implementation of trigger strategies and so on. The new institutionalists have been slower to acknowledge that the creation of economic institutions takes place not on the 'level playing field' of the market but rather within the political arena, in which some are endowed with greater power than others. The image conveyed in the new institutionalism is that of economic actors, frustrated in their efforts to transact in markets, structuring non-market institutions that will enable them to transcend their dilemma and thereby attain welfare-enhancing outcomes. The reality is that non-market institutions are often created in the legislature or the court room or by economic actors who anticipate the appeal of others within such political arenas. Property rights, contract law, the power to regulate the production and exchange of commodities – these and other economic institutions are created by the state.

In attempting to construct an economic theory of non-market institutions, then, the new institutionalism commits major errors of omission: it underplays or ignores the importance of politics. The significance of this omission can be illustrated by turning, once again, to a discussion of marketing boards. Research in East Africa suggests that, at least under the government of Jomo

Kenyatta, the first President of Kenya in the post-independence period, the Kenyan Coffee Marketing Board operated as a relatively efficient organisation. It provided public goods to farmers: research into new varieties, assistance in combating pests, marketing services, technical advice and so on. It also regulated the marketing of coffee, but not in ways that greatly distorted prices in markets. Coffee sales took place in competitive auctions. And the prices paid to farmers compared favourably with those prevailing in international markets (International Coffee Organisation 1978a). In the same period, the Coffee Marketing Board of Tanzania behaved in a strikingly different manner. It provided little by way of services, and those that it did provide, it supplied inefficiently. It regulated the exportation of coffee, but it did so by acting as a monopsonistic purchaser of the crop, imposing non-competitive prices on producers and extracting the difference between the domestic and international prices for coffee (International Coffee Organisation 1978b).

The two marketing boards shared a common historical origin: both were created under the guidance of the British during the colonial era. They regulated industries producing the same kind of coffee, produced in nearly identical physical environments.[11] Their statutes reveal that they shared common economic objectives: the efficient provision of services and a fair return to producers. Both were endowed by their governments with legal powers to attain these ends. But their performance was strikingly different.

This example underscores the range of possible departures from the status quo that economic institutions can provide. It also suggests the importance of politics in explaining these variations in outcome. The two boards, similar in so many ways, inhabit different political environments. In the immediate post-independence period, the coffee industry in Kenya fell within the core constituency of the Kenyatta regime, which was based in the Central Highlands. Top politicians and bureaucrats became the owners of coffee farms, thus attaching their personal fortunes to the performance of the industry (Njonjo 1974). In addition, the coffee sector included both plantations and peasant producers; and the plantations, many owned by top political officials, dominated the representative body that shaped the policies of the coffee board. By contrast, in Tanzania, the government's political base was located in the urban areas and the semi-arid zones. It did not include the highlands, where coffee was produced; indeed, it regarded these regions as a hotbed of opposition to its socialist policies. Under the guidelines governing the behaviour of public officials in Tanzania, none could own farms; and there were no plantations, only peasant farmers, in the coffee industry.

The economic institutions of the coffee industry in Kenya thus lay within a political setting that created incentives for its officials to employ their powers in ways that would promote the efficient operations of that industry and enhance the returns to producers. The economic institutions of the coffee industry in Tanzania, by contrast, lay within a political setting that created few political incentives for its officials to defend the coffee industry; and, indeed, they employed their powers in a way that extracted resources from the industry, even at the cost of reducing producers' incomes.

Taking political factors into account thus provides explanations for the direction and magnitude of the departures from the status quo that economic institutions make possible and yields insight into the source of the variability in their performance. The new institutionalism originates in economics. To fulfil its own agenda, however, it must move into the study of politics. It needs to take into account the allocation of political power in society and the impact of the political system on the structure and performance of economic institutions.

Errors of commission

The new institutionalism seeks to complete the neo-classical programme by 'reducing' social organisation to the choices of rational individuals. Two major failures bedevil its efforts. Taken together, they reveal that this attempt to extend the neo-classical paradigm founders on a contradiction: it fails to adhere to two of the basic axioms of neo-classical reasoning, the commitment to the individual as the unit of analysis and to rationality in the making of decisions.

As can readily be seen in Arrow's formulation, quoted above, the new institutionalists locate the causes of non-market forms of organisation in their consequences, that is, in their ability to solve market failures. This form of reasoning suggests a deficiency in the attempt thus to extend the neo-classical paradigm, leaving the level of explanation at the social rather than at the individual. The approach is functionalist (Stinchcombe 1968; Elster 1978). It is the needs of society – deficiencies in the social welfare – that call forth non-market organisation. This form of reasoning therefore abandons the individual level of explanation and bases its explanations on the welfare of society. Hence, explanations advanced by the new institutionalism depart from the standard form of explanation used in neo-classical economics. Rather than representing an extension of the paradigm, it represents a departure from it.

The 'account' of the origins of institutions provided by new institutionalists also violates the assumption of rationality. By their reasoning, should people encounter a social dilemma, they would forge new institutions in an attempt to transcend it. But, given that the new institution would make all better off, the institution itself constitutes a public good. Would not the act of its provision also generate incentives to free ride? And why, then, would individuals, behaving rationally, be willing to pay the costs of its provision? Viewed in terms of the incentives faced by individuals, then, it appears that the demand for institutional solutions to collective dilemmas does not imply their supply; the solutions themselves pose collective dilemmas (see Bates 1988; Ostrom 1990). Individuals, behaving rationally, would fail to provide them. The approach thus appears to be ensnared in a basic contradiction.

CONCLUSION

This chapter has traced the origins of the new institutionalism. It has isolated the core arguments of the approach. It has criticised the new institutionalism, stressing weaknesses in policy analysis, an unwillingness to acknowledge the fundamentally political nature of its arguments and the failure to fulfil its own agenda: creating a theory of non-market institutions based upon neo-classical foundations. These shortcomings – particularly the neglect of the political – are highlighted in a famous parable which is introduced in one of the canonical texts of the new institutionalism, Ronald Coase's 'The Problem of Social Cost' (1960).

Consider a situation in which a single railway line runs through a valley populated by a multitude of small farmers. Each train run through the valley generates revenues; it also inflicts costs in the form of soot, smoke and noise. One of Coase's fundamental contributions to the new institutional economics was to demonstrate that in the absence of transaction costs property rights – any form of property rights – would make it in the private interests of the operators of the railway to make efficient use of the line. In the absence of property rights, the railway would run trains until the revenue from the next train equalled the costs to the railway of running one more train. With a system of property rights, however, the railway would then have to take into account the full social cost, including the costs imposed upon the farmers; it would run fewer trains. Should the structure of property rights favour the farmers, then the owners of the railway would have to compensate the farmers for the external costs imposed upon them. Should the structure of property rights favour the railway, then the farmers, in an effort to reduce the externalities inflicted upon them, could in effect 'bribe' the railway to run fewer trains; they could compensate the railway for the loss of profits from running fewer trains. Either system of property rights would thus create incentives for the railway to reduce the number of trains out of a regard for the value of the negative externality inflicted upon agriculture.

To summarise, the 'Coase Theorem' suggests the power of an institution – in this instance, property rights – to produce an efficient allocation of resources. But, in such a situation, where is the solution itself likely to come from? And which legal system is likely to prevail: that favouring the rights of firms or that favouring the rights of the railways?

As has been repeatedly stressed, the answer of the new institutionalism to the first question – where do solutions come from? – is fundamentally flawed. There is a second possible answer, however: that their origins lie in politics. As a new institutionalist, Coase answered the second question – which system of property rights would prevail? – by stating that it would depend upon the costs of transacting. Once again, there is a second possible answer, namely, that it would depend upon the structure of politics. For the origin of the legal system is the state. And the nature of the costs of guaranteeing and structuring property rights is determined in large part by the nature of political institutions. In the state, then, and in the study of politics, we can find answers to both questions.

The new institutional economics is profoundly apolitical. Institutions represent agreements or conventions chosen by voluntarily transacting parties in efforts to secure mutually welfare-enhancing outcomes. Each agent is assumed to be autonomous; each agreement voluntarily entered into by mutually assenting parties. The emphasis is upon choices, not constraints; even slave 'contracts' are analysed from the framework of Pareto optimality (Barzel 1989).

What is omitted from the accounts of the new institutionalists, then, is that institutions are often imposed rather than chosen; that the choice of institutions takes place within a pre-existing set of institutions; and that, being backed by the power of the state, institutions provide means whereby agents can extract involuntary transfers of resources. The sort of marginalist choices studied by the new institutionalists take place within structures. They may yield Pareto optimal outcomes, given the constraints imposed by these structures (including the initial endowments that each actor is allowed to bring into the social arena). However, when social dilemmas are solved and non-market solutions chosen, some people benefit more than others; indeed, some may benefit at the expense of others. These are key features of outcomes which the voluntaristic and marginalist approach cannot explain. Explaining them requires political, not economic, analysis.

To extend the 'Coase Theorem', consider a world in which elections are banned, the state rules by decree and laws are made by bureaucrats after consulting with major economic interests. One could easily infer that in a political system thus structured, the structure of property rights would favour the railway. Indeed, political theories based upon the very reasoning explored in this paper would predict that outcome. For the railway is the more highly concentrated interest; given its level of concentration, it stands to capture privately the full social benefits of lobbying and therefore encounters weak incentives for free riding. By comparison with the farmers, the railways would therefore be the superior lobbyist (Olson 1965). And the state, structured so as to respond to interest groups, could be expected to be biased in its favour.

Now consider another state: one in which politicians make the laws, but only after capturing a majority of the votes in competitive elections. Provisioned with additional assumptions – about the number of rural dwellers voting in the electoral district containing the railway and the proportion of rural as opposed to urban districts in the legislature – an alternative outcome can be easily inferred: one in which property rights would favour the farmers as opposed to the railway. In electoral systems, numbers count; political incentives spur efforts by politicians to secure majorities; and politicians will champion laws that favour the numerous small, even sometimes at the expense of the 'big interests'.

Politics involves coercion; the state, in Weberian phrasing, is the human institution that possesses a monopoly of violence. The institutions that promote social rationality are generated and put in place by the state. The structure of political institutions affects which economic institution is chosen. Behind every Pareto optimal outcome, then, arrived at by marginal adjustments among maximising agents devising institutional solutions to problems of market failure, lies a previous act of coercion.

Using the bloodless language of the new institutionalism, Coase was right: the choice of institution depends upon the structure of transaction costs. But it is the state that determines the allocation of these costs. The costs of agreement among the multitude of farms are lower, for example, if vote-seeking politicians help them to organise in opposition to the railway. Once politicians are seen as determining the magnitude and distribution of these transaction costs, then a different vocabulary becomes relevant: that of political science. And the problem itself acquires a different coloration. It is no longer one of pure economics. The new institutionalism thus stands as an important addition to the development literature. However, it will achieve its full promise only when it becomes a part of a broader field, the field of political economy.

NOTES

I wish to thank Alberto Díaz, Catherine Elkins, Brian Loynd and Beatriz Magaloni, and participants in seminars at Rutgers University, Haverford College, the Society for Economic Anthropology and the London School of Economics and Political Science for comments on this paper. The paper draws on my contribution to J. Acheson (ed.) *The New Institutionalism and Modern Anthropology*, Boston: University Presses of America, 1994. It was prepared under Cooperative Agreement No. PDC-0095–A-1126–00 between the Institute for Policy Reform (IPR) and the Agency for International Development (AID). The views expressed are those of the author and not necessarily those of the IPR, AID or any individual.

1 See the early contributions to the theory of labour and tied contracts that came out of research into agrarian institutions in India. Some are collected and many are cited in Bardhan (1989).
2 Its most notable proponent is, of course, Douglass North (see e.g. North 1981, 1990a).
3 This literature builds as well on the work of Friedrich Hayek, Ronald Coase and Frank Knight. See the useful overview contained in Putterman (1986).
4 It should be noted that flows of payments from the person who is harmed by the infliction of negative externalities would also work. Such 'protection money' would provide a benefit that would make it in their financial interests to refrain from inflicting external, physical costs. For an elaboration, see the classic article, Coase (1960).
5 The phrase is from Frohlich and Oppenheimer (1978). The locus classicus remains Olson (1965).
6 Too great a differential in education would suggest a difference in preferences, rendering the source of information an unreliable guide to appropriate decisions.

7 The classic remains Katz and Lazarsfeld (1964).
8 If the signal were cheaper for those with lesser abilities, less able workers would disguise themselves.
9 Arun Agrawal, 'Community Safeguards for Natural Resources: A Study of Village India', PhD Dissertation, Duke University, Durham, North Carolina, 1992. Agrawal's dissertation received the award for the best dissertation in the field of political economy from the Political Economy Section of the American Political Science Association.
10 Similar problems also arise in repeated games, a form of analysis that is commonly employed in the new institutionalism. As stressed by the well-known Folk Theorem, repeated games yield an infinite number of equilibria and so encounter similar problems of indeterminacy. See Gibbons (1992: 56).
11 I am referring here to the arabica portion of the Tanzanian industry. Both Tanzanian and Kenyan washed arabicas fall within the 'Colombian Milds' grade in international markets.

4

THE NEW INSTITUTIONAL ECONOMICS AND ITS IMPLICATIONS FOR DEVELOPMENT THEORY

John Toye

HISTORICAL PROLOGUE

The Western tradition of political theory, at least from the time of Plato and Aristotle, has identified personal greed as the dominating cause of injustice.[1] The implication of this identification is that justice in society results from the virtuous behaviour of individuals. The role of institutions then is to prescribe and promote virtuous behaviour. But what to do when insufficient people understand or feel compelled to follow the path of virtue, or, worse, when the institutions of society themselves are tainted with moral corruption? What if the people, when understood 'as they really are', are not capable of the degree of virtue which the just society requires?

In the eighteenth century, these questions were addressed by a number of social philosophers, including Montesquieu, James Steuart and John Millar. They made a central distinction between private passions and private interests. They believed that the former could, even in the absence of personal virtue, be effectively restrained and disciplined by the latter. They also believed that certain forms of economic growth, particularly the development of trade and industry, were strengthening the power that interest had to discipline passion. Finally, they argued that this would have beneficial consequences in the realm of politics and statecraft, since the complexities of a modern economy would both strengthen the material basis of the state and, at the same time, limit the scope for oppressive action even by amoral rulers. This line of thinking was, however, closed off by Adam Smith, who put private interest and private passion back together into a unified concept of 'self-interest' (Hirschman 1977).

In the nineteenth century, the accelerating progress of industrialisation in the aftermath of the French Revolution gave the reconciliation of private strivings with public good much greater urgency in the minds of the thinkers of the day. Hegel ignored the passion/interest distinction when he posed the reconciliation problem thus:

Passions, private aims and the satisfaction of selfish desires are ... tremendous springs of action. Their power lies in the fact that they respect none of the limitations which law and morality would impose on them; and that these natural impulses are closer to the core of human nature than the artificial and troublesome discipline that tends towards order, self-restraint, law and morality.

(Hegel 1837/1953: 26)

Nevertheless, since private interests had eventually to be reconciled with the common interests embodied in the state, the development of appropriate institutions was for Hegel a major historical task:

A state is then well constituted ... when the private interest of its citizens is one with the common interest of the state ... a most important proposition. But in a state many institutions are necessary – inventions, appropriate arrangements, accompanied by long intellectual struggles in order to find out what really is appropriate, as well as struggles with private interests and passions, which must be harmonised in difficult and tedious discipline.

(Hegel 1837/1953: 30)

Hegel's reconciliation device was the famous 'Cunning of Reason', the exhaustion of private passions by and through their real historical conflicts.[2]

The Cunning of Reason, however, engenders an unresolved paradox. While it may have been intended as a secular theodicy that would encourage the virtuous to persevere in virtue despite the worldly disasters which they actually experience, logically it could have the opposite effect on behaviour. If selfish actions (the pursuit of passions) ultimately have unintended good consequences, a justification is provided for the abandonment of virtuous behaviour. The belief that Reason will enthrone itself through history, even if justified, could thus as easily undermine as reinforce the moral agent's incentive to create appropriate institutions to reconcile private and common interests (Smith 1989: 209–13).

John Stuart Mill also saw the need for appropriate institutions, and offered a different solution to the problem of how they could be built up. He began by criticising his fellow political economists because:

they attempt to construct a permanent fabric out of transitory materials ... they take for granted the immutability of arrangements of society, many of which are in their nature fluctuating or progressive, and enunciate, with as little qualification as if they were universal and absolute truths, propositions which are perhaps applicable to no state of society except the particular one in which the writer happened to live.

(1872/1987: 92)

He illustrated this criticism by pointing out that the results of the Ricardian analysis of distribution depended on specific assumptions about property rights. As a matter of fact, he argued, property rights in the factors of production were radically different in different societies. India, France and Ireland all had laws of property which were different from each other with regard to factor ownership, and from those of England and Scotland, where the Ricardian assumptions applied. Mill inferred from this cross-section evidence an important general conclusion about development, that 'the arrangements of society' were inherently 'fluctuating and progressive'.[3]

Under the unfamiliar heading of 'political ethology', Mill then enquired about the relation between institutions (laws and customs) and the 'collective character' of a nation. He sketched a relation of interdependence. A nation's (or people's) present collective character was strongly influenced by its past institutions. But nevertheless inherited institutions could be moulded by collective action in the present. Mill granted that 'speculation, intellectual activity and the pursuit of truth' were much weaker propensities of human nature than selfish motives. Nevertheless, he believed that the former determined whether and how institutions could be improved. This sociological notion of a 'clerisy' of higher minds devoted to the rational education of inferior minds underpinned his familiar arguments for maximum liberty (Mill 1872/1987: 92–3; Cowling 1990: 106–61). But, as a reconciliation device, the rational clerisy was no less paradoxical than Hegel's Cunning of Reason, while the idea that interest could bridle passion and promote good government was long forgotten.

Mill, however, was the last of the classical political economists. Starting with the publication of Cournot's *Recherches* (1838), and moving on through Jevons to Walras, a new discipline of 'economics' now began to emerge, characterised by a narrow focus and a commitment to mathematisation (Debreu 1984: 267–8). The commitment to rigorous mathematical methods is stated in Walras's intellectual manifesto:

There are today heaven knows how many schools of political economy .... For my part, I recognise only two: the school of those who do not demonstrate; and the school, which I hope to see founded, of those who do demonstrate their conclusions. By demonstrating rigorously first the elementary theorems of geometry and algebra, and then the resulting theorems of the calculus and mechanics, in order to apply them to experimental data, we have achieved the marvels of modern industry. Let us follow the same procedure in economics, and, without doubt, we shall eventually succeed in having the same control over the nature of things in the economic and social order as we already have in the physical and industrial order.

(Walras 1926/1954: 471)

The Enlightenment goal of a universal science aimed at control over the future is restated plainly here, but the narrowing of focus is shown in the choice of harmonisation problem to which mathematical methods were now to be applied. The reconciliation or harmonisation problem addressed by this neo-classical economics was quite different from Mill's and Hegel's concerns for appropriate institutions to reconcile the selfish individuals with state and society. Instead, it consisted of a purely economic reconciliation of the actions of profit-maximising producers with those of preference-maximising consumers under the requirement that, for every commodity, its demand must equal its supply. The presentation of a theory of general equilibrium of markets, showing that, in rigorous terms, an equilibrium price vector was calculable (Walras), then the normative evaluation of such equilibria of perfectly competitive markets to derive the fundamental theorems of welfare economics (Pareto), and the first solution to the problem of the existence of such equilibria (Abraham Wald) all but monopolised the following century of economic theorising. Even Marshall, who repeated Mill's complaint about assuming the constancy of the institutional structure in his Inaugural Lecture at Cambridge, did little – except by way of description – to restore the problem of institutional change to a central place in economic thought (Matthews 1986: 903).

What was the institutional content of Walrasian general equilibrium theory? On the one hand, it presupposed a number of markets (without physical infrastructure or modes of regulation) and on the other hand a ghostly 'auctioneer'. The role of the auctioneer was to communicate to each market price information implied by the potential exchanges in all the other markets, and to prevent any actual exchanges until all the re-contracting that was desired by market participants, in the light of the available price information, had been completed. The auctioneer was a coordinating (harmonising, reconciling) device to rule out the possibility of 'false exchanges' – exchanges made with incomplete information – which would have been incompatible with the achievement of a general equilibrium of markets.

It is not surprising that just as the Walras–Pareto theory of general equilibrium moved on to its comprehensive and mathematically-watertight restatement in the hands of Arrow and Hahn (1971) and Debreu, new questions arose, gaining attention precisely because they were insoluble within that majestic structure. This historical prologue has brought us to the point where we are now able to offer a definition of the new institutional economics (NIE). The new institutional economics is 'new' because it starts from logical puzzles which the Arrow–Debreu theory cannot solve. It is 'institutional' because it comprehends other types of institutions than Arrow–Debreu markets and the ghostly auctioneer. It is 'economic' because – unlike earlier attempts at 'institutionalism'[4] – it retains many of the axioms and assumptions of the tradition which Arrow–Debreu completed, most notably methodological individualism (see Platteau 1990a: 19).

Nineteenth-century political theory posed the problem of reconciling individual and collective interests through appropriate institutions, but failed to resolve it, either by Hegel's Cunning of Reason or Mill's rational clerisy. The earlier passion/interest distinction of Montesquieu remained buried until recently disinterred by Hirschman. Economics (of the Arrow–Debreu type) simply assumed the problem away. The essential significance of the NIE is that it provides a new style of economics which attempts a new resolution of the problem of appropriate institutions.

BASIC IDEAS OF THE NIE

The theory of general equilibrium threw up numerous logical puzzles. The particular puzzle which acted as the catalyst of the NIE centred on the economic theory of the firm. On the one hand, the firm's economic activities were believed to be central and integral to the Walras–Pareto theory. Hicks (1946: 84) stated that dislodging the firm from its existing position in economic theory would involve the 'wreckage' of 'the greater part of general equilibrium theory'. On the other hand, the 'firm' that was so entrenched in general equilibrium theory was 'a strange bloodless creature without a balance sheet, without any visible capital structure, without debts, and engaged apparently in the simultaneous purchase of inputs and sale of outputs at constant rates' (Boulding 1950: 34). An unbridgeable gap existed between the firm as an economic actor in general equilibrium theory and the firm as an administrative and financial organisation, as it was comprehended in the 'real world'. Those bold enough to discuss the growth of the firm had to preface their models with warnings that 'the "firm" is not a firm' and with doubts about whether their subject might lie 'outside the pale of economics proper' (Penrose 1966: 1, 13). Some theorists – including the young Kaldor – felt obliged to analyse the growth of the firm through the ingenious fiction of a succession of different 'firms'.

The pioneering contribution of Coase (1937) was not merely to realise that general equilibrium theory had no explanation for the existence of firms, but also to provide a more satisfactory one than previous theorists of industrial organisation. Firms clearly do exist. Indeed they are the dominant organisational form on the production side of the economy. Yet this form has no rationale in general equilibrium theory. 'Producers' in that theory could just as well be individuals as firms. Coase theorised the nature of the firm while boldly departing from the Walrasian assumption of costless and timeless *tâtonnement* (or recontracting), organised by the ghostly auctioneer.[5] In the real world, he asserted, transactions are not costless. 'The main reason why it is profitable to establish a firm would seem to be that there is a cost of using the price mechanism' (1960: 390). Transactions involve the 'cost of discovering what the relevant prices are' and the 'costs of negotiation and concluding a separate contract' and the costs of monitoring and enforcing the contract *ex post*. This is the basic idea of 'transaction costs'. The objective of the firm is to minimise, not just production costs, but the sum of production and transaction costs, and corporate organisation, may, in given conditions, allow the reduction of the second term in that sum.[6] Thus, the discovery of transaction costs solved the puzzle of why firms are administrative organisations as well as economic actors within the explanatory framework of marginalist micro-economics.

At first sight, it seems odd that it was not until 1937 – the year after Keynes's *General Theory* – that the concept of transaction costs was incorporated into the theory of the real economy. Walrasian general equilibrium was constructed in a way that minimised the impact of money on the economy. Money is only introduced into the theory once relative prices have been determined, so that it affects only the absolute level of prices, and nothing else. Keynes, by contrast, integrates the theory of money with the theory of value. For him, but not for Walras, 'money matters for the functioning of the real economy and is not simply the determinant of the absolute price level' (Thirlwall 1993: 329). Although the Keynesian integration of monetary and value theory does not appear to have influenced Coase, it is worth recalling that monetary theory itself had for many years already used the idea of transaction costs in order to explain the unpopularity of barter and the use of money as a medium of exchange.[7]

Having challenged Walras, Coase (1960) turned to Pareto's fundamental theorem of welfare economics. This states that where perfectly competitive markets are in equilibrium (and externalities are absent, along with various other prior conditions), each equilibrium is optimal. That is to say, in those conditions, no-one's welfare can be increased without reducing someone else's welfare. Coase pointed out that, on Walrasian assumptions of zero transaction costs, resource misallocations would never persist. Rational people would continue the costless process of bargaining in the market until all misalloca-tions were eliminated. Coase argued that to account for the admitted persistence of resource misallocations, it was necessary to acknowledge the existence of transaction costs.

But once this is done, the strong Paretian claims for the efficiency of perfectly competitive markets as a device for resource allocation are impaired. The impairment arises not from the existence of transactions cost *per se*, but rather from the existence of economies of scale in transaction technology. In other words, the efficiency problem arises because transaction costs are not equi-proportional to the value of the goods exchanged. As with scale econo-mies of production, scale economies of transactions leads to a misallocation of resources. At the same time, the mere fact of misallocation does not necessarily indicate market inefficiency. Efficiency now requires the minimisation of the sum of production and transaction costs. However, this situation raises the question of whether another social device than the market, e.g. a government, could make the required reallocation of resources at lower cost. If it can, the market is shown to be a *relatively* inefficient social instrument. The market thus becomes one type of social device, whose performance is to be judged against that of others. It becomes the object of social cost–benefit analysis, on a case by case basis. Economists with strong pro-market commitments find this parity of position uncomfortable.

The realisation that transaction costs (and especially the costs of negotiating and enforcing contracts) are a pervasive phenomenon of the real as well as the monetary economy produced a large subsidiary literature on the behaviour which Williamson (1975) labels as 'opportunism', defined as 'self-interest seeking with guile'. Economists who had previously tended to assume that the enforcement problem could be overcome by a government using taxes to establish police forces and law courts, now see it as much more complex than that. The study of opportunism is not precisely the exploration of that form of rational self-interest which respects, in Hegel's words, 'none of the limitations which law and morality would impose'. Limits remain, but the opportunist will take advantage of all legal loop-holes, braving moral censure of 'sharp practice'.

The economics of agency can be used to analyse opportunism (Pratt and Zeckhauser 1985). Many types of contract specify the relationship between an agent and a principal, in furtherance of whose interests the agent is supposed to act. Unless the principal is perfectly informed at zero cost about the actions of the agent, this relationship becomes problematic, in that the agent is given scope for opportunistic behaviour which benefits himself or herself and usually also reduces the welfare of the principal. This contrasts with rational self-interest in Walrasian and Arrow–Debreu models which benefited the individual, but had no spill-over effects on other individuals. This agency problem was, however, familiar in nineteenth-century political theory. Hegel elaborated his dialectic of the master and the slave, as did Nietzsche. Marx's account of the proletarian revolution could be reinterpreted as a catastrophic agency loss for capitalists. The NIE now re-examines this old theme of political theory in the light of (several variants of) micro-economics.[8]

While many different forms of contract or business practice can be analysed in the light of the agency problem, insurance contracts have been an important model, because the asymmetry in information between the parties to an insurance contract is so substantial that a language for describing the incentives problems arising therefrom has been well developed. Two concepts in particular taken from the insurance world have been given more extended application by the NIE. *Moral hazard* arises when an insurance contract is so drawn that it encourages (or permits) behaviour by the insured that increases the probability of the event insured against. An example is an insurance policy which will pay for a replacement car, even if the insured decides no longer to bother to lock his existing car at night, once he has insured it against theft. *Adverse selection* arises when an insurance contract is written in a way which is particularly attractive to purchasers bearing above-average risk of the event insured against, and unattractive to those with below-average risk. Life-insurance policies which fail to ask different premiums from the well and terminally ill would be an extreme example.

At the theoretical level, it does not matter whether one views the NIE as a 'transactions cost' or an 'incentives' approach. The ubiquity of incentives problems (as against earlier attempts to confine them to the economics of labour bargaining and executive remuneration) is the reason why transaction costs are high. But at the empirical level, it does make a difference, for the reason pointed out by Cheung (1987: 2, 56) – that incentives are not in principle observable. That is why, if testable propositions are to be derived from theory, the problem should be cast in terms of the costs of enforcing performance. Since the derivation of testable propositions is essential to the progress of scientific enquiry, it is preferable to keep the focus on transaction costs and the terms of contracts if the research programme of the NIE is to succeed.

MICRO-LEVEL APPLICATION OF THE NIE TO DEVELOPMENT POLICY

What are the implications of the NIE for development analysis and policy? They can be divided into two broad categories – the grand theory of the role of institutions in development, elaborated further below in the next section, and the application of NIE concepts to specific micro-level problems, which are featured in this section. Transaction costs analysis applied at the micro-level is used to elucidate contractual phenomena, to explain why some contracts exist and others do not and why the details of contracts vary in the ways that they do. This is not, however, an entirely straightforward exercise. The collection of factual information about contracts is straightforward (in principle) and corresponds to the programme of descriptive realism pursued by the old institutionalists. Explaining the manifold characteristics of existing contracts relies, however, on positing an underlying structure of incentives and risk-preferences, which is not directly observable and for which evidence of an indirect kind is usually scarce. The explanations, therefore, are constantly in danger of being rationalisations, or justifications for contractual forms which are irrational or non-functional.

Nevertheless, it now appears that certain forms of contract which prevail in the developing world have in the past been taken rather too easily to be irrational and non-functional. One such is the agricultural share-cropping contract, which gives the landlord a fixed share of the crop, regardless of the proportions of the two parties' contributions to the expenses of production. Share-cropping contracts in agriculture had been dubbed 'inefficient' by Marshall, and exploitative by modern neo-Marxists, and their prohibition sought in the interests of both efficiency and equity. A vigorous debate about share-cropping in the 1970s suggested that it was not necessarily inefficient and moreover, it had features favourable to the share-cropper, compared with a simple rental contract. Specifically, its risk-spreading character is beneficial in the high-risk environment of peasant agriculture for an operator who, because of poverty, is highly risk-averse. A wage contract, on the other hand, shifted all the risks to the landlord, and provided no incentive for the worker to work, unless workers were closely monitored, incurring high transaction costs thereby. Share-cropping represented a compromise between the risk and incentive effects (Stiglitz 1989: 21). What remains puzzling is the constancy of the shares over space and time (Byres 1983).

A similar discussion has taken place over the phenomenon of interlinked contracts for land and credit. The starting-point was a contractual practice whose efficiency could not be defended by appeal to the criterion of Pareto-optimality, where markets are separated except through income effects. This was followed by an interpretation based on coercive class-based power, and a re-examination which suggested a less extreme view, once agents' attitudes to risk and transactions cost are reckoned with. This less extreme view says that 'peasants are rational, but they are not fully informed .... [I]mperfect information (as well as a variety of other transaction costs), besides limiting the effective degree of competition, creates institutional rigidities, allowing the persistence of seemingly inefficient institutions' (Stiglitz 1989: 27).

Share-cropping contracts in marine fishing have also been extensively scrutinised, notably by Platteau and Nugent (1992). They have shown that the differences of circumstances in which adverse selection and moral hazard might arise in marine fishing (as compared with agriculture) result in important disparities in typical forms of contract, notwithstanding the prevalence of share contracts in both activities. These differences of circumstance include the fact that, in fishing, the possibilities of asset misuse by workers are much greater than in agriculture, because boat owners do not go to sea and poor performance by the crew can have much more disastrous consequences. This is reflected in contracts which effectively make crew members share with the owner the costs of fuel and maintenance. Another contrast with agriculture is the need for close worker cooperation while at sea. This is reflected in provisions to allow considerable mutual consultation between owner, captain and crew in the recruitment of captain and crew. A further contrast is the need for flexibility of working hours arising from tides and weather conditions. This need is addressed by contracts of short duration. Platteau and Nugent also suggest that certain anthropological features of marine fishing, such as extensive reliance on ethnic and kinship networks, can be explained by the reductions in transaction costs which it brings about.

Nabli and Nugent (1989: 1341) believe that there is considerable scope for using the transaction costs approach outside agriculture and fishing, for example, to analyse mining, manufacturing, transport and tax collection. It may be that rather more has been accomplished already in these areas than they suggest. But even so, there is no doubt more that can be usefully done, provided that researchers remain on guard against the constant danger of imputed functionalism, or finding a good reason for every last detail of existing social practices. Imputed functionalism is, after all, only the other face of that particular style of radical social criticism which manages to find fault with everything, however apparently innocuous.

The recognition of transaction costs, and the consequent retreat from the Walras–Pareto view of markets, disposes of the automatic preference for provision of goods and services through the market. Equally their presence undermines an ideal view of governments as benevolent and omnicompetent. Market failure is clearly with us, to a greater or lesser extent. But so is government failure. So the questions of public policy become more complicated. Should imperfect governments be used to correct imperfect markets, or contrariwise should imperfect markets be brought into play to improve the resource misallocations of imperfect governments? What the NIE tells us is that neither answer is invariably correct. Rather, the task is to estimate the respective net changes in transaction costs in comparison with the anticipated allocative improvement, to find out whether policy should be favouring additional government intervention or further privatisation.

Since in many developing countries, but especially those of sub-Saharan Africa, the state has experienced institutional decay, the transaction costs associated with the goods and services it provides have increased dramatically. It is clear that privatisation of some of those functions is appropriate in such circumstances, but only if the new privately provided goods and services themselves have low transaction costs. It cannot be assumed that this will necessarily be so in every case. A privatised service should be designed and legislated for, just as a nationalised service is designed and legislated for. The NIE offers a set of tools to inform this kind of institutional design.

Leonard (1991) shows how the concepts of the NIE can be used in designing appropriate forms of privatisation (or semi-privatisation) for veterinary services in Africa. He argues, for example, that if the private service is allowed to be run by a few fully qualified vets located in urban areas, the transaction costs will inhibit its use by herders, increase the likelihood of epizootic diseases, and eventually compel a return to state intervention. If, on the other hand, the state contracts private vets to patrol at stated times routes known to be used by herders, and if the state additionally allows vets to practise privately, the public interest aspect of a veterinary service will be adequately performed. Another dilemma which arises in the design of a private veterinary service is whether paraprofessionals should be licensed, in order to lower service costs, or excluded in order to eliminate the high agency costs of proper supervision. A third design problem is whether the state should turn its control of animal drugs over to private vets, to help them supplement earnings, or not do so because this allows them to make monopoly profits. The many complexities of contractual design for the privatisation of services are exposed once the underlying structure of incentives is mapped out.

One very important type of transaction costs is the cost of excluding those who are not parties to a contract from the enjoyment of the goods or services that are provided under it. With many goods and services, exclusion is entirely straightforward under existing property rights, so that markets for them can operate normally. But for others the costs of exclusion can be high (in some cases, infinitely high) leading to the problem of free riders – those who benefit from provision, but do not contribute to financing it. Even when consumption is non-rival, this causes market failure, as existing payers have an incentive to try to become free riders themselves, and market provision progressively collapses. Where property rights have not been legislated, as with common land, air, common water, there is no right to exclude and that is itself likely to raise the costs of (illegal) exclusion. Here the users all constitute free riders, with no individual willing to bear the expense of conserving the resource.

What can be done in such situations? This depends on the prospects of overcoming the free rider problem in non-market forms of action. Although free-riding causes market failure and 'the tragedy of the commons', it also plagues alternative forms of action aimed at overcoming them. Government intervention often has to be prompted by campaigning interest groups, which are hard to organise for reasons explained by Olson (1965). Community organisations aimed at self-regulation suffer from the same difficulties of constituting and sustaining themselves as do interest groups. Part of the answer may lie in the restructuring of the incentives which interest groups and community organisations offer to their members. That would be the economist's approach. But there is evidence that other factors are also at work when collective action is successfully organised (Nabli and Nugent 1989: 1338; Platteau 1990a: 23–4).

Wade (1988) examined two classic externality problems (damage to crops by grazing cattle and congestion in the use of irrigation water) in South India, enquiring into the conditions under which collective action to prevent them was successful. These covered a wide spectrum. The nearness of the affected fields to users, and the obviousness of their boundaries; the smallness and solidarity of the user group and its aptitude for communication; the existence of inter-group obligations and sanctions against their breach; the visibility of the offence against common rules of usage and the willingness of the state to tolerate locally based authority – all these were favourable factors for the success of collective action to prevent the abuse of common-pool resources. Evidently, these factors reduce the transactions costs of community self-policing and help to explain why in some communities it is feasible, but in others it is not, to resort to it when grazing land or irrigation water become scarce.

A final example of the relevance of NIE concepts can be taken from the international arena. The current practice of making certain types of international aid conditional upon specific policy changes by the recipient government can be analysed as a contractual relation. The contract here is the structural adjustment loan agreement. As formulated in the early 1980s by the World Bank, the loan contract failed to close off the option of opportunistic behaviour by the borrowing government. It was possible for borrowing governments to take the loan, and then fail to make any of the required policy changes, after having agreed to do so. This was because the changes in any case required reasonable time to accomplish, and the Bank could not monitor very closely whether genuine progress was being made. Agency problems of monitoring and enforcement were, therefore, considerable. Worse than this, one could argue that the structural adjustment loans incorporated an element of moral hazard. By offering loans which did not have adequate monitoring and policing provisions, the Bank was tempting countries to be opportunistic. The loan finance provided a way of easing the pressures for policy change, while the conditionality was drawn in such a way that it could be ignored with impunity.

The structure of incentives in this (and other) forms of contract can be modelled using game theory. With the help of certain simplifying assumptions – for example, that the game has only two players, the World Bank and the borrowing country – the choices facing each party can be formally modelled and a solution derived. The key features of the game can be identified, so that both players come to understand better the environment in which they are acting. Either or both may then want to renegotiate the rules of the game. In the case of the structural adjustment loans, the key feature of the game turned out to be whether or not the borrowing country required a further round of finance from the Bank. If Bank re-finance was not needed for any reason (a favourable movement in the terms of trade or interest rates, or the availability of non-Bank finance), the Bank was left without any sanction on opportunistic behaviour by the borrower. The Bank responded to this, in the mid-1980s, by slicing the loan into 'tranches', giving itself opportunities to stop further payment at fixed intervals inside the disbursement period of the loan. Then, when even this failed to put a stop to all reneging, the Bank asked for prior compliance with the policy conditions, thus going to the heart of the incentive problem.

These four examples of the application of NIE concepts to development issues are meant to be merely illustrative. They by no means even begin to exhaust the possible fields of application. The chief reason for choosing them was to show work that has already been done, and to indicate the breadth of the issues that can be treated with the NIE approach. More general comment on these examples follows in the penultimate section.

THE GRAND THEORY OF INSTITUTIONS AND DEVELOPMENT

Does the NIE provide a different and better solution to the problem of the development of appropriate institutions than those proposed over a century and a half ago by Mill and Hegel? Does it illuminate micro-economic problems of the kind that have been illustrated above and, more importantly, offer a grand theory of social science? Exciting intellectual possibilities abound, and have evoked some over-excited responses. Development used to be defined as economic growth plus structural change. The NIE suggests that development should be redefined as economic growth plus appropriate institutional change, meaning institutional changes which facilitate further economic growth. Appropriate institutional change has been elevated by the NIE to a central place in the theory of development, by contrast with neo-classical growth theory's central focus on saving and population growth.

The neo-classical answer to the question of how institutions can develop 'appropriately' is that market forces not only generate the most Pareto-efficient outcome possible in a static framework, but they also do so in a long-run dynamic framework. The unrelenting pressure to improve economic performance which they produce means that institutional adaptations which favour Pareto-efficiency are favoured over the long term, while those which do not are abandoned. The NIE rejects this simple view of unilinear institutional progress driven by the market itself. It is right to do so, but for reasons which do not derive specifically from NIE assumptions. The neo-classical view involves an implicit appeal to the biological analogy of natural selection, in which institutions which are ill-adapted to their conditions become gradually extinct. The process of natural selection of living organisms in the natural world is based on a mechanism which has no place for conscious motivation, decision-making or choice. It is, therefore, most implausible to suggest that it can be applied to social practices which reflect human aspirations and endeavours. All discussion of the survival or development of institutions has to be placed in this context of human willing and striving. It is idle to think that an evolutionary 'mechanism' could be found outside this context. The existence of norms, customs and organisations does not require that people have no choice about how to relate to them. People surely have to choose how conventional to be and whether they want to join certain institutions, or to try to subvert them. The problem with the biological analogy is not that people cannot choose between institutions, but the exactly opposite one – that they can.

When we contemplate the survival of institutions we have to ask whether they are desired or desirable from a human point of view. We know that undesirable institutions do survive – untouchability, female circumcision, institutionalised racism, cruel and unusual punishments, for example. Explanations of these survivals is given in terms of human decisions – perhaps that it is rational for an individual to suffer unpleasant institutions because individual attempts to subvert them would bring down on his or her head even more unpleasant consequences. Explanations of the non-survival of undesirable institutions often include martyrdom – the willingness of individuals to suffer those even more unpleasant consequences, in order to break through the social defences of undesirable institutions. In short, people can and do choose how they address their institutions and that is precisely why there can be no general presumption that institutions will become 'appropriate' (or when), and that it will be market forces alone that work the trick.

The NIE approach to the grand theory of institutional development distances itself from the market-driven, natural selection explanation of long-run development. It stresses, by contrast, the limited information available to different groups and the diverse mental modelling of available information within distinct ideologies and cultures, which in turn generates their own institutional arrangements – including both organisations and social practices. The question is then posed: how do societies with different cultures and institutions adjust to new opportunities for trade and technological innovation? It is assumed (as with the market-driven model) that competitive pressures are ubiquitous, but the rate of learning both about the nature of these pressures and how to adjust to them will differ. The incentives embodied in existing organisations will also influence the process of adaptation. Thus change will be on the one hand slow and incremental and path dependent, hardly able to deviate much in the short run from a trajectory set by the initial institutional arrangements. Since the state is a central part of the institutional complex, given its ability to define property rights, it will be weighty in determining the path of development that is followed. But the state may be too concerned with maximising its own revenues to be willing to change property rights in a way that will lead to more efficient dynamic outcomes for society. In that event, the eventual outcome will depend on the size of the 'political transactions cost' of changing the nature of the state (North 1989b).

The NIE theory of development, as expounded by North, has a distinctly eighteenth-century flavour, and indeed represents a repetition of many of the views of Montesquieu. North, like Montesquieu, takes as a major theme, 'how Commerce Emerged in Europe from Barbarism'. Both share the perception of trade as the engine of economic growth. Both perceive the development of new institutions which facilitate trade to be powerful sources of increased prosperity: recall Montesquieu's admiration for the inventions of the bill of exchange and of foreign exchange arbitrage. Both see institutional advances in the economic sphere as cumulative. Both note spillover effects from economic progress facilitated by institutional change to political progress, through the pressures for better (more limited) government which ensue. Both believe that, where reason is weak, men's interests can bridle their passions – Montesquieu's thesis of *doux commerce*.

But eighteenth-century optimism needs to be tempered. Additional reasons why any institutional adaptation will be slow and incremental are adduced by Matthews (1986). One of these is discussed under the heading of 'inertia', although that term perhaps gives a misleading impression of what is involved. The problem is better seen through Matthews's explanation of this 'inertia'.

Institutional arrangements are about interpersonal relations and ... there are inherent reasons why it should be more difficult to make changes where other people's consent is needed than where they can be made by individual *fiat*.

(1986: 913)

The purpose of every institution – not always achieved, needless to say – is to create settled expectations both for those inside and outside it, over a wider sphere of action than would be possible without it. The process of doing this inevitably creates conflicts between the interests of the institution (in achieving its purpose) and the interests of the individuals who compose it, which are only partly convergent. Hence the need for the patient negotiation of any change. The institution, as an embodiment of collective action, experiences all the problems which the theorists of collective action have identified.

It is worth noting, parenthetically, that the acceptance of this view leads to a criticism of Williamson's 1975 account of the firm. He views the firm as an authority structure defined as a 'command system', proposing that the division of activities between the firm and external markets will be determined by their respective transaction costs. The criticism is that the idea of the firm as a command system is an over-simplification. The firm is an institution like others – including military forces, which have a 'command system' *par excellence* – in which the effective exercise of authority rests on (partial) consent and (sufficient) trust. The firm which disregards the state of its interpersonal relations will soon experience transaction costs of a magnitude that will put it out of business.

If this is so, it is clear why institutional change driven from the inside can only be gradual. Externally imposed change can be much faster, and this is why reforms to institutions are so often externally driven. The external pressures for change can originate either from markets or from non-market sources. Market pressures will tend to winnow out firms that fail to minimise the sum of production and transaction costs. But this does not guarantee the survival only of firms with low transaction costs. To take an example, aluminium producers who put intensive effort into negotiating special low-cost power sources can succeed in driving out minimally administered competitors who pay normal power rates.

The main source of non-market external pressure is the state. One of its roles is to set the framework within which the market pressure can operate. In our aluminium company example, the state is likely to regulate the activities of the power companies, perhaps setting the rules under which special deals may be concluded by them. The state often mediates the operation of market pressures, and can do so in a way which is not conducive to the survival of the most efficient companies. The state also intervenes directly to reform institutions which are not subject to market pressures. But such reforms are typically plagued by information problems, as argued by Niskanen (1971). One way of overcoming them is to begin by establishing a committee of enquiry, on which impartial representatives of the community exhaustively compile the relevant information – historical as well as current – before making recommendations for change. This itself militates against rapid externally driven reform. The other option is to reform on the basis of political intuition. This is rapid but not likely to be conducive to efficiency, particularly in view of the complexity of most institutions.

The complexity of institutions is the third of Matthews's reasons (after inertia and the pervasive role of the state) why reform is so difficult, and why therefore the evolution of efficient institutions is so problematic. One facet of the life of institutions which tends to be forgotten once we lose sight of its human context, is its constant search for fresh recruits to replace those who have resigned, retired or died. The purposes of some of its internal rules is unlikely to be understood by all of the individuals who compose it, and the practices which have become habitual may be at variance with its rules. The very purpose of the institution may shift subtly over time, without any overt acknowledgement, in response to the creative activities of its leading figures. The reforms imposed on it by external non-market agencies may simply be misconceived because these complexities are not understood.

In summary, there are many reasons why one cannot presume that institutions will evolve efficiently, even over long periods of time. They are all rooted in the fact that individuals can and do choose to address existing institutions in a multitude of different ways. Even those political philosophers like Mill or Hegel – or, even earlier, Kant – who had confidence that people would learn (in different ways) from accumulated experience did not say whether the learning process would take generations, centuries, millennia or aeons.

THE WEAKNESSES OF THE NIE

A comparison of the discussions of the two preceding sections suggests that, while the NIE appears to have a wide and varied range of applications to micro-level or sectoral level development problems, it is much less successful as a grand theory of the development process in its entirety. In this respect, the NIE is simply another example of the unfortunate tendency of some theorists to inflate a useful low-level theory until it becomes an unsuccessful global-historical generalisation.

The main weakness of the NIE as a grand theory of socio-economic development is that it is empty. As a critique of other theories which altogether ignore the role of institutions in long-run change and growth, it is welcome. Institutions (cultures, ideologies, property relations, particular organisational forms) are important determinants of economic performance. But when it comes to new general insights about how that determination works, the theory adds nothing to what we already have. No new predictions can be derived; no new policies can be recommended. No historical episodes can be explained better now than they were by the historians who have already studied them. At the macro-level, the whole idea of transaction costs becomes blurred and problematic, especially when 'political transaction costs' are added to economic transaction costs (Khan, this volume).

It is much easier to slide into this micro-to-macro transformation because of another much remarked weakness of the NIE. Very little effort has been given to the definition and measurement of the concept of 'transaction costs' in relation to the weight of theorising which has been developed from it. By now, this has become a well-rehearsed complaint (*inter alia* by Matthews (1986: 917) and Platteau (1990a: 28–29)). Within monetary economics, the concept has been better served by applied researchers. Studies have measured the non-interest and repayment costs of taking agricultural credit (Adams and Nehman, 1979). This good example has been very little followed as the concept has been developed by the NIE outside the monetary context. Walras, who saw rigorous demonstration as a prelude to applications to experimental data, would not have been satisfied with this state of affairs.

Since the NIE opens up the possibility that non-market social devices may be more efficient than reliance on market forces, much has been said about the vindication of government intervention by appeal to a cost-effectiveness analysis, comparing the transaction costs of market forces with those of government action (Chang 1991: 67). In fact, it has been 'the school of state intervention or socialism of the Chair' (to use Walras's terms) that has investigated this possibility most thoroughly. The problem here is the temptation to try and justify state intervention on too grand a scale, by concentrating on extensive state action of the type that appears to have successfully accelerated development in Korea and Taiwan. But actually performing a cost-effectiveness calculation for state intervention on this national scale makes the tasks of measurement quite prodigious. The best that can be done is to produce theoretical arguments about why, in such cases, the transaction costs of the state's intervention may well have been low. These difficulties reinforce the case for restricting NIE theory to micro-level analyses. The quantification tasks are much more likely to be manageable.

If this possibility is ignored, transaction cost ends up as an all-purpose tool of explanation, pressed into service to 'solve' any and every puzzle – but in fact empty of explanatory power. Even at the micro-level, it is quite possible for the concept to support a tautological functionalism of the sort beloved of many conservative economists. When market outcomes appear to be inefficient according to traditional economic analyses – i.e. those which ignore transaction costs – some will be tempted to argue that they are as efficient as they can be once transaction costs are taken into account. This is usually done without any quantification, just by admitting the possibility of their existence theoretically. Unless transaction costs are quantified, they are not being 'taken into account' properly. They are only being conjured with, to evoke the spirit of Dr Pangloss for whom 'everything is for the best in the best of all possible worlds'. It will often be the case that market outcomes remain inefficient, even after transaction costs have been accounted for. We then have to seek for the residual causes of these inefficiencies. To say that we must bring 'history' back into the explanation is but a first step. 'History' is just another portmanteau concept which has to be unpacked, to make clear whether one is appealing to pure contingency, class power, culturally formed expectations or whatever. Moreover, history is particularistic, the validity of any one of these lines of enquiry needing to be tested in a specific context.

The NIE retains from the Arrow–Debreu framework the postulate of methodological individualism and the concern with static equilibrium solutions. As argued in the section on 'The Grand Theory of Institutions and Development', these features make it an approach which is ill-adapted to provide adequate global-historical theories. The NIE in this respect is in much the same predicament as Marshall was a century ago – stressing the centrality of dynamics and evolution to an understanding of economics, while providing only static analyses.

CONCLUSION

A recital of the weaknesses of the NIE should not be read as a vote in favour of rejecting or ignoring it. Despite these weaknesses, the NIE represents an important breakthrough for development theory. This breakthrough has two facets, one linguistic and psychological and the other substantive. In the first place, the NIE has brought about a major shift in the terms of the discourse about development. Those approaching this discourse from the orthodox or neo-classical side have found, in the NIE, a means of extending the scope of 'economics' as they understand it, and therefore also of widening the range of thoughts which it is permissible and legitimate for them to engage with. Before the NIE, structuralist theories of development were 'too ill-defined' for neo-classicals to understand. They were given the intellectual status of 'things which left-wing development economists say', remarkable chiefly for their incoherence (see Matthews, 1986: 903, 907). The NIE represents an escape hatch through the wall of incomprehension which has separated the school of those who demonstrate their conclusions mathematically from the school of those who do not. The mathematical demonstrators can now talk about institutions, too, because they have found a language to do so with which they feel intellectually comfortable.

Should the school of mathematical non-demonstrators feel threatened by this, or should they welcome it? Some will undoubtedly interpret it as a new phase of the imperialism of economists. Some will contend that intellectual accommodation will prove possible only on oppressive terms. They fear that cohabitation will occur only if they agree to abandon their old language, as in nineteenth-century Wales when an improved education was provided, but only in English, and Welsh-speaking children were whipped and expelled from school if they did not learn the new language. Such apprehensions are surely too pessimistic. The non-demonstrators are in better shape than such a defensive view of future prospects of intellectual exchange imply. As is shown in the section on 'Micro-level Application of the NIE', many previous lines of 'structuralist enquiry' have investigated issues in the manner of the NIE, even without having used its terminology. To change the linguistic metaphor, many structuralists have been talking prose for a long while without knowing it. They should be well placed to engage with the NIE's conceptual vocabulary, and need not fear that such an engagement would necessarily occur on disadvantageous terms.

The substantive point is that the NIE (however the encounter of concepts develops) does address a problem of very fundamental interest, which orthodoxy and structuralism alike have until recently tended to shy away from. The exploration of 'opportunism' – rationally self-interested behaviour in conditions of strategic interaction of decision-making, deficiency of information and uncertainty – has far-reaching consequences beyond the realm of game theory to which it has been traditionally confined. It is inconceivable that development theory will not benefit from being rethought to accommodate the pervasiveness of 'opportunism'. It has been politically convenient for development theorists to attribute opportunism to a few selected organisations – multinational companies, international financial institutions, *compradors* – when it has a much more general application to human behaviour than has yet been reckoned with. The pursuit of this enquiry should appeal not only to the new institutional economists, but to development sociologists, economic anthropologists, political scientists – indeed, to the whole range of social science disciplines which have created multidisciplinary development studies.

NOTES

1 'If Aristotle is to be our guide, the unjust person ... is dominated by only one vice, greed. That is why he breaks the rules of law and fairness. He just wants more of everything, material goods, prestige and power. And the impact of his greed falls entirely on others, who receive less than they deserve, thanks to his grasping conduct' (Shklar 1990: 28).

2 Hegel explained this as follows: 'The special interest of passion is thus inseparable from the actualisation of the universal; for the universal results from the particular and definite and its negation .... It is not the general Idea that involves itself in opposition and combat and exposes itself to danger; it remains in the background, untouched and uninjured. This may be called the *Cunning of Reason (List der Vernunft)* – that it sets the passions to work for itself, while that through which it develops itself pays the penalty and suffers the loss' (Hegel 1837/1953: 43–4).

3 Mill's inference involves a logically invalid leap from observed differences at one point in time to a process of change through time. This leap is still made by many modern students of development, especially when long runs of historical data are lacking. Note that Mill's observation of institutional differences between countries, or areas within countries, did not lead him to abandon the use of the deductive method in the science of political economy. Rather he argued that 'though many of its conclusions are only locally true, its method of investigation is applicable universally' (1872/1987: 92). In other words, a knowledge of local institutional

circumstances would allow deductive conclusions to be drawn correctly. This is the more appropriate message from Mill to modern students of development. For further clarification of these points, see Hollander (1985: I, 83–6, 121–2, 134–6; II, 770–1).

4   The old institutionalism in economics, which flourished particularly in the United States between the 1890s and the 1930s, followed a research programme which was largely descriptive in character. A recent sympathetic critic has commented on this as follows: 'The error here was largely methodological and epistemological, and committed by many institutionalists with the exception of Veblen himself and a few others. It was a crucial mistake simply to clamour for descriptive "realism" .... Contrary to the empiricist view ... science cannot progress without a theoretical framework, and no observation of reality is free of theories or concepts' (Hodgson 1988: 22). From this it does not follow that the only methodological alternative to realism is methodological individualism, however.

5   The interpretation of the precise mechanics of *tâtonnement* is various. Apart from the version already given in the main text, it could also operate by allowing potential contracts to be made but also to be cancelled without the consent of the other party whenever prices change; or while making false exchanges contractually binding, by allowing unfavourable consequences for one party (arising from any price changes) to be automatically nullified in subsequent contracts. The point to note is that none of these three interpretations corresponds with normal contractual arrangements in a capitalist society.

6   Coase considered not merely why firms exist, but also why, if organisation confers advantages, all production does not occur within a single large firm. His answer was that 'a firm will tend to expand until the costs of organising an extra transaction within the firm become equal to the cost of carrying out the same transaction on the open market or the costs of organising another firm' (1960: 395).

7   A more obvious Cambridge influence on Coase was Austin Robinson. He had recognised that 'the hypothetical business ... is as rare as snakes in Ireland' and had proposed that the size of the firm was determined by the costs of coordinating its activities (Cairncross, 1993: 42–9; Coase, 1937: 395–7).

8   In this connection, note that Coase showed that his economic concept of a firm (production directed by an entrepreneur/coordinator) corresponded with the British legal definition of a firm (a master's right to control the work of a servant) (1937: 403–5).

Part II

NIE: THEORY AND POLICY

5

STATE FAILURE IN WEAK STATES

A critique of new institutionalist explanations

Mushtaq Khan

This chapter examines the implications of the new institutional economics (NIE) for analysing state failure in developing countries. The NIE approach aims to identify the institutional causes of state failure. In their chapters Bates and Toye have argued that the economic consequences of particular institutions depend on the social and political context in which they are placed. The question is whether the results of the NIE analysis can be grafted on to data about political differences across countries or whether recognising political differences requires abandoning the NIE approach.

It will be argued that the performance ranking of institutions is specific to the inherited political power of classes or groups subject to the institution. By ignoring this, NIE authors have come up with competing rankings. *Explaining* institutional performance requires an analysis of the inherited balance of power or 'political settlement'. The institutional structure which is best for a particular society depends on its political settlement. *Responding* to institutional failures requires not just an understanding of the balance of power but also requires us to take political positions. This is not only because there are a multiplicity of potential improvements with different class and group implications. It is also because all solutions to institutional failure involve 'political costs' or 'transition costs'. It is necessary to be explicit about these costs and recognise that their incidence is not equal or inevitable. In attempting to sanitise the analysis of state failure by removing political judgements and political positions, NIE may have clouded rather than clarified this issue.

The first section defines institutions and state failure and distinguishes between two types of state failure which have been addressed within the NIE approach. The second and third sections discuss the two types of state failure and examine the NIE approach to each type of failure. The final section draws some conclusions.

TWO VARIANTS OF STATE FAILURE

An institution is defined as the set of formal and informal rules which constrain

71

and govern the interaction of agents subject to that institution (Schotter 1981: 11; North 1990a: 3; Knight 1992: 2). The formal institutional structure includes conventional property rights but also any other enforceable constraints such as taxes and subsidies. State regulation in general creates or attenuates property rights and is therefore part of the formal institutional structure. The state is also the body responsible for the enforcement and protection of all formal property rights. Both formal institutions and informal or voluntary ones affect economic outcomes because they condition the opportunities and incentives of agents. Institutional failure refers to some judgement about the potential improvement in performance if institutions could be restructured.

This chapter is primarily concerned with formal institutions. The state is closely associated with the protection and maintenance of formal institutions and the processes through which they are changed. This is reflected in the close relationship between the literature on state (or government) failure and institutional failure. In the following analysis, the terms state failure and institutional failure are used interchangeably to *describe* the economic performance of formal institutions. State failure is therefore a descriptive term involving only a judgement about the potential benefits of alternative institutions. It does not necessarily imply that the state *decides* which institutions to protect and how. The state or parts of it can under some circumstances act autonomously, in others it simply responds to pressures from competing classes and groups.

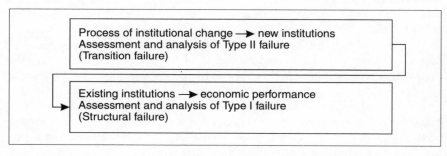

Figure 5.1 Type I and Type II state failure

Two types of institutional and state failure can be distinguished in the NIE contributions. The distinction is between the performance of the existing set of institutions and the efficiency of the process through which institutions are changed. Type I state failure in Figure 5.1 refers to a comparison of the *outcome* generated by the existing structure of constraints on economic agents with the outcome generated by a hypothetical alternative structure of constraints. Thus Type I failure is referred to as structural failure. Outcomes may be compared in terms of a chosen criterion such as utility, net output or growth. The most general objective is to maximise the level of net benefits for society. *Type I state failure or structural failure occurs if a particular formal institutional structure results in lower net benefits for society compared to an alternative structure.* The lost net benefit indicates the magnitude of Type I failure. The better set of institutions could be theoretically identified or empirically observed. NIE uses transaction cost and rent-seeking analysis to compare net benefits under alternative sets of institutions to analyse the possibility and magnitude of Type I failure.

Type II failures refer to failures in the *process* through which institutions change relative to alternative processes. Type II failures are therefore failures of transition. If Type I failure exists, then it is instructive to compare alternative paths to a better structure. The existing process may be less satisfactory than an alternative specified by theory or observation and indeed the existing process of change may be increasing the magnitude of Type I failure. If an alternative process could have carried out a transition to a better structure or carried it out faster, the *cumulative* difference in net benefits over a period of time gives a measure of Type II failure. *Type II state failure or transition failure occurs when the process for changing the structure of institutions attains a lower cumulative set of net benefits for society compared to an alternative process over a given period.* For Type II failure, NIE relies on 'higher level' transaction costs such as Douglass North's political transaction costs (North 1990a) or the costs of organising collective action to explain differences in the processes of change.

TYPE I STATE FAILURES

The NIE analysis of Type I or structural failure draws on the analysis of rent-seeking and extends it using an analysis of transaction costs. It aims to analyse the contribution of different institutions to economic performance. This understanding aims to aid the identification of the institutions responsible for structural failure across countries. This section examines the consequences of the NIE attempt. Different NIE analysts have identified very different institutions as being critical for success or failure. It will be argued that these contrary rankings can be explained by making explicit the political balances of power required to make different institutions work efficiently.

Rent-seeking models (Krueger 1974; Posner 1975; Buchanan 1980; Bhagwati 1982) emerged in trade theory and the New Political Economy (which is reviewed in Toye 1993). Proponents of such models argued that the cost of state intervention was more than the traditional deadweight welfare losses associated with the divergence of prices from marginal costs. This is because state-created rents create incentives for agents to leave productive activities for so-called unproductive ones to try and acquire credentials which give access to the rents. The withdrawal of resources from productive uses continues until the expected marginal return to a factor from productive and unproductive

activities is equalised. The cost of rent-seeking is the use of productive resources in unproductive activities. Type I state failure is associated here with
state intervention. Moves towards *laissez-faire* are predicted to reduce the
incidence of rent-seeking and hence Type I failure.

Transaction cost analysis derived from the seminal work of Coase (1937).
Transaction costs are the costs of agreeing a contract (including measuring all
the attributes relevant for the exchange) and the costs of enforcing the contract
(including the costs of detecting infringement, policing and punishing) (Matthews 1986: 906; North 1990a: 27; Eggertsson 1990: 14). Coase's insight that
transaction costs differ across institutions underlies the NIE analysis of Type
I failure. Type I failure is attributed to high transaction cost institutions.

Transaction costs are detrimental for net social benefits because they prevent gainful transactions from occurring which might otherwise have taken
place. The failure to exhaust gainful transactions is, of course, market failure.
Consequently, transaction costs are simply a way of describing the causes of
market failure. If finding the best technologies, organising the process of
production, finding markets, arranging insurance and writing credible and
fully enforceable contracts for all of these were costless, every society would
be on the notional production frontier. Since all such costs must be transaction
costs, the gap between the neo-classical production function and reality can
always and tautologically be attributed to transaction costs. To proceed beyond the conventional analysis, the transaction cost approach has to identify
an attainable set of alternative institutions with lower transaction costs.

How are these institutions identified by NIE? In what respects does the
transaction cost approach extend the rent-seeking framework? Varian (1989)
showed that if rent-seeking only resulted in pure transfers there would be no
social cost in the conventional sense. The social cost derives from the effects
of rent-seeking on the vector of net products. If rent-seeking results in a
lower-valued vector of net products with unchanged endowments this is
equivalent to production inside the production frontier. This in turn can be
described as an increase in the transaction cost of organising production and
exchange. Thus rent-seeking results in Type I failure by increasing transaction
costs. Since rent-seeking is only one of the sources of transaction costs, the
transaction cost framework can be used to show why the rent-seeking argument may be one-sided in its simple versions.

First, all property rights confer privileges on their possessors. Compared to
the alternative where an individual did not have a particular right, these
privileges have the character of rents (Roemer 1982, 1988). Rent-seeking type
activities can, therefore, be expected to be associated with any structure of
rights as people would spend resources trying to change or maintain them
(Samuels and Mercuro 1984). Compared to a situation where such contests did
not take place, any right structure has rent-seeking costs due to contestation.
Type I failure, however, only exists if lower rent-seeking costs are *attainable*.
Comparing the real world with a contest-free *laissez-faire* which is unattain-

able is irrelevant. The relevant transaction cost difference between intervention and non-intervention may be much smaller than suggested by rent-seeking theory.

Second, intervention can *save* transaction costs by changing incentives or enabling coordination and monitoring. What matters therefore is the net effect on transaction costs. For instance, if infant industry protection allows cheaper coordination of technology acquisition, the net effect on transaction costs after rent-seeking may still be favourable. If so, intervention with rent-seeking may have lower overall transaction costs than *laissez-faire* with lower rent-seeking.

Although one-sided, the rent-seeking analysis showed that there may be real social costs as a result of contests over property rights. But by concentrating on and overstating the costs it ignored the improvements in net benefits which changes in institutions (or rights) could bring. The transaction cost framework enables this point to be made, although the precise social cost of contests over rights in different contexts is still imperfectly understood. In the early models it was assumed that the social cost was exactly equal to the size of the rents being contested. This was soon shown to be based on assumptions about the political institutions governing rent-contestation (Congleton 1980). Two complementary approaches emerged in the NIE literature to preserve the mapping from institutions to Type I failures. Both attempts ultimately fail.

The first of the two approaches incorporates the effects of formal political institutions. It argues that by looking at the effects of formal economic and political institutions jointly we can preserve the mapping from institutions to economic outcomes. Examples of such analyses are Congleton (1980), Rogerson (1982) and Chang (1994). The problem is that in each case it is easy to imagine alternative situations where the results suggested are overturned.

Congleton compares rent-seeking expenditures under majority voting with those under a dictatorship. He finds that if legislators in a majority vote setting can be cheaply bribed, there is less rent-seeking expenditure than under a dictatorship. He points out, however, that if legislators demand high minimum bribes, a dictatorship is cheaper (Congleton 1980: 177). Rogerson compares political institutions which limit access to rents to a small group with political institutions which allow unrestricted access. He finds that limited access might lower rent-seeking transfers. This result too can be overturned if the excluded have the power to heavily contest their exclusion. In Chang the costs of contestation can be reduced if the state is less vulnerable (1994: 38–40) and if the rent-seeking process is less competitive (1994: 41–4). However, as he points out, an invulnerable state can sometimes result in large social costs and restricted access to rents at one level can simply lead to rent-seeking spilling over to other levels. It appears that the costs of contestation cannot be deduced from the formal political rules under which the protagonists operate.

The second approach, associated in particular with North (1990a and in this book), is to introduce politics through an analysis of informal institutions while retaining the analysis of formal political institutions. Informal institutions are the norms and conventions which also constrain agents but are not enforceable by third parties. They are important for the functioning of formal institutions because they determine the intensity of contests and therefore determine how cheaply and effectively existing rights can be enforced. Thus a formal institution (such as private property) is likely to have very different consequences if important informal norms (such as the commitment to honour contracts) are absent. The conclusion is that it is not enough to create the formal institutions which lower transaction costs, we also have to create the political conditions which sustain the appropriate informal institutions. This argument is very similar to the previous one, except now it is a combination of formal and informal institutions which determine Type I failure.

In North's (1990a) analysis, the best formal economic institutions are well defined private property rights. These formal institutions work best with particular informal institutions which support trust in (and therefore reduce contests over) private property rights. The analysis identifies the best economic institutions and then deduces the best informal institutions necessary to support them. For North (Ch. 2, this volume), the importance of the polity is in ensuring that the required informal institutions come into being.

The critical assumption is that the choice of the best formal institutions is independent of the polity. If the best formal institutions are indeterminate, so are the best supporting informal institutions. For instance, if lifetime employment can be the best institution for some contexts, the best cultural norms would be appropriately different. If the ranking of formal institutions depends on characteristics of the polity, this would undermine the NIE project of attributing performance to institutions and require an analysis of the relative performance of institutions under well-specified political conditions.

The strongest support for such a critique paradoxically comes from the work of institutional economists themselves. North's analysis of institutions is supported by a comparison of the British–North American path with the Spanish-Latin American one (1990a: 112–17). In contrast, the evidence from the East Asian NICs has been interpreted by a number of observers as supporting the case for intervention particularly for technology acquisition (Wade 1990; Amsden 1989). Using the NIE analysis, Chang (1994) argues that state intervention in South Korea *reduced* transaction costs by enabling the coordination of technology acquisition at a lower cost. These analysts thus reverse North's institutional ranking by suggesting that attenuated private rights might perform better than well-defined ones.

The evidence suggests that the political balance of power conditions both the problems institutions have to solve and the costs of solving them in particular ways. The Industrial Revolution in Britain and early North American industrialisation occurred in fairly similar societies. Political power was relatively dispersed and technical opportunities required relatively small investments. Well-defined property rights and the market resulted in growth. These institutions can therefore be *described* as having low transaction costs.

76

In contrast, South Korea and Taiwan in the 1960s were societies where political power was effectively centralised and both faced the opportunity of catching up by coordinating technology acquisition. In these countries centralised coordination proved effective and interventionist institutions can be *described* as having low transaction costs. The NIE explanation is misleading because in neither case does this describe anything intrinsic to the institution but only its performance in a particular context.

Looking at the experiences of less successful countries demonstrates why this is critically important. Pakistan in the 1960s, for instance, had an interventionist state quite similar in its modernising motivation to the one in South Korea. It also had political exclusion under a military regime. Its economic performance was initially promising but not good enough to satisfy all demands and the experiment ended with civil war and the dismemberment of the country in 1971. In Pakistan, as in many other developing countries, although political power was formally centralised, effective political power remained dispersed and was used to challenge formal political and economic rights. Here a strategy which required the centre to coordinate the interests of political organisations rapidly became prohibitively conflictual (Khan 1989).

Both rent-seeking analysis and the subsequent transaction cost models are in effect correcting implicit assumptions in conventional models regarding the social costs of contestation over different sets of rights. The net effects of an institution depend not just on the institution and the production technologies it coordinates but also and critically on the balance of power between the classes and groups affected by that institution, that is, on the *political settlement*. North is quite right in pointing out that the informal institutions which can be supported in an economy depend on the polity. However the same is true for formal institutions. The contestation over particular institutions can vary across polities. If so, an institution which is theoretically superior in a model which keeps these costs constant may not be superior when we allow for differences in the political settlement.

One consequence of recognizing differences in the political settlement is that it is possible to explain why performance rankings of institutions in one political settlement may not be transportable to another. The related but more serious problem is to devise a methodology which will allow us to isolate important questions about institutions and to develop analytical models which can address the performance of institutions in specific settlements. The NIE methodology summarised in Figure 5.2 assumes that it is possible to separate the transaction costs associated with an institutional structure into the 'institution effect' of each institution and a residual 'political effect' to be attributed to the political settlement. Instead it is more likely that the balance of power determines the net benefits particular institutions or structures can deliver by determining the contestation costs of maintaining the institution.

If so, a more appropriate methodology would be to begin by trying to identify important aspects of the political settlement in the country where

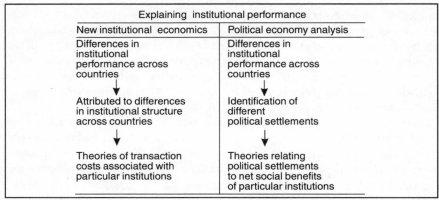

Explaining institutional performance	
New institutional economics	Political economy analysis
Differences in institutional performance across countries ↓	Differences in institutional performance across countries ↓
Attributed to differences in institutional structure across countries ↓	Identification of different political settlements ↓
Theories of transaction costs associated with particular institutions	Theories relating political settlements to net social benefits of particular institutions

Figure 5.2   NIE versus political economy methodologies

Type I performance is being assessed. Information about the political settlement can come from historical and sociological sources. It can also be based on comparing institutional performance in the country with others which attempted similar institutional changes. If performance differed substantially, this would alert us to the relative power of classes or groups adversely affected by the institution in the two countries. The alternative methodology is also summarised in Figure 5.2. Here the analysis of the relative economic effects of institutions is concerned with the effects of a specific political settlement on the net social benefits associated with alternative institutions.

The implications in terms of policy assessments are quite substantial. Comparing Pakistan with South Korea does more than simply point to conclusions about the transaction costs associated with particular institutional arrangements. Instead a comparative exercise and a reading of history facilitates an understanding of differences in the balance of power between the groups relevant for each set of institutions across these countries. A comparison of industrial policy in Pakistan and South Korea in the 1960s suggests that the former had much stronger clientelist linkages between middle- and lower-middle-class groups and the state. These linkages prevented the Pakistan state from making centralised decisions except at a much higher cost in terms of lost net benefits compared to South Korea (Khan 1989).

Industrial policy would be 'responsible' for Type I failure in Pakistan if it is possible to identify alternative institutional arrangements which would imply higher net social benefits *given the balance of political power* in that country in the 1960s. The Pakistan variant of industrial policy, like the South Korean one, was based on the state deciding the industrial activity of a small number of large conglomerates. There are a great number of alternatives which may have reduced the costs of contestation emanating from a large, well-organised but excluded middle class. For instance, the Taiwanese strategy allowed small capitalists to compete vigorously in a relatively free market while technology acquisition was organised by the public sector (Whitley 1992 compares the sociological differences with the South Korean strategy). This may have absorbed many more members of the contesting middle class in Pakistan into capitalist roles. The role of multinationals is also interesting because it may allow a clientelist state to prevent contestation in critical areas. The Malaysian strategy of limiting most of its clientelism to sectors where important technology decisions were not involved is instructive. Other more radical institutional alternatives could also be considered. Thus industrial policy may have been responsible for structural failure in Pakistan even though it played a dynamic role in South Korea. Why did the Pakistan state follow such a strategy? Was it a weak state? These questions are addressed in the next section.

TYPE II STATE FAILURES

Why should the executive branch of any state not introduce growth-increasing rights? After all, even a predatory state could benefit from growth. The failure to change institutions to improve net social benefits is Type II state failure or transition failure. Explanations of Type II failure can be classified under three heads. The first looks at the objectives of the political leadership and in particular their time horizon compared to that of society. The second concentrates on errors of calculation and the correctness of the models of the world used by agents including the political leadership. The third and potentially most interesting approach looks at the costs of change. The NIE contribution here has been to model these costs as a variant of transaction costs (as in *political* transaction costs, North 1990a). The remainder of this section will concentrate on the implications of applying transaction costs to the analysis of change and briefly indicate why the other two approaches are of limited interest.

If policy-makers desire lower growth than society, this is a failure of political representation. Problems emerge when an attempt is made to identify systematic reasons why political leaders may not want growth. One explanation is in terms of the time horizon of leaders. This is implicit in the revenue-maximising state discussed in North (1981). Such a state is not interested in introducing output-maximising property rights if this lowers short-run tax revenues. Casual observation suggests that predatory leaders do not always have short time horizons. Marcos in the Philippines or Ershad in Bangladesh behaved until the very end as if they expected to last forever. Moreover, even if some predators have high discount rates, is this an exogenous variable? For instance, the Kuomintang in China in the 1940s could only be described as predatory (Moore 1991: 187–201). The very same Kuomintang in Taiwan in the 1950s established a developmental state (Wade 1990). It is unlikely that there was an exogenous change in the time preference of Chiang Kai Shek and his party between these two dates. It is more likely that the behaviour of the KMT in China followed from an inability to impose their programme on the population. Type II failure has to be explained by something other than the time preferences of the leadership.

The problems with the knowledge-based arguments are quite similar. Wrong models of the world and imperfect knowledge have been identified as a cause of stagnation (North 1990a: 8). For instance, policy-makers may have introduced tariffs to protect domestic industry but, by taxing their raw material imports as well, the net effect may be to disadvantage domestic industry. However, if knowledge was the source of Type II state failure, why does it persist? It would be hard to argue that leaders of less successful countries have lagged behind in *wanting* to learn policies and ideologies from more successful countries. Nor is there any evidence that they persistently make a greater number of mistakes. But less dynamic countries *do* find it more difficult to correct mistakes once made. Failure may have more to do with the costs of changing institutions rather than imperfect knowledge or inadequate vision.

Even if there were substantial differences in the models used by leaders, there are good methodological reasons for focusing on the costs of change in analysing Type II failure. The relative importance of subjective and objective factors in explaining the performance of the state is an old issue in social science. In the case of firms which share the same environment, the differences in the subjective creativity of entrepreneurs (Schumpeter's entrepreneurial vision) may be fairly important in explaining their relative performance. In comparing the relative performance of states, the objective differences in their environments are likely to be far more substantial. The environment refers not just to technological possibilities but also to political settlements. Subjective differences between leaders may still be important but may in this case be *relatively* less important. Good analysis should therefore begin by asking how objective factors might determine Type II failure.

The third set of explanations focuses on the objective political differences between societies. If growth-enhancing institutions do not emerge there must be resistance to change. The NIE approach is to model institutional change as a series of voluntary contracts. It is therefore exactly analogous to the neo-classical model of market exchange. In the latter transaction costs may prevent all the gains from trade from being exhausted. In exactly the same way, the costs of organising institutional change may prevent all socially beneficial institutional changes from being implemented. Institutional change involves losers, and if it is to be freely negotiated, the losers must be compensated. In the NIE literature, the compensations are referred to as side-payments (Libecap 1989) or participation bribes (Dow 1993). Political transaction costs are the costs of *organising* the side-payments which allow institutions to be changed through a process of voluntary contracts (North 1990a: 49–51). Type II failure is then explained by high levels of political transaction costs:

> The efficiency of the political market is the key to this issue. If political

transaction costs are low and the political actors have accurate models to guide them, then efficient property rights will result.

(North 1990a: 52)

The critique of the NIE approach to the costs of change applied in this chapter makes two related points: (a) if all institutional changes were voluntarily negotiated with compensating side-payments, all Type II failures would be due to failures of knowledge alone. The costs of change then become irrelevant as an explanation of Type II failure. However, (b) most important institutional changes are *politically* resisted by the losers because compensation is either not offered or, if offered, is not accepted. The intensity and extent of resistance is the real 'cost of change' faced by its initiators, namely, the *transition cost*. This is a cost of change but it is not the political transaction cost. The transition cost is the political cost faced by initiators of new institutions. It depends on the change attempted, the gainers and losers from that change and the balance of power in that society. Thus, it can be concluded that the NIE approach does not in fact explain Type II failure. It is possible to have Type II success with high political transaction costs. It is equally possible to have Type II failure with low political transaction costs.

First, it is necessary to establish why political transaction costs are not relevant for the transacted institutional changes analysed by NIE. Suppose voluntary contracts were the only available procedure for organising institutional change. Then the only *attainable* institutions would be those which could be created through voluntary negotiations between individuals. If agents had full information they would always contract into the best attainable institutions given their costs and preferences. Attainable institutions would only be 'lost' if the political transaction costs were higher than they need be. Is there any reason why political transaction costs should be higher than attainable?

Like ordinary transaction costs, political transaction costs are specific to institutions, in this case political institutions. Consequently, individuals could contract to create new political institutions to lower political transaction costs if *they* were attainable. With full information, this too should automatically happen whenever there are potential gains in net benefits from such a change. For North, democratic institutions may not have zero political transaction costs (1990a: 51) but they are the most favourable institutional structure approximating that condition (1990a: 109). For others in the NIE tradition, the costs of negotiating can be lowered by *restricting* political access (Rogerson 1982; Chang 1994: 38–40). In either case, an explanation has to be found which shows why individuals do not negotiate the creation of *political* institutions with the lowest political transaction costs.

It may be that such political changes are blocked by even higher level transaction costs ('constitutional transaction costs'?). These may include the costs of making credible commitments of compensation to those disadvantaged by the proposed political changes or the costs of monitoring new types of free-riding behaviour once the new institutions are created. Either these constitutional transaction costs are unavoidable and prohibitive in which case political institutions cannot be changed to reduce political transaction costs. In this case we have no Type II failure. Or political transaction costs *can* be lowered. In this case political transaction costs are indeed responsible for Type II failure but this should be transitory. As soon as agents are informed of the possibility of reducing political transaction costs they should freely negotiate the institutional changes which would remove the Type II failure.

With full information, the best institutional world attainable through individual contracting (apart from transitory blips) can be realised (Dahlman 1979). Consequently political transaction costs can only explain Type II failure during the transitory blips when agents have not caught up with new knowledge. Only persistent failures of knowledge can result in political transaction costs being persistently higher than necessary. In that case this explanation collapses into the lack of information explanation discussed earlier.

But in fact important real world institutional changes are rarely accompanied by the compensation of losers. Human history may not be a history of class struggle alone but it is certainly not a history of negotiated institutional change. Modelling institutional change 'as if' it were a negotiated process with compensation allows the importation of sophisticated tools developed in the neo-classical analysis of market exchanges but makes the analysis seriously deficient. Real-world institutional change involves path changes. These are discontinuous breaks in the paths that would have been negotiated through compensation. Even relatively minor institutional changes such as changes in tax rates are typically not negotiated through compensating side-payments. The NIE in contrast is 'explaining' path dependence which involves negotiated transitions along a defined path which may have many branches.

The costs of change become relevant with path changing. The relevant costs of change are not the transaction costs of organising side-payments. By definition, if side-payments are not on offer, the cost of organising them is not relevant. The relevant costs of change are what we shall call transition costs. *Transition costs measure the political costs which potential losers from a proposed institutional change can impose on the proponents.* Proponents of change can rank potential projects in terms of the political opposition they are likely to face. This ranking reveals their assessment of the transition costs of projects. The ranking may turn out to be wrong and have to be revised over time. But at any given time, the transition cost ranking indicates which if any of the projects are politically feasible given the tolerance level of the proponents to absorb transition costs.

Unlike political transaction costs which are an economic cost, transition costs cannot be measured using an economic numeraire. The political costs they measure are the 'costs' inflicted on a specified group by political events such as physical violence or defeats in elections. Some of these costs may have

	HIGH POLITICAL TRANSACTION COSTS	LOW POLITICAL TRANSACTION COSTS
HIGH TRANSITION COSTS FOR GROUP PROPOSING GROWTH	LOW TRANSITION Pakistan 1960s	SLOW TRANSITION South Asian democracies
LOW TRANSITION COSTS FOR GROUP PROPOSING GROWTH	RAPID TRANSITION East Asian NICs China 1980s	RAPID TRANSITION US and UK 19th century

Figure 5.3 Political transaction costs versus transition costs

an economic counterpart in damage to property or losses to production but even here what matters is the ranking of composite bundles of costs associated with each strategy. One important determinant of the transition costs political contenders can inflict on one another is the balance of power described by the political settlement. Given the transition cost ranking of each group, the feasibility of particular projects depends on the critical level of transition costs the group can absorb. The ability to absorb transition costs and change rights in turn changes the political settlement since the relative political power of classes depends to some extent on their formal economic and political rights.

Although transition costs are not directly related to political transaction costs, organising cooperation within a class or group with similar interests does depend on the costs of organising side-payments. In turn, the ability of the contending groups to organise collectively is one factor determining the political costs they can impose on others. The relationship between transaction costs and transition costs is shown in Figure 5.3.

High transition costs for classes proposing growth-enhancing institutional changes are shown in the top row in Figure 5.3. Transitions will be slow regardless of the political transaction costs of negotiating change. Implicitly the balance of power is in favour of groups who would be hurt by the growth strategy proposed. Here low political transaction costs may paradoxically allow cheaper organisation of resistance by the dominant group. The stagnation in the top right-hand cell may be deeper than in the top left-hand cell! This would be the case, for instance, if institutional changes proposed by an emergent industrial class are being successfully resisted by clientelist groups which stand to lose from these changes. In such a context, political arrangements with low costs of negotiating collective action (such as an efficient democracy) may help the dominant clientelist groups further (Khan 1989).

83

On the other hand, if the political settlement favours classes who are initiating growth-enhancing institutional changes, they will face low transition costs along the bottom row in Figure 5.3. Once again, the effects of political transaction costs are indeterminate. Low costs of negotiating political transfers may further help the already dominant class to coordinate their strategies and to suppress political opposition. The emergence of Parliament as a committee of enclosing landlords may have played just such a role in seventeenth-century England (Moore 1991: 19). However, if universal suffrage is the only democratic option, an emerging capitalist class may prefer *high* political transaction costs. With more efficient political institutions, they may find it easier to coordinate their own actions but they may also have to compensate losers much more. The experience of the East Asian NICs and China in the 1980s demonstrates this. The Chinese experience also shows that well-defined property rights are not necessary for Type I success. If the initial allocation hindered capitalist development, with an appropriate political balance of power, weakly defined rights may simply indicate rapid transition and Type II success.

Type II failure or transition failure can happen for two sorts of reasons. Given the political settlement, it may be that some beneficial changes with acceptable transition costs are lost because of problems of knowledge or vision or avoidable political transaction costs. These factors result in a failure to negotiate improvements which could have been contractually attained. NIE explanations of Type II failure address this aspect of the transition problem. A second possible reason for Type II failure is that transition costs for a *specific* class or group result in potential institutional changes not being selected. This much more important possibility is the one which needs to be seriously addressed.

The identification of Type II failure due to high transition costs could in turn be based on a number of comparisons with different political implications. First, it should be possible to compare the existing *institutional structure* with an alternative (with lower Type I failure) *holding the political settlement constant*. Type II failure exists if the existing process of institutional change does not lead to the emergence of this alternative structure. Second, a comparison might be made between the existing *political settlement* and an alternative (with lower Type I failure) *holding the existing structure of institutions constant*. Type II failure follows in this case from the state and the classes associated with existing institutions not being able to change the political settlement in the appropriate way. Finally, it may be possible to compare existing performance with an alternative with different institutions *and* a different political settlement. Type II failure in this case follows from not being able to change both institutions and the settlement in appropriate ways.

While it is relatively simple in each case to *describe* the location of Type II failure, by focusing on one possible location rather than the large number of potential alternatives, the analyst is making a political judgement about the transition which is desirable. This is a political judgement because there is no arithmetic to compare alternative sets of potential net benefits with transition costs which vary in their intensity and incidence and which are ordinal rankings specific to particular groups. Nevertheless such judgements have to be made. It is then necessary to be explicit about the political values and notions of justice informing the particular choices being suggested.

Differences in political implications can be seen by referring to the example of structural failure in Pakistan in the 1960s. The first type of comparison would locate transition failure in the inability of alternative sets of capitalists (small capitalists or multinationals for instance) to establish alternative institutions more appropriate to the political settlement. The focus here would be on the inability of these groups to absorb the transition costs involved or to reduce the ability of existing groups to inflict these costs. The policy implication would be to mobilise and strengthen these groups for such a contest. Alternatively, a comparison could be made between the political settlement in Pakistan and an alternative which would allow industrial policy of this type to work. Transition failure here would be attributed to the inability of the military regime to change the political settlement by absorbing the transition costs involved or reducing them through political deals. The Ayub Khan regime in Pakistan did in fact attempt such a transition through a process of suppression and selective incorporation of clientelist groups. The experiment was abandoned after the uprising of 1969–71 and a civil war in which possibly a million people died. If the state is judged to have been a 'weak state' the subsequent policy implications are clear. Finally, a comparison with an alternative set of institutions with a different political settlement could result in radical conclusions and the identification of alternative political programmes.

The analysis of transition failure is therefore quite separate from the political judgements involved in selecting a particular strategy of transition. The great danger with the NIE approach is that by ignoring transition costs it presents what are essentially transitions as processes which can be managed judiciously by states which have the right models or the right 'vision' (Chang and Rowthorn 1993). States, when they are involved in processes of transition, are attempting some transitions rather than others. The justification for this must be based on a politics which should be made explicit. Moreover, transitions which had low transition costs in one context may not in another. The difference between South Korea and Pakistan had little to do with the quality of their leaders or their conflict management skills. The real difference was in the balance of power in these societies in the 1960s. A political assessment of the transition costs which were inflicted by the Pakistan experiment of the 1960s suggests that other strategies of transition must have been preferable even if Pakistan had managed as a result to achieve the South Korean rate of growth.

CONCLUSIONS

The aim of the NIE is to analyse the economic implications of institutions and to suggest policy. It has been argued that a mapping from institutions to economic performance cannot be sustained either theoretically or with reference to history. This conclusion holds even if the institutional specification includes political and informal institutions. An analysis of the political settlement is required for assessing the contribution of specific institutions to Type I failure. It is even possible for the ranking of institutions in terms of their economic performance to be reversed under different political settlements. The alternative research methodology suggested is to analyse the implications of institutional structures under specified political settlements.

The analysis of transition or Type II failure is even more seriously affected by the absence of a political analysis. The NIE analysis is either correct and trivial or incorrect and misleading. It would be correct if real-world institutional changes were voluntarily negotiated between contracting parties. It would nevertheless be trivial because in such a world all transition failures would be due to information lags. In fact, institutional change does not involve compensation and the NIE analysis turns out to be seriously misleading. The relevant cost of institutional change is a political cost, the transition cost. The transition cost is closely dependent on the political settlement. Transitions which were possible with low transition costs in one context may be unacceptably costly in another. But this is not all. To select between strategies which have different intensities and distributions of transition costs requires a political judgement about the acceptable incidence of transition costs. Finally, it is worth remembering that a 'mistake' in the assessment of the transition costs involved in implementing particular programmes of institutional change can ultimately result in civil war and large-scale loss of lives. The false sense of objectivity in the NIE analysis could not be more serious.

NOTE

I would like to thank John Toye for his support. Many colleagues and friends read and gave very useful comments on earlier drafts. Particular thanks are due to Stephanie Blankenburg, Wendy Carlin, Ali Cheema, Andrew Glyn, Asma Khan and Rathin Roy whose help in different ways was invaluable.

6

MAPS AND LANDSCAPES OF GRAIN MARKETS IN SOUTH ASIA

Barbara Harriss-White

INTRODUCTION: THE NATURE OF MARKETS

'The market' is conventionally seen as perfectly competitive. It is operational-ised as an atomistic realm of impersonal economic exchange of homogeneous goods by means of voluntary transactions on an equal basis between large numbers of autonomous, fully informed entities with profit-maximising be-havioural motivations and able to enter and leave freely. It is the supreme medium for the expression of individual choice (Hodgson 1988: 178). Models of other stylised market structures (monopoly, oligopoly) alter certain criteria, retain others and predict the consequences for prices and quantities.

These abstractions do not contribute greatly to an understanding of spatial variations in the structure and behaviour of real markets (Olsen 1991). Real markets have indeed proved awkward to define; but their definition enables us to discern the mass of exchange that is not mediated by the market. A restrictive definition of market exchange in which voluntarism, egalitarianism and infor-mational availability are stressed has been offered by Pandya and Dholakia, 'the simultaneous transaction of valued goods and services between two parties [who are] capable of accepting or rejecting the values offered ... and [who are] uncoerced and capable of communication and delivery' (1992: 24). By contrast, Fourie sees a real market as 'an economically qualified, purposeful interchange of commodities on the basis of *quid pro quo* obligations at a mutually agreed upon exchange rate ... in a cluster of exchange and rivalry relations' (1991: 43,48). Here, the social relations unique to market exchange require the combination of 'horizontal' and adversarial competition between populations of buyers (and populations of sellers) on the one hand and a mass of 'vertical', exclusive, mutualistic, bilateral transactions between one buyer and one seller on the other. The implications of this definition (*pace* the voluntarist defini-tion) are that exchange rates mutually agreed on may not be mutually beneficial, that vertical contractual arrangements may prevail over horizontal competition, and that purposeful bargaining and the obligations resulting from it may rest on and reinforce a highly unequal base or fall-back position.

Non-market exchange will then be of two principal sorts: redistribution and reciprocity. Polanyi contrasted such non-market exchange with that of a stylised modern society where commercial logic rules and an unembedded price-making market dominates economic life (Polanyi *et al.* 1957/1985; see also Platteau 1990b: 10 for a similar dualism). But as Braudel has observed, 'It is too easy to reduce one phenomenon to sociology and another to economics' (1985: 223). And John Davis is the most recent of many to argue against Polanyi's dualistic schema on the empirical grounds *not* that reciprocity and redistribution did not, or do not, characterise underdeveloped exchange but that they are deeply pervasive in what he calls OECD economies (Davis 1992). With reference to markets for staple food, with which we are principally concerned here, it is likely that both redistribution and reciprocity are of quantitative importance in themselves and further that when market relations are entered into in order to acquire an input to a relation of reciprocity (for example, grain) it is the logic of reciprocity not the profit- or utility-maximising market logic that is the motivation for marketing.

Fourie's kind of market is conventionally distinguished from other types of economic activity, for example firms. Although some theorists have depicted firms as clusters of individual market-like contractual relationships, firms are better seen as 'a command economy in microcosm' (Folbre 1994: 45). Their internal structure of authority is understood by some primarily to minimise transaction costs and by others primarily as a coercive mechanism. The point is that firms cannot be reduced to markets. Firms are a type of economic institution and a conventional characterisation contrasts institutions with markets. Markets must then be understood as '*not-institutions*' (Folbre 1994: 24).

But markets cannot exist in a de-institutionalised form: no economic phenomena do. It is only possible to construct supply and demand schedules on the assumption that buyers and sellers react as though any price could be the equilibrium price. Prices are therefore formed in logical time as if expectations and memories were eliminated. This is a necessary condition for perfect competition. But perfect competition not only does not exist, it would not be viable for long if it did exist because entry, exit, investment and disinvestment depend in the actual world upon the belief or the fact that information regarding opportunities is restricted. Two central tenets of the neo-classical project, 'methodological individualism' involving voluntarist and individualist subjective preference and instrumental rationality on the one hand and the market (as an actually existing bundle of 'legal, customary, political and other social arrangements' in which parties act with procedural rationality (Hodgson 1988: 174)) on the other are incompatible.

'Institution' is a notion used in at least three rather loose ways. The first is sociological. Any behavioural regularity is the manifestation of an institution (Fourie 1991: 52). Thus a conference is an institution but so also is the way in which biological sex becomes social gender or norms of justice and other aspects of ideology and social rules are developed and reproduced. The second is micro-economic. Institutions are understood in 'special case' terms. North argues that organisations are distinct from (social normative) institutions and examines the tensions between them. Organisations are groups of individuals bound by some common purpose to achieve objectives (North 1990a: 5). The organisations or micro-economic institutions of interest to economists are those concerned with production and exchange: firms and contracts. The third sense of institution is macro-economic, encompassing the definition of rights, the scope of economic behaviour, the mechanisms to protect exchange, penalise miscreants and through taxation ensure state legitimacy (Giddens 1992; Shaffer 1979). The word will be explored in all three senses here.

The questions addressed in this chapter concern the theoretical, methodological and substantive means whereby we can understand how real markets are institutionalised. The substantive territory is an 'actually existing market' which is arguably the most crucial for state legitimacy and social survival – that for grain – and in a country with two-thirds of recorded global poverty in which social survival for many is painful and time-consuming: India. The efficiency of actually existing markets in the agricultural sector is both an unexamined theoretical assumption of, and a practical prerequisite to the success of, the economic liberalisation reforms enacted since 1991 (Parikh 1993; Pursell and Gulati 1993; Cassen *et al.* 1993). The substantive landscape will be somewhat stylised from the insights of field research on grain markets in Tamil Nadu and West Bengal. We present empirically observed regularities which are vulnerable to falsification. Our account is based on primary field material gathered in North Arcot District over the period 1972–94 (Harriss 1981) and Coimbatore District in 1980 (Harriss 1991a) both of which are in Tamil Nadu; and in Birbhum District in 1982 (Harriss 1982) and Bardhaman District in 1990 (Harriss 1991b) both in West Bengal.

As a starting point, it may be argued that markets *are* institutions, contain bundles of other institutions and are nested in yet others. If the institutionalised nature of markets is accepted, there is still a world of difference between regarding these institutions as imperfections or as constraints to a commercial logic based on profit maximisation and voluntarism on the one hand (North 1990a; Ensminger 1992: 6; Folbre 1994), and regarding the institutions of markets as inherent and essential characteristics of their functioning on the other: what society *is* (Etzioni 1988: 9).

The former approach invites normative policy advocacy in the form of interventions making individual markets more closely resemble perfect competition (with its assumption that efficiency is an uncontested primary value and with its implications for Pareto optimality (Clarke 1982: 165)). A methodological trap is set here, because under conditions of deviation from perfect competition, changes are necessary to all factor and product markets in order to achieve optimality and empirical research in the economics of agricultural marketing generally assesses the allocative efficiency of one commodity market alone (Rudra 1992). The latter, 'enabling' approach to institutions questions the value for policy-making of conventional 'market purism', is not necessarily normative and endogenises the policy process itself.

What *are* the key institutions of real markets? How do we come to understand how a real market works? What are the projections, scales and keys to the maps which depict this landscape?

SOCIAL INSTITUTIONS OF MARKETS

In a recent book, Folbre (1994) has convincingly sustained her hypothesis that production and reproduction are shaped by a variety of types of institution of collective action. These institutions can be ascribed, acquired, multiple, not coordinated and non-monitored. Returns to participation in such institutions are not consciously calculated. It must be noted, however, that social institutions are of two types, first, social groups and, second, the social norms, ideologies and conventions underlying such groups.

One point about social norms in Indian grain markets is necessary. Although space does not permit a detailed discussion of 'mercantile norms', a singular feature of trading ethics in Indian grain markets is that notions of right and wrong are usually context-specific. Many practices can only be justified by the existence of an ethic which places the material interests of a merchant's family before any other moral consideration. At the same time collective action based on the material and moral interests of castes has only recently been challenged by morality based on acquired qualities. Formal law and the interests of the abstract community will also be morally referred to and adhered to by grain traders. For this moral multiplicity to be possible there has also to be a fourth mechanism for shifts between referents and for recognition of the appropriateness of the various norms. The social result is that in the Indian grain trade, grossly exploitative and/or technically criminal economic activity thus coexist with legal compliance and with piety, religiosity and (within limits) a redistributive charity.

Here, although social groups may encompass family, caste or ethnicity, the discussion will concentrate on class; and, although for Folbre sexual preference is as important analytically as class and race, the focus we will be on social convention not through sexuality but rather through the prism of patriarchy.

Class and markets

Theory and methodology

The institutional phenomenon of class is identified in three ways. Classical Marxists define class in terms of relationship to the means of production – class in itself. Class is also used to refer to explicit political alignments defending a collective material interest – class for itself. The word is also used more loosely to refer to habitual rather than conscious behaviour to defend collective interest (Etzioni, 1988; North, 1990a). We shall deconstruct these ideas in relation to grain markets. Most analyses of class are focused upon production, not the least because of its theoretical primacy and determinacy in political economy. 'Merchant's capital' is the Marxist analogue to 'the market'. In its abstract form merchant's capital is used for buying and selling which does not change the nature of the good traded. This form of capital is therefore necessary but unproductive and by extension unable to affect production relations. Actually existing commercial capital is as far removed from 'merchant's capital' as real markets are from 'the market'.

The first useful contribution made by political economy to an empirical framework for the analysis of agricultural markets concerns the determination of institutional forms taken by markets. In political economy, the question of historical determination of institutions of the market has been addressed by examining their relation to forms of production: 'a definite form of production ... logically ... determines the forms of consumption, distribution and exchange, and also the mutual relations between these elements' (Marx 1971: 33). Yet Marx also argued that changes in modes of distribution, which he attributed to both exogenous factors (such as the expansion of demand, or the locational readjustment of rural and urban populations) and endogenous (such as the concentration of capital) would change production in a process of 'mutual interaction', hedging his bets both over the direction and the nature of determination (Marx 1971: 22).

Contemporary political economy theorists of South Asia have succeeded in analysing mercantile power as manifested structurally in property relations resulting from specific forms of production (Blaikie et al. 1981, for Nepal; Chattopadhyay 1969; Chattopadhyay and Spitz 1987, for North East India; Djurfeldt and Lindberg 1974; Nagaraj 1985 for South India). More controversially, the property relations of commodity exchange have been theorised to be manifested in an indirect control over production via a variety of modes of surplus appropriation as well as via control over interlocked markets, such that production relations are determined by exchange relations and the direction of determination is reversed (Bhaduri 1986). However, while it may be possible to explain market forms by reference to institutions of production, this empirical practice has not yet moved below high levels of generality towards the interesting details of institutions of production and distribution.

In this context, Leplaideur (1992) has proposed a class analysis of agricultural market systems. Classes are defined, as classically, in terms of forces and relations but here they are of distribution as well as production. The forces of distribution are defined as assets, information, activities and access to the state. The relations of distribution are organisational networks (kin, friends, neighbours), contractual behaviour and the internal social relations of firms.

Classes within markets are then proposed in terms of (a) access to the means of distribution (transport, sites, capital or credit, stock (inventory) information and patents, etc.) and (b) status in terms of surplus appropriation. From this potentially highly complex classification, Leplaideur has developed a four class schema according to these criteria: pauperising traders, marginal and assetless traders, simple-reproducing firms and surplus accumulating firms.

This is a methodological advance on a par with that proposed some time ago for the empirical analysis of production by Deere and de Janvry (1979). It also offers a framework within which micro-economic institutions may be analysed. Key expressions of power may be located. The theoretical and empirical question whether markets can be analysed as entities or whether they have to be contextualised and whether, if so, not just in production relations but also within national and international marketing systems, are posed.

A few comments are in order. First, the two notions of class and surplus appropriation are used heretically by Leplaideur. They are Marxist terms but as used here they do not invoke a Marxist teleology. In practice, surplus accumulation would be indistinguishable from proxies such as total returns, profit, or savings and investments which are easier to measure. Second, time is inadequately specified. Insofar as markets enable the daily survival of small firms the time-frame will be on a micro-scale. Insofar as the accumulation dynamic is an analytical fundamental, the time-frame could be generational. In between, seasonal variability in structure and behaviour will introduce much indeterminacy into any analysis based on this framework. Third, the current taxonomy has immense possibilities for disaggregation. Unless the various criteria are congruent they will generate an untractable complexity. Since marketing systems exhibit considerable institutional autonomy, such a congruence is unlikely.

Exchange relations and class-in-itself in the Indian grain economy

The terms and conditions of exchange relations have been discovered to be complex. There have been two influential attempts to model them. First, Bharadwaj (1974, 1985) has located exchange in production relations, modelling its terms and conditions for an agrarian structure comprising a differentiated owner occupancy with four agrarian classes.

At the apex, prices are created by the speculative exchange of the class of large farmers who are not only subsistence producers *par excellence*, but who also dominate the marketed surplus. Middle cultivators respond competitively to the prices established by the exchange behaviour of large cultivators. Small cultivators are modelled as long-term self-sufficient and engaged in sporadic marketing. At the base are two classes – small peasants and landless labour which are compulsively involved in markets in order to obtain the means of subsistence. The implications of such exchange relations for supply and price schedules have been modelled by Sarkar in a theory of multi-stratum price formation (1989).

The distinction between normal or voluntaristic marketing and that under conditions of coercion provoked Bhaduri (1983, 1986) into theorising forced commerce for a share-cropping agrarian structure wherein relations of debt cause producers to part with subsistence requirements immediately post-harvest on disavantageous terms of (disguised) interest and price only to buy it back pre-harvest using loans on terms and conditions where the risk of default is transferred to the borrower. Distress commerce of this general type has been widely observed empirically coexisting with normal commerce under a variety of agrarian structures in South Asia (Nadkarni 1980; Harriss *et al.* 1984; Crow 1991; Olsen 1991).

The institutional attributes of commodity markets in these models are never specified. In Bharadwaj's formulation 'the market' is implicitly competitive and in Bhaduri's it has to consist of a strategic alliance of landlords, money-lenders and traders (whose internal conflicts of interest are then explored, and have been subsequently thoroughly criticised). Yet it follows from these models that resource appropriation via 'the market' is far more complex than a mere redistribution resulting from buying and selling. The terms of buying and selling will be affected by those of interlocked markets. Commonly, agricultural commodity transactions are interlocked with credit contracts in ways which can sometimes be shown to depress commodity prices below levels resulting from unconstrained transactions and to raise interest above 'market' rates. Cases have been analysed of the triadic interlocking of water, grain and money through three agents: merchant-moneylenders; moneylending and borrowing sellers of water and grain; and purchasers of water and grain who borrow money (Janakarajan and Subramaniam 1991). It is clear, however, that interlocked commerce renders irrelevant both a comparison with a competitive alternative (should it be identifiable) for a subordinate party deprived of choice, and the separation of interest and price. Buying and selling on class-specific terms and conditions may also be further affected by opportunistic speculation and hoarding. Resources may also be appropriated through capitalist relations in agroprocessing and other productive activities necessary to the post-harvest commodity system abstracted as 'the market'. Resources are also commonly appropriated from producers in underdeveloped agricultural markets in primi-tive ways through crime and coercion (via fraud on weights and measures, arbitrary deductions, misinformation about price, etc.) as well as through the corrupt subversion of regulatory interventions of the state (Janakarajan 1986; Harriss 1991a; Harris *et al.* 1984).

Within grain marketing systems, large numbers of agents coexist with a distribution of mercantile property combining massive polarisation and con-centration. Gini assets and output coefficients of 0.6–0.75, are normal – considerably greater than those for land and production. 'Oligopolies', for want of a better word, coexist with crowded, petty trade. Major entry barriers to the latter subsector are gender and caste rather than capital or information, though there are high and rising barriers of the last sorts protecting the local oligopolies. Important fractions of petty trade are not independent but tied. The mercantile oligopolies strive to set the terms and conditions of accumulation of the petty sector by relations of finance. Small firms are also dependent on large ones for information, and physical facilities such as storage, processing and transport for which rental markets commonly evolve.

Markets are not only economically but can also be spatially and temporally differentiated. Common patterns in India involve periodic markets with concentrations of petty trade, wholesale markets with a range of institutional diversity and wholesale sites arranged dendritically for regional (occasionally international) export (Bohle 1992). Although these market institutions maintain a varying degree of autonomy with respect to forms and institutions of agricultural production (such that real markets are not related deterministically to production relations) some of the variation in market institutions and behaviour is regional and seems a response not only to the technical requirements of the crop and the agrarian structure, but also to the specificities and serendipities of distributions of capital and information and to the actual substance of state intervention.

Political alignments: class-for-itself

Fox's pioneering anthropology of the commercial economy of a North Indian town drew a portrait of merchants as politically isolated, socially marginalised and defensive in their sporadic and minimalist collective activity (Fox 1968). Our field research on the political activity of grain traders has to an extent challenged this characterisation.

Formal political involvement on the part of grain merchants is indeed minimal and fragmented, although almost all big merchants are motivated coercively and by fear (which neo-classical economists would identify as self-interest and the transaction costs school as opportunism) lavishly to fund all political parties. Political parties are not class-based and no political party has a coherent operational policy on the private grain trade. Political power is exerted in more subtle ways through the manipulation of ostensibly non-political institutions such as those of social service (for status), of religion (for control over urban property) and of local government (for control over urban administration). Grain merchants wield their political clout through elaborate federations of trade associations. Fox's hypothesis that mercantile politics is defensive has been corroborated. It is the elite oligopolistic fraction which is well defended in this way. Grain merchants' politics is reactive, defending this class of accumulators primarily from claims from organised male labour within the marketing system (which is in turn provoked to create a range of labour unions by a range of political parties). It also defends this commercial class from state regulatory activity, of which more later. Such associations can and do organise the physical protection of marketplace sites from theft by grain consumers. And the formal group interests of large landed merchants have been observed to prevail over those of non-mercantile producers where a conflict of institutional objectives arises (as when Farmers' Movements sought the regulation of credit and of grain transactions in Coimbatore in 1980, a move suppressed by collusive action with the local judiciary by grain merchants who were members both of the farmers' movement and of the grain association). Grain traders are too heterogeneous to form one *political* alignment but their regular and indirect politics is usually supportive of the interests of those most economically powerful.

Habituated collective action

Considering patterned behaviour which is not formally organised, the most important expression of such action is via the reciprocal aspect of market mediated commodity exchange – the relations of money and credit. Three examples follow, but there are many more. First, the grain trade is financed, both in terms of investment capital and working capital, through networks derived from the ascriptive institution of caste. Depending on the relationship of caste to agrarian structure, such financial networks may mitigate the intensity of class-exploitative exchange relationships (as in South India where trade and agriculture are more often than not undertaken by similar castes) or they may intensify such relationships (as in West Bengal where the reverse is true). Second, acquired characteristics such as 'reputation' and 'loyalty' (increasingly replacing the ascription of caste as the grain trade becomes more complex, fast moving and long distance) are individual essentials which develop social patterns, on the basis of which creditworthiness is evaluated. Capacity to repay is more important to the earning of 'reputation' than capacity to lend *per se*. Third, trading requires acts of purchase and sale, but the length of delay of the payments for goods may be, first, unsymmetrical (for example, paying for purchases within 10 days but being repaid for sales within 90 days); second, variably compensated for by price and, third, extremely systematic such that certain positions within a marketing system, certain towns within a spatial market, may be points of economic power and others of economic weakness.

Thus, although Folbre writes accurately that 'shifting definitions of self-interest and changing possibilities of pursuing group interests create a strategic environment far more complex than any simply duality based on class and gender alone' (1994: 38), in historical fact, local mercantile oligopolies rarely make tactical errors.

Gender and grain markets

Theory and methodology

Aspects of culture have been argued to be more resilient to pressure for change than other social institutions, none more so than patriarchy (Ensminger 1992; Folbre 1994). Folbre argues that both gender ideology and gender relations are 'sticky' social institutions because of the macro-social ascription to women of the nurturing and protection of life, the affective work for which role massively compromises the capacity of women to resist male ideological domination and their control of property. Just as household reproduction is gendered so is market reproduction. The new home economics has done to the household what transaction costs economics has done to the firm. Comparative advantage within the household is inferred from values based on labour markets outside the household. The origin of the gender division of tasks in (and out of) the labour market is analytically externalised. It is a matter of debate whether intra-household activity is structured by markets or by patriarchy, and if by markets, then whether market valuations are gender-neutral and the result of productivity differentials and supply availabilities (which may be conditioned by prior patriarchally determined reproductive imperatives) or whether market wage rates are the 'independent' result of the operation of patriarchy in the market itself.

Gender in Indian grain markets

The grain trade is highly gendered. Extreme lack of ownership or control over property, or any 'means of circulation' (which determine creditworthiness), strongly gendered notions of space and of proper conduct for men and women enable women to participate in the grain trade in three ways according to their social caste position and economic class position. First, directly, women from pauperised, female-headed and/or low caste households are confined to petty and often seasonal operation, to subsistence orientation and 'simple reproduction', particular positions and activities within the system (especially processing and retailing), local territorial linkages, weekly marketplace sites and unlicensed and/or illegal transactions in cash.

Second, women are used for the caste-based reproduction and expansion of larger and higher caste firms by means of their dowries on marriage and through the (rare) practice of fictitious 'benami' registration of a trading company in a woman's name generally for purposes of tax avoidance. In these cases, the higher education of such women is a good example of the economic inefficiency of gender institutions. For such women education is a status good and leads neither to economic participation nor control over assets or over major economic decisions. Female education certainly leads to a lowering of birth rates (though not to reduced gender discrimination in regions where this is practised). But it is primary rather than tertiary education which achieves this result. Educated mothers are thought to educate their own children better, but the structure of ownership of large mercantile companies, framed by the pre-emption of tax laws, frequently requires strong male control of young male adults and discourages migration for advanced education.

Third, in the recent past in smaller family firms, unwaged female family members have provided that part of the wage to labour in trading firms which takes the form of prepared food (though with the commercialisation of labour, this practice of payment in tea and meals is dying, or itself being commercialised). Female labour will then subsidise the firm. It has to be added that a large rice milling and trading firm will almost certainly 'subsidise' some of the costs of reproduction of their male labour force such that the social reproduction of male labour is not entirely borne by female labour within their households. Accidents on site are usually compensated and medical expenses often paid at times of sickness. Both male and female labour receive at least one month's extra pay at a major festival. Often this is given in kind as cloth. It can also be argued that such payments both retard the formation of labour markets because of their informational opacity and reflect 'backward' relationships of patronage rather than market exchange by dint of their discretionary element.

Fourth, female casual wage workers from the assetless class form the large substratum of labour in rice milling and pre-milling processing. Outcaste women are allowed to turn paddy on the dry yards because the kernel is still protected from ritual pollution by its husk. Female coolie is prevalently regarded as a household supplement. Wage differentials of two-thirds to a half that of male wages in rice mills in no way reflect productivity (which in any case would be impossible to measure accurately since the division of tasks in milling is sex sequential). Female mill work is deliberately casualised: unionised female labour is never encountered. The sexual exploitation of the mill work force by management is not unknown.

Indian grain markets present themselves superficially as male domains but they reflect in vivid ways the gender subordination characteristic of Indian society as a whole. Resistance to these arrangements is rare.

MICRO-ECONOMIC INSTITUTIONS/ORGANISATIONS

Theory and methodology

Several types of systematic attempt have been made in order to remedy the theoretical reductionism pertaining to markets and in order to answer the question about key institutions. The methodological contributions of industrial organisation theorists, new institutional economics, and commodity systems approaches are reviewed briefly below.

Industrial organisational analysis

The earliest empirical framework was borrowed from the economics of industrial organisations where J. S. Bain and his school set out to explore through careful description the possibility of regular predictable relationships between market structure and behaviour (Bain 1959). Bain's empirical question concerned the welfare and efficiency effects of monopoly and oligopoly. To answer this required definitions of structure, conduct and performance (SCP) so that they were consistent with theory, empirically measurable and amenable to comparison. Market structure consists of organisational characteristics which can 'influence strategically the nature of competition and pricing' (Bain 1959: 8). These are the degree of seller and buyer concentration, the degree of product differentiation and entry conditions. Conduct consists of mechanisms of adjustment of firms to the market. These are firm-level price formation policies; and interfirm interaction. Market performance was defined as 'the character of end adjustments to the effective demands for sellers' output' and vice versa for buyers (Bain 1959: 11). Four main criteria were: the efficiency of production relative to firm size; size of profits; relation between production costs and marketing costs; progressiveness in industrial innovation.

The method underwent certain corruption on its translation to agricultural commodity markets (see Cummings 1967; Lele 1971; and Jasdanwalla 1966 for India; and Gilbert 1969; Illori 1968 and Jones 1972 for Africa). Problems with its use have included, first, the reification of Bain's SCP descriptive characteristics (which were carefully derived in the first place from price theory and welfare theory) to an efficiency norm (even though increased competition will not necessarily increase allocative efficiency because structure and performance are only linked theoretically under perfect competition, which does not exist) and, second, the interpretation of irregular deviations of large numbers of variables from an unrealisable ideal. Third, the evaluation of performance has been reduced to the analysis of price series (the more distorting, the more vertically extended the post-harvest system) with integration (a statistical concept) proxying for efficiency and competition. So far the prices of by-products have never been included in price integration analysis even though they are well known to have a crucial impact on allocative efficiency. Other problems include, fourth, vagueness of definition; fifth, aggregation problems and acute measurement difficulties such that only arbitrary subsets of Bain's SCP framework have been compared; sixth, the historically contingent lack of comparative analyses and, seventh the ideological deployment of the method to justify a minimalist role for the state (Harriss 1979; Pujo 1993).

The original project has failed both theoretically and practically in an important way. It has not proved possible to predict real performance from real structures. Nor the reverse. Price behaviour was not empirically relatable to structures. This does not mean that the method need be jettisoned provided the rigorous comparative project is relaxed and the method is deployed not only to describe SCP but also to examine the wider institutional framework.

Transaction costs economics (TCE)

The second approach draws upon insights of transaction costs economics (TCE) and stylisations of markets and firms. Institutions of the market are conceptualised as responses to problems of the organisation of information, of transactions and of property rights, under conditions of environmental and biological lags and uncertainty, opportunistic behaviour and bounded rationality.

Under certain conditions – either of specialisation in production and marketing and informational opacity, or of lack of specialisation and under-development of information infrastructure – information may be costly to obtain, to control and transfer. It may also be insufficient to enable calculations of the results of alternative actions. Information asymmetry and impactedness are argued to lead to 'opportunistic behaviour' and to high monitoring and enforcement costs. Such information and monitoring and enforcement costs are components of a broader set of costs necessary to the making and protection of contracts now known as transaction costs. These costs include the costs of search and screening, of negotiation and of transfer of property rights, of coordination, and safeguarding (Jaffee 1990; Marion *et al.* 1986; North and Wallis 1987). Micro-economic institutions will reflect these costs, uncertainties and economic relations and have been theorised as being the means of minimising such costs and uncertainties (Bardhan 1989; North 1989b; Williamson 1985). It is argued that under certain conditions, namely high degrees of asset specificity, transactional idiosyncrasy and uncertainty derived from incomplete information and from opportunism, the transaction costs of marketing are most cost effectively internalised within firms. Inside the firm market relations yields to a hierarchical arrangement of authority (Williamson 1985). Hodgson (1988) counter-argues that the firm may protect a social space where the calculus of transaction costs is unnecessary.

Testing these alternative propositions in the environment of agricultural markets which are plausibly TC constant yet within which coexist many combinations of capital and labour and many variations in the internal organisation of labour (all of which are far removed from the stylised form of TCE) has not proved possible. As with SCP in its agricultural incarnation, there are problems with both the theoretical consistency of TCE and with the derivation of an empirical methodology. The theoretical argument that existing institutions minimise transaction costs because TC minimisation is their function is tautological and Williamson has pre-empted its falsification (Sanghera 1992). TCE also requires agents to devise TC-efficient institutions while labouring simultaneously under bounded rationality and cognitive incompetence.

It has been pointed out that the designers of economic institutions also labour under a canopy of historically evolved norms and habit patterns – a set of social institutions which filters the choices available by reducing into tractable forms the enormous superabundance of information that exists. TCE also wrenches institutions from their contexts of property distribution and power. As Weber pointed out, markets that are formally free are actually influenced by the distribution of economic power, by which he meant the legally sanctioned power of control and disposal: 'money prices are the products of conflicts of interest and of compromises and ... they result from power constellations' (Weber 1979: 68, 108). For Williamson, power is reducible to 'self-interest with guile' and to the problem of designing organisational forms which would replace ones where such opportunism is practised. To this it can be objected that between and within firms institutions generate systems of rights and values which can as easily reinforce power as replace or challenge it and that 'opportunism' is not restricted to employees.

Transaction costs have often been invoked residually for results inexplicable in other ways. Irrespective of the issue of whether firms minimise transaction costs, a series of empirical hypotheses have been generated (Marion *et al.* 1986) that transaction costs increase, *ceteris paribus*, with increasing distance; market concentration; systemic complexity; and decreasing clarity of property rights, and that TCs decrease with relational contracting; the degree of standardisation of measurment technologies for quantity and quality, and lack of specificity of investment. Some of these propositions are too indeterminate to bear empirical investigation (e.g. clarity of property rights or systemic complexity) and all require large-scale surveys to test. It is often asserted that TCs cannot be measured, but some can (North and Wallis 1987). With respect to the Indian grain trade the latter include (some limited sorts of) information, travel and communication costs, hospitality and the costs of inspection to cover default risks and contract enforcement (Harriss 1991a). With caution, Marion's propositions can therefore be empirically investigated and have been broadly upheld. There is an essential unreliability about such costs, however, because of inter-firm variation in the extent to which grain-trading firms employ wage labour or alternatively unvalorised family labour for such activity. And to date, wide-ranging institutional research on rationales for contractual arrangements in a wide range of horticultural and agricultural markets has shown these cannot be related in a deterministic way to technical characteristics of crops, to conditions of agricultural production or to performance outcomes (Jaffee, 1990).

Commodity systems

The third methodological framework arose from the empirical recognition of the greater institutional complexity of markets than of production. Whereas SCP was developed for one layer of transactions, markets are here conceived 'vertically' in systems form: as multiple and interdependent sequences of industrial and trading activities, decisions, transfers of ownership and price formation. A series of technical activities form the skeleton of such systemic analyses: assembly, storage, transformation, redistribution and consumption, lubricated at all points by transport and credit. Three types of analysis flesh out this skeleton: the costs and margins at each stage; the spatial flows (involving places, volumes and directions) and, lastly, the social relations of trade involving the identification of key points of economic power (Leplaideur 1992).

The immense empirical scope of the first two kinds of analysis are well illustrated in the stack of crop marketing reports produced by colonial provincial governments in the inter-war period in South Asia, and the approach has been used recently in Indonesia to evaluate technical and policy changes to the system (Ellis *et al.* 1991). In its Anglo-Saxon incarnation the commodity systems approach has tended to focus on the rationale for vertical integration, upon economies of scale and on institutional responses to market imperfections (Goldsmith 1985; Jaffee 1990; Minot 1986). The Francophone version (*filières*) traces descriptively the organisational, contractual forms taken by a commodity system, their costs and profits (CIRAD 1990). There are also some problems with this approach. First, to date the method has not been used for rigorous hypothesis testing. Second, the costs and profits of a variety of organisational forms are in practice reduced to a priori archetypes – private firms, MNCs, cooperatives, marketing boards. Third, the differences in competitive conditions within the system are hard to research using the 'vertical' or systemic field methods such as 'follow a sack' which are necessary for this approach. Fourth, it has proved hard empirically to distinguish structural and relational elements in a marketing system and between exogenous and endogenous sources of change (García 1984).

Organisations and contracts in Indian grain markets

A measure of the value of these old and new institutional approaches is that there is a certain overlap in the key institutions identified. Product differentiation, property rights and organisation, entry conditions, activities, information and price formation and performance indicators are considered below.

Product differentiation

Rice is far from being a homogeneous commodity. In South India, 120 varieties of rice have their prices tracked. Prices are increasingly sensitive to varietal and quality characters with constrained substitution possibilities and increasingly complex, seasonally changing, spatial flows. The market for rice is therefore a bundle of economic markets.

Property rights

Patterns of control over the fixed and variable capital which comprises a grain trading firm are very complex. Common organisational forms include :

1 self-employment, on a petty scale or in a family firm. Petty trading can be seen as a commercial analogue to petty commodity production, and not a capitalist form for lack of wage equivalents and for lack of the capacity to engage in expanded reproduction;
2 private firms, with combinations of family and wage labour, with private or corporate ownership, with national or international capital;
3 cooperatives commonly with but sometimes without wage labour;
4 state trading institutions whose ownership varies from complete dependence on the state to partly privately owned, joint stock companies independent of the state.

A striking feature is the coexistence of varied organisational forms and control over property in environments which would be considered transaction-costs constant.

Competitive conditions

Likewise, the competitive conditions within the post-harvest production and trading system vary at each of the multiple stages of transfer of property rights. Entry barriers are social (caste and gender) rather than economic, though attenuated periods of apprenticeship or clerkship are required to master the informational, financial and relational aspects of grain trading. Within-system micro-variation in competitive conditions is manifested in the asymmetry, degree of delay and degree of compensation for delay in payments for grain. The power exerted over agents if payment is unsymmetrically delayed is exacerbated by lack of compensation.

Activities

The functions performed by firms constituting actually existing markets are not confined to buying and selling. At the very least, trading firms may buy, sell, broker, store, transport and process, produce, finance the production of others and finance trade. There are thus 9 (362,880) possible combinations of these activities. From the simplicity of vernacular classification systems of trading firms it might be assumed that activity combinations are highly patterned, but this is not so. Combinatorial Q-analysis (Atkins 1977; Johnson 1990) reveals that grain trading firms tend towards uniqueness, as well as diversity and complexity in their activity combinations. Types of activity combination do not correlate closely with stage in the marketing system or even with competitive conditions. The evaluation of performance is thus seriously compromised by lack of comparability. Just as products have 'niches' so too do firms in markets.

Price formation

The possibility of non-market price formation in agricultural markets has to be allowed. The idea that transactional decisions are voluntarily taken (irrespective of the completeness of information) is mistaken. If decisions were voluntary, every decision would be preceded by a decision to decide (a potentially infinite regression which fortunately only ever occurs in Oxford college meetings). The conditions under which decisions happen is an empirical issue. A study of price formation in coastal fish markets in West Africa revealed that price was not determined by supply and demand, instead prices oscillate around a price which is politically and socially determined which covers the cost of production and the subsistence wage of sellers (Jorion 1988). In Indian grain marketing subsets of settlements can be distinguished where local paddy purchase prices are formed backwards from rice wholesale prices. Costs of transactions and production are subtracted. So also is a net profit margin which is downwardly rigid. But other subsets of settlements can be found where rice prices appear to be formed from paddy prices in a reversal of this process. Much more purely speculative gains are to be had from the important trade in the major by-product of rice: bran for solvent oil extraction.

Contracts

Common contractual forms range from spot contracts through advance and/or futures agreements, through attached, repeated or relational forms to internalised transfers. They may effect the transfer of rights of control not only over tangibles (commodities) but also over intangibles (reliability, 'quality', loyalty) (Jagganathan 1987). Contracts may be written (but if written, not in a form recognised as a written contract by a court of law). A formal bill of contract is only created under circumstances of state vigilance and inspection (such as when movement restrictions obtain). Usually they are verbal. Rules of adherence may be formal and legal, or customary norms (Basu 1990).

Repeated trade and relational contracting is particularly common. These have been explained as TC-efficient institutional responses to certain conditions: first, a medium- to long-term time horizon; second, strong inter-organisational linkages or social networks; third, complex informational requirements; fourth, exchange in intangibles coexisting with and dependent on trade in tangibles (Pandya and Dholakia 1992). We would add poor physical security and insecure property rights. Screening, information provision, negotiation and enforcement are highly institutionalised by caste and location, by contractual routine and 'standard operating practice'. Few of these institutional attributes happen to be 'correct' according to the law. But to conclude that these firms and contracts are 'efficient given the environment' is both tautological and ideological. The social networks associated with relational contracts are mechanisms for consolidating market power, for preventing entry, for controlling information flows and for bonding labour.

Performance

Innovative performance has been of three types – technological, organisational and financial. Technological change has been adopted in stages by the largest rice millers. The steel huller mill is replaced by a rubber roll sheller – which requires paddy-stone separators and cone polishers as well. In rarer cases the sundrying of paddy is replaced by a batch drier. Technical innovation increases operational scale both physically (in increases in throughput per hour) and economically (in terms of the capacity utilisation required to break even given far higher capitalisation). It has been characterised by state-subsidised capital, by large-scale displacement of labour (particularly female labour) and by increasing concentration of control over gross output in rice markets. More widespread is the adoption of the telephone which has had radical economic and social consequences, reducing and streamlining transaction costs, increasing the velocity of transactions, dissolving ascriptive trading relations and replacing them with relational contacts acquired through reputation, experience and loyalty.

Organisational innovation is low level, continual and requires the destruction or modification of old institutional structures. In 1993/4 in a small grain marketing town in South India, there has been a rapid increase in the number of small firms entering the grain marketing system. It would seem that the process of accumulation is being decentralised. Manifold institutions of the (black) financial economy in a marriage of convenience with state production credit have finally enabled producers to loosen credit ties with paddy dealers. Those with marketed surplus prefer to pawn jewels for urgent post-harvest cash needs, to delay grain sales and to calculate that the post-harvest price rise in paddy will exceed the (illegally high) interest rate on pawn-loans. In retaliation, paddy merchants have innovated and are buying standing crops and organising the harvest in their effort to capture supplies of local paddy. It would be wrong to infer that the independence of intermediaries has improved, however. Rice mills challenged by the development of small custom hulling businesses are simply turning their finance to the unregistered money-lending institutions which supply working capital at high interest to these emergent firms.

Performance evaluated by average rates of return to marketing hides a great range of returns which are affected by the extent to which wage labour is used. Rates of return also vary with activity combinations. Wherever they can be compared, however, returns to pure 'trade' exceed those from agricultural production, agroprocessing and from segments of the informal money mar-

kets. Close links between grain marketing and grain production in the investment portfolios of mercantile firms take two forms. One is where production
is controlled directly through the ownership of land. Though subject to great
variation the landholding of traders is greater than in the population as a whole
and also likelier to be rented out (or latterly put directly to long duration
orchard crops with low supervision requirements). The other linkage leads to
an indirect control over production through pre-harvest credit tied to post-
harvest sales. This latter can involve several tiers of more or less tied trading
intermediaries who lend onward at higher (implicit) interest until the post-
harvest supplies of financially dependent producers are captured. Under these
conditions, market performance as judged by price integration analysis
(Palaskas and Harriss-White 1993) applied to date to three staples in West
Bangal and Tamil Nadu is short-term inefficient. Spatial price margins exceed
transport costs. Price differences in form exceed processing costs. These
differences are far greater in West Bengal in the northeast than in Tamil Nadi
in the southeast.

MACRO-ECONOMIC INSTITUTIONS: THE STATE AND
MARKETS – INSTITUTIONALISING REGULATION

The other major arena of non-market relations pertaining to real markets
concerns the state. State interventions in pricing, stock holding and physical
distribution are classic examples of non-market exchange about which much
has been written. As Etzioni has emphasised (1988: 256) unrestrained competition will destroy market exchange. But for a market to be able to function
efficiently and competitively, there have to be established:

1 rights to exchange property rights,
2 conventions about the scope of economic behaviour,
3 definitions of legitimate tender,
4 rules about price formation,
5 conventions about liability,
6 penalties for delinquency.

These are the elements of a regulatory system. The regulation of markets is
also understood as being a proper activity for the state. In fact there is argued
to be a synergy between regulatory public investment and private investment.
Definitions of this regulatory activity range from the full pattern of government intervention in markets (including taxes and subsidies) (Dahl 1979) down
to the range of statutory and common law defining the operation of a private
market economy (Joseph 1984). At the same time the state finds in markets a
milch cow for its revenue needs and the security and infrastructural aspects of
regulation can also be perceived as a strategic quid pro quo for this revenue.

The regulation of Indian grain markets

That regulation based on abstract markets has unintended outcomes when applied to real markets is exemplified by the Indian Regulated Markets Acts. These pertain to the transactions between producers and merchants. Under these Acts minimal barriers to entry are created (licences); legal conduct is specified as open tender, spot pricing, immediate cash payment. The state provides information, infrastructure, a site (and some storage) and a democratic and participative form of management, in return for which fees are to be paid by traders and accounts and inventory statements supplied to the committee.

These laws were introduced and enforced by the colonial state in order better to control the assembly of export crops. Much later on they were extended to food crops and given transaction cost minimising types of justification. The marketing acts are based on assumptions of abstract market logic and voluntarism. They are also based on the legal-deterministic assumption that law can mould behaviour (in this instance in the direction of perfect competition) in considerable ignorance of the actual power relations between traders, producers and the state and within the market system. In historical practice the ubiquity of interlocked contracts between credit and grain, and relational trade, prevent the operation of the open auction, spot price and centralised siting clauses. Traders have also refused to provide the information on quantities stored and traded required by the state in return for its price information, which is usually too localised and *ex post* to be of value to traders. The low benefit–cost ratio of compliance and the weak legitimacy of state regulatory practice has led to the evolution of a pervasive ideology of disrespect for the state. Lastly, the democratic and participative committees have proved no match for the vigilance needs of markets, and are deeply structurally compromised by their membership. The committees are weak in relation to other state institutions (municipalities, parastatals, etc.) and are debilitated by the unequal power and conflicts of interest of members within them and by the conflicts between public and private interests of individual members.

The intervention is successful in raising revenue, despite systematic evasion and underdeclaration. In response to actually existing markets states have centralised their administration, spawned specialist parastatal institutions (Directorates, Departments and Boards) in order to manage the administrative cadre for marketing and to deal with the parastate and international funders. The law has thus been transformed in implementation beyond all recognition. The law works most approximately as intended under three conditions: where markets were relatively competitive anyway; where non-local traders need a site; and where sellers are unindebted to traders. These conditions are rare.

Recently in Bardhaman District of West Bengal (studied in 1990) there has mushroomed a meso-level set of multipurpose collective institutions. They did not arise to minimise transaction costs, instead they were a collective institutional reaction to political representations from collective labour institutions. Once in place, in addition to rate fixing (for labour, transport, sometimes processing), lobbying and responding to the state, these groups have rapidly evolved a variety of other roles: ownership of market sites as group property; exploiting scale economies (for example, transport); putting up entry barriers; collusion over prices; risk spreading and insurance; reduction in the transaction costs associated with trading (information not just about price but about production, supply big deals, fraud and deliquency (the circulation of which is confined to the group); calibration of weights and measures, dispute resolution, enforcement); and expressions of social coherence, philanthropy and piety.

The role of these collective institutions is distinctly ambivalent. Markets cannot function without them, yet they protect their own interests, exclude potential entrants and often deprive the excluded of voluntary action and of the capacity to accumulate. Any reforming state would have to reckon with the existence of these collective institutions. And because of their socially undesirable attributes and activities, a state might find it necessary to reform its regulation rather than leave it to civil-social associational forms.

While the normative policy advocacy derived from marginalist economics allows no reformist insights, indeed is the basis for many of the current problems in the first place, an empirical framework for the analysis of regulation (Shaffer 1979) provides useful insights into the scope for reform. Its elements involve: the degree of specification; the degree of contingency; the nature of (legal) incentives; enforcement mechanisms; jurisdiction at the boundaries. Using this framework we can see that market conduct ought to be less specified. Implementation should be more contingent on local capacity and need (which depends on the conduct of civil society institutions). Positive incentives should replace negative legal strictures. Enforcement needs centralisation and muscle. And jurisdiction at the boundaries, where open markets meet other institutions and other law, needs tighter definition than exists now.

CONCLUSIONS

Real food-grain markets in India are therefore far from any of the theoretical archetypes and reveal the latter's ideological nature. Markets for a given commodity are actually bundles of separate economic markets. Real markets do not reduce to firms with comparable organisational forms and, more controversially, with comparable objectives. The activity of firms in markets is contingent. Markets are not devoted to trading, but to trading and many other activities. Accumulation from trade cannot be distinguished from accumulation generally. Institutions which are usefully theoretically separate (and for some in contradiction) are in practice enmeshed: state, civil society and market, firm and family.

An empirical analysis of South Asian grain markets poses real unanswered challenges to theory, particularly with respect to: the explanation of diversity and complexity coexisting in the same TC environments; the relationship between market and non-market exchange and other kinds of distribution; and the explanation of determination and change. Each of the approaches reviewed, with the possible exception of the systems approach, has been inspired directly by theoretical questions and is not independent of theoretical moorings. SCP is concerned with the welfare and efficiency impacts of market structures, TCE with the role of institutions in minimising transaction costs, political economy with the role of markets in the transformation of production and thus with the determination of structure and behaviour. An eclectic empirical method which used the horizontal framework of SCP alongside the vertical systems framework, was sensitive to transaction costs and analysed economic and gender differentation within the marketing system would have to accept the validity of all these theoretical issues and the varied empiricist and deductivist relationships posited between these frameworks and the real markets whose representation they facilitate.

It is equally clear that all these taxonomies are merely first-stage frameworks within which lies the arena for the development of institutional theories of exchange, of theories of institutional interaction and of the empirical research with which they may be evaluated. These methodological frameworks all carry the same implications for scale and mode of empirical enquiry. They require intense scrutiny at the level of firms and localities. There is no short cut.

NOTE

With thanks to Meghnad Desai for his comments.

7

INSTITUTIONAL THEORIES AND STRUCTURAL ADJUSTMENT IN AFRICA

Howard Stein

INTRODUCTION

Central to the process of economic reform is the role of institutions in the formation of markets. This chapter examines the theory of institutions embedded in three different traditions in economics, the neo-classical/structural adjustment viewpoint, the new institutional perspective found in the work of Douglass North, Oliver Williamson and Ronald Coase and the old institutional approach that was generated by Commons and Veblen and more recently in the writings of people like Geoffrey Hodgson and William Lazonick. For this purpose the chapter looks at a series of institutions central to the development of markets in Africa including property rights, property rights in agriculture, money and financial institutions, markets and prices, firms, and markets and states. The nature of each institution is examined from the perspective of the neo-classical/adjustment model, new institutionalism and the old institutionalist tradition.

The argument in the chapter is that structural adjustment, because it is derived from neo-classical economic theory, is basically a-institutional and therefore ill-equipped to promote the development of market institutions in Africa.[1] If African governments are interested in economic reform that develops market institutions then they would be best advised to consult the institutionalist literature. The chapter begins with a discussion of the Walrasian general equilibrium roots of neo-classical economics which underlies structural adjustment. In this view markets are seen as a product of the spontaneous interaction of atomistic self-seeking individuals. As Ronald Coase (1992: 714) has aptly put it, this model 'only lives in the minds of economists but not on earth'. While there are no reasons for institutions in the original model, in the more relaxed version of structural adjustment there is a need to legally ensure property rights and for monetarist type guarantees of the stability of the currency.

In the new institutionalist model institutions are more broadly defined as a means to reduce transaction and information costs. However, the new institutionalists still rely on the 'choice theoretic approach that underlies [neo-classical] micro-economics' (North, Ch. 2, this volume). The old institutionalists reject the emphasis placed on rational-maximising self-seeking behaviour of individuals which is at the heart of both neo-classical economics and new institutionalism. They believe that institutions are less instrumental and more 'settled habits of thought common to the generality of man' (Veblen 1919: 239). This requires a more detailed examination of the relationship between institutions, neo-classical economics and structural adjustment.

INSTITUTIONS, ADJUSTMENT AND NEO-CLASSICAL ECONOMICS

The neo-classical model, which provides the theoretical underpinning of structural adjustment, is a seriously flawed representation of how markets operate. Exchange, in the neo-classical model, arises spontaneously from the atomistic interaction of self-seeking individuals. Goods traded in every market are assumed to be homogeneous so that prices provide the only information needed to make the decisions on production and purchasing. No individual has sufficient market power to affect the market price. Markets must exist for all goods and services for now and in the future so that individuals can make completely informed rational decisions based on perfect information. Finally, to ensure that equilibrium is reached, neo-classicals posit the existence of a Walrasian auctioneer who gathers and processes the information from all these markets so that individual agents through a *tâtonnement*, or groping process, can adjust their decisions to remove excess demand and supply from all markets. The result will be that Pareto optimal conditions will be reached thereby maximising the welfare of society (no one will be able to be better off without making someone worse off).

In the strict model no institutions are necessary since exchange is simply driven by utility considerations or, as von Mises has put it, 'an attempt to substitute a more satisfactory state of affairs for a less satisfactory one' (Mises 1949: 97). In more relaxed versions, as Brett argues (Ch. 12, this volume), there is the recognition that property rights are also transferred in exchange and therefore require some external guarantor like the state. In addition, while monetary institutions have never been adequately explained in a general equilibrium framework (since one must have reasons for holding money which requires an assumption about uncertainty), there is some recognition that money is needed as a means of payment (Hodgson 1992: 753). This then sets preconditions for a monetary institution like a central bank which, like the guarantor for property rights, would play only a neutral role (or in Friedman terms, would ensure that money expansion does not cause inflation or deflation by putting it on automatic pilot so it only expands at rate of real growth in the economy 3–4 per cent per annum in the long run).

The aim of structural adjustment in Africa (and elsewhere) is to remove the impediments caused by state interference in the operation of these markets.

Capitalism would be promoted in Africa by removing the distortions that have disrupted prices from equalising supply and demand. The nature of these reforms are well documented (Quarco 1990). Tax and tariff concessions needed to be removed or, at a minimum, lowered and equalised, so that firms can choose inputs based on prices that reflect the relative scarcity of the factors of production in the country. The government needs to scale back by reducing social subsidies (introducing user fees), deregulating the conditions of private sector operation and privatising or closing state run public enterprises. Private property rights need to be carefully defined and guaranteed so that there is no risk of state nationalisation at a later date.

Exchange rate controls need to be removed and currencies should be permitted to float so that the exchange rate reflects supply and demand conditions and permits the free flow of investment in and out of the country. Financial reforms focus on the need to introduce real positive interest rates to attract savings and to ensure that only projects with a high rate of return will be undertaken. Overall credit constraints in the banking system are necessary to reduce price levels and to lower balance of payments deficits. Reducing government expenditures in the manner discussed above helps to lower credit expansion and ensure that credit to the private sector can expand with the real growth in the economy.[2] In general, once price distortions and other impediments are removed, the private sector driven market economy will naturally occur and prosper.

Hence, the model of structural adjustment mirrors the neo-classical view of how markets operate. This view of state institutions is also limited to seeing them as guarantors of the rights of private property and the money supply.

FLAWS IN THE NEO-CLASSICAL/ADJUSTMENT VIEW OF INSTITUTIONS AND CAPITALISM: TWO PERSPECTIVES

As indicated in the introduction, there are two somewhat competing views one can use to criticise neo-classicals and their model of structural adjustment from an institutional perspective. New institutionalism (NIE), which derives from the work of Ronald Coase, Douglass North and Oliver Williamson, does not fundamentally challenge the precepts of neo-classical economics but criticises it for failing to explain the nature of institutions and the role they play in supporting the existence and operation of markets. Institutions exist as a means of reducing transaction and information costs so that markets can operate with the kind of fluidity and efficiency projected in the neo-classical model. To quote Douglass North, 'Information processing by the actors as a result of the costliness of transactions is what underlies the formation of institutions' (North 1990a: 107). A second, older, institutional tradition (OIE for old institutional economics) arises from the work of Thorstein Veblen, Commons and others, which rejects much of the neo-classical tradition with

111

its emphasis on rational-maximising atomistic agents. Instead they focus on economic outcomes as a product of entities like large corporations operating in a complex historically specific environment of social, economic and legal institutions (Veblen 1919: 240). Institutions are seen as much less instrumental and more as 'settled habits of thought common to the generality of man' (North 1990a: 239).[3]

PROPERTY RIGHTS

It is easiest to understand the weakness of the neo-classical/adjustment view of reform in Africa by focusing on a number of issues deemed vital by institutionalists to develop capitalism in Africa. Perhaps at the centre of adjustment, from an institutional perspective, is the question of property rights. The World Bank in principle recognises the need to protect property and contract rights to build African entrepreneurship (World Bank 1989: 134). In practice, however, the emphasis has been on specifying conditions of deregulation and privatisation in structural adjustment programmes, which is consistent with the neo-classical notion that impediments created by the state are the single most important factor inhibiting the expansion of the private sector. Thus scaling back the state will allow capitalism to flourish.

NIE is critical of this perspective, since it does not put sufficient stress on the role of a systemic state-sponsored legal system in encouraging and enforcing market exchanges in a world of positive transaction costs. As Ronald Coase has succinctly put it:

> If we move from a world of zero transaction costs to one of positive transaction costs what becomes immediately clear is the crucial importance of the legal system in the new world ... what are traded on the market are not, as is often supposed by economists, physical entities, but the rights to perform certain actions and the rights which individuals possess are established by the legal system .... As a result, the legal system will have a profound effect on the working of the economic system and may in certain respects be said to control it.
>
> (Coase 1992: 717–18)

NIE takes this one step further to emphasise the need to design a system so that 'these rights should be assigned to those who can use them most productively with incentives that lead them to do so' (Coase 1992: 718). Unlike neo-classical economics, assigning property rights to the private sector is not necessarily viewed as an improvement in all cases. Toye, arguing in a NIE vein (Ch. 4, this volume), is critical of the neo-classical/adjustment view of privatisation. In Africa, where both market and state failures are present, the decision should be based on whether the act of reassigning property rights will lower transaction costs. Thus to NIE, within the context of reform, one should add a concept of efficient property rights.[4]

This emphasis on legalism and efficiency is what differentiates NIE from the old tradition of institutionalism. It is what makes NIE an addendum to neo-classical economics rather than an alternative.[5] OIE emphasizes the need to differentiate the *legalisation* of property rights emphasised by NIE from the *institutionalisation* of property rights (Koslowski 1992: 684). In particular, property rights must not only become established but legitimate. NIE shares the same weakness as the neo-classical model in the sense of having a common belief in the naturalism of markets. In the neo-classical case with its assumption of zero transaction costs, market exchanges will naturally arise due to the inherent actions of self-seeking individuals. However, to NIE positive transaction costs provide an impediment to these actions. Once the state properly designs and enforces contract rights then transaction costs can be reduced and markets can naturally proliferate.

To OIE property rights are much more than legally recognised entities. They are part of a whole *weltanschauung* that involves a particular mode of thinking that is historically specific. Their view, then, fundamentally questions the naturalism of neo-classical theory. To OIE the concept of property inherent in the functioning of capitalism is very different from the ideas of what constitutes legitimate property under socialist regimes both in Africa and Eastern Europe. In parts of Africa, private property and accumulation is seen as evidence of exploitation, which often entails the enrichment of visible minorities at the expense of the local African population. For capitalist-type exchanges to operate and become widely acceptable, both the polity and the society must reconceptualise the legitimacy of markets. The expansion of market activity and the encouragement of investment and accumulation requires stability in the concepts which represent property rights. Once a particular mode of thinking becomes habitual, markets will operate with greater fluidity. Both the society and the polity will then be committed to an acceptable form of property rights which will ensure their reproduction.

Structural adjustment largely misses this crucial dimension of reform. Since the superiority of the private sector is axiomatic to the neo-classicals, resistance to privatisation, which has been widespread in Africa, is deemed to be the product of entrenched interests where parastatal and government officials do not want to forgo opportunities for patronage and pilferage (Samuel 1990). However, in countries like Tanzania, state ownership and control have been part of the prevailing ideology (*ujamaa* in this case). While the ruling elements have utilised the ideology to enhance their hegemony over civil society, they have also legitimised state forms of ownership. In Tanzania, the problem with inefficient parastatal enterprises has not been perceived as being inherent in the form of the property right but in the exercise of property rights. This is why the anti-corruption campaigns have been so popular in Tanzania and why the government has introduced so many minor organisational shifts to try to deal with the problems.

Moreover, private ownership has been presented as the antithesis of the national ethos. During colonial times, legal barriers impeded the ability of Africans to engage in commerce.[6] After independence, the choice was often to recognise and extend the dominance of groups like the Asians in the economy by guaranteeing their property rights or to utilise newly formed bureaucracies to usurp those rights on behalf of the general African population. Thus, encouraging private property rights has become synonymous with the negation of the economic rights bestowed on the local population by nationhood. All of this points to the need in many African countries to consider less alienating paths of property right reform, including employee stock ownership, distribution of stock vouchers, or retaining formal state ownership with more democratic forms of control. If nothing else, this will enhance the identification of the general population with the reform process in a manner which is more consonant with the prevailing ideology. The distinction between structural adjustment, NIE and OIE can also been seen in the question of property rights and agriculture.

PROPERTY RIGHTS AND AGRICULTURE

Structural adjustment policies emphasise the need to provide farmers with the permanent right to cultivate and bequeath their land. The World Bank argues that secure rights will provide incentives for individuals to improve land and help credit markets develop as land is good collateral (World Bank 1989: 104). Once again, implicit in this analysis is the universal neo-classical notion that efficiency can only be achieved by ensuring that impediments are removed to the rational decision-making of self-seeking individuals. In the atomistic world of neo-classical economics the right to decide what, when and how to produce must be vested in individual production decisions.

NIE also supports reforms that redistribute land to individual owners, based on slightly different reasoning. The notion of efficient property rights in agriculture arises from the need to reduce transaction costs and to avoid principal–agent problems that can arise in other forms of agricultural relations such as hiring labour (Newbery 1989: 288). OIE, on the other hand, is more sceptical of the capacity of shifts in land ownership to have the efficiency properties suggested by both the neo-classicals/World Bank and the NIE school. In particular there is a scepticism that there is a singular relationship between the security of property rights and the patterns of the use of that property.

In Africa, there is a variety of coincidental and competing claims based on clientage and kinship that do not disappear after a shift toward private property rights. The literature from anthropology is replete with examples (Shipton 1987; Barrows and Roth 1990). When looking at land and property rights, one needs to distinguish between the right to ownership, the right to claim ownership, the *ius utendi et abutendi* (right to use and dispose of land) and the usufruct (the right to use and enjoy the fruits of the land). In the African countryside merely shifting to titled ownership will have little impact on the other rights which are a product of a complex web of social interaction. The unification of *ius utendi et abutendi* and the usufruct under a generally recognised singular right to ownership is the *sine qua non* of the institution of private property. This, however, implies an entirely different set of societal norms, values and structures which entails much more than new categories of legally defined property rights. The other forms of socially defined property rights are in many cases more legitimate than the new definitions of private property rights superimposed in the rural areas. Economic reform efforts need to fully comprehend the basis of the existing legitimacy and the transformative prerequisites (and implications) of moving towards new forms of legitimacy. Structural adjustment, with its neo-classical concepts, is not well equipped for this task. There are other problems with the neo-classical/World Bank view of the measures to develop markets in Africa.

MARKETS AND PRICES

The discussion above focused on the role of property rights in the reform process. Central to the strategy of structural adjustment is the promotion of efficiency through the encouragement of market prices which reflect scarcity value:

> If the economy is producing efficiently, scarcity values must be equal to opportunity costs, and their common value is the efficiency price .... An economy is efficient, as opposed to just production efficient, if it is impossible to make anyone better off without making someone else worse off. In addition to producing efficiently, the final consumers must have exhausted all possibilities of mutually beneficial exchange. This in turn requires they all face the same market prices and that these are equal to efficiency prices .... The case for removing distortions and moving market prices closer to efficiency prices rests on the argument that prices influence production efficiency and the reform will increase production efficiency.
>
> (*World Development Report* 1983: 42)

This revealing quote from the 1983 *World Development Report* (*WDR*), illustrates the World Bank view of the role of prices in reform. Markets will operate with efficiency as defined by neo-classical Pareto criteria, if certain distortions are removed. The source of the distortions is the state:

> In most instances ... price distortions are introduced by government directly or indirectly in pursuit of some social or economic objective, sometimes deliberately, sometimes incidentally.
>
> (*WDR* 1983: 57)

115

The thrust of structural adjustment, then, is to remove the state's interference so that markets can operate to produce efficient prices.

NIE is critical of this view of building markets. In particular, markets require more than simply the absence of any hindrances to individual maximisation decisions; markets require an institutional structure that supports the exchange process. As Douglass North puts it: 'Institutions provide the structure for exchange that (together with the technology employed) determines the cost of transacting and the cost of transformation' (North 1990a: 34). As economies become more sophisticated the institutional structure of markets must also evolve. North distinguishes between three levels of market development; personalised exchange involving small-scale production and local trade; impersonalised exchange that involves some long-distance and cross-cultural trade; and the impersonal exchange of modern economies. The institutions of the first type focus on repeat dealings and cultural homogeneity (common values). In the second case the exchange requires kinship links, bonding, the exchange of hostages or merchant codes of conduct. Finally, modern economies require third party enforcement. Central to the success of modern markets is the creation of a set of rules that make a variety of informal constraints operational, otherwise continual enforcement would make transactions too costly (North 1990a: 34–5).

This view has a number of implications for the model of structural adjustment. North emphasises the gradual nature of the evolutionary process and the impediments that exist to rapid change:

> institutions typically change incrementally rather than in a discontinuous fashion. How and why they change incrementally and why even discontinuous changes (such as revolution and conquest) are never completely discontinuous are a result of the embeddedness and informal constraints in society.
>
> (North 1990a: 6)

Resistance to change is even more acute in the first type of exchanges which would characterise many African markets where '[t]ransaction costs are low but because specialisation and division of labour is rudimentary, transformation costs are high' (North 1990a: 34). What this suggests is that the time horizons for reform are much longer than those typically embedded in the targets of structural adjustment/stabilisation programmes. Second, different policies need to be designed for different market structures. In Africa, one often has the three types of market North describes in a parallel existence. If higher levels of growth are to be sustained then one needs to examine not only how policies can assist markets at the three levels, but how one can design policies that will expedite the transformation of type one and two markets into the third type, which would assist in the expansion of growth and accumulation.

Where NIE and the neo-classicals/World Bank converge is on the importance of prices and their impact on the choices of individuals. This should not be surprising since both share the same micro-foundations, e.g. exchange is a product of the atomistic interaction of self-seeking individuals. However, in the case of NIE, institutional change is also the result of individual preferences reacting to shifts in relative prices: 'Institutions change and the fundamental change in relative prices are the most important source of that change ... relative price changes alter the incentives of individuals in human interaction (North 1990a: 84). As a result, NIE and structural adjustment would agree that 'getting prices right' would assist economic reform. However, in NIE's case the conduit for improving conditions would include not only prices for current decisions on what to produce and consume but prices that could be used to encourage more efficient types of institutional transformation.

OIE relies on different micro-foundations which doubt the impact of getting prices right. OIE rejects the notion that prices are the *ex post* product of the equilibrium of supply and demand and perfectly reflect scarcity value once hindrances are removed. Instead prices are seen as providing norms or conventions. They are the product of historical time and 'depend in part on expectations and the legitimizing and informational functions of institutions' (Hodgson 1988: 187). Prices are only one aspect of markets. To OIE, markets are social institutions which structure, organise and legitimate contractual agreements and the exchange of property rights. They not only provide price conventions but are a means to communicate information regarding products, quantities, potential buyers and potential sellers (Hodgson 1988: 187). Thus OIE would concur with the NIE argument for policies that are more broadly defined than the narrow focus of structural adjustment on distortions. However, since the causal movement is from institutions to the formation of price conventions, and not the reverse, OIE rejects the notion that a change of relative prices will lead to some predictable more efficient economic outcome.

MONEY AND FINANCIAL INSTITUTIONS

Closely linked to the notion of prices and markets is the concept of money and financial institutions. We saw above that money in the more relaxed neo-classical model is needed as a means of payment. However, to the neo-classicals the real sector should be distinguished from the monetary sector. Following Say's Law, production is determined by the supply side of the economy. Money then is 'a veil' which can have no impact on the real side of the economy and therefore simply determines the price level.

As indicated above, a central focus of adjustment is to provide price stability through proper regulation of the money supply. The focus of financial liberalisation should be strengthening the institutions that can be used to control the rate of expansion of the money supply. This can best be achieved by allowing the commercial banking sector to operate free of government intervention while building institutions such as bond markets to control the money supply through open-market operations. Beyond open-market operations, the monetary authorities should focus on regular audits and enforcing reserve ratios. State intervention should be reduced by privatising banks, prohibiting the government allocation of credit and subsidising of interest rates to prioritised sectors, and curtailing the use of the commercial banking sector to finance the government debt (World Bank 1989: 170–3). In general, the private sector should be used to funnel investment funds to credit worthy individuals while the state is restricted to properly expanding the money supply:

> Banks or informal savings and credit associations should be entrusted with the task of assessing the commercial risks attached to individual requests. Monetary authorities will need to ensure that the pace of money creation is consistent with broader economic objectives. This equilibrium should ideally be reached with interest and foreign exchange rates that clear markets and avoid the need for rationing.
>
> (World Bank 1989: 171)

NIE largely rejects the neo-classical view of money as a 'veil' pointing to the central role that credit and finance play in firm investment decisions. Building on his critique of Modigliani and Miller, who argued, in very neo-classical terms about the unimportance of a firm's financial structure to their investment decisions, Stiglitz argues that the financial structure affects the probability of bankruptcy, the perception of potential profitability of the firm by possible investors, managerial incentives, tax liabilities, how the firm's managers were monitored, to some extent who controlled the firm and the flow of funds under different exigencies (Stiglitz 1992a: 17).

However, NIE does not accept, a priori, the superiority of market over non-market forms of capital and financial allocation. Stiglitz rejects the notion that the move historically to more market forms of finance (such as junk bonds) has necessarily provided a more efficient way of providing funds, lowered transaction costs and increased the potential for risk diversification. Since privately motivated historical changes have not necessarily been efficiency enhancing, government direction may be needed:

> If, as we suggested, the evolution of financial institutions has entailed a movement from more to less control of borrowers ... and if markets are not necessarily efficient ... this may suggest a potential role for government intervention.
>
> (Stiglitz 1992a: 30)

NIE rejects the treatment by neo-classicals of capital and financial markets as mere auctions. Banks do not simply allocate credit to those that are willing to pay the highest interest rate. There are real questions concerning the type of institutional arrangements that are best suited to enhance the climate of investment. Stiglitz views the Japanese system, with its interlocking directorships between banks and other companies, as one way of dealing with the multiple-principal–agent problem (the manager is the agent, the banks and the workers principals). Banks as both the lender and shareholder are more likely to pursue actions that will improve the overall return to capital to the group (Stiglitz 1992b: 181–3).

Stiglitz also warns of relying on indirect mechanisms like open-market operations to control the volume of credit, particularly in reforming economies with high levels of uncertainty. He suggests the use of more direct forms of allocation such as the central bank issuing rights to loans to commercial banks who would then have the option of inter-bank trading (Stiglitz 1992b: 175–6). Thus the government's role, as suggested above by the World Bank, of simply ensuring monetary expansion that allows market clearing equilibrium interest rates, ignores broader questions such as the appropriate design of financial structures.

OIE like NIE questions the neo-classical treatment of money as a veil:

> the core of classical and neo-classical economic theory has been the economics of neutral money. Like God in Unitarian theology, money is there, but it does not do very much. This is ironical since capitalism is above all a monetary economy, yet it was presumed to behave as if it were a barter economy.
>
> (Dillard 1980: 256)

However, OIE goes beyond NIE's focus on the role of money and credit in the firm's investment decisions. To OIE money is the strategic institution of modern capitalism and is so central to the determination of output that it might be represented as an institutional factor in the functional relation between factors of production and output (Dillard 1980: 255, 265).

While the neo-classicals and NIE concentrate on defining money in terms of its uses, OIE focuses on the 'source of money: how is money created, and how does it enter a capitalist economy?' (Wray 1992: 2). Money to OIE is any balance sheet item which transfers purchasing power across time and was created when private property arises and an individual becomes a creditor or potential debtor (Wray 1990: 2, 8). Money largely pre-dated markets. Dating back to the Greek cities, the earliest form of money was used as a unit of account and appeared when private property was loaned with the expectation of a return of a sum exceeding the original loan. Thus, unlike the neo-classical view of barter arising naturally out of the utility-maximising behaviour of individuals and money simply evolving to facilitate exchange, we find that money was in existence well before the development of markets. Barter was never an important economic activity nor did barter exchange lead to the development of markets. Thus money could not have developed out of markets. This is quite clear from the research of the economic anthropologist Karl Polanyi.[7]

To understand OIE's concept of money one needs to focus on the evolution of financial institutions associated with the rise of capitalism. What is absolutely crucial to capitalist development is the movement to fiat money which

119

is 'currency issued by the state whose value is purely nominal' (Wray 1990: 27). One of the important steps to developing fiat money was the evolution of giro banking institutions. A giro was a payment society whose members agree to accept credit issued by other member(s) as a medium of exchange and a means of payment. Typically, an English exporter would sell wool to a Flemish importer for one-third cash and a bill of exchange covering the other two-thirds. The Flemish importer would sell the wool and purchase a bill of exchange issued by a Flemish merchant who exported goods to London. The bill of exchange could be retired and the London wool exporter could be paid once these Flemish goods were sold in the London fairs. The early expansion of banks was linked to their role as a guarantor of bills of exchange and as a transfer point between debtors and creditors in giros. Once bank debt became generally accepted as payment, the expansion potential of the giro was greatly enhanced and trade would not be limited by the circulation of commodity money.

The demand of the state for revenue (in the early stages to finance wars) and the restrictions of relying on finance through commodity money led them inexorably toward entry into the giro network. Once the state accepted bank liabilities for tax payments from the general public, the liabilities issued by banks became acceptable to citizens outside the giro, greatly expanding economic activity inside and outside the state. The key to enhancing state power and modernising the banking system was by organising a central bank and enforcing a mono-reserve system. Once fiat money replaced commodity money the state could issue currency and increase spending without fear of a depreciation of the value of state money relative to giro money. The transition to a modern financial system based on credit creation and fiat money was absolutely central to the development of modern capitalism. This was not the product of the spontaneous evolution of the private sector as some neo-classicals would like us to believe, but the product of conscious state directed policy intervention (Wray 1990: 54). Just as the state was critical in the development of financial institutions during the rise of capitalism, it will be argued below the role of the state in finance must go well beyond simply 'guaranteeing' the money supply.

As already indicated, a core element of structural adjustment, following the monetarist doctrine, was to ensure that the money supply expands at the rate of real growth in the economy so that prices remain stable. A second important element was that investment cannot expand without an increase in savings which will only rise if interest rates are greater than zero in real terms. OIE questions both of these policies. At the heart of the OIE theory of money and financial institutions is that money is basically endogenous, which means that loans make deposits, deposits expand reserves and money demand induces money supply. From the perspective of a firm, money demand represents the inducement to go into debt while money supply is the IOU which it issues. From the bank's perspective money demand represents the willingness of a firm to enter into debt while money supply is representative of the bank's acceptance of the IOU and to issue liabilities to purchase the IOU of the firm. This is simply two sides of the balance sheet. In the US, if it is profitable, the bank will find the reserves to cover the additional loans by using asset and liability management, the Fed funds market, international sources or the discount window (Wray 1990: 73–4). The central bank can make this more costly by raising the discount rate or it can influence reserves via open market operations or it can refuse to loan sums through its discount window. However, it can hardly set the rate at any specific target (as monetarists would have it in their exogenous money supply concept) and is likely to need to flood the system with reserves as lender at last resort if interest rates become too high.

Moreover, there is not likely to be any predictable relationship between money supply and inflation rates. To OIE, money cannot be neutral in a credit economy, only influencing prices via the monetarist real balance adjustments. The concern for nominal monetary values does not arise out of money illusion but the fact that credit–debt relations at the heart of economic growth are denominated in money. Neo-classicals tend to confuse money with the medium of exchange. In their view, an exogenously determined stock of money as a medium of exchange leads to a particular spending flow. However, one needs to distinguish between money and the medium of exchange, money and spending and the medium of exchange and spending. Money is created in the process of facilitating flows and is representative of the conditions of debt generation. The medium of exchange allows one to spend without incurring a debt. The usage of money as a medium of exchange permits one to use someone else's debt to make a purchase. Money can also be used by another as a means of payment to settle debt, reduce balance sheets and destroy other money. This has absolutely nothing to do with spending.

Similarly, many types of transactions have little to do with the broadly accepted medium of exchange (such as demand deposits and currency). Credit card purchases involve the generation of debt which might or might not be settled at the end of the month by the payment of demand deposits (Wray 1990: 14–15). Overall given the complexity of money (even where financial institutions are less developed as in Africa), there is likely to be a variable relationship between a given stock of money as a medium of exchange and a particular level of prices and nominal expenditures. OIE is also critical of the structural adjustment/neo-classical view of interest rates and savings. First, as mentioned above, behaviour in economies is not inherent as neo-classicals would suggest, but learnt. Neo-classicals would have us believe that banks evolved to act as the intermediaries to channel the deposits of savers to investors. OIE citing historical evidence disagrees:

> [T]he true order of events show that orthodoxy clearly has reversed the process through which investment is funded. Banks do not begin as intermediaries which accept the deposit of 'savers' and then make loans

121

to 'investors', for this would assume that the public has already developed the 'banking habit'. This habit is the end result of public experience with short term bank liabilities which have been created as banks extend short term credit to finance working capital expenses.

(Wray 1990: 58)

In Africa, the institution of banking is not particularly well developed and in many areas is restricted to large urban centres. Arguing that raising interest rates to real levels will lead to some predicted increase in savings is untenable to OIE, even in the context of more ubiquitous banking habits in developed countries. The causal direction between savings and investment is reversed in the view of OIE. Spending on investment goods financed by credit creates profit income which becomes the basis of savings. Just as capitalism requires that it not be constrained by commodity money, savings cannot impede the production of investment goods (Wray 1990: 53). What is required is well developed financial institutions that can provide credit for growth and accumulation.

The heart of the OIE alternative to structural adjustment must focus on the development of finance. There are serious structural impediments to this undertaking. Prior to independence African countries relied on banks created by the colonial power which typically maintained 100 per cent reserves against any currency issued. Currency could expand only if they were able to run a trade surplus (or if they were given grants or loans from the home country). Money was thus largely in a commodity form. In many ways in the post-colonial era, African countries have had difficulty breaking out of this particular mode of money. While the state can freely issue currency, the fiat money of developed countries is generally preferred. As a result external sources via aid or balance of payment surpluses have provided much of the finance. The focus of economic reform in the financial sector should not be on interest rate or money supply targets as the neo-classicals would like but on developing endogenous banking institutions that will lead to the acceptance of domestically based fiat money. This will occur where state money gets integrated into domestic and international giros and banking habits become more universally adopted (Stein 1995).

THEORY OF THE FIRM: STRUCTURE AND INNOVATION

The firm in neo-classical theory has often been described as a 'black box' (Coase 1992: 714). Since prices are the only element necessary to make production and consumption decisions, there was no apparent reason for the existence of the firm in mainstream theory. Similarly, we have seen that the focus in structural adjustment is also price reform. In the case of firms the only focus is in ensuring publicly owned corporations are privatised. The key is to make sure that decisions with regard to production are put into private hands or, in other words, that the public 'black box' become a private 'black box'. In the real world of modern capitalism corporations, not individuals, play the central role in the production and distribution side of the market. Understanding the nature of the firm and the role that it plays in innovation and growth would seem to be an important part of designing a strategy for Africa's future development.

To NIE corporations exist as a means of reducing transaction costs. Coase in his classic 1937 article uses a marginal cost approach in describing the decision of using the market versus the firm in undertaking an additional exchange transaction:

> The question always is, will it pay to bring an extra exchange transaction under the organising authority? At the margin, the costs of organising within the firm will be equal either to the costs of organising in another firm or to the costs involved in leaving the transaction to be 'organised' by the price mechanism. Business men will be constantly experimenting, controlling more or less, and in this way equilibrium will be maintained. This gives the position of equilibrium for static analysis.
>
> (Coase 1937: 404)

Williamson (1985) takes the transaction cost concept one step further by formulating a theory to explain the factors responsible for transaction cost differences. For this purpose, he draws on the work of Herbert Simon and Kenneth Arrow. Arrow, a strong proponent of general equilibrium theory, argued that market failure can arise from the problem of information. In particular, since the price cannot capture all the information relevant to transacting parties, when the integrity of one of the parties is suspect, transaction costs will arise. Williamson terms this source of transaction costs as 'opportunism'. Various governance structures of firms have the capacity to contain opportunism thereby economising on transaction costs. Without opportunism there would be no reason for the existence of internal organisations in firms. Simon, on the other hand, emphasises that decision-making, given the limited computational capacity of the human brain and incompleteness of knowledge, is undertaken in a world of bounded rationality. Unlike the neo-classical maximiser including all possible information, Simon argues that decisions are taken from a small set of prerogatives. These cognitive limitations also create transaction costs since it limits their ability to achieve global objectives.

To Williamson, both concepts are necessary to present the analytical complexity of his transaction costs construct. Opportunism is not sufficient to explain transaction costs since in a world of unbounded rationality the information about which participants were opportunistic would be known. Similarly without the opportunism of participants in exchanges, the costs entering transactions with limited cognitive capacity would also be minimized. According to Williamson, there are two branches of transaction costs, the 'governance' branch and the 'measurement' branch. The former is concerned with the capacity of firms to organise transactions to adapt to disturbances in the external environment of the firm. The second focuses on the capacity to bring goods and services to the market at a cost which is justified by the price. Thus what links opportunism and unbounded rationality is uncertainty created by both the cognitive limitations of corporations and the unforeseen disturbances which create opportunities for one party to the exchange to take advantage of the other.

The focus here is to create an organisation which can respond rapidly and efficiently to the shifting external environment. This is complicated by the degree of 'asset specificity' which refers to the extent that physical and human assets are tied to particular transactions in economic organisations. The more transaction-specific assets in the organisation, the less the capacity of the firm to respond to uncertainty in the face of opportunism and bounded rationality. Williamson also recognises that the 'frequency' of transactions is also important since it allows one to spread fixed-cost governance structures over a greater number of units (Lazonick 1991a: 206–13).

OIE is very critical of the focus on firms as transaction cost minimisers. First, OIE rejects the concept of the firm as a calculating subject adding a structure on the margin when the transaction cost warrants it. Again this illustrates the neo-classical roots of NIE. Second, while pricing norms are available to calculate transaction costs in a market setting, it is much more difficult to calculate the costs of organisational structures in the non-market setting of the firm. How can one make the kind of rational calculus implied in NIE? To OIE, firms are seen as social institutions which provide a refuge from the vicissitudes of the market. They embody the habits and routines that allow corporations to deal with the complexity of production and exchange and to develop expectations of the future in a world of uncertainty:

> The nature of the firm is not simply a minimizer of transaction costs, but a kind of protective enclave from the potentially volatile and sometimes destructive, ravaging speculation of a competitive market. In the market the rational calculus depends upon the fragile price convention which can often depend on 'whim or sentiment or chance'. Habits and traditions within the firm are necessarily more enduring because they embody skills and information which cannot always or easily be codified or made subject to a rational calculus. What the firm achieves is an institutionalisation of these rules and routines within a durable organisational structure. In consequence they are given some degree of permanence and guarded to some extent from the mood waves of speculation in the market.
>
> (Hodgson 1988: 208)

OIE also rejects the notion of hierarchy implied in Williamson's corporate structures of governance. The problem is that human behaviour from Williamson's perspective utilises a neo-classical view of individuals as acquisitive and self-seeking. Thus at all points one will have to guard against the natural tendency toward opportunism. OIE points out that while opportunism exists, the successful corporation will not rely on hierarchy and supervision but on the capacity to encourage other human traits like loyalty and trust. In simple terms it will be impossible to supervise and monitor every activity in a corporate structure. This loyalty and trust also spills over to the market place. In places like Japan long-term arrangements between suppliers and producers have avoided the uncertainty (and therefore transaction costs) of open-market interactions (Hodgson 1988: 209–10). This is one of the reasons for the relative success of some forms of industrial organisation and arguably helps explain the relative rise of Japan over the US, where there is less reliance on trust and loyalty inside and outside of the firm. The failure to differentiate different types of capitalism based on the organisation of firms is one of the weaknesses of structural adjustment and is a reflection of the atomistic focus of its neo-classical roots. However, for reform to be successful it will not only have to address questions of ownership but also questions of the internal and external structure of firms. The organisation of firms also has implications for the question of innovation which is central to economic growth and development. Williamson and the NIE have no adequate explanation for why innovation occurs in the firm. Hodgson emphasises that since innovation cannot occur in a market setting (e.g. how could you design a futures market for something chanced upon or where the nature and application of the project will be unknown in advance?) one cannot point to the transaction costs that would be saved by using an internal corporate structure. He points to the role of the firm as a refuge for research and development and the importance of the scale of operation:

> The firm as a relatively durable organisational structure is able to deal with the lack of knowledge about the future fruits of research and development and innovation. Its relative internal stability means that it can carry unquantifiable risks which would be eschewed in the volatility of the market. In particular large firms are able to set up and sustain R&D departments with their own funds. It is widely recognized that atomized, small-scale private enterprise is not well able to make such long-term commitments.

> (Hodgson 1988: 213)

Lazonick also doubts the capacity of Williamson to explain innovation in his framework. To Lazonick, Williamson provides a theory of adaptive organisation, one where firms react to a given economic environment as opposed to an innovative environment where the firm attempts to change its economic environment. A crucial difference in the two approaches to organisation is that asset-specificity in Williamson's adaptive organisation creates difficulties in dealing with uncertainty (Lazonick 1991a: 218). However, in the more dynamicinnovative organisation, asset-specificity is created by the organisation and is a symbol of success not failure.

Through the augmentation of fixed costs associated with asset-specificity, the innovative organisation chooses to create uncertainty with the knowledge that it could produce a superior product at a competitive cost (product innovation) or an existing product at lower cost (process innovation). Higher fixed costs are taken in order to reap the potentially higher generation of revenue. The firm organises its operations to deal with the productive and competitive uncertainty created with a potential innovation. Productive uncertainty is internal to the firm and is linked to the unknown impact of the innovation on new products and methods of production. Competitive uncertainty is external to the organisation and is associated with the incapacity of the firm to know the availability of the supply of factors and the demand for their products both of which are necessary to reap financial returns from the fixed costs. To reduce productive uncertainty, the successful innovative organisation will invest in a managerial bureaucracy that is capable of the planning and coordination of physical and human resources. In addition the organisation must develop not only the technical skills to deal with the innovation but also a 'collective force' that permits the planned coordination of the horizontal and vertical division of labour required to generate an innovation (Lazonick 1991b: 203). This is best accomplished with the reduction of barriers to the mobility of labour within the firm, the free flow of ideas between all levels of the company and incentives that ensure that the participants receive the benefits of innovations (such as through long-term employment guarantees). The Japanese companies with their absence of craft unions, the *ringi* system which encourages the two-way movement of ideas up and down the corporate ladder and the permanent employment guarantees provide a quintessential example of the collective force (Lazonick 1991a: 39–43). To reduce competitive uncertainty the innovative firm needs to push forward and backward integration. Production facilities must be sufficiently large to lower unit costs. Thus the firm will be tempted to expand into mass marketing to ensure that there are sufficiently large sales. It will also need to move into material supplies to ensure a high quantity and quality flow of inputs (Lazonick 1991a: 204). Again the Japanese have been most successful at reducing competitive uncertainty with their vertically integrated enterprise groups which have evolved from the family run *zaibatsu* of the pre-war period. Large banks have played an important role in reducing financial uncertainty at the production and marketing stages of innovations.

As African governments search for models of economic reform, they will be well advised to study the experience of institutions that have successfully spawned innovation and growth models that are conspicuously absent from structural adjustment. A final issue is the view of the state and the role it can play in supporting the development of market institutions.

THE MARKET AND THE STATE

Strictly speaking, as we have seen above, in the pure neo-classical model as represented by Walrasian equilibrium, there is no need for a state since society's welfare is maximised. In the less extreme model of structural adjustment, the state is the guarantor of property rights and the money supply. Implicit in this notion is that the state will benignly intervene in these matters. State intervention in any other matters sets up the opportunity for predation (following the public choice literature) and is inferior to the operation of the market.

NIE defines the state in more consistent terms. North sees the state as an organisation with a comparative advantage in violence. This is important if it is to enforce property rights since 'the essence of property rights is the right to exclude and an organisation which has a comparative advantage in violence is in the position to specify and enforce property rights' (North 1981: 21). Handoussa (Ch. 8, this volume), writing in an NIE vein, sees the state operating in an institutional framework that governs economic activity and centres on property rights, on the enforcement and execution of the law and on the resulting transaction costs. To Handoussa, total factor productivity should be the measure of the efficiency of state intervention to change institutional structures.[8] OIE, on the other hand, sees the state as playing a much broader role in support of markets that goes beyond principles of efficiency. To OIE markets did not arise out of the spontaneous activities of utility-maximising individuals but from direct state intervention. To quote Polanyi:

> [W]e have evidence of organisational and financial activities initiated by kings, generals or governments responsible for the military undertakings .... Go-ahead generals devised up-to-date methods of stimulating local market activities, financing sutlers to wait upon the troops and engaging local craftsmen in improvised markets for the supply of armaments. They boosted market supply and market services by all means at their disposal, however tentative and hesitant local initiative sometimes may have been. There was, in effect, but little reliance on the spontaneous business spirit of the residents.
>
> (Polanyi 1971: 85, quoted in Wray 1990: 5)

OIE believes that focusing on violence defines the state too narrowly. In particular it not only defines and enforces rights, but broadly supports the whole process of exchange and is thoroughly involved with the social distribution of goods and services while also monitoring performance. Dugger argues that the state and exchange as they developed through the city-state to the territorial-state to the nation-state have evolved together in a mutually enforcing manner. To Dugger and the OIE, *laissez-faire* is a myth which has no historical basis (Dugger 1992: 24). The state has also not lived by coercion. It possesses and uses its authority not due to force but due to legitimacy.

Following John R. Commons's emphasis on sovereignty, OIE defines the state as an agent that exercises sovereignty (Dugger, 1993: 4).

Above it was argued that markets, according to OIE, are social institutions which require broadly defined forms of intervention to operate. Even the so-called free-market experiments of the Thatcher and Reagan era involved continual juridical, political and institutional intervention by the government. As Hodgson, puts it 'the main argument is not really between intervention and non-intervention, but which type of intervention is to be carried out and for which ends' (Hodgson 1988: 253). Innovative organisations, vital to growth and development, have thrived under a fostering environment supported by the state. In Japan the state has protected home markets to permit innovative industries to attain competitive advantage. It has also maintained high levels of employment, and an equal distribution of income to encourage a market for manufactured goods. It has created incentives for individuals and companies to purchase goods that embody new technology. It has limited the number of enterprises in each industry to permit a sufficient market size for companies to incur the fixed costs to make them competitive internationally. It has also encouraged cooperative research efforts among competitors and provided cheap sources of financing. Finally, it has invested heavily in educating its labour force which has prepared it for the internal generation of innovations (Lazonick 1991a: 37). This is a long way from structural adjustment and its attempts to create competitive markets by removing the 'distortions' created by the state.

CONCLUSIONS

The chapter opened with a discussion of the model of structural adjustment and its neo-classical economic roots. In the strict neo-classical model, there are no reasons for the existence of institutions. In the relaxed version there is some need for a central authority to guarantee property rights and the stability of the money supply. Following the neo-classical model, structural adjustment focuses on removing state sponsored impediments to the private sector driven market economy. State institutions should also be limited to guarantors of the rights of private property and the money supply. Two competing perspectives on the nature of institutions are discussed. The new institutionalists, who use the same theoretical precepts as the neo-classicals, see institutions reducing transaction and information costs. The old institutionalists define institutions more broadly as 'settled habits of thought common to the generality of man' and generally reject the neo-classical emphasis on rational maximising-atomistic agents.

The chapter considers a number of institutions deemed vital to the development of markets. NIE sees legally guaranteed property rights as vital to reducing transaction costs. OIE interprets property rights in broader terms as a mode of thinking which is historically specific and not guaranteed merely through shifts in legally defined terms. This is particularly the case in the African countryside where there are a variety of coincidental and competing claims to land based on clientage and kinship. Both NIE and OIE are critical of the adjustment claim that markets will operate efficiently by simply removing hindrances to individual maximisation decisions. Both see markets as broad institutional structures that support the exchange process. However, OIE is more sceptical of the impact of a change in relative prices on the evolution of institutions as suggested by NIE arguing that the causal movement is from institutions to the formation of price conventions.

NIE and OIE reject the neo-classical notion that money is a veil and has no impact on the real side of the economy. NIE focuses on the role of finance in investment decisions and questions the neo-classical assertion that the movement to more market forms of finance is necessarily efficient. OIE goes beyond the role of money and credit in firms' investment decisions arguing that money is the most central institution of modern capitalism. While neo-classical economics and NIE focus on the uses of money, OIE focuses on its sources. While the neo-classicals focus on the evolution of money as a medium of exchange arising spontaneously to assist utility-maximising barter activities, OIE points to the role of credit creation which has nothing to do with barter. To OIE money is endogenous, banking habits must be learned and do not come naturally and investment generates savings. Thus structural adjustment's focus on the monetary rule and real interest rates is likely to prove ineffective. To OIE the problems of finance in Africa are more deeply structural and will require the state to find ways to integrate its fiat money into national and international giros.

While NIE focuses on a transaction cost explanation of firms, OIE is more critical of the assumption of individuals as opportunistic when describing the rationale for the hierarchical structure of the firm. OIE emphasises the role of trust and loyalty in the organisation both in internal and external company relations. Links based on encouragement of these attributes are vital to the creation of the innovative firm which should be one of the prime considerations of reform in Africa.

Finally, states play a very vital role in the support and development markets and other capitalist institutions. The state is the primary agent of institutional intervention. It has the capacity to stabilise or transform institutions including markets. At this vital juncture the debate over the direction of policy in Africa must be based on a historical understanding of the institutions underlying the development of markets. African countries should choose their future economic strategy fully informed of the institutional options that exist. Structural adjustment with its neo-classical roots is rather ill-equipped to meet this challenge.

NOTES

An earlier version of this paper was published as 'Theories of Institutions and Economic Reform in Africa', World Development 22, 12, December 1994.

1   Elsewhere I have discussed some of the pitfalls of basing structural adjustment on neo-classical economic theory both in terms of the impact on industry (Stein 1992), basic needs (Stein and Nafziger 1991) and through the misinterpretation of the policy lessons from Asian development (Stein 1994). This chapter extends that critique by focusing on the institutional implications of relying on neo-classical economic theory.

2   Khan et al. in their 1990 article lay out the explicit monetarist assumptions at the heart of the IMF's model of stabilization. In particular the rise in the money supply is a product of the aggregation of the growth in foreign reserves (a positive balance of payments), the rise in private sector credit and the increase in public sector credit. Using the strict monetarist assumption that velocity is constant (or at least predictable), the demand for money rises with the increase in money income, and the money market is in flow equilibrium, then it is easy to show that the balance of payments will improve with a fall in private sector and public sector credit growth. The model completely falls apart with any real-world adjustments to the assumptions including the endogeneity of money, a lack of constancy or predictability of velocity, the introduction of other reasons for demanding money (e.g. Keynes's speculative motive), the existence of partitions between reserves and the money supply (when you relax the assumption that the central bank is the only financial institution), etc.

3   The new institutionalists like to project themselves as being superior both to neo-classicals and the old institutional tradition. In a recent article on new institutionalism and development economics the authors quote Stephen Langlois to buttress their point, ' ... the problem with many early Institutionalists is that they wanted an economics with institutions but without theory; the problem with many neoclassicists is that they want economic theory without institutions; what NIE tried to do is to provide an economics with both theory and institutions' (Nabli and Nugent 1989: 1336). While there might be some problems with elements of the microfoundations of institutionalism (e.g. no unified theory of price formation), the problem with the NIE is that it is captured by the precepts of neo-classical theory which, we will argue below, limits its understanding of how capitalism operates and by implication how to design institutions to build markets in African countries.

4   It should be noted that not all proponents of NIE agree that efficient property rights will be created in practice. North argues that there is a tendency for the state for political reasons to produce inefficient rights. He refers to transaction cost and competitive constraints on polities which often produce inefficient rights. Transaction costs are related to principal–agent problems insofar as rights need to be defined in a manner which will augment revenue collection by the state. Competitive constraints arise due to the need by political parties to avoid defining property rights in a manner which would antagonise constituents (North 1989a: 665). Still, embedded in this framework is some hypothetical measurement of efficient property rights which would lead to maximising behaviour and higher levels of economic growth. As he states in his contribution in this book, the heart of development policy must be the creation of polities that will create and enforce efficient property rights. The concept of efficient property rights is not found in OIE.

5   In this book Bates takes a rather different view of NIE. He argues that NIE

abandons the premises of neo-classical economic reasoning (e.g. the commitment to the indiviual as a unit of analysis and the usage of rational choice as a theory of decision-making). NIE, according to Bates, locates the origin of all non-market institutions in the need to deal with market failures. Since it arises from societal needs rather than individuals they have abandoned the first premise. Second, since all non-market institutions are public goods they will encounter a free-rider problem (e.g. they cannot arise if the principle of rational choice is operational). To Bates, NIE must be a departure rather than an extension of neo-classical economics. The argument is not very cogent. Not all non-market institutions are public good solutions to market imperfections. Coase's firms are created by individuals as a means of reducing transaction costs. The benefits of a firm as a governance structure are privately accrued. As noted below, the aproach used is marginal, individually derived and rationally determined. There will be no 'free-rider problem'. However, Bates is quite correct in classifying much of NIE as functionalist. This is indeed one of the weaknesses of NIE which OIE avoids. Interestingly enough, Bates uses cultural symbols like 'shared belief systems' to explain how honest business transactions can evolve which begins to sound like OIE (in the case he presents, culture is not a product of an n-person game but helps move the game toward a suitable resolution).

6   The extent of private property and markets in the pre-colonial period has of course been subject to extensive debate. Authors like Anthony Hopkins (1973) have compiled impressive data to present a complex economy with extensive trading networks, capital markets and general purpose currencies. While much of this places doubt on a strict substantivist interpretation of the period (that exchange was culture-bound) it hardly supports the opposite formalist extreme of the universality of economic behaviour (along the lines of the neo-classical 'homo economicus'). Iliffe (1983: 53–4), for example, argues that Robert Harms's observation that the Bobangi traders of the middle Congo perceived the acquiring of wealth as a zero sum game (it could only be acquired by typically sacrificing one's relative to witches) was fairly widespread in Africa. He also details the colonial period's disarticulation of indigenous accumulation, particularly in the rural areas. McCarthy (1982) systematically documents colonial policies such as stiff graduated licensing, credit restrictions, controls on itinerant trading and the directing of commerce toward official markets, which inhibited the growth of indigenous accumulation in British Tanganyika. The impact of these measures can be seen in the small participation of Africans (as opposed to Asians) in the retail and wholesaling sectors at independence (Hawkins 1965). What one sees at independence is generally a weak indigenous private sector, without widespread legitimacy, which can do little to resist the policies of the post-independence governments. For a discussion of the case for Uganda see Brett's chapter in this volume.

7   Polanyi's work on the origin and nature of money and its relationship to states has come under considerable criticism by economic historians like Robin Law. In 1966, writing on Dahomey, Polanyi argues that the state was a prerequisite for the development of archaic forms of money which in turn supported early 'state building'. In the case of the kingdom of Dahomey, the state regularly issued cowrie helping it to remain stable both in domestic price terms and relative to the foreign exchange between cowrie and gold. Law (1992) counters that the money supply was not controlled by the state but by market conditions including the volume of slave exports, the proportion of slaves purchased by cowries and the price of slaves. Prices of commodities showed enormous variation as did the cowrie value in gold (particularly after 1845). Law provides an impressive amount of data to illustrate the vicissitudes of prices in a variety of commodities. Whether this was a product of supply and demand as Law argues or the result of adjustments in the institutions

of price-setting hypothesised by Polanyi is difficult to assess from the evidence. What is remarkable, however, is the extraordinary stability of exchange between gold and cowrie for 150 years, up to the mid-nineteenth century, which would seem to be unlikely if cowrie supply was simply a reflection of market conditions. In fact as Lovejoy (1974) (a strong critic of Polanyi) has pointed out, the instability of the currency system in West Africa, as illustrated by the devaluation, should be correlated with European imperialism. In particular, the growing European presence in West Africa (and by implication the displacement of the power of local states) initially led to an increase of East African cowries and later as cowrie imports diminished their value fell as they were displaced by new coinage in transactions. What is important from this discussion is that in West Africa, the evidence indicates that money (in its archaic form) did not spontaneously evolve to facilitate exchange, as neo-classicals would have us believe, but was the product of conscious state intervention.

8   Handoussa, in the theoretical section of her chapter, defines a broad array of objectives including incentive and institutional instruments, which is very OIE like. However, the emphasis on transaction and information costs and efficiency indicators places the argument in a NIE framework. Her discussion of structural adjustment in Egypt is very neo-classical with a heavy emphasis on wholesale not piecemeal reform (shades of shock treatment?), transparency in regulations, prices that are undistorted and reflect opportunity costs, deregulation and the promotion of the informal sector to counter some of the social costs of adjustment. It leaves one wondering how some proponents of NIE and neo-classicals differ in policy terms.

8

THE ROLE OF THE STATE
The case of Egypt
Heba Handoussa

INTRODUCTION

This chapter considers the redefinition of the role of the state in a developing country undergoing liberalisation and structural adjustment. After three decades characterised by central planning and regulation, the dominance of public enterprise activity in the productive and tradables sectors, and the operation of an elaborate system of welfare, the scope and degree of state intervention is now being questioned in Egypt. The problems of delineating the economic boundaries of the state and of analysing the structure of incentives and organisation with which it guides economic activity are common to many countries in the Middle East which adopted similar growth and development policies in the 1960s and which are now beginning to make the transition towards a market economy.

Egypt represents a consistent model of development which has attempted to blend the neo-classical precepts of a market economy with those of a highly socialist orientation. This model was applied to a considerable extent by many of its neighbouring countries, with similar repercussions on performance. Halfway through the period under study, Egypt inaugurated its Open Door Policy (October 1973), with a partial liberalisation of the incentive and institutional structure. However, the three underlying themes characterising the Egyptian model have persisted throughout the period: an import-substituting strategy imposed through central planning and macro-economic policies; a dominant state sector (dominated by a top-heavy bureaucracy) in key areas of the economy; and an extensive institutionalised system of welfare transfers operating mostly via implicit and explicit subsidies and guaranteed employment.

An important distinction is made throughout this chapter between the instruments wielded by the state in providing an optimal incentive structure for efficient performance of the economy and those used in providing an enabling institutional environment. The first concerns the package of macro-economic policies and corrective measures that affect the operation of markets and resource allocation and the second addresses the system of laws and regulations which govern the operation of economic agents. Together, these two sets of tools have determined the pace and direction of economic growth. Yet neo-classical economics is mostly concerned with the manipulation of the incentive set of instruments, and tends to take the institutional setting of the economy as 'given' and determined by the configuration of social and political circumstances about which the economist has little to say.

The analytical approach adopted here is therefore based on the neo-institutional view of economic theory whereby the state and its institutions play a pivotal role in determining the performance of the economy. The standard neo-classical model – with its focus on market orientation as the essential ingredient to the efficient allocation of resources – ignores the major role which institutions play in reducing (raising) uncertainty and promoting (impeding) the acquisition of knowledge. Just as efficient institutions can provide an enabling environment which enhances competitive behaviour and an efficient growth path, inefficient institutions may persist over time because of the symbiotic relationship between them and the organisations that have evolved in response to their sub-optimal structure. Organisations – firms, trade unions and other economic, political, social and educational bodies – come into being and take advantage of the opportunity set as determined by institutions and by the standard constraints of economic choice theory. These organisations are therefore likely to maintain and reinforce an inefficient institutional system and can be seen as the major source of resistance to its evolution along a path that improves economic welfare (North 1990a).

The first part of this chapter provides an analytical framework which links the nature of state intervention in the economy with the performance of that economy over time. It is based on the approach of the new institutional economics (NIE) which recognises both the theoretical framework of neo-classical economics as well as the limitations of its assumptions (Hodgson 1988, 1993; Langlois 1986a). The main questions to be considered are: why the neo-classical model of growth has failed to explain the differential growth performance of developing countries; how the institutional approach can help remedy the weaknesses of the neo-classical model; and what are the boundaries of the state that are implied by the NIE? The second part of the chapter uses the new institutional framework to analyse Egypt's development experience since the 1960s and to identify the strengths and weaknesses of the Egyptian model of intenventionism. Four hypotheses are formulated which can be tested using the combined neo-classical/institutional apparatus of analysis. The third part of the chapter presents a critical review of Egypt's current programme of structural adjustment and institutional reform in order to appraise the consistency of the reform process which is designed to put the economy back on a path of sustainable growth. It also focuses on the future role of the state.

THEORETICAL FRAMEWORK

Standard neo-classical analysis is based on the rational-maximising behaviour of individuals and firms, with a focus on the functioning of markets to bring about equilibrium where all marginal conditions obtain. Simultaneous equilibrium in all markets leads to the static general equilibrium model which can then be aggregated to obtain a growth model. The neo-classical growth model provides a neat and rigorous framework. Yet it is ahistoric, taking as its determinant the production function and using highly stylised assumptions about human and organisational behaviour. The simple model cannot explain the differential performance of countries over time and space. Recent extensions of the model have tried to incorporate variables such as structural change on the demand and supply sides, the pattern of industrialisation and the internal and external policies which affect resource allocation. Another line of enquiry has focused on the nature of technical change and its correlation with firm size, research and innovation (Syrquin *et al.* 1984). Yet whatever refinements are attempted, the neo-classical model is built on some fundamental assumptions which have long been criticised for their lack of realism. Foremost among these is the assumption of perfect information. In fact, as indicated elsewhere in this volume, both transactions and information costs have been shown to constitute a major and growing share of total costs in a modern economy and it is the nature of the state and its institutions that determines the level of these transaction costs and hence the level of performance of the economy.

A second weakness of the standard neo-classical model has been the comparatively static nature of the equilibrium growth path which makes it difficult to incorporate the all-important process by which firms acquire knowledge and adapt to the ever-changing circumstances of the global economy. No economy is resting in a stationary state or moving frictionlessly along a steady state. Circumstances on the global scene are changing at an accelerating pace and in order to adjust, enterprises are forced to either innovate, to specialise or to reorganise. Although inventions and innovations have been responsible for the outward shift of production frontiers over time, there is growing evidence that a country can have a higher rate of growth and productivity than its trading partners without necessarily being a leading innovator, as long as it has superior institutions which promote the best use of this new technology through efficient organisation. In the context of developing countries this gives added strength to the argument that the role of the state should not simply be confined to the elimination of market distortions and ensuring a competitive environment (static efficiency) but should also encompass the promotion of innovation and change (dynamic efficiency) via its education, science and industrial policies so as to facilitate the process of 'catching up'.

Another departure from the standard neo-classical approach that is deemed appropriate in analysing the role of the state in Third World countries is in the treatment of the notion of competition. In mature capitalist economies, neither domestic markets nor external markets can be described as fully competitive, a necessary assumption for equilibrium conditions to be Pareto optimal. For a typical less developed country, the setting is even worse: markets are incomplete and highly segmented, and the mobility of factors of production a great deal lower than in mature economies. What is equally serious is that government intervention has more often than not aggravated the problem of market failure by superimposing a 'modern' institutional structure which serves only one part of the economy, thereby accentuating the degree of dualism across public and private sectors, large and small scale, urban and rural, formal and informal.

Hence, the new institutional economics is an appropriate complement to the neo-classical framework when evaluating the role of the state in a developing country. First because it helps identify those aspects of the system of property rights which raise transaction costs and hinder the smooth functioning of market forces. And the evidence would seem to be that transaction costs and information costs are positively correlated with the degree of bureaucratic intervention in the economy, a common feature of developing countries (de Soto 1989; Portes *et al.* 1989; Chickering and Salahdine 1991). The second reason is that institutional analysis is interdisciplinary and seeks to incorporate the historical context in which growth takes place. The NIE recognises that social and political evolution is an integral part of economic development. This is particularly relevant to the study of the role of the state in countries that are still in the process of reformulating their national identity. Rather than insisting on one identical blueprint for the economic role of the state in all developing countries, institutional analysis is sufficiently flexible to admit of country specific institutional structures that can serve to enhance the efficiency of the growth path.

A third justification for using institutional economics in the treatment of state intervention in developing countries is that it brings in more explicitly the question of income and wealth distribution which is automatically ignored by standard welfare economics. Instead of relegating the income distribution role of government to second-stage transfers via taxes and subsidies, the institutional model deals with property rights from the outset. The state can therefore play a pivotal role in the assignment or reassignment of property rights according to society's preferences for equity and justice. A fourth, final reason why it is useful to incorporate the institutional parameters into a discussion of the role of the state is that it avoids the trap of having to take a polarised position as between the extreme right and left ideologies.

Figure 8.1 presents four alternative but extreme models of state intervention in the economy, ranging from minimal intervention on the incentive and institutional fronts (the mature capitalist model) to maximal intervention (the mature socialist model). Although experience shows that the majority of developing countries have opted for neither of the extreme models (Min/Min or Max/Max), two main groups can be distinguish according to their choice between the High/High position (extensive intervention with market forces combined with a heavy dose of bureaucratic intervention) and the Low/Low position (a selective degree of intervention with the free market system coupled with a minimum interference in the system of private property rights). Examples of the High/High model would include a large number of countries in Latin America, the Middle East (including Egypt), Africa and South Asia whereas the Low/Low model is a useful approximation of the successful Southeast Asian countries. An elaboration on the instruments used and their relationship with the functions of the state will show that the alternative models are in fact far more varied and complex than implied by Figure 8.1.

Intervention via institutional instruments

		Minimal	High	
Intervention via incentive instruments	Minimal	Price mechanism rules Private property rights	Distorted price mechanism Highly bureacratic system	High
	Low	Selective protection Private property rights	Central planning rules Maximum state ownership	Maximal
		Low	Maximal	

Figure 8.1 Degrees of intervention by the state in the economy

In order to analyse the role and size of the state in a developing economy it is necessary to enumerate the set of functions which it should perform and then show whether the incentive (allocative) and institutional frameworks adopted in fact coincide with the efficient conduct of these functions. This implies that the state intervenes in the economy in order to fulfil four major functions: stabilise the macroeconomy, correct for market failure, redistribute income and enhance the 'catching up' process. The first three are conventionally accepted by neo-classical and Keynesian theory, the fourth follows from the reassessment of the competitive nature of global markets, the dynamic implications of growth and the resulting importance attached to the 'knowledge' and 'organisational' dimensions of development by the NIE theory when applied to Third World countries (Beckerman 1990; Hyman 1990).

Correcting market failure may involve any one or all three of the following functions: regulation of economic activity; provision of public and merit goods (based on principles of non-excludability and non-rivalry); and the ownership of natural monopolies. 'Catching up' strategies may embrace planning, industrial policy and organisational development. These are critical areas of intervention where the effectiveness of state action can be analysed to determine whether or not the state is responding to the needs of society as a whole and not to any one group in society. But the potential for inconsistency among the functional objectives or methods of state intervention is great and provides the key to understanding the performance of the state in the economy. Table 8.1 illustrates the multitude of objectives and variety of tools that can be manipulated by the state in a developing country. The distinction between incentive and institutional tools is real, not only conceptually but also in practical terms. The degree of openness of an economy as reflected under the incentives column may not necessarily translate into a corresponding degree of decentralisation under the institutional column.

The tools and methods subsumed under the incentive framework are easily recognised by an economist trained in the mainstream tradition, they are all centred on the operation of the price mechanism and are designed to influence the allocation of resources in production, consumption and investment. Allocative efficiency can thus be used as the indicator of performance of state intervention in the market via the signalling mechanism. Yet, while much of the debate has revolved around the effectiveness of the chosen degree of market intervention by the state, particularly in price controls and in planning, the institutional framework that governs the economy has long been taken as 'given'. Only recently have development economists drawn attention to market failure that is caused by bureaucratic obstruction in the legal and administrative domains. The literature is especially rich when analysing difficulties faced by traditional sectors of economic activity which hamper their integration into the modern economy and retard their growth potential (de Soto 1990; Portes et al. 1989; Chickering and Salahdine 1991; Hopkins 1992). The debate over public ownership of enterprises in the tradables sector has also arisen over the past decade, support for privatisation being derived from the experience of developing countries (Helm 1990; Galal et al. 1992). These arguments must be questioned as the evidence for the superior performance of private over public ownership is far from conclusive. In most cases where state-owned firms have operated in the tradables sectors of developing countries, they have responded to a deliberately distorted set of incentives and institutional regulations. Reforms of the policy and control environments that surround the public sector are therefore much more likely to bring about the type of market response that is being called for than simply transferring their ownership rights to the private sector. Moreover, privatisation will be especially risky in instances where the institutional and regulatory environments have not been suitably adjusted to avoid private sector monopoly behaviour and agency problems.

By focusing on the institutional framework that governs economic activity and centres on property rights, on the enforcement and execution of the law and on the resulting transaction costs, it is possible study of the response of economic agents in terms of the organisational arrangements they choose and how these translate into an efficient or inefficient growth path. The evolution of the institutional structure will determine total factor productivity change

138

Table 8.1 Objectives and instruments of state intervention

Objectives	Incentive tools	Institutional tools
1. *Stabilisation*		
Full employment	Tax policy	Tax and customs administration
Price stability	Expenditure policy	Controls on trade and distribution
Budget balance	Monetary policy	Banking and credit laws
External balance	Exchange rate policy	Exchange controls
2. *Regulation*		
Promoting competition		Anti-trust legislation
Regulating monopoly	Administered prices	Protection of property rights
Consumer protection	Tariff levels	Entry and exit rules
		Investment licensing
Labour protection	Non-tariff barriers	Consumer protection legislation
		Labour laws
3. *Public and merit goods*		
Defence and security	No direct charge	Government monopoly
Population control	No direct charge	Government monopoly
Environment protection	No direct charge	Zoning and pollution controls
Legal structure	No direct charge	Independent judiciary
Education and research	Free vouchers/subsidies	Public /private mix
Health services	Selective support	Public/private mix
Integrating informal sector	Selective incentives	Public/NGO mix
Regional development		Public/NGO mix
4. *Natural monopolies*		
Providing infrastructure	–	Public monopoly
and utilities	–	Public monopoly
5. *Redistribution*		
Transfers to poor and vulnerable groups	Taxes and subsidies	Guaranteed employment
Basic needs	Social security (same as merit goods)	Social contract (same as merit goods)
6. *Planning*		
Information and forecasting	Information dissemination	Indicative/central plan
Industrial policy	Selective protection	Investment licensing
7. *Organisation*		
Responding to global oligopolies and enhancing knowledge acquisition	Autonomy, transparency and accountability of national oligopolies	Discrimination in favour of national oligopolies (public or private)
		Institution building to promote information, education and technology

(the traditional black box) via the flow of knowledge it promotes and the economy with which knowledge is acquired by new organisational patterns. Total factor productivity (TFP) can therefore be considered as an indicator of the efficiency of the changing institutional structure as impacted on by state intervention and societal responses. In mature economies, a growing body of evidence suggests that neither size or expenditure on research can explain the differential TFP performance among firms in one country or across countries, but rather the ability of firms to reorganise along both internalisation and externalisation directions (Scherer 1982, 1986; Mansfield 1988; Griliches and Maitresse 1990). This evidence is also supported by the twin global trends whereby giant firms are still increasing their share of the market and are also increasing their level of specialisation (Best 1990).

Third World countries would seem to be in the precarious situation whereby the process of catching up becomes progressively more difficult. Yet there may be cause for optimism. First, the information revolution is making knowledge a great deal cheaper to acquire. Second, structural change in world demand is making scarce capital a lot less important in the growth industries of the future. Third, technical economies of scale have turned out to be much less important than judged by economists at mid-century (Best 1990; Thurow 1992; Portes et al. 1989; Madnick 1991). This means that the state can play a crucial role if it develops an active industrial policy after the East (and possibly South East) Asian model where deliberate interventionist regimes have used four major tools to promote rapid structural change and productivity growth: selective protection for targeted subsectors at high levels but of limited duration (although the length of infant status would seem relatively long); a comprehensive assault on all institutional fronts in order to maximise the knowledge flow to all economic agents (market information, technology, education and training) and to minimise bureaucratic obstacles; a deliberate avoidance of foreign direct investment except in those fields where knowledge could only be obtained through that route; and a discriminate institutional policy favouring the creation and operation of giant conglomerates (at least in Japan and South Korea).

THE CASE OF EGYPT

The pattern of the country's evolution over the last two centuries (Egypt's modern economic history begins with the reign of Muhammad Ali in 1805) can be characterised as cycles of growth followed by stagnation. During this period there were two major attempts at structural transformation and growth: the first between 1805 and 1845; the second following the 1952 revolution. Both attempts were made possible by the existence of a strong state capable of keeping foreign intervention at bay and of mobilising domestic resources for development. In each case, the state adopted highly centralised administrative controls for the pursuit of an import-substituting, closed economy model.

During the second phase there was also a concern to achieve an equitable distribution of income. The century-long interval between the two experiments was marked by foreign domination, neglect of education, the absence of protective tariffs (until the 1930s) and the integration of Egypt into the world economy as a primary exporter of raw cotton which accounted for 80 per cent of total exports until 1950. The growth path became unsustainable and per capita GDP which had been higher than Japan's (about $50) until 1913 grew negligibly thereafter (Issawy 1990; Owen 1969; Mead 1967: Hansen and Marzouk 1965). Meanwhile, the most damaging result of this lopsided pattern of development was an irreversible change in the nation's resource equation, with population turning from shortage to surplus (10 million in 1900 to 52 million in 1990) and water and cultivable land becoming effective constraints threatening the country's future economic viability and ecological balance.

Today and over the past forty years, the persistence of poverty reflects the most daunting challenge to Egypt's policy-makers – how to harness the country's vast pool of human resources and turn it from burden to mainstay of consistent growth and rising living standards. The task has been all the more difficult because of the conflict between domestic and external demands made on the state's modest resources. Throughout the period since the late 1940s, the trade-off between defence and investment expenditures has been one of the most striking features influencing the country's record of economic growth (Handoussa 1991; Handoussa and Shafik 1991). Another has been the drastic shift in political alliances from the West to the East and back to the West in the space of less than twenty years. Between 1956 (the Suez War) and 1973 (the October War), the country's institutional structure was twice traumatised: first with a series of radical socialist measures, transferring to the state the ownership of, or control over, a dominant share of non-agricultural activity; second, with the Open Door Policy (ODP) or *Infitah* policy that reinstated private ownership albeit within a highly bureaucratised and inconsistent institutional framework.

It can be argued that throughout the socialist period, and in spite of the far-reaching nationalisations of the 1960s, the 'incentive' framework was not as seriously disrupted as the 'institutional' framework. Import restrictions rather than tariffs were the main tool providing protection for import-substituting industries. Relative prices continued to reflect world prices – subject to controls designed for the purpose of income redistribution and the mobilisation of savings by the state – and central planning never effectively overstepped the boundary of allocating the bulk of the country's investment resources to projects selected and executed by the public sector, itself responsive to the price mechanism. State intervention on the incentives front was thus high but not extreme and serious price distortions did not arise until after the ODP had been initiated (Hansen and Nashashibi 1975; Handoussa 1979a, 1979b, 1980). The fact that the state refused to relinquish control over prices despite the inauguration of the liberalisation era in the mid-1970s reflects an attachment to a policy of income transfers even though the net effect of artificially imposed prices was a substantial and growing loss of state revenues which ran counter to the second objective of mobilising savings. Nevertheless, when the state was forced to abandon price controls after 1986, the speed and smoothness with which this reform was accomplished confirms the fact that the price mechanism had functioned relatively smoothly during the preceding thirty years.

In contrast, state intervention on the 'institutional' front as practised in the 1960s had a far more profound impact on economic, political and social relations by interrupting the normal development of domestic capitalist enterprise, preventing democratic participation in the decision-making process and promoting negative attitudes towards individual initiative, risk taking and profits. The drastic reduction in property rights was accompanied by an exponential growth in the size of the bureaucracy which was to take over as the dominant power exercising control over the economy. The bureaucratic state, with its rigid and centralised rules and regulations, its lack of transparency and its internal inconsistencies, became deeply entrenched and intractable.

Starting in the early 1970s, new legislation was enacted to encourage Arab, foreign and later Egyptian private sector investment and to allow domestic capital to engage in foreign trade (Fahmy 1988). This legislation was added to the existing body of corporate, labour, foreign exchange, stock market and other laws governing property rights as modified during the socialist era with little if any amendment to these laws to suit the requirements and spirit of the declared *Infitah*. The result was glaring contradiction across the laws, the proliferation of new bureaucratic agencies superimposed on the older bodies to 'simplify' transactions for new investors and traders and increased discretion for civil servants to interpret and execute ambiguous set of rules and their related procedures. By 1991, even foreign investors whose interests were given top priority in the formulation of the investment encouragement code (Law 1943 of 1974, modified in 1977 and 1989) and the creation of a specialised investment agency (the Authority for Foreign Investment and Free Zones) could still complain that two major impediments to an increased flow of foreign direct investment (FDI) were 'a discretionary investment regime with an inappropriate incentive package and a lengthy screening and approval process; and an archaic bureaucracy' (Foreign Investment Advisory Service 1991: i).

In evaluating the role of the state since ODP, four hypotheses have been formulated which follow from the analytical framework set out above. These are designed to ascertain major sources of weakness in the current Egyptian interventionist model. The classification of functions performed by the state – set out in the theoretical framework above – will be followed, except that analysis of stabilisation strategies is deferred until the final part of the chapter which considers the comprehensive stabilisation and structural adjustment programme currently being implemented.

Hypotheses 1 and 2 on the regulatory role of the state

The Egyptian state has not provided a regulatory framework which ensures competition, a major function of any modern state.

1 Under-regulation has been a major feature of the partial *Infitah* implemented since the mid-1970s. Limited liberalisation of product and factor markets has only accentuated distortions and encouraged the growth of highly protected and often monopolistic private entities.
2 Over-regulation has continued to characterise the institutional structure in spite of the Open Door Policy. Legislative and bureaucratic reform has failed significantly to reduce transaction and production costs. Agency problems have now become a major source of resistance to reforms.

In dealing with these two hypotheses, it is useful to remember the distinction between incentive and institutional instruments, set out above, available to the state in performing each of its functions. The first hypothesis relates to the manipulation by the state (via the executive branch of government) of the package of policies that have a direct or indirect bearing on the system of relative prices guiding the allocative process. Both private and public economic agents are continuously responding and adjusting to these relative prices and the regulatory function of government should ensure that this system of prices best reflects scarcity. In the case of Egypt, the transition from the socialist to the *Infitah* era was accompanied by only a partial liberalisation of the incentive regime, with significant departure from the initial Second Best situation. The second hypothesis deals with the legal and administrative rules that govern market entry and exit which were also only partially revised to allow more competition from the private sector. An incomplete liberalisation of the incentive structure means that the market is under-regulated, making it possible for agents to behave monopolistically and for factors of production to be misallocated. In parallel, insufficient reform of the institutional structure means that agents are prevented from responding and adjusting to the changing market signals because of the institutional impediments. Hence the institutional structure is over-regulated.

Over the period of the *Infitah*, the three major producers of tradables (agriculture, manufacturing and energy) experienced a significant deterioration in the structure of relative commodity prices in their input/output relations and in the real cost of primary factors of production. The exchange rate became increasingly overvalued and the real rate of interest increasingly negative, while real wages in the flexible labour markets first shot up (until 1982) and then declined gradually to present levels. The outcome was a significant decline in effective rates of protection from high levels set in the late 1960s and early

143

1970s. Some subsectors (agriculture and public sector manufacturing) experienced negative protection but others (energy intensive and consumer durable industries) still enjoyed positive protection (World Bank 1983).

The link between the incentive structure and economic performance can be found in the indicators of allocative efficiency of the various sectors of economic activity and in the distribution of aggregate investment over time. The evidence shows that during the period 1975–92, as a result of the highly distorted structure of relative prices, sectoral performance – as measured by domestic resource cost and economic rates of return – has worsened. There has been an inefficient use of capital resources, an under-utilization of labour, and ineffective decision-making in terms of output mix. The allocation of investment to sectors has also been sub-optimal. A detailed analysis of TFP performance over the *Infitah* period demonstrates a striking acceleration in the use of capital relative to labour in formal private and public sector manufacturing enterprises. In real terms, after deflating the capital series, the capital/labour ratio was shown to have increased at an annual rate of 10 per cent, at a time of rapid growth for the manufacturing sector as a whole (Handoussa 1991; Richards 1991). The slowdown in the absorption of labour in the manufacturing sector (annual employment growth of about 2 per cent between 1970 and 1984 compares with 9.6 per cent in 1960–65 and 3.7 per cent from 1965/66 to 1970/71) contrasts with the average annual growth in manufacturing output of about 7 per cent over the period as a whole. As to the impact of the growing price distortions on product mix, the sector with the most significant supply response would seem to have been agriculture where the reallocation of land use was unprecedented in terms of the departure of actual from optimal crop mix, with huge losses in opportunity cost to the economy and, to a lesser extent, the farmer (Moursi 1980, 1986: Kheir El-Din and Clark 1979). Distorted price signals in the agricultural sector also led to a wave of large-scale investments in what became known as 'Food Security Projects' in animal husbandry and dairy farms. These had negative real returns to the economy but generated huge profits for the capitalists involved (Handoussa and Kaldas 1986).

In terms of the impact of the incentive structure on the overall allocation of aggregate investment, over time the increasingly distorted price system which accompanied the partial opening of the economy was responsible for a lopsided distribution of private investment. The increased rate of inflation (up from an average of 5 per cent in the 1960s to 15 per cent in the 1970s and 20 per cent in the 1980s) was partly responsible for the flow of savings into inflation hedges, mostly property. But the most serious distortion in relative prices arose from the rigid system of administered prices applied in sectors controlled or operated by the government, especially services, intermediate goods and centrally marketed agricultural commodities. The distribution of private investment between the periods shows a significant decline in the share of the commodity sectors (excepting petroleum) and rapid growth in non-productive services

(Handoussa 1989b, 1991). Those subsectors characterised by excessive protection (due to tariffs or domestic subsidies) were those where large capitalists could reap abnormal profits by maintaining a monopoly position.

This shows that the initial structure of relative prices is likely to worsen in an under-regulated economy unless liberalisation is undertaken simultaneously on all fronts. The private sector is especially responsive to the price mechanism and its production, investment and consumption behaviour will adjust rapidly to new constraints and opportunities. The resulting allocation is not only inefficient in terms of lost output but also creates a new class of vested interests that will try to maintain the distorted price structure and the rents it generates. The creation of a rentier class among importers and manufacturers of highly protected consumer and intermediate goods during the *Infitah* has attracted adverse criticism (Abdel Khalek 1982; Biblawi 1992). But it was state imposed market failure that caused the apparent private sector failure.

The second hypothesis links the institutional structure with economic performance. Due to the incomplete nature of the reforms concerning property rights, the bureaucracy assumed new discretionary powers to interpret contradictory legislation while powerful elements of the private capitalist class exploited inconsistencies in the legal system to their own advantage. Agency problems ensued, the new rentier class and bureaucracy combined and conspired to maintain an inherently monopolistic environment and resisted further reform. For those agents who are unable to capture the potential rents – the bulk of the capitalist class – transaction costs are prohibitive and result in high barriers to market entry, reduced competition and lower growth.

The disjuncture between stated objective and outcome of legislative reform illustrates how the non-rationalised structure of institutions that has persisted throughout the *Infitah* has worked to prevent the economy from achieving its potential growth rate. The two most prominent objectives that have been consistently pursued since ODP have been the growth in private sector investment and in exports. By isolating and examining those segments of the institutional framework that pertain to the incorporation of private firms and export activity it is possible to identify a number of explicit and implicit constraints that have raised transaction costs and hampered market entry by potential producers and exporters. Explicitly, seven years elapsed between the start of the ODP and the reform of corporate law. The old code, as modified during the socialist era, provided for the equal representation of labour on company Boards of Directors and the distribution of 25 per cent of corporate profits to labour. This legislation was only repealed in 1981. The new company law cut worker participation in profits to 10 per cent. But the provisions of the new commercial code conflict, in some respects, with the twice-amended law on foreign investments which also regulates business enterprises. Moreover, the foreign investment law categorises companies in terms of the currency of investment rather than the 'nationality' of capital thereby causing further confusion as to what legislation applies to which enterprise (Handoussa 1989b). The provisions of the code and law have yet to be harmonised. Ill-defined jurisdictions between national and local government or amongst ministries also generate friction and create opportunities for bureaucratic discretion and special treatment, especially in sectors such as tourism and food security.

Implicitly, legislation discriminates in favour of large investors, partly on account of the centralised nature of the administrative departments, particularly in areas such as taxation, customs concessions, overseas trade, credit and access to land (Handoussa and Shafik 1993b; World Bank 1991b; GATT 1992). Another major barrier to market entry for all potential competitors – public or private, large or small – is the discretionary nature of the investment and import licensing system which lacked any transparency before 1991. For the 'typical' firm, additional transaction costs are encountered in dealing with the securities market, employment, taxation, purchasing 'quota' intermediates, and selling to government agencies. Such a costly institutional environment makes it far more difficult for smaller firms to absorb fixed transaction costs which constitute an effective barrier to their entry and competition. In Egypt, micro-enterprises (defined as establishments with fewer than 10 employees) account for 90 per cent of total private sector employment outside of agriculture. They face not only the usual problems of market failure that characterise underdeveloped markets for capital and labour but also those created by an inefficient and over-centralised bureaucracy (Integrated Development Consultants 1989; Handoussa and Potter 1992).

Under-regulation on the incentives vector and over-regulation on the institutional vector of state intervention in the economy have both been very high in Egypt since the introduction of ODP. The impact of these two dimensions on the growth of monopolistic private sector tendencies, of agency problems and of transaction costs has been positive and significant. These tendencies can only retard the growth process and sustain the two hypotheses that the poor performance of the economy is related to a sub-optimal regulatory framework imposed by the state. The policy implications are clear: both sets of inconsistencies on the incentive and institutional fronts have reinforced one another over the past two decades, and neither partial nor complete reform of the one without the other can rid the economy of the significant burdens that they impose. Rationalisation of the institutional structure will now be even more difficult to achieve given the significant rents that accrue to some elements of the bureaucracy.

Hypotheses 3 and 4 on the role of the state as owner and producer

The state is in the process of reducing its role as owner and producer in the tradables sectors of the economy. How much privatisation should take place and in which subsectors should be based on an understanding of the strengths and weaknesses of public enterprise.

3 Centralisation of the control structure over public enterprises in the face of partial liberalisation has led to a dual economy where state-owned organisations have not been allowed to respond to market signals. The deterioration in performance of the public sector is therefore directly related to the degree of centralisation imposed by the state. Hence reforms will only improve efficiency if the state is willing to enforce the spirit and letter of the law.

4 In the context of privatisation, the extent to which the state should retain its role as producer is intimately related to its willingness to sever links between the bureaucracy and public organisations. Managerial X efficiency is not significantly different between public and private firms in those activities where products are homogeneous and processes are subject to a slow rate of technological change. But those activities that require product differentiation, a high degree of flexibility and individual initiative should be turned over to the private sector.

In addressing the question of state ownership beyond sectors of natural monopoly, the optimum role of the state been subsumed under the 'catching up' function presented in the first part of this chapter. Three conditions must obtain for public enterprises to fulfil this objective: they must enjoy full autonomy and flexibility to design and implement their individual strategic plans; they must abide by the regulatory rules that ensure that they cannot exploit their oligopoly advantage in monopolistic pricing or in preventing market entry; and they must be accountable for their performance via a transparent system of evaluation and penalty/reward.

In spite of ODP, Egyptian state-owned firms lacked autonomy in all key areas of decision-making until 1991. These included production planning, wage and price determination, labour recruitment and promotion, and investment and finance. The state has used and abused the public sector for income distribution purposes. These policies have imposed unsustainable costs on public enterprises, reflected in high rates of disguised unemployment, low productivity, falling real wages and increasing losses. They have also undermined the potential role of this vast sector to act as an engine for savings, growth and diversification. The centralised and bureaucratic nature of the organisational structure governing public enterprises has also stifled managerial initiative and inhibited aggressive, market oriented behaviour (Handoussa 1980, 1991; Ministry of Industry 1990, 1991).

All these constraints were institutional in character and were supposed to disappear with Law 203 of 1991 and attached executive decree. As of March 1993 seventeen state holding companies and their affiliated enterprises were separated from direct supervision by individual ministries and the ministry of planning. The new mandate for the holding companies is to maximise the present value of the state's portfolio of shares in each group of enterprises. The holding company has the right to sell shares, assets or entire enterprises or to even liquidate them. Law 203 has guaranteed the freedom of affiliated firms to respond to market forces and has raised the level of operational transparency and accountability (Handoussa 1989b: Table A.10.1) Whether the legislative (and incentive policy) reforms will allow Egypt's 309 state-owned enterprises to extricate themselves from the bureaucracy after thirty years of rigid subservience to it will depend on the state's willingness to enforce the new rules of the game and allow a true separation between business and the state administration.

State planning has been another major source of institutional constraint on the efficient performance of public enterprises. Central planning was conceived as an alternative to market forces but enterprise decisions in the allocation of the bulk of public investment used a system of surrogate prices that contradicted a system of price relations dictated by opportunity cost. There are three ways in which the role of planning can support efficient economic growth in developing countries. The first is in tackling the information problem by using the sophisticated techniques available to expert individuals and specialised equipment in providing all agents in society with valuable predictions and forecasts. The second is in identifying sectors where market failure is important and designing alternative strategies for the long-term solution to these problems including manpower and education plans as well as plans for regional development and for the protection of the environment. The third is in coordinating macro-policies and public investment in the fields of public goods and natural monopolies so as to support an active industrial policy which selectively intervenes with market forces to promote dynamic comparative advantage. Nevertheless, a central plan cannot efficiently perform the role of prices in a constantly changing environment, it cannot possess all the information dispersed among individual agents involved in decision-making. Since planning is the complex of interrelated decisions about the allocation of resources, all economic activity is planning, and the dispute is not about whether planning should be done but about whether it is to be done centrally, by one authority on behalf of the whole economic system, or divided among many individual agents. This suggests that the planning authority should only interfere selectively with the price system and only out of a conviction that prices matter and that changes in the incentive structure should produce an organisational and allocative response that satisfies the longer-term objectives of dynamic efficiency. In sum, judicious government intervention should minimise the role of the state and allow organisations to make decisions in the light of a stable, coherent and transparent system of institutions (Coase 1937: 390–1, 394; 1960: 17).

The current transition to indicative planning, as expressed in the *Third Five-Year Plan* document for 1992/93 to 1996/97 (Ministry of Planning 1992), goes a long way towards reforming the institution of the Plan. Commodity balances are no longer the means to justify the implementation of projects that will fill the gap between projected domestic consumption and production (the long-lived import-substitution criterion) and the entire public enterprise sector has in fact been excluded from the government's public investment budget. The public 'business' sector is now expected to make its own investment plans and to find its own sources of finance – on market terms – independent of the rigid controls to which it has been subjected to over the past thirty years. Enterprise profits – a major potential source of finance – are now also subject to the same rules of distribution and tax liability as for the private sector. The emphasis of public investments is on the provision of public goods (social services) and natural monopolies (infrastructure and utilities). Well over half targeted aggregate investment in commodity and goods production is projected to be undertaken by the private sector, especially in the critical activity of manufacturing. Nevertheless, the attempt to shift the focus of planning 'from the planning of projects to the planning of policies' can only bring about the forecasted acceleration in private sector activity if all of the institutional problems are resolved. This is being done within the context of a reforms of the incentive structure implemented as part of the programme of structural adjustment.

The second hypothesis links efficiency levels in the public enterprise sector to the incentive framework. On the assumption that institutional reforms are successful in breaking the hold of the bureaucracy over public organisations, what factors will determine the level of X efficiency of these firms? What functions can still be performed by these firms now that they are neither instruments for income redistribution nor for fulfilling a centralised national plan? Hypothesis 4 asserts that there is no inherent difference in the managerial behaviour of public as opposed to private enterprises in Egypt. Evidence to support this argument can be found in two early studies of the operation of public enterprises, before they became subject to the totally inconsistent set of constraints that dictated inefficient behaviour in response to distorted market signals. It can also be found in a detailed analysis conducted in 1981/82 of a large sample of private and public enterprises in the manufacturing sector which showed that there was no significant difference between the two sectors in terms of allocative efficiency (Handoussa 1974, 1979a, 1980; World Bank 1983). Moreover, TFP analysis of the comprehensive data set on formal public and private manufacturing firms over the 1970–80 period shows no consistent superiority of private over public sector. It also shows that in those branches of economic activity where direct competition occurs (textiles), the public sector rates of TFP growth were higher than those for the private sector (Handoussa 1991).

The performance of public enterprises in Egypt's manufacturing sector has been shown to be allocatively efficient for the majority of industries in which they operate and benefit from scale economies, namely, most branches of textiles, food processing, basic metals, chemicals and engineering. In the 1960s, many of these public sector enterprises created a comparative advantage for Egypt in sectors such as of basic metals, fertilisers, paper, pharmaceuticals, railway rolling stock and some lines of electrical equipment and consumer durables. Their strength derived from the quality of managerial and technical personnel, their oligopoly position in the domestic market (which enhanced bargaining power with multinationals) and scale. Those enterprises that suffer from low rates of return or negative domestic value added at international prices were few in number. Most either utilised obsolete technology or assembled foreign branded goods and were dependent on the acquisition of know-how and capital equipment via licensing agreements. Their financial viability was due to high levels of effective protection and state subsidies, often cheap energy (Handoussa 1979a).

Egypt adopted a sophisticated system of unified accounting for the public sector in the 1960s and since then the performance of public enterprises has been judged by standard profit and loss criteria, unlike establishments in Eastern Europe (Wahba 1986). While the growth in price distortions of the 1970s and early 1980s made published financial results irrelevant as a means of judging efficiency, gradual price liberalisation in 1986 (which has accelerated since 1991) will soon allow profit and loss statements of public enterprises to be reinstated as an effective tool of accountability.

The essential hypothesis to be verified is that public enterprises have maintained their responsiveness to market forces notwithstanding exogenous constraints imposed on their behaviour via controls in their incentives and institutional frameworks. Measures of allocative efficiency were calculated for a sample of thirty-one enterprises affiliated to the Ministry of Industry representing the subsectors of manufacturing and accounting for more than half of capital employed in 1990/91. The results of the analysis show that industries which displayed comparative advantage in 1980/81 were still highly efficient, notably food processing, tobacco, fertiliser and cables. The exception was the textile industry which would seem to have suffered from the relative increase in international prices for extra-long staple cotton (World Bank 1983; Kheir El-Din et al. 1989). The World Bank survey also shows that the performance of some enterprises which suffered from low allocative efficiency in 1980/81 had significantly improved by the middle of the decade. A third feature of the study was that within each subsector the variance in performance across firms was extremely high, a characteristic of the Egyptian public sector throughout history.

These results are consistent with the hypothesis that public enterprises are inherently responsive to the price mechanism but that the absence of a system of evaluation and enforcement of penalties for the chronically sick firms means that those that should die (or be restructured) have instead been allowed to survive indefinitely. The challenge to the newly formed public holding companies is to use their mandate and move to rationalise portfolios via all of the legal tools which have been instituted, including mergers, liquidation and privatisation.

STRUCTURAL ADJUSTMENT AND THE FUTURE ROLE OF THE STATE

The legacy of four decades of heavy state involvement in the Egyptian economy has been more negative than positive, culminating in the rapid growth of unemployment, a food deficit and savings gap. Basic human needs are not satisfied, population growth is still too high and at least a quarter of the population is living below the poverty line (World Bank 1991a). Starting with the *Infitah*, the state's gradualist approach to liberalisation has been very costly in terms of delayed responses by economic agents to a reformed structure of incentives and the growth in foreign indebtedness. The piecemeal approach to reform has also aggravated the social and political costs of stabilisation and structural adjustment for the mass of the population. The partial nature of ODP meant that growth was dictated by an environment of excessive protection and distorted prices, leading to an anti-export and anti-labour bias and substantial investments in non-tradables, low value-added activities and speculation. The positive potential of a generous package of investment incentives was neutralised by the persistence of import-substituting trade and investment regimes.

The four hypotheses have also tried to bring the institutional dimension of state intervention more explicitly into the analysis, illustrating how the incomplete nature of legislative reform and deregulation and decentralisation have obstructed competition, raised transaction costs and retarded economic growth. The delayed or inadequate revision of property rights and especially the body of laws pertaining to financial markets, incorporation and employment have inhibited the flow of private investment into productive sectors of the economy. Moreover, glaring inconsistencies between existing and new laws and regulations, lack of transparency in many of the new provisions and failure to reform the administrative apparatus of government and introduce strict but simple operating procedures have together encouraged the growth of agency problems. A new class of powerful capitalists and elements of the bureaucracy now wield new powers in interpreting the contradictory legislation and exploiting the high degree of discretion it provides. Although the structural adjustment programme addresses a number of institutional issues, the state must correct identified defects even though it is likely to face resistance from well entrenched interest groups.

In appraising Egypt's 1991 Economic Reform and the Structural Adjustment Programme (ERSAP), it is useful to distinguish between each function which the ERSAP is designed to address (these are identified in Table 8.1). Stabilisation policy (under IMF Standby) is designed to restore equilibrium in the budget and external accounts and bring inflation under control. These objectives have been achieved by significant reductions in government expenditure (including subsidies investment), revenue raising measures (mostly indirect tax and public utility price hikes) and increased receipts from energy sales (IMF 1992). The effects on economic growth are – as expected – highly negative. Yet these measures are being applied at a time when the economy has been suffering from six years of recession, in contrast to normal practice whereby expenditure-reducing measures are used to stabilise an overheated economy. The restoration of GDP growth according to the IMF/World Bank model is predicated on an upsurge in private sector investment in the medium term, a task made difficult when public investment is mostly of the 'crowding in' type, and when a major element of the stabilisation component of ERSAP has been to maintain real rates of interest well above international levels (the real interest rate reached 7 per cent to 8 per cent in 1993), in order to neutralise foreign capital flows (World Bank 1992b).

While structural reforms of the real economy are still in progress, the ERSAP has been completed in the area of liberalisation of the exchange rate, financial markets and capital markets. This sequencing is quite different from that effected in most economies and has resulted in substantial reversal of capital flight and in the de-dollarisation of the economy. Against the positive impact which this has had on the balance of payments and on business confidence, unexpectedly large inflows of capital have led to an appreciation of the domestic currency which is contrary to the policy objective of maintaining a competitive exchange rate (IMF 1992). A weekly auction of Treasury Bills was introduced in January 1991 and has since served as the determinant of the Central Bank discount rate. Only part of the proceeds of these sales have been used to finance the shrinking budget deficit, the balance has served to neutralise capital inflows which in turn foster high interest rates. The cost to the budget of interest payments on the cumulative stock of Treasury Bills (LE 25 billion by end of 1992) threatens to exceed debt relief charges. It is therefore difficult to justify a neutralisation policy which continues to encourage massive and volatile capital inflows in response to the interest rate premium achieved on Egyptian, as opposed to foreign, currency deposits over the past two years, a period during which the unified, flexible exchange rate has been very stable.

Nevertheless, stabilisation has been highly successful in terms of restoring Egypt's international creditworthinesss, bringing inflation under control, and removing the elements which have discriminated between public and private sector enterprises in the markets for finance and for foreign exchange. The system of Treasury Bill sales, as a new tool of government monetary policy, is another achievement. So is the application of a unified exchange rate to all items in the government budget and to all public sector transactions, a reform which will enforce transparency and avoid inconsistency and distortions. The positive roles of low inflation and a stable exchange rate on the real economy are also significant since business expectations and confidence are highly sensitive to these indicators.

The structural adjustment component of ERSAP (under the World Bank SAL agreement) aims to liberalise the incentives framework and to deregulate the institutional framework for all sectors of the real economy (IMF 1992). In fact, reforms were begun in 1986 with a 'gradual' correction of relative prices. By end of 1990, price liberalisation had been completed for more than half of public enterprise production. Energy prices had increased by 43 per cent, and the agricultural sector was entirely decontrolled except for cotton, sugar cane and rice. By mid-1992, cotton prices had been raised to 66 per cent of their world price equivalent, petroleum prices had reached 80 per cent of world prices, electricity 69 per cent of long-run marginal cost and the percentage of public sector output value subject to price control had been reduced to 22.4 per cent. Another component of liberalisation has been the trade and protection regime. Maximum and minimum tariffs have been revised so as to reduce effective nominal protection. The list of tariff exemptions was revised downward from 49 per cent of potential tariff revenue equivalent in 1986 to 17 per cent in 1990. The coverage of import bans was reduced from 52 per cent in 1990 to 37 per cent in 1991and to 10 per cent in 1992. Deregulation has also proceeded swiftly with the dismantling of public sector monopolies in most foreign trade and agricultural distribution systems. The investment licensing system has also been reformed. New legislation has granted full autonomy of public enterprises and public holding companies. Rationalisation of the regulatory function of the state is thus well underway, and the completion of ERSAP will remove all of the remaining areas of state imposed monopolistic behaviour, especially with the expected dismantling of the public sector export monopoly for raw cotton and the projected revival of the domestic cotton exchange.

While discrimination between public and private enterprise is gradually disappearing, the dualistic structure of the economy in terms of the large/modern and the small/traditional dichotomy has not been addressed. The state has failed to correct for market failure in the micro-enterprise sector, providing these firms with access to credit. Basic education and training, with a 60 per cent rate of illiteracy among the urban self-employed and 78 per cent among the rural self-employed, is also deficient. Traditional institutions are being supplanted by ineffective modern bodies that are costly and likely to impede the gradual integration of the informal sector into the formal economy (Handoussa and Potter 1992). And the ERSAP has grave equity implications. Mechanisms utilised to combat poverty and unemployment since the 1960s have been abandoned or weakened (Handoussa 1989a). The campaign to reduce the budget deficit has concentrated on measures such as squeezing explicit and implicit subsidies and raising indirect taxes. This has a regressive impact on income distribution. Similarly, the reduction in employment opportunities, particularly in the public sector, is bound to hit those segments of the population that rely more heavily on wages and salaries as their sole source of income. Egypt has no general system of social insurance nor does the state provide any form of unemployment benefits. In effect a social safety net system which has endured for thirty years is being dismantled, while no apparent substitute is emerging. The state has not addressed the need to design a new social contract in the absence of open-ended subsidies and publicly guaranteed employment for educated entrants to the labour market. Nor has it forged an arrangement to meet minimum demand for targeted support for the most vulnerable groups in society. The Social Fund component of ERSAP is an emergency tool to ease the social and political burden of structural adjustment that can only reach a very small proportion of the population.

The analytical framework employed in this chapter has given prominence to the role of the state in assigning property rights. The state enacted a series of land reforms at the beginning of the Nasserite revolution, turning over a significant part of agricultural land to landless peasants. In the 1960s, property rights were reassigned from the capitalist class of industrialists and merchants to the state. Now that private enterprise is the order of the day, the state has the option to reallocate some of its property rights to the poor and the unemployed. Poverty alleviation could thus be combined with promoting income generating activities amongst the two million unemployed and measures to raise the incomes of close to another two million working in the informal sector. The potential of the informal sector as an engine of growth has been largely ignored by the state. Four decades of concerted effort at promoting Egypt's economic growth with equity have altogether bypassed the traditional small-scale business element of the economy because of policies and institutions which have discriminated in favour of the large, modern and unionised sectors of activity, especially in the form of tariff protection, fiscal incentives, subsidised credit and access to subsidised land. There are much larger externalities to be reaped by government intervention that targets small business and provides it with access to education and training, to serviced land and to credit. To date the government has tolerated informal activity as a means of reducing open unemployment. A more proactive approach might result in improved rates of economic growth and, possibly, greater political participation at grassroots level. The notion of private individuals willing to risk their meagre capital and to allocate their labour towards providing a decent living for themselves and their families must replace that of the rich and all-powerful provider state.

NOTE

I am deeply indebted to Sahar Tohami for providing me with much of the recent literature on the New Institutional Economics and for her many useful comments on my research outline. I am also grateful to Ismail Shoukry, Dalia Khalifa and Ahmad Ghoneim. Ismail Shoukri was responsible for collecting the necessary detailed information on a large sample of public sector enterprises and for calculating measures of allocative efficiency for the group. Dalia Khalifa prepared a short appraisal of the public sector hotel industry and Ahmad Ghoneim made a thorough search of the local press for articles on the new public sector law and collected and adjusted data on wages.

Part III

NIE: INSTITUTIONS AND ORGANISATIONS

9

COCOA PLANTATIONS IN THE THIRD WORLD, 1870s–1914

The political economy of inefficiency

W. G. Clarence-Smith

Economic rationality suggests that smallholder cultivation of cocoa should prevail over estate production. The growing and primary processing of cocoa have varied little over the centuries. Barriers to entry are low, and there are no obvious economies of scale. Even in the 1980s, there was hardly any mechanisation of cultivation on the most advanced estates. Recent improvements in yields of planting material are of questionable practical value, and can in any case be adopted by both large and small agricultural units. Fermenting beans in a heap and drying them in the sun produces cocoa of a quality often superior to that processed in expensive and complicated fermentation and drying machines (Wood and Lass 1989).

Logical economic reasoning further counsels that the key role of the state in a cocoa economy should be to strive to guarantee the existence of an open and competitive private marketing network. This was the case in South Sulawesi (Indonesia) in the 1980s, where smallholder production boomed in spite of the depressed world price of cocoa. A partly Chinese group of private traders competed fiercely for supplies from smallholders, who benefited by receiving a remarkably high share of the world price (Ruf 1993: 31–3, 35). In contrast, the intervention of marketing boards or cartelised private sector trading systems have created gross distortions in smallholder cocoa economies. State marketing boards have played the most pernicious role, for they have destabilised world prices by sending the wrong price signals to small farmers, resulting in alternating gluts and shortages (Bauer 1954; Bates 1981). Competitive private marketing, in association with an effective futures market, cannot iron out price fluctuations altogether, but experience suggests that this is the best way to stabilise a volatile market.[1]

The cocoa plantation boom of the late nineteenth century thus needs to be explained. Planters consolidated their position in established foci of cocoa cultivation in the New World, Venezuela, Trinidad, Surinam, Central America and, above all, Ecuador (Preuss 1901/1987; Guislain and Vincart 1911; Chiriboga 1980; Crawford de Roberts 1980; Deler 1981). New plantations also

157

sprang up around the world's equatorial belt (Hunger 1913: 384, map). In the Asia Pacific zone, Ceylon (Sri Lanka), Java and German (Western) Samoa stood out as centres of cocoa estates (Wright 1907; Hall 1946–50; Reinecke 1902: 193–208, map). São Tomé e Príncipe's planters dominated Equatorial Africa, briefly making the little Portuguese island colony the world's largest supplier of cocoa in 1905 (Hodges and Newitt 1988: 27–48; Mantero 1910: annexes). Plantations flourished on a more modest scale in Fernando Póo (Equatorial Guinea), Cameroun, French Equatorial Africa, the Belgian Congo and Angola (Sanz Casas 1983; Michel 1969; Claessens 1914; Chalot and Luc 1906; Lopo 1963). Even in British West Africa, where it was later claimed that a smallholder strategy had always prevailed, the authorities initially shared the general belief in the superiority of estates, and a few cocoa plantations were laid out by Europeans (Phillips 1989: 11–12, 27, 72–5, 86–9; McPhee 1926: 44, 145, 197–8).

The 'golden bean' undeniably brought great wealth to some planters around the turn of the century. A dozen or so Ecuadorean families spent a life of luxury in Paris and the French Riviera (Crawford de Roberts 1980: 65–8). Rags to riches stories abounded. José Constantino Dias came out to São Tomé in 1871 to work in a small shop, a poor boy of 16 from the interior of northern Portugal. By the end of the 1900s, he had become the Marquis of Val Flor, owned a domain of over 10,000 hectares, and produced some 3,500 tons of cocoa a year (Mantero 1910: appendices; *Grande Enciclopedia Portugesa e Brasileira* 33: 856; *Der Gordian* 1898, 3: 1170). His vast palace in Lisbon still stands as a monument to the new rich cocoa planters of his day. Max Esser represented a corporate plantocracy more common in German, Belgian and Dutch colonies. He headed the giant Westafrikanische Pflanzungsgesellschaft Victoria (WAPV), which in the late 1900s owned some 15,000 hectares of land in Cameroun, with an output of around 1,000 tons of cocoa a year. Esser was on the board of half a dozen other Camerounian companies, and was personally decorated by the Kaiser for 'fructifying Cameroun with capital' (Hausen 1970: 311–15).

PRICES AND PLANTATIONS

The most obvious explanation for the late nineteenth-century plantation boom is that estates flourished when cocoa prices were high, but could not cope when prices fell. Cocoa prices bucked the trend afflicting most tropical agricultural commodities in the late nineteenth century, rising fast in the late 1870s and staying at a fairly high level till around the First World War (see Figures 9.1 – 9.4). This reflected a steep increase in world consumption, as technology transformed the production and range of cocoa products for the newly urbanised masses (Othick 1976). Prices began to fall gently from around the mid-1890s, however, and were only artificially driven up to two new peaks by market manipulations, the first time by unnamed 'speculators' in 1896–7

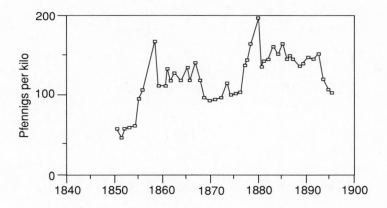

Figure 9.1 Average cocoa import prices, Hamburg 1850–96
Source: *Der Gordian*, vol. 3: 1108

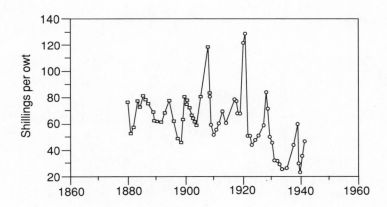

Figure 9.2 Highest price paid by Cadbury, 1880–1941 (São Tomé, 1880–1908;
British West Africa, 1907–41)
Source: Cadbury papers, file 304

(Stollwerck 1907: 49–53). The second price manipulation was carried out by a
shadowy international cartel of planters and merchants from Ecuador, Brazil,
the Dominican Republic, Trinidad and São Tomé, who temporarily withheld
cocoa from the market at various times between 1906 and 1911 (Crawford de
Roberts 1980: 98–9; *Der Gordian* 1907, 12, 283: 1010–17; *Portugal em Africa*
1909, 16,199, *Suplemento*, 110–1). This short-sighted manoeuvre merely triggered off a rush of planting by smallholders, bringing prices crashing down in
real terms after the First World War. Planters became disenchanted with cocoa,

159

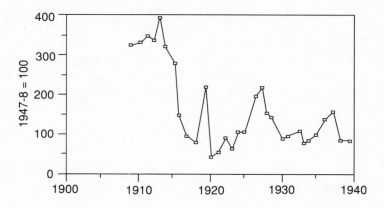

Figure 9.3 Deflated Lagos export prices for cocoa, 1909–39
Source: Berry (1975: 223–4)

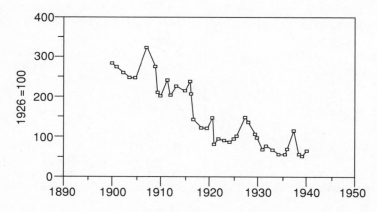

Figure 9.4 Deflated UK import prices for cocoa, 1900–40
Source: Gunnarson (1978: 177) from FAO

and often switched to more remunerative crops, while West African smallhold-ers, with lower overheads, cornered the market (Harwich 1992: pt. 2).

Official intervention to boost prices in home markets was not common prior to the First World War. Spain was something of an exception, in regard to cocoa from Fernando Póo (Clarence-Smith 1994). This factor did become important after the war, however, and probably explains why estate cultivation of cocoa persisted in São Tomé and Angola, and actually expanded in Fernando Póo until the Spanish market was saturated in the 1930s (Hodges and Newitt 1988: Chs. 2,3; Teixeira 1934: 371–2; Sanz Casas 1983: 196–9; Nosti 1948).

Similarly, the protection of the large urban market of south-central Brazil may have been a factor in the extension of plantations in the cocoa zone of Bahia in the 1930s (Caldeira 1954: 29–30).

The problem with the price argument is that it can only account for the ability of plantations to coexist with smallholdings, leaving estate dominance and its irregular geographical distribution to be explained. Estate dominance was profound in some territories, and yet was successfully challenged in others. Small farmers, often migrants, quickly took the lead in British West Africa from the 1890s (Hill 1963; Berry 1975). Even two neighbouring colonies within a single empire might evolve in a significantly different manner. Thus, cocoa smallholders developed faster in Togo than in Cameroun, though both were German possessions (Sebald 1988: Ch. 4; Clarence-Smith 1993b). In the New World, smallholders were prominent in the frontier lands of southern Bahia, and dominated production in the Dominican Republic, Haiti and Grenada (Caldeira 1954; Abel 1985: 340; Lundahl 1979: 42; Williams 1964: 189). In Asia, the original cocoa lands of Eastern Indonesia and the Philippines remained the fiefs of smallholders, producing mainly for the local market (Clarence-Smith 1993c; Blink 1905/7: vol. 1, 522; Hall 1932: 493).

THE ROLE OF THE STATE AND NEW INSTITUTIONAL ECONOMICS

As prices do not tell the whole story, it is necessary to turn to the new institutional economics. As Douglass North stresses in his chapter in this volume, institutions are not usually set up to be socially or economically efficient. They reflect the bargaining power of social and political actors, and predominant cultural forms tend to maintain 'institutional path dependence'. Plantations fit neatly into this institutional approach. Planters were socially and politically powerful individuals or firms. They justified their dominance by manipulating influential ideologies, which claimed to prove the 'scientific' superiority of plantations over smallholdings and of Europeans over non-Europeans (Beckford 1983; Graham and Floering 1984).

Official support for planters took many forms. In Java and East Sumatra, the state in the so-called 'Liberal period' from 1870 to 1900 helped to cut the production costs of estates, channelling land, labour and capital to planters on preferential terms (Booth *et al.* 1990, especially chapters by O'Malley, and Barlow and Drabble). In contrast, the British rulers of West Africa quickly became disillusioned with the much trumpeted efficiency of plantations. They were also responsive to pressures from the commercial sector and well organised African political forces, so that plantations never achieved much importance in the Gold Coast (Ghana) and Nigeria. The British West African authorities were precocious in the colonial world of their day in refusing to supply planters with land and labour on special terms, but it should be noted that their views did not extend to their colleagues in Ceylon (Phillips 1989).

The French only came to similar views at a later stage in the Ivory Coast and Madagascar (Blanc-Pamard and Ruf 1992: 11–12).

Smallholders were also actively obstructed from competing with estates. In Cameroun, Governor von Puttkamer deliberately manipulated export regulations in 1901: 'to protect the plantations from the wild and completely unsuitable expansion of cocoa cultivation by natives' (Puttkamer 1912: 233). In the Dutch East Indies smallholders were blamed for spreading the dreaded 'pod borer' pest to estates, and the Dutch authorities thus ordered the uprooting of nearly half a million diseased peasant cocoa trees in 1868 in northern Sulawesi (*Koloniaal Verslag* 1869: 154). In Ecuador, where smallholders accounted for no more than a fifth of cocoa output in 1890, the planter class set out to monopolise all suitable land, in part in order to prevent smallholder competition (Chiriboga 1980: 140, 176–7; Ayala 1982: 44). Heavy-handed attempts to encourage smallholders sometimes had the opposite effect. Thus, in the Ivory Coast, the French Congo and the Belgian Congo, peasants were put off cocoa cultivation by official attempts to force them to grow the crop for sale at fixed prices (Groff 1987; Coquery-Vidrovitch 1972: 471–2; Leplae 1917: 177–8).

This explanation for planter supremacy has almost achieved the status of an established orthodoxy, but it is argued here that it is somewhat flawed, as cocoa smallholders may have remained competitive in spite of all that the state did for planters. There are three main reasons for suggesting that this was the case. The most significant is that plantation labour, so often assumed to be cheap, was generally much more expensive than the labour employed by smallholders. Second, many planters employed a great deal of unnecessary fixed and working capital in their operations, in stark contrast to smallholders. Finally, planters tended to pay more for their land than smallholders. And yet, the generally higher quality of estate cocoa did not attract a price differential sufficient to compensate for these three sets of higher costs.

While these propositions hold good at a high level of generalisation, estates were far from uniform in their utilisation of the factors of production, and Douglass North's notion of 'mental models' discussed in his chapter in this volume is useful in explaining such differences. African and Asian plantations were particularly rigid and high cost in their organisation, whereas Latin American planters tended to approximate more to a smallholder pattern. While local conditions played a part in each case, there may have been a deeper ideological reason for the 'technological' approach of planters in the colonised world. Colonialists legitimised the conquest and subjection of Africans and Asians in large part by claiming to be bringing 'progress to benighted peoples', and Western science played a key role in this process. For European planters to 'stoop to native methods', as rational economic calculation suggested they should, thus proved extremely difficult from a psychological and social point of view (Austin 1995).

THE COST AND UTILISATION OF LABOUR

The constant complaint of cocoa planters scattered round the globe in this period was that unskilled labour was expensive and in short supply, although this was also a frequent complaint of smallholders. The crucial difference in response was that planters were able, at least in some cases, to resort to coercion on a large scale. This sometimes involved the authorities conniving at the continuation of slavery and the slave trade, most notably between the Portuguese colonies of Angola and São Tomé e Príncipe (Duffy 1967). In other cases, the state provided prisoners of war, convicts and impressed villagers to the planters as forced labour, a technique brought to a fine art by the German administration in Cameroun (Ruger 1960). In Fernando Póo, Spanish officials allowed planters to obtain labourers who had been forced into accepting contracts by the administration of the independent republic of Liberia (Sundiata 1974). On the Banda islands of the Dutch East Indies, where cocoa was a minor crop, convict labour sent from Java helped to save the planters during the difficult transition from slavery after 1860 (Republik Indonesia, Arsip Nasional 1863).

Coercion failed to reduce labour costs much, if at all, for planters. Recruitment payments were substantial and rose steadily, as international and metropolitan pressure forced the restriction of slave raiding and punitive expeditions. Initial disbursements were considerably higher for slaves than for forced labour, but slaves remained on plantations and acquired skills. The real problem was that in both cases recruitment payments had to be made before any labour could be obtained from workers. Given that mortality rates were appallingly high, reflecting poor sanitation and the movement of labourers from one disease environment to another, these initial payments were frequently lost before being amortised. The cost of a slave on Príncipe rose steadily to a maximum of £40 by the mid-1900s, but mortality rates only slowly declined from a horrendous peak of 22 per cent a year in 1902 to 7 per cent on the eve of the First World War (Clarence-Smith 1990: 155–7). Labourers ran away with monotonous regularity, typically shortly after arrival at the plantations. Humanitarian pressures forced the payment of wages, even to *de facto* slaves, as well as an improvement in the non-wage element of income, especially food, housing and clothing.

As important as the high costs of procurement and maintenance was the fact that the productivity of coerced workers was abysmally low and that supervisory costs were excessively high. Brought to the estates against their will and subjected to continual violence, labourers did as little as they could possibly get away with. They actively resisted their oppression through a wide range of day-to-day sabotage, theft, flight and occasional rebellions, further reducing productivity. This necessitated a large retinue of supervisors, many of them expatriate Europeans, who had to be hired at exorbitant rates of pay (Clarence-Smith 1993a).

Coercion played a smaller part in the recruitment of labour in Asia, reflecting higher population densities in 'labour reservoirs', and the gang labour system was more flexible than that operating in Africa. Ceylon planters employed temporary migrants from south-eastern India, who came recruited by their own headmen (Kurian 1989). The permanent work force on cocoa estates was kept to a minimum, day labour was commonplace, and tasks such as weeding were done on a piecework basis (Hall 1914: 400, 404, 469). In Java, cocoa planters relied almost entirely on local supplies of labour from surrounding villages, for land shortage was already acute by the late nineteenth century and the island was fast becoming a labour exporting area. Most workers were paid by the day, and the work force was overwhelmingly female. Piecework was common, especially for harvesting operations, with women receiving a fixed sum per tin of wet cocoa beans (Hall 1914: 406–7; 1946–50: 312, 336; Roepke 1922: 66–9, 77–8, 155 (photo)).

This said, estate labour costs in both Asia and Africa were pushed up by an over-employment of workers, in the name of agronomically defined rationality. Moreover, the tendency was for such economically dubious practices to increase over time. Just as neurotics might wash their hands even more often when less frequent washing failed to relieve anxiety, so planters intensified their cultivation methods, in a kind of collective scientific neurosis. Planters clear-felled the forest, dug large holes for the young cocoa trees, and did not interplant. West African smallholders, in contrast, thinned the forest, did not bother with plant holes, and interplanted food crops between the young cocoa trees. Modern research indicates that the latter was the better tactic. Planters usually spaced their trees far apart, potentially improving yields per tree, but yields per hectare were lower, and wide spacing greatly increased the need for weeding and pruning. Again, modern research shows that the West African smallholder practice of close planting was in many ways more sensible (Wood and Lass 1989: 145–58; Hall 1914). In Java, terracing on estates was also quite common, and planters adopted highly labour intensive ways of attempting to eliminate the pod borer pest by stripping all the pods from diseased trees (Roepke 1922: passim).

Labour on cocoa estates in the New World seems to have generally worked out cheaper than in Africa, with Asia somewhere in between. Calculations as to the relative cost of labour in different parts of the globe became common in the 1900s, as planters felt the chill wind of falling profits. For all the pitfalls involved in such calculations, they certainly seemed to favour American and Asian plantations over African ones (Sociedade de Emigração 1915: 104–5, notes 1 and 2 for a set of partial figures). The overall cost of labour in Surinam plantations, by no means the cheapest of the New World producers, was estimated at about £1.3 per month in around 1910, compared with £1.6 in the neo-slave system of São Tomé (Hall 1914: 317).

Low costs in the Americas reflected flexible forms of labour utilisation. Under the *redención* contract in Ecuador, workers received a cash advance and land, with an obligation to sow cocoa and shade trees. They planted their own food crops between the young trees, and were paid a fixed sum for each healthy cocoa tree at the end of five years, from which advances were deducted. If debts were not cleared, the workers would enter into a further five-year contract. The work of caring for mature cocoa trees was generally performed by day labourers (Chiriboga 1980: 200–3; Guislain and Vincart 1911: 66; Deler 1981: 167). A share-cropping system also operated in southern Bahia, with the added proviso that any early maturing cocoa could be sold by the worker for his own benefit. Piecework was the norm for other tasks. Planters advanced food, tools and cash, and agreed on a given price for a fixed task, leaving workers to accomplish it in their own time (Caldeira 1954: 39–40). A similar mix was found on Trinidad, with four-year written contracts to clear and plant cocoa. Piecework was almost exclusively employed to tend the mature trees (Preuss 1901/1987: 31–2).

These forms of labour contract went together with extensive methods of cultivation, which saved on labour inputs. Paul Preuss, the head of the Cameroun botanical gardens, was horrified by the 'forests, in place thickets' which constituted Ecuadorean estates at the turn of the century. All sorts of forest trees were left standing when the land was cleared, wild cocoa trees were incorporated into the groves, and seeds were put directly into the ground with no preparation of the soil. Several seeds were planted in each place and there was no thinning of seedlings, so that up to ten trees grew together. Trees were close planted and hardly pruned at all, so that they grew very high. And yet, he had to admit that Ecuador was the world's largest producer of cocoa and that its estates were profitable. In contrast, he praised 'the regular lay out and perfect maintenance' of Surinam plantations, while admitting that their output was low and falling, their costs were high, and their owners were hopelessly in debt (Preuss 1901/1987: 19–29, 78–91).

Yet it is hard to see in what ways the methods of most Latin American planters before the turn of the century were superior to those of smallholders. Ecuador's landowners constituted a parasitic superstructure, dependent for economic success on their immense political power, which was greater than that of any planter group in the colonised world. Indeed, it could be argued that cocoa planters actually were the state from 1895 to 1925 (Crawford de Roberts 1980: 117–19). The 'cocoa barons' of Guayaquil used their political power to engross so much land that potential and existing smallholders were obliged to work for them as share-croppers (Ayala 1982: 44 passim). Arguably, their 'success' in the cocoa economy amounted to no more than a kind of 'political rent'.

Moreover, sensible New World labour systems on estates came under strain from around the turn of the century. Scarce demographic resources usually proved insufficient for planters' needs as the cocoa boom took off, and migrants had to be attracted by relatively high pay. Venezuelan cocoa planters drew on ex-slaves from densely populated Caribbean islands, but then suffered severely from a ban on West Indian immigration in 1903, enacted for social and political reasons (Rangel 1974: 79; Norbury 1970: 137–8). Trinidad had access to indentured labourers from the Indian sub-continent, but these were mainly employed in the larger and better capitalised sugar estates (Williams 1964: 118). Southern Bahia probably had the best supplies of labour, freed slaves from the sugar lands and cowboys from the drought-stricken backlands of the north-east, but these immigrants were keen to set up on their own account (Caldeira 1954: 11, 37–8).

The most pernicious changes in labour organisation came in Ecuador, where planters began to turn away from the old *redención* contracts, adopting labour intensive methods with migrants from the Andean *sierra*. This may have been because migrants from the *sierra* lacked the skills of the local population in cocoa cultivation. Wages three to five times higher than in the *sierra* were a magnet for the impoverished Indians of the Ecuadorean highlands, where hereditary debt, the subdivision of land, taxation and the decline of the artisanal textile industry acted as 'push factors'. Indeed, Ecuadorean landowners, swept up in the euphoria of the cocoa boom, went beyond Asian and African models, mechanising some field operations to save on labour (Chiriboga 1980: 17, 61, 185–9, 200–3; Crawford de Roberts 1980: 77–80; Deler 1981: 167–9). The collapse of Ecuadorean plantation cocoa from the early 1910s is usually attributed to outbreaks of witches' broom disease in the cocoa groves (Chiriboga 1980: 415; Crawford de Roberts 1980: 150), but it may rather have reflected the folly of abandoning earlier practices of share-cropping and extensive cultivation.

Smallholders probably paid less for labour, due in particular to efficient and flexible forms of share-cropping, as suggested by both Robert Bates and John Toye elsewhere in this volume. In the Gold Coast, the fastest growing centre of smallholder cocoa cultivation, Hill (1963) estimated that there were 'as many farm labourers as farmers' in cocoa cultivation by 1910. Workers were mainly share-croppers, with piecework restricted to clearing, weeding and transport. Labour services were rarely remunerated prior to the harvest, in contrast to the situation on plantations. Share-cropping had the immense advantage of motivating workers, hence increasing their productivity, and keeping recruitment and supervisory costs down to an absolute minimum. Family members, for whom opportunity costs but not wages as such were incurred, made up another substantial part of the work force. Some slave, pawn and forced labour was also used, for instance by Ashanti chiefs, but not on a major scale (Hill 1963: 17, 187–90; Austin 1984: 379, 454–6, 523).

THE COST OF LAND

Planters' expenditure on land was considerably less than for labour, but it was often higher than might appear at first sight. Assoumou's contention that land was free for cocoa planters in Equatorial Africa is certainly incorrect (Assoumou 1977: 169). Even when, exceptionally, public land was ceded for nothing by the state, as was the case for a short time in Fernando Póo, planters found that they had to pay burdensome taxes and survey fees (Africa-Guinea, Alcalá de Henares, Archivo General de Aministración 1926). Plantation companies in Cameroun frequently paid for their land twice over, first buying it from African chiefs, and then paying concession fees to the state to make sure their title was recognised in law. Ignorant of local conditions, planters also bought huge areas of worthless land, while speculative intermediaries pushed up prices. After a decade in which the Germans allowed a fair amount of land alienation near the coast, checks were imposed from Berlin in the early 1900s, essentially to avoid rebellions of the kind that had rocked German East and South West Africa. The supply of fresh land was thus curbed, driving up prices for existing freehold land (Clarence-Smith 1993b: 191–2, 197–200, 207–8).

Restrictions on planters acquiring land were common in colonial situations, especially in British and Dutch possessions, because planters did not directly control the state. A major reason for the failure of plantations in British West Africa was that the authorities refused to decree the existence of crown lands which could be ceded to planters, because they feared the social and political consequences of doing so. Planters thus became bogged down in endless court battles over the legality of land purchases and leases from Africans (Phillips 1989: Ch. 4). In directly ruled parts of the East Indies, the Dutch forbade land sales by 'natives' and only granted long leases on 'waste grounds' (Booth *et al.* 1990: 198). In indirectly ruled areas, they refused to force reluctant indigenous rulers to lease land to aspiring cocoa planters (Republik Indonesia, Arsip Nasional 1873). This all tended to push land prices up.

Even in independent Latin American countries, where landowners exercised far greater power over the state, land costs were not necessarily low. In Ecuador, concessions of uncultivated land were at first free for any person prepared to clear and cultivate, but by 1911 this was no longer the case. The government sold *sitio* shares in uncultivated land, presumably driven by fiscal necessity, and these were changing hands for considerable amounts (Guislain and Vincart 1911: 66). Whereas in the early nineteenth century the great Ecuadorean planters had expanded their estates by social and political means, by the end of the century they had to buy land (Deler 1981: 167–72). Land prices rose steadly during the cocoa boom years prior to the First World War, driven up by speculation, although land prices were still considered to be low in 1900 (Chiriboga 1980: 177; Preuss 1901/1987: 91). In the chaotic frontier zone of southern Bahia, where the authority of the state was shadowy, land disputes between settlers were generally settled by violent means, so that landowners had to keep expensive bands of armed men to obtain and retain their domains (Caldeira 1954: 29; Pereira Filho 1959: 67–8).

The land costs of smallholders were not nil, as is sometimes said, but the indications are that they were lower than those of the planters. In areas characterised by high land to labour ratios, as in most of West Africa, the opportunity costs of planting communal or family land in cocoa were probably insignificant compared to those of employing labour to plant and tend the trees. Communal lands were neither taxed nor surveyed at the inhabitants' expense, owing to the administrative and political problems involved (Phillips 1989: Chs. 4, 6). Smallholders sometimes bought plots of land from planters in Ecuador, but, as often as not, they squatted on remote parts of great domains (Chiriboga 1980: 415). Even when smallholders did buy land, they may have managed to pay less than planters for it by exploiting local knowledge and personal connections. Thus the migrant 'stranger farmers' of the Gold Coast disbursed between £0.7 and £1.4 per acre in the mid-1900s, whereas the firm of Cadbury had to pay £7 to £8 per acre in 1909 for their experimental cocoa plantation (Hill 1963: 50; Southall 1975: 81).

THE COST OF CAPITAL

Capital was in notoriously short supply in the tropics and risks were high, so that borrowing tended to be very expensive. Planters required a great deal of money in advance, long before they saw any return from their slowly maturing cocoa trees. It was calculated that a planter purchasing 50 hectares of forest in Fernando Póo in 1906 would incur losses in the first four years, break even in terms of current expenditure in the sixth year, and only begin to make an overall profit in the thirteenth year (Africa-Guinea, Alcalá de Henares, Archivo General de Administración 1906). However this calculation was based on an assumed interest rate of 5 per cent a year, whereas in reality agricultural interest rates on the island tended to be between 10 per cent and 12 per cent (Liverpool Central Libraries, John Holt Papers 1910). In contrast, a smallholder plot of communal land cleared and sown with family labour only required the cost of seeds or seedlings and a few hand tools.

The capital resources of planters were further stretched by official insistence that labourers be paid monthly. This made it impossible to wait until the proceeds of the harvest were available to pay the work force. Colonial regulations stipulating regular payments were often ignored in the 1880s and 1890s, but they were increasingly enforced from the turn of the century (Clarence-Smith 1990: 158–9). The over-utilisation of labour by estates in Africa and Asia only made matters worse. From this perspective, the share-cropping arrangements of smallholders and Latin American planters made a great deal more sense.

Ill-judged investment in machines and buildings made problems of credit yet more severe for planters. The surfeit of fixed investment reflected an optimistic belief in the benefits of the application of science and technology, particularly in the colonial territories of north-western European powers (Kemner 1937: pt. 2 for one example). There was little or no mechanisation of field operations, but expensive drying machines worked badly in this period, frequently imparting a smoky flavour to the beans. The use of drying machines also reflected a poor choice of location for the growing of cocoa, in regions where it was difficult to benefit from a fine spell after the main harvest to dry the beans in the sun. Installations for fermentation at controlled temperatures were less expensive than drying machines, but it is far from clear that they resulted in better fermentation than the tried and tested method of heaping wet cocoa beans under banana leaves. Much capital was also tied up in transport, from mules to railways, in part a response to labour shortages (Preuss 1901/1987: passim). Even in Ecuador, some wealthy planters were swept up by the enthusiasm for 'progressive' methods in the mid-1900s, and introduced harrows, disc ploughs and similar equipment, which made intercropping between young cocoa trees impossible (Chiriboga 1980: 202–3).

Not only were machines and buildings expensive in their own right, but they required a small army of skilled labour to install and maintain them. These workers were partly drawn from Europe, especially in the colonial territories. They could only be tempted out to the tropics at immense expense, including putting up yet more costly buildings to meet their housing requirements. Europeans had little understanding of local conditions and they tended to succumb all too easily to tropical diseases, so that their productivity was low. They added considerably to the needs in working capital of plantation enterprises, without clearly improving profitability. Not surprisingly, German plantation companies in Cameroun were trying hard to reduce the number of their European employees before 1914 (Clarence-Smith 1993b: 202–3, 211).

This said, it is important to exercise care in comparing the investment costs of planters and smallholders, in that estates tended to 'internalise' many economic functions which intermediaries undertook, at a price, for small producers. African smallholders in Fernando Póo and Cameroun sometimes sold wet beans at a low price to the trading house of John Holt & Co. (Liverpool Central Libraries, John Holt Papers 1907, 1911). Intermediaries then dealt with fermentation, drying, sorting, packing, warehousing, insurance, transport and sale, a whole range of operations which plantation companies might perform themselves (Sociedade de Emigração 1915: 106–7 for a detailed set of calculations). Whether it was efficient for estates to perform these functions is unclear, but there was no obvious economic logic for it.

One is on firmer ground in saying that the much vaunted superior quality of plantation cocoa was rarely worth all the costs involved. The price differential between 'fine' and 'bulk' cocoas was narrowing fast before the First World War, making extra investment in improving quality steadily less rewarding (*Portugal em Africa* 16, 213, 7 Nov. 1909, *Suplemento*: 327). Best Ceylon cocoa fetched F105 per 100 kilos in Le Havre in 1913, but best Accra cocoa (Gold Coast smallholders) had actually overtaken best São Tomé, at F86 to F84. Even the worst Haitian smallholder cocoa was worth F68 (Tosta Filho 1957: 3). It is true that the highest price for Venezuelan cocoa was F200, but, as Preuss noted with some irritation, Venezuelan planters obtained such prices for their famous *criollo* cocoas in spite of their 'primitive' cultivation and processing techniques, and not because of any application of allegedly progressive and scientific methods (Preuss 1901/1987: 64–77). The survival of Central Java as the only significant Asian example of plantation cocoa after 1918 was also something of an exception, in that Dutch planters concentrated on a grade of cocoa for which world demand was low but relatively stable. They thus survived by exploiting a particular niche in the market, although production was on a very small scale in world terms (Roepke 1922: 80–1, 84).

THE TEMPORARY COMPARATIVE ADVANTAGE OF ESTATES

Cocoa planters may generally have been high-cost producers, but they had the advantage of speedy reaction to favourable market situations. This derived from the organisation of estates, and their ability to gain the backing of the state. Planters had excellent access to market information, were able to obtain planting material with great speed, and could raise capital relatively easily. They were thus well placed to react quickly to any surge in demand and prices, as long as the state facilitated their access to land and labour. In such conditions, planters could clear massive swathes of forest and plant millions of cocoa trees in a very short period, albeit at a relatively high cost (Companhia da Ilha do Príncipe 1895ff, for one notable example in the 1890s).

Smallholders are undoubtedly able to react quickly to favourable market conditions, as they have proved time and again in world history, but in the specific case of cocoa in Africa and Asia in the late nineteenth century, they appear to have hesitated to commit themselves. Cocoa was not a familiar crop in Africa, and was little diffused in Asia. It was not eaten at all by Africans, and only to a limited extent by Asians. Food crops were normally planted between cocoa trees until they came into full production, but once the canopy had formed, further inter-cropping became impossible, closing off the land to food production. Cocoa took some five years to come into full production and could continue to bear for decades, so that it represented a weightier production decision than planting annual crops, or even other perennials such as coffee. Smallholders found it hard to obtain good information and planting material, as agricultural support from governments or private bodies such as religious missions hardly existed. It is particularly important to beware of anachronism in this respect, in that the ability of smallholders in many parts of the Third World to obtain information and planting material in the 1870s and 1880s was far less than it is today (Berry 1975, for a Nigerian example).

Hesitation on the part of smallholders was short-lived, however, when cocoa offered a way out of difficulties affecting another commodity. Thus, the palm oil crisis of the mid-1890s served as a trigger for cocoa planting in the Gold Coast, and the wild rubber slump of the early 1910s set off a similar cocoa boom in south-western Nigeria (Hill 1963: 15, 164–9; Berry 1975: passim; Gunnarsson 1978). Once they had decided to commit themselves to the cocoa market and had made investments in information, trees, land and labour, smallholders were reluctant to withdraw again. They thus persisted long after their efficiency had caused prices to come tumbling down in the inter-war years (Ruf 1991). This explanation may also account for the puzzling lack of a smallholder cocoa boom in Asia comparable to that in West Africa before the 1970s, in that coconuts, rubber and other smallholder crops provided viable alternatives in maritime South East Asia.

CONCLUSION

The abnormal salience of cocoa plantations in the period from the 1870s to the First World War would not have been possible without high cocoa prices on the world market, but the New Institutional Economics helps us to understand both the intensity and the uneven geographical incidence of planter dominance. Planters were generally politically powerful men, but their relative bargaining power varied from territory to territory. The ideology of science and 'progress', at times degenerating into Social Darwinist racism, underpinned the support given to plantations by the state, but such ideas were prone to considerable local variation. Estates as organisations enjoyed certain advantages over smallholders, especially in terms of access to information. However market factors generally overcame institutions and organisations over a period of a few decades, and the demise of the cocoa estate over much of the world after 1918 stands as a reminder that markets can effectively erode the obstacles created by institutions and organisations. This said, the rebirth of the cocoa estate in the 1970s in South East Asia also shows how quickly historical lessons can be forgotten (Ruf 1993).

NOTES

I would like to thank Robert Bates and François Ruf for their useful comments on the first version of this paper.

1   See Hanisch (1991) for a discussion of these issues. The opinion is my own.

10

PRODUCTIVITY AND POWER

Institutional structures and agricultural performance in India and China, 1900–50

B. R. Tomlinson

It is easy to press history into the service of the new institutional economics. Historians have long studied the development of economic institutions, and the social and political contexts in which public choices are made by markets, states and other agencies. But the results of this work are complex and contradictory. History is about change – it is about discontinuities and disjunctions; its purpose is to show that the past can be different from the present and the present different from the future, and that the processes that link them are not necessarily coherent. In the Third World, in particular, public economic choices have often been determined by social and political constraints, while pervasive risks, incomplete markets, information asymmetry and moral hazard have shaped economic behaviour in complex ways, and helped to create and sustain market-interlinking (interlinked transactions between economic agents) especially in rural areas (Bardhan 1989: especially Chs 1, 12).

In the mid-twentieth century India and China were both poor countries, heavily dependent on rural economies with low levels of output and unequal distribution of resources. Access to food and other basic goods, secured through landownership, tenancy, share-cropping or wage labour, was distorted by a number of economic and socio-political institutional barriers. The majority of cultivating families did not command enough resources of their own to ensure social reproduction, and had little control over the marketing and supply of the inputs and outputs needed to ensure adequate returns from their farming activities. The fundamental problems of agricultural development in both countries were the same – capital investment and infrastructure were extremely poor, and labour productivity was distressingly low. Since there were few alternative employment prospects outside agriculture, most labour was confined to the land, but without the capital inputs needed to raise output and efficiency.

In such circumstances, agrarian institutions, notably systems of land and labour control and exploitation, operated in conditions of economic subsistence, market imperfection, political uncertainty and ecological fragility. Markets for capital, commodities and labour were heavily interlinked, and skewed against the vast majority of peasants who did not have unencumbered access to the minimum land-holding needed for subsistence. Yet, while the agrarian systems of India and China suffered from constricting institutional rigidity, they were not static, timeless or 'traditional'. Indian agriculture expanded considerably in some areas in the late nineteenth and early twentieth centuries, while the Chinese rural economy (in politically stable areas) probably grew faster between 1920 and 1935 than in previous or subsequent decades. Peasants and agricultural decision-makers seem to have been 'rational' – optimising output where possible in conditions of economic uncertainty, market imperfection and political instability (Keyes *et al.* 1981: 753–878). Where productive investment and sustained demand for staple crops was well established, market networks could emerge that offered economic opportunities to a wide range of participants, although with structural biases that usually favoured the holders of political influence and social power. However, problems of national political control and of international economic instability, as well as the constraints of local political, economic and social institutions, meant that change was often more circular than linear, and that alternatives to subsistence crop production could never provide sustained improvement in the prevailing low levels of labour productivity, income and welfare.

INDIA: RURAL PRODUCTIVITY AND DEVELOPMENT

Inadequate agricultural production lay at the heart of India's development problems in the late nineteenth and early twentieth centuries (Tomlinson 1988, 1993). Athough several regions experienced some growth in per capita output and expansion in cropped area before 1913, a steady rate of population increase from the 1920s onwards resulted in an emerging subsistence crisis by the middle of the twentieth century, caused by both poor availability of food and skewed entitlements. Market demand did stimulate some increases in crop production and productivity, and commercial crops with favourable market opportunities, such as cotton and sugar, achieved considerable yield increases, and had consistently higher average productivity per acre than did food-grains. However, yields of the subsistence crops that provided the basic needs of the rural population were much less responsive to new stimuli. Food-grain and non-food-grain output may both have risen faster than population from 1860 to 1920, but even optimists accept that food-grain output lagged behind population growth after that (Heston 1984: 387; McAlpin 1983: 360 ff). Static overall yield figures do not mean that productivity everywhere was stagnant, but rather that progressive forces were always cancelled out by regressive ones, and that periods of dynamism were interspersed with periods of enervation. Considerable agricultural growth, underpinned by technological change and capital investment, occurred in some parts of the sub-continent, but such growth was rarely sustained and it failed to transform the locality through a process of long-term social or economic change. The crucial issue for historians of Indian agricultural performance is not to explain the absence of growth, but to discover why such growth as did take place remained isolated, spasmodic and short-lived. To answer this it is necessary to investigate the institutional structures of colonial agriculture, and the interaction of social control and economic power that shaped rural productive systems for most of the nineteenth and twentieth centuries.

The question of how profits were made in the rural economy, and what use they were put to, is perhaps the most crucial issue in the history of Indian agricultural development, defined in terms of increases in labour productivity and a rise in labour's share of the product. Those who see in Indian rural economic history the victory of capital over labour seek to explain why increased profitability, and the structural benefits that capital derived from colonial rule, did not lead to increased investment and the modernisation of production processes, but instead created a form of non-dynamic capitalism in which profit was realised and sustained by the exploitation of ever-larger amounts of labour employed at very low rates of productivity. Their conclusion is that the dominance over the rural economy exercised by local elites with access to social control was in itself anti-developmental, since it discouraged any investment that might improve labour productivity and hence increase labour's power to bargain for the rewards of production (Washbrook 1988: 89–91). These issues have been approached in a very different way by those historians who doubt the existence of a large enough surplus, or a sufficiently vigorous market stimulus, to encourage or maintain productive rural investment. They suggest that sustained agricultural development required investment in production, and such investment had to be fuelled by profits; although growth from below in the rural economy may have been possible in the nineteenth century at times of maximum market growth, this form of development was overwhelmed after 1900 by adverse circumstances and Malthusian traps (Stokes 1978: 13–14).

These rival interpretations of peasant society cannot be tested easily or reconciled fully. Few historians of rural India would accept that there was never a surplus over subsistence anywhere that could have been used for productive investment, while it is clear that agricultural growth was constrained by the weaknesses of the market economy as well as the social relations of production. 'Stratifiers' (following Lenin) conclude that the role of social stratification in determining access to resources such as land, water, carts, and credit, and in allocating rewards for their use, was intensified in areas where such resources were scarce. 'Populists' (after Chayanov), on the other hand, argue that not all changes in the supply of such resources necessarily led to an unequal distribution of rewards and punishments. Both schools agree, however, that the interaction between political systems, social structure and economic opportunity in creating the interconnected markets that determined access to those resources, were a key set of variables that underpinned the process of agricultural change under colonial rule. It is this institutional context that must now be considered.

By the second half of the nineteenth century British administrators in the Indian countryside had helped to create and sustain a wide band of privileged groups who benefited from state action over land revenue, tenancy and agricultural investment. Favouritism by the state brought some direct economic advantages, such as the privileged land tenures that gave tax-free or tax-favoured status and formed the personal holdings of village officials, local landlords and peasant farmers with occupancy rights. More important, however, was the role of social power, reinforced by the privileges of a position in local organs of the state such as the land revenue hierarchy and village administration, in giving control of production by manipulating the scarce resource of land, and the local markets for employment, rural capital and sales of output. Returns from agricultural production and trade provided by far the largest share of rural income, but farm profits were often used to spread the risks that resulted from practising under-capitalised agriculture at times of ecological adversity and unstable market conditions. Given the limited and unstable nature of the market opportunities that faced the agricultural sector, maximising security was often more important than maximising output. Consequently, some dominant groups invested the surplus derived from their economic strength in reinforcing their social power, and the dominance of local state agencies, on which their command of scarce resources ultimately depended.

During the late nineteenth and early twentieth centuries, new crops, markets and institutions gave some agricultural operators the opportunity to challenge and overcome the control networks of established elites. Although the colonial state clearly favoured certain groups in the revenue settlements of the nineteenth century, it did not consistently reinforce them thereafter, and those who found their position usurped had little redress. Between 1860 and 1930 dependent cultivators had a number of opportunities to produce commercial crops directly on their own account, and thus move partially out of the subsistence and into the cash economy. The peasants of the cotton-growing areas of the Khandesh in western India, for example, were able to control production and marketing of their crop from the 1870s onwards, and got good terms for output and credit from a competitive service economy. In Bengal the jute boom of the 1900s temporarily freed peasants in districts such as Faridpur and Dacca from debt, and enabled them for a time to market their crop independently, without resort to *dadan* (the taking of loans against a standing crop hypothecated at half the market price of the previous season). The opening-up of groundnut cultivation on the plains of Tamilnad offered a similar opportunity (Guha 1985: 216–17; Goswami 1984: 337–8; Baker 1984: 151). The benefits of rising demand could help weaken the ties of the social hierarchy in other ways. In boom times the price of land rose faster than interest rates, so that peasants could hope to recover some of their land-holding by selling or mortgaging another part at a higher value. Where agricultural profitability increased, demand for labour also rose, returns to labour increased accordingly and freer wage-labour markets grew up to replace older custom-based systems.

The market networks of rural India operated as part of a complex mix of particular local economic, social, political and ecological circumstances. Economic growth from below was possible in some circumstances, and such growth was able to trickle down, or by-pass, the social hierarchy to a significant extent. The history of wheat in the Punjab, of cotton and tobacco in Gujerat, of jute in Bengal, and of garden crops everywhere, suggests that where market mechanisms and demand stimuli were the strongest, the influence of social networks on the allocation of factors of production and economic choices was weakest. Overall, however, there was often no clear link between investment and profitability, nor were there universal returns to scale or to scope waiting to be captured. Equally, commercialisation did not lead to any major changes in the distribution of owned land-holdings by size. Large farms secured no significant advantages over small ones, provided that smallholders could super-exploit their own labour and obtain off-farm employment. Absentee landlords faced severe difficulties in controlling production; rich peasants rarely became rentiers; poor peasants did not often lose access to land entirely. Possession of even a tiny holding of land retained considerable psychic and cultural advantages for Indian villagers, as well as assuring them of a more favourable relationship with the local labour market.

For these reasons, economic growth in the Indian countryside did not necessarily lead to changes in social structure or in the factor-mix used to produce staple crops. Opportunities for market-based expansion were always limited, and probably only existed in ecologically balanced areas growing crops for which there was a substantial export demand. This stimulus virtually came to an end with the onset of the prolonged depression that hit the Indian rural economy in the late 1920s. The collapse of international demand for primary products after 1929 weakened the Indian rural economy considerably and disrupted the capital and labour markets based around export-led production that had grown up since 1900. The most corrosive and lasting effects came from the liquidity crisis that undermined the market for rural labour both in cash and in kind. Dominant cultivators did not retreat from cash-crop production, but they looked for ways of minimising costs – especially those of labour. This was done by switching to less labour-intensive crops, or to less labour-intensive methods of cultivation, and by employing family rather than hired labour on the farm. Erstwhile labourers were, in turn, thrown back onto their own, inadequate, family plots, or had to migrate to the cities in search of work (Charlesworth 1985: 230; Guha 1985: 220; Bhattacharya 1985: 120–2).

As a result of all these changes deficit food producers could no longer earn enough to meet their subsistence, rent, revenue and capital costs by growing commercial crops for market on their own account. During the 1940s urban demand for consumption goods rose sharply, fuelled by the wartime inflation, and the real cost of rent and capital probably fell. These changes pushed up the price of food still further, and meant that entry into various forms of tied labour became a crucial mechanism for securing subsistence goods. The vicious circle of under-consumption of basic wage goods tightened still further once the rural poor had to compete directly with urban demand in the domestic food-grain market (a food-market severely distorted by procurement, transportation and allocation difficulties throughout the 1940s), and could no longer benefit from windfall gains in international prices for exportable crops. In these two decades it became significantly more difficult for those with inadequate unencumbered holdings of land, or with insufficient access to credit and employment, to obtain surplus produce. Thus the market failures of the 1930s and 1940s, coming on top of the inadequate institutional development of colonial India before that, helped to establish the particular problems of poverty, poor infrastructure, absence of public investment and low labour productivity in Indian agriculture that have constrained rural development ever since.

CHINA: AGRARIAN SURPLUS AND RESOURCE ALLOCATION

Market structures, social organisation, state action and ecological circumstance were all also important in determining the response of Chinese agriculture to economic opportunity, although the way in which these factors are weighted and mixed often differs from the Indian case.[1] The agrarian history of modern China is dominated by a long-running controversy about the existence of an agrarian surplus and its distribution. As in the case of India in the first half of the twentieth century, the classic contemporary account of Chinese agricultural backwardness (with obvious political overtones) stressed distributional problems as the source of stagnation and growing poverty. This interpretation asserted that a large percentage of agricultural income was taken from the peasants in the form of rents, interest charges, taxes, and unfair terms of exchange by a broad class of exploiters comprising landlords, industrialists, merchants, usurers and officials. This process left the peasants with little surplus for investment or consumption, while those who acquired the surplus used it for conspicuous consumption, or in buying up more land to rent out at a profit. The result was an increasingly unequal pattern of land distribution over time, and a land-hunger fuelled by rising population and inflated prices. In consequence, the capital costs of expanding agricultural production increased, pushing up rents and further deepening debt bondage. With a larger and larger share of the surplus going to reward those who controlled the scarce resources of land, capital, power and employment, incentives for cultivators to increase productivity were weak. This led to the stagnation of agricultural technology, resulting in a decline of output to below the rate of population increase.

The alternative to this 'distributionist' interpretation of agricultural backwardness has been termed the 'eclectic' or 'technological' approach. It also derives from data collected in the 1920s and 1930s, especially that provided by the work of John Lossing Buck and the Department of Agricultural Economics at the University of Nanjing. Buck's (1937/1982) data on the rural economy suggested that peasant agriculture was backward because of inefficient allocation of factors of production. In particular, farms were too small, land was used uneconomically, peasants had too little capital and access to new technology, little control over natural forces, poor transport, high marketing costs and so on. His conclusions suggested that land reform on its own would have had little effect, since the main problem was the low productivity of existing peasant-owned plots. What was needed instead were measures to improve efficiency through extra investment and the diffusion of new techniques. Others, notably Ramon Myers (1980, 1991), have gone on to suggest that this would have been done best by the development of produce and factor markets. Thus the commercialisation of agriculture was associated with increasing productivity and returns, rather than with increasing exploitation and pauperisation.

Some of Buck's arguments were later expanded, and given a specifically technological twist, by the work of Mark Elvin (1970b), Dwight Perkins (1975) and others which argued that pre-industrial technology had already raised yields in Chinese agriculture as far as was feasible by the mid-eighteenth century. After that, only access to virgin land, new crops and the enjoyment of comparative advantage as a result of commercialisation could help output keep pace with population growth. By the early twentieth century all these expedients were failing, and agricultural development was now dependent on inputs that could only be supplied by a domestic industrial sector. Since the emergence of such a sector was constrained by the weak supply and demand stimuli associated with a stagnant agricultural sector, this amounted to a 'high-level equilibrium trap' that could not easily be escaped. Without new arrangements for organising large-scale investment in infrastructure and agricultural technology, the level of rural surplus would remain too low to resolve the problem of low productivity.

The case for the 'high-level equilibrium trap' in twentieth-century China has been weakened by direct calculations which purport to show that in 1933 the economy produced a substantial surplus, as indicated by the use of available resources for non-essential purposes (including the undesired idleness of agricultural labour) (Riskin 1975: 74, 1978; Lippitt 1978). If there was a large potential surplus in the Republican economy, then rural poverty cannot be attributed simply to the exhaustion of natural resources, and hence the lack of technical change in agriculture and industry was not an inevitable result of a shortage of investible funds. Further, in this account, the chief consumers of the surplus, and hence the main impediments to productive investment, were Chinese rather than foreign. Thus the domestic socio-economic structure and its institutions were more important than the incursions of foreigners alone (even of the Japanese) in explaining China's economic backwardness before 1949.

In China, as in India, the crucial question to face in analysing the rural economy is this: if there was a substantial rural surplus over consumption needs in the first half of the twentieth century, then how was it utilised, and how far did it lead to substantial investments in productivity-enhancing agricultural development that could raise the output and consumption of the large numbers of cultivating families who had to exchange their labour for food, since they did not have enough unencumbered land to meet their subsistence needs? The classic debate over the problems of Chinese rural development focuses on two main issues. First 'distributionists' and 'technologists' divide critically over whether agricultural production was higher than that needed for consumption. 'Distributionists' argue, as already indicated, that there was a significant rural surplus in the first half of the twentieth century. The agrarian problem was therefore that of control over the surplus, and of the growing divide between rich and poor that led to low investment in agricultural improvement and little productivity increase. 'Technologists', on the other hand, argue that there was little surplus in the first place – rural poverty represented a productivity failure brought about partly by technological constraints, and partly by social choice in perpetuating inefficient systems of agricultural production and organisation. Second, the two schools differ over the extent of centralisation and decentralisation of economic institutions and market networks in the rural sector. Here the 'distributionists' argue that the problem is the result of the hegemonic control over the economy by one small sector, with a coherent group of landlords, officials and merchants dominating the rest, especially when using alliances with foreign firms and governments to cement their local and regional power. By contrast the 'technologists' tend to stress the pettiness of economic organisation, and the absence of forward or backward linkages within agriculture, or between agriculture and the rest of the economy.

Recent literature on the Chinese rural economy has explored some of the same themes in a new way, using a different perspective based around the effects of commercialisation on rural income and labour productivity.[2] Optimistic re-assessments of the economy of Republican China have suggested that agriculture enjoyed an annual growth rate of between 1 and 2 per cent from 1918 to 1937, leading to an annual increase in peasant incomes of 0.5–0.8 per cent, and a per capita GDP growth rate of 1.2 per cent. This growth is thought to have been caused by a process of increased commercialisation that made the economy of mainland China more 'modern', bringing more employment for labour and better returns for capital used in cash-crop production, and leading to rational utilisation of family labour in peasant households and competitive markets which bred efficiency and welfare benefits for ordinary farmers. All of this has been contested, in turn, by those who doubt the validity of any income figures gathered before the 1930s, who find few indicators of increased labour productivity in agriculture, and who interpret the agricultural production data to show that output growth barely kept up with population increase in the first half of the twentieth century. These pessimistic conclusions have been encapsulated in Philip Huang's Chayanovian concepts of 'involuntary commercialisation', the 'familisation of rural production' and 'rural involution', in which labour productivity in food-grain, cash-crop and handicraft production were so low that wages and living standards remained depressed. Thus increases in output were secured only by increased inputs of labour, with declining returns per work-day, while 'peasant marketing consisted chiefly of the exchange of subsistence necessities' without any effective supra-local product, factor or labour markets (Huang 1990: 112).

The nature and extent of land control was crucially important in shaping the institutional framework of the Chinese rural economy. Landowners played a major role in the management of cultivation – recent reworking of the land-ownership statistics shows that 42 per cent of the land farmed in the 1930s was rented-in by tenants, and 4 per cent of all rural households owned 39 per cent of the land.[3] What is still unclear, however, is how the Chinese squirearchy secured the economic surplus of the countryside, and to what extent they invested significant sums in managerial farming and improvements in agricultural infrastructure, or lived simply on rentier profits, usury and the proceeds of government office. The rural elite of the late imperial and early Republican period combined landed power with gentry status and government office, but there were considerable regional variations. In landlord-dominated counties of Anhui, for example, land-ownership by itself gave the key to rural power throughout the nineteenth century, with the local gentry forming a broad social class comprising about 20 per cent of the population, based around a system of lineages whose wealth and status were derived mainly from the ownership of land. In Hebei, on the other hand, land control in the nineteenth century was determined by access to government office, and income from land was seen as merely one way of buying into the top echelons of wealth and power enjoyed by successful merchants, degree-holders and office-holding bureaucrats. These routes to advancement were supplemented by a wider range of commercial opportunities and by careers in the military in the Republican period (Chang 1955; Ho 1962; Huang 1985: 178–9; Beattie 1979: 131).

The most powerful local groups of late imperial China were those that combined access to government with participation in the rural economy. Gentry status gave landowners crucial advantages in the nineteenth century – according to Chung–li Chang, 'a gentry landowner enjoyed a better income per *mou* than did a commoner landowner because he was in a position to receive more in rent and pay less in taxes'(Chang 1955: 147). The operation of the 'landlord bursary' system identified by Yuji Muramatsu in one district of Jiangsu province represents another way in which access to state power was important in the organisation of the rural economy. Here, absentee landlords in the 1910s and 1920s hired the services of gentry-landlords who established landlord bursaries to extract rent from the scattered parcels of land that made up their estates. These bursaries used the official authority of gentry families and the local law enforcement system to discipline defaulting tenants. It was the gentry-official status of the owner of the bursary that gave such institutions their advantage in farm management – landlords could only exercise effective social control over their tenants if they were able to secure official backing (Muramatsu 1966: 571–2, 584–5). At the village level, power and wealth differentials between families in Guangxi depended more on institutional position and socio-political status, especially in the management of collective bodies for water control and the corporate land that belonged to clans and temples, than on private ownership of land (Elvin 1970a: 108–9; 1970b: 166–7).

Direct access to state power was closely associated with social aggrandisement and wealth accumulation throughout the Republican period and the GMD political system itself became an important agency for rural success. On the North China plain, where local notables sought to insert a buffer between themselves and state authority so that they did not have to answer directly for tax arrears, the New Policy reforms of the early twentieth century strengthened of the position of village headmen thanks to their state powers. The possible exception was the Yangzi delta where the state continued to deal with villages through their urban landlords (Huang 1990: 153–4). In frontier regions of north China in the 1930s, military officers and government institutions built up large estates out of new land brought under cultivation as a result of public irrigation schemes. After the severe famine in Shaanxi in 1928–31, landlords in the Guanzhong area were only able to secure their land with government support – which meant donating a piece of it to the military or the state (Vermeer 1988: 43–5). Fei Chung-sen, one of the prominant gentry bursary owners of Jiangsu, was forced out of business by low profits and a rapid increase in official exactions through taxation after 1927 (Muramatsu 1966: 573–5, 596). The history of the rural economy under the Republic was the history of state power, its agents and usurpers, but those who controlled the scarce factors of production did so in conditions of high levels of risk and uncertainty. As access to the state power on which their economic position depended became more difficult for many established landlord families in the 1930s, so the incentive to maximise productivity weakened still further.

Chinese estimates of the extent of managerial farming in the 1920s and 1930s suggest that less than 10 per cent of landlord holdings were farmed on capitalist principles, using profits to invest in agricultural improvements and cultivating with significant amounts of hired labour (Ding 1992: 135–7). Commodity market institutions alone were not strong enough to support commercialised agriculture by landlords and market-oriented peasants, so that markets in power and social status dominated agricultural production, especially at times of uncertainty. Local studies point to local circumstances as all-important in determining whether increased market opportunities and commercialisation would lead to managerial agriculture or a rentier system. As Huang has pointed out, paradoxes abounded and simple causal relationships cannot be assumed:

> In Michang, the higher returns of cotton farming powered the rise of successful managerial farms; in Sibeichai, that same commercialisation drew merchant capital to the land and tipped the local scales of power in favour of landlordism, which was then able to set rent rates high enough to block the development of managerial agriculture.
>
> (Huang 1990: 72–3)

In Jiangsu, rentier profits increased sharply between 1905 and 1917, but flattened out and declined in the 1920s as taxes and other expenditure rose (Muramatsu 1966: 598–9). In the 1930s, rising real costs of labour, fertiliser and other inputs everywhere led to less intensive cultivation and a reversal of previous productivity gains. This, and the political difficulties caused by the Japanese invasion after 1937, probably caused a sharp decline in the number of commercially oriented 'rich peasants' and landlord entrepreneurs between 1929 and 1949 (Buck 1937/1982: 14; Ding 1992: 141–2; Muramatsu 1966: 598–9).

INSTITUTIONS AND ECONOMIC CHANGE

Studying the comparative history of agricultural performance in India and China identifies a common pattern in the interaction of institutional structures and economic change. In both economies there was some surplus over subsistence, but this was not used to improve agricultural productivity enough to cope with population increases. Recent estimates suggest that per capita food-grain availability in the 1930s was between 417 and 446 grams for India (falling to 395 grams in the early 1950s), and between 281 and 307 grams in China, with grain productivity levels in both countries static over the first half of the twentieth century as a whole (Heston 1984: Table 4.6; Chaudhuri 1978: Table 38; Xu 1992: 129).[4] Capital was often invested to ensure social status and political power, rather than directly in raising labour productivity. This was done to overcome uncertainty, rather than as part of an inherently exploitative feudal social structure, or an inappropriate 'traditional' culture. Alternative allocative systems, provided by the operation of commodity markets for agricultural products, and state initiatives to improve agricultural practice and infrastructure, did give incentives for productivity increases in some areas and at some points in time – but these forces never created a developmental push strong enough to overcome the problems of backwardness. Furthermore, the processes of historical change did not go in straight lines, and opportunities for agricultural development became much more limited after 1930. Market failures in the 1930s, associated with the fall of export demand, led to a crisis of employment for those without enough land to feed themselves directly, while the institutional collapse and political uncertainty caused by war and insurrection disrupted the power relations around which many local production and distribution systems were organised.

By the 1940s the failings of the rural economies of both India and China were obvious, but their causes were complex and remain somewhat obscure. The institutional networks of the rural economy were an important variable determining performance, since the social mechanisms for allocating capital and credit, and for providing access to land and employment, distorted other market relationships. Rural power relationships helped to set boundaries to productivity increases, because those who controlled land and capital often used their surplus to secure political and social stability, rather than economic maximisation. However, there was nothing inevitable about the dominance of social structure over economic opportunity in Indian agriculture, nor about the control of political elites over market institutions in China; the apparent shortage of productive resources and increase in man:land ratios in both countries were not insurmountable barriers to sustained development. Social and political mechanisms for controlling the land and its surplus were strong because market stimuli were so often weak and corrupted, and because of the vacuum caused by the virtual abdication of formal public institutions. With more favourable and stable market networks, and more coherent state policies to extend and supplement these, agricultural growth in colonial India and mainland China in the first half of the twentieth century could have been stronger, more universal and more consistent. In the event, market failure and institutional collapse exacerbated the problems of agricultural production, preparing the way for policies in the 1950s that limited productivity still further.

NOTES

1 This account is largely based on survey material, notably Riskin (1975), Myers (1980), Ho (1959: Chs 8, 9) and Feuerwerker (1980, 1983). For more recent literature see Chao (1986); Brandt (1989), Eastman (1988), Faure (1989), Rawski (1989) and Huang (1985).

2 For a convenient introduction, see Myers (1991: 604–28), Huang (1991: 629–33) and Little (1989: Ch. 4). The conventional Chinese view remains that traditional feudalism and a natural economy dominated agricultural organisation right down to 1949 (see Wright 1992: 16–18, 113–51).

3 This alters the perception, gained from Buck's surveys of the 1930s, that owner-occupancy was relatively well-established, with less than 30 per cent of land rented-in. See Esherick (1981: 396–400) and Buck (1937: Table 22, pp. 57–9).

4 The Indian estimates are for 1941 and 1951; the Chinese estimate is for grain production only.

11

STATE INTERVENTION IN THE BRAZILIAN COFFEE TRADE DURING THE 1920s

A case study for New Institutional Economics?

Robert G. Greenhill

Ideas about international growth and development have been strongly influenced by Western European and North American economic ideas as well as by their actual experience. In the nineteenth century the prevailing body of economic knowledge, although not static, was broadly the classical philosophy of *laissez-faire* and Free Trade (see, for example, Taylor 1972). It emphasised the importance of markets to formulate prices and minimised the ability of organisations to influence resource allocation and income distribution. The essence of classical economics is that the small size of individual firms ensured that markets were not dominated by any single organisation. The philosophy emphasised the mobility of resources via markets where individuals have free rein. In short, individual pursuit of self-interest would lead to the highest common good, and so unfettered capitalism would promote economic growth. In a world of economic rationality institutions hardly mattered; efficient markets, which were costless in their transactions, characterised economies (North, Ch. 2 this volume).

Criticisms of this economic orthodoxy, in theory and in practice, are not hard to find. There are already reservations about the efficacy of the market solutions imposed by the International Monetary Fund on the republics of the former Soviet Union or in Brazil. Indeed, at the start of the twentieth century the ideas of classical economics were in the real world already becoming outmoded. In the United States, if not in the United Kingdom, the primacy of individual responses and the philosophy of market coordination has for some time been shown to be flawed through Alfred Chandler's work (see, for example, Chandler 1990) on the role of the 'visible hand' of corporate decision-making. The atomistic and individual approach of small-scale British firms was no match, argues Lazonick (1991b), for the organisational coordination which American companies achieved through their vertical integration and greater capital intensity. As Britain continued to rely on market coordination so economic leadership passed to the United States.

Of course, the attribution of economic success to a particular form of business organisation may overlook other factors which explain the relative success of the United States against Britain (see Church 1993). Indeed, the organisational and competitive difficulties facing very large firms today and the preference for de-merger and buy-outs may have taken some of the gloss from the Chandlerian sheen. But, what both the United States as well as the British approaches to capitalist development have ignored, however, may be the importance of collective institutions in achieving prosperity. The late twentieth-century experience of Japan, it has been argued, suggests that a constructive capitalism provided by a developmental government may be a better route to economic growth and development (Lazonick 1991b). The unevenness of development between advanced countries may be explained in terms of institutions and organisations. Although critics have suggested that Japan might have performed even better without MITI's intervention, conventional wisdom continues to assert its key role. If so, the lesson for Western growth could be that concerted collective action by means of economic institutions capable of coordinating organisations may offer a better way forward than the return to individualism and deregulation presently urged on both sides of the Atlantic.

The possibility that a developmental government may organise institutions to promote economic well-being, defined as both growth and a fairer distribution of income, and achieve an outcome superior to that of leaving matters to market forces is not new. There are nineteenth-century instances of this process in Latin America's commodity trades. The Peruvian government, for example, took control of the guano deposits from the 1840s (Mathew 1981) and in the 1870s developed a monopoly over the nitrate industry (Greenhill and Miller 1973). The benefits of such state intervention did not necessarily match the expectations of those who formulated policy. What the initiatives did indicate, however, is that no understanding of the two trades or of Peru's development path is possible without taking account of the role of the Republic's organisations and institutions. In both cases the state was not exogenous to developmental policy and practice.

This emphasis upon the role of institutions lies at the heart of the new institutional economics which have arisen in dissatisfaction at the explanations for growth and development supplied by neo-classical theory. The new institutional economics 'extends economic theory', writes Douglass North (Ch. 2, this volume), 'by incorporating ideas and ideologies into the analysis, modelling the political process as a critical factor in the performance of economies'. Institutions are not merely bodies or organisations designed to achieve certain outcomes but may include formal conduct ('the rules of the game'), legal property rights and informal norms of behaviour, and are established to reduce economic uncertainty. Economic performance, continues North, 'depends crucially on the setting in which market exchange occurs – on complex institutional arrangements which neo-classical theory takes for granted'.

In particular, new institutional economics stresses the importance of transaction costs which, typically, may be regarded as the costs of specifying what is being exchanged and of enforcing agreements, such as property rights, over time and space. At the heart of neo-classical analysis lies a frictionless static world of zero transaction costs. Such a world does not, of course, exist. 'In reality', wrote Michael Prowse (1993: 12), 'the impersonal exchange between millions of participants ... in a dynamic market economy imposes formidable transaction costs'. Their existence is, in fact, well-known. Ronald Coase's (1937) work on the origin and development of firms in modern market economies long ago pioneered the use of transaction costs which, more recently, business historians have exploited, to explain, for example, the development of multinational companies in preference to using agents abroad (see, for example, Nicholas 1983). Incomplete information represents a form of transaction cost which institutions may be developed to make up for. Transaction costs, a form of market failure, emerge because information is costly and is asymmetrically held by parties in any exchange.

Deeper examination of institutional and organisational change is, of course, crucial for economic historians in their search to understand past economic performance and earlier growth strategies, and the development of new institutional economics sheds fresh light on issues of interest to economic historians. This chapter uses the new body of economic ideas to explore a case study of state intervention in the Brazilian coffee trade before 1929, a policy intended to improve the coffee planter's market conditions. The essay raises a number of issues. How efficient was the market for coffee? In what ways did market conditions disadvantage Brazilian growers? What interventionist programme was pursued by officials? How did foreign capitalists react to policy formulated in Brazil? The chapter is in four parts. The first describes coffee's market structure in Brazil up to the turn of the century and the problems it posed native planters. The second describes the policy responses of the state and national governments to these problems. The third part analyses the reaction of foreign businessmen to the institutional changes established in Brazil and the fourth draws some of the threads together into a tentative conclusion.

COFFEE MARKETING

What were the market conditions for Brazilian coffee in the late nineteenth and early twentieth centuries? The first point to make is that there was no single market to transfer goods but a series of linked markets, between planter and local intermediary, between local intermediaries, between local intermediary and exporter and, of course, between exporter and buyer in the consuming countries. The classical analysis of nineteenth-century commodity markets is that they are characterised by conditions of perfect competition. There are, it might be posited, large numbers of profit-maximising buyers (merchants) and sellers (producers) transferring an homogeneous product, who possess perfect knowledge and experience low barriers to entry and to exit. They are price-takers in a market where the decisions to buy and sell are coordinated by the 'invisible hand' which determines prices.

In fact, the real world of buying and selling coffee in Brazil at the turn of the century was nothing of the sort. First, coffee planters were not an homogeneous group. They comprised, of course, large landowners (*fazendeiros*) who at first dominated marketed supplies but increasingly in the twentieth century included smaller immigrant farmers who settled in the State of São Paulo. The differences in landholding also exhibited a variety of cultivation systems (Aranha Correa do Lago 1978). The bigger estates used slaves until the 1880s and thereafter hired labour and various forms of share-cropping were to be found. The smaller farms had generally to make do with family labour supplemented at peak times by paid workers. There were also a small number of so-called model farms, sometimes owned by merchant houses or foreign estate companies like the Fazenda Dumont,[1] but these were very much the exception before 1914. The result was that large producers may well have had more influence in forming contracts with buyers than smaller farmers who simply depended on market forces. On the other hand, the overheads and fixed costs on the smaller farms were almost certainly much lower than those on the large estates. By the 1920s, the differences in perceptions and priorities between large and small farmers were considerable (Font 1990). From this description emerges two further points to notice. First, barriers to entry existed for aspiring coffee planters in Brazil. Although share-croppers and tenant farmers did slowly emerge among coffee producers, access to land was largely dependent on the willingness of the large *fazendeiros* to sell or let. Second, supply of coffee was not perfectly elastic. Given the availability of labour and capital farmers might harvest more intensively as a short-run response to any upward movement in prices but in the medium-term new coffee trees took some five years to produce additional output. This lag presented particular problems if the price had fallen again in the meantime.[2]

Buyers in the Brazilian coffee trade were not homogeneous either. There was not a single layer of intermediaries between producers and final consumers but a bewildering variety of traders. A hierarchy of native middlemen and foreign traders can be detected. Farmers generally marketed their crops to *comissários*, Brazilian or Portuguese brokers and general merchants, who not only provided credit but also performed a range of agential services, despatching supplies, settling transport charges, checking weights and storing produce (Stein 1957a; Ridings 1982). Once a buyer among the exporters was found, the *comissário* deducted his expenses and commission, forwarding the balance of the sale price to the grower. In Rio de Janeiro, but not in Santos, a further middleman, the *ensacador*, intervened before coffee reached the exporter. The origin of the Rio system is obscure but the later development of Santos, which permitted a more streamlined practice, may explain its absence there. The *ensacador* bought lots from several *comissários* which he bagged in suitable quantities and qualities for overseas shippers. He was generally a broker of greater resources than the *comissário*, possessing storage and handling machinery (van Delden Laerne 1885: 231; *Brazilian Review* 10 July 1900: 436).

The intervention of successive factors each performing a specialised function added to costs which diminished the margins received by growers and exporters. In times of rising prices and buoyant market conditions, which for coffee peaked in the mid-1890s, such intermediation could be sustained. In any case, local dealers performed a useful function in the days before railways when foreign shippers could not easily travel far from ports. But by the early twentieth century conditions were very different. Falling prices meant that traders sought to make economies and the improved railway network allowed middlemen at the ports to venture further afield in their search for business. Some *comissários* by-passed up-country agents and were also seeking to cut out the *ensacador* (*South American Journal* 20 July 1901: 71; *Brazilian Review* 23 July 1901, 13 March 1909).

The final buyers in Brazil, the foreign exporters, also sought to eliminate local middlemen and deal directly with farmers up-country in local markets where it was an established custom to sell coffee on the spot in various contractual forms. It became the foreign exporters' policy not only to pay for coffee on delivery, but also to provide advances if a farmer was well-known and the quality of his crop good.[3] The elimination of local middlemen could have benefited Brazilian coffee planters since they might retain part of the fee hitherto charged by the *comissário*. However, the *comissário* was able to play upon the farmers' fears that such elimination merely reduced the competition for and the price of the coffee crop (*The Times* 5 August 1909: 3f).

These business strategies furnished anecdotal evidence about the expanding role of foreign shippers in the Brazilian coffee trade but the degree of their market leverage at the ports was of even more concern. The shippers were relatively few in number and exports were concentrated at two main ports, Rio and Santos. At the turn of the century the fear was that an oligopsony of large shippers controlling a huge share of the market would combine to offer artificially low prices to local traders and producers. Although the number of exporters was actually large – in the 1870s the *Jornal do Comércio* named about 100 at Rio de Janeiro as well as 90 unknown *diversos* responsible for very small quantities – the bulk of shipments was handled by a small group of firms. And the degree of domination appeared to be increasing. Five-firm concentration ratios increased from about 40 per cent of shipments from Rio in 1885 to up to 65 per cent thereafter. Ten-firm concentration ratios similarly rose from about 60 to 90 per cent.[4]

In practice the degree of exporter concentration may have been exaggerated. More qualitative evidence suggests that the barriers to entry and exit were not insurmountable. From the 1880s a regular supply of German and United States houses competed with the British shippers.[5] There is evidence, too, of domestic exporters emerging – although this development only became pronounced after the Second World War. Further, the impression is of strong rivalry between the firms as exporter lists are full of names which appear for a few years as important shippers only to retreat later into a minor role or even extinction. The changing population of firms was sometimes the result of ill-judged business decisions or of the retirement of a senior partner who had made insufficient provision for his successor. Moreover, falling prices from the 1890s and the problem of exchange movements were bound to lead to a high turnover of firms. Nevertheless, the perception was that the export houses controlled the trade. Coffee, explained Richard Morse, was delivered in Santos to a 'half dozen exporters' who set their own price (Morse 1951).

Credit relations, it is often argued, enhanced the market power of coffee buyers, especially the export houses. It is a well-known feature of many commodity trades that the supply of credit by intermediaries to producers provides a tie which binds the producer to the merchant and removes the former's discretion over pricing and quality (Stein 1953). There were also credit relationships between intermediaries. Farmers who borrow at one stage of the farming year use the next crop as a security for the loan and are pressed to market it through their creditor. Merchants generally have access to cheaper credit than farmers and the foreign exporters, especially British with links in the London money markets, were particularly well placed to borrow cheaply and lend more dearly.

Foreign capital, too, gave the merchant further advantages over the producer in the form of investment in storage capacity, processing and transport. In the absence of storage capacity up-country, farmers had to ship coffee quickly once it had been harvested; if there was a bumper crop which would reduce prices, coffee could not be held to await an upturn; in succeeding short crops, when unit costs were higher, prices tended not to rise in sympathy since merchants released stocks onto the market (Greenhill 1977: 210ff). Foreign exporters invested in warehousing at the ports of shipment – although storage was not without its own risks which could turn against its suppliers.

Similarly, the multiple processing operations of cleaning, drying, sorting and bagging coffee were increasingly being financed by foreign capital which exploited economies of scale in these functions. Moving up-country not only enabled the exporters to buy coffee cheaply it also encouraged them to invest in milling capacity to enjoy the value-added functions traditionally performed by local middlemen.[6] Rail transport from up-country to Santos was provided independently of foreign shippers – although the railroads were largely foreign-owned – but a crucial function was also to transport coffee from the railhead to the warehouse in Santos or to the dockside by mule cart or, later, by lorry, and this, too, was financed by expatriate merchants.[7]

Once more, the expatriate merchants' access to low-interest capital might help the producer who could, perhaps, borrow more cheaply than when he depended more on local intermediaries – although the anecdotal evidence does not suggest that the cost of borrowing was particularly low. It is difficult, anyway, to determine whether rates charged to producers by exporters were excessive or not – given the risks involved, the delays in repayment and the possibility of default. Similarly, foreign investment in storage and ancillary services for the coffee trade might also help farmers – but, again, access to cheaper facilities could only have been to the advantage of the coffee planter if he *shared* in the value-added component.

The Brazilian coffee trade was also one in which transaction costs might be substantial. Neo-classical theory may assume that efficient markets were costless with regard to transactions but there are always transaction costs and individuals act on incomplete knowledge in their decision-making. Although farmers may know as much as traders about local crop prospects, Brazil's coffee trade was not characterised by perfect knowledge of demand conditions abroad or of quality and standards. Nor was coffee an homogeneous product although in up-country Brazil grading was rough and ready. There was, for example, no single world price for coffee set in New York or Europe but a series of prices determined by different qualities.[8]

The asymmetrical pattern of knowledge and understanding favoured the foreign export houses like E. Johnston & Co. 'We know so much more about coffee', one of the firm's partners informed head office, 'and are so much better informed that we can afford to let alone lots which are undesirable.'[9] Farmers were particularly disadvantaged owing to the well-known lag between planting and harvesting coffee. Their investment decisions had to take account of what prices would be in five years time.

The nineteenth century marked an increased striving for better information. Certainly, large *fazendeiros* might be reasonably well-informed but smallholders were unlikely to possess good market intelligence. In Santos and Rio knowledge of international market conditions was probably more widely available by the turn of the century. Information travelled by word of mouth on the *praça*, in newspapers, through the market intelligence news-sheets produced by many merchants and by means of regular steamship communications. Moreover, the telegraph had linked Brazil to Western Europe and North America commodity markets by the last quarter of the nineteenth century (Ahvenainen 1986). What Brazil lacked, however, was a formally established coffee exchange without which farmers and local merchants would remain less well-informed about prices and qualities than the foreign houses who enjoyed quicker and more direct links with commodity exchanges overseas. Such access to information gave foreign capital a head-start in making investment decisions.

Douglass North (Ch. 2, in this volume) argues that it is exceptional to find markets which approximate to the conditions of efficiency. And, on balance, it seems that market structures in the Brazilian coffee trade painted a picture which bore little resemblance to models of perfect competition. Alliances between large landowners and traders undoubtedly existed but *fazendeiros* considered that the balance of power lay overwhelmingly in favour of the merchant, especially the foreign shipper. It is very difficult to be certain about who took what portion of the total coffee product but what mattered was that it was believed that foreign merchants unscrupulously exploited the market.[10] The lack of warehouse accommodation did not allow farmers to store their crops to await higher prices and the absence of a formal commodity exchange was keenly felt. Producers sold on unfavourable terms, made worse in the series of bumper harvests early in the twentieth century. Further planting decisions in the early 1890s when prices were at their peak were being undermined by falling prices thereafter so that the share taken by the farmer seemed to be decreasing. Finally, the diversified investment portfolio of the merchant may have allowed him to set terms and conditions in related and complementary activities. Could the welfare of planters be raised through the introduction of political and social devices? In other words, could official action create a better outcome? The case for reform, through both official intervention and market regulation, seemed overwhelming in the Brazilian coffee trade.

PLANTERS AND POLITICS

Government intervention is often the outcome of successful campaigning by interest groups. The identity between plantation and political elites in Brazil is a matter of debate. Normano's view that 'the entire history of the First Republic is dominated by the interrelationship between coffee and politics' probably overstates the case (Normano 1935: 42). Nevertheless, land represented political power and the political activity of planters, if not at a federal level, was significant on a provincial or state platform and probably greater than that of other exporting elites (Graham 1969: 106–11; Hill 1947: 629). A relatively small body of rich planter-oligarchs in São Paulo and Minas Gerais filled local official posts and controlled the machinery of government in their own interests, enjoying a 'political' as much as an economic rent. Within Brazil's decentralised federal structure, Paulista and Mineiro politicians held many of the highest offices of the Republic, although the federal authorities did not invariably act in coffee's interests (Monbeig 1952: 122–3). Nevertheless, the importance of coffee's export earnings for overseas debt settlement and government revenues was not lost upon officials.

One solution to the problem of market failure was to improve the working of the markets. Policies might have been introduced to reverse the existence of cartels and collusion which seemed to prevent markets from functioning. The encouragement of competitive private marketing in association with the establishment of an effective commodity exchange with all the facilities of hedging and futures trading might have gone a long way to solve some of the perceived problems, even if they could not be entirely eliminated.[11] In the years immediately before the First World War private enterprise, mainly expatriate, as we have seen, formed warehouse companies and there were several commodity clearing houses or *caixas* which supplied the usual exchange services (Bacha and Greenhill 1992: 206–18).

However, officials also intervened directly in the coffee trade. Douglass North's notion of 'mental models' (Ch. 2, this volume) in his explanation of new institutional economics and the significance of policy may be useful in explaining why there was such official intervention in Brazil's coffee trade and, perhaps, more importantly, what form it would take. Planters used to slave labour constantly complained that unskilled workers were both in short supply and expensive. Thus, subsidised immigration to provide cheap labour as well as public works to improve transportation, both financed by the São Paulo State Government, bore the hallmark of the coffee-grower's influence (see, for example, Lewis 1991).

The fact that the state, if not the federal, government believed in the primacy of the coffee planter and that his interests were being compromised by foreigners resulted in the evolution of a *defesa* policy of protecting coffee. How could Brazilian farmers gain greater control over the coffee trade? Initial responses which involved controlling costs, encouraging demand and cutting supply, produced no long-term solution. Lower export duties merely reduced government revenue; devaluation to cheapen exports simply made imports and debt-servicing dearer; discriminatory duties against low-grade coffee were resisted by vested interests; permanently lower production levels were unpopular among farmers facing high overheads. Barriers to entry in the form of a tax in 1903 on new planting would show no effects for four or five years and, despite propaganda, it was difficult to increase demand by much, given its low response to falling prices.[12]

A bumper crop in 1906, which lowered prices to less than half those ruling a decade earlier, brought matters to a head. Those in Congress and the press advocating a minimum price plan – advanced but not implemented in 1902 – now had the ear of government. Thus, representatives of the states of São Paulo, Minas Gerais and Rio de Janeiro met at Taubate to formulate what became known as a valorisation plan to stabilise coffee markets.[13] Minas Gerais and Rio de Janeiro later backed out leaving the state of São Paulo to operate the policy alone.

The plan exploited fluctuations in coffee harvests to regularise shipments and thus equalise crop variations. Valorisation replaced the merchant's stockholding capacity by reserving that function for the farmer. Officials would buy coffee at minimum prices and store it until under-supply again occurred, anticipating that the withdrawal of stocks would soon influence prices upwards. Valorisation differed from crude restriction schemes in that it was not designed to raise prices *per se* nor permanently to reduce supply. The intention was to prevent fluctuations in price and supply, an important advantage to consumers, as well as to producers. The release of stocks during shortages would prevent undue price rises and stabilise planters' incomes (see Rowe 1932, 1965).

At first, valorisation undoubtedly worked. Serious consumer resistance was avoided when stocks were discreetly reduced and from 1908 crop returns showed welcome reductions which brought a reversal in price trends so that levels ruling in 1912 were the highest for twenty years. By the outbreak of the First World War, six years after valorisation began, the loans had been repaid and stocks profitably liquidated. Moreover, valorisation stabilised prices and supplies and it protected farmers' incomes, thus achieving one of Brazil's main objectives, market control (Greenhill 1977: 225–6).

Critics suggested that it was external factors – soil exhaustion, bad weather and planting prohibitions – rather than valorisation which subsequently reduced coffee crops, but the scheme *anticipated* that shortfalls would succeed bumper crops. Farmers attributed their improved fortunes to the policy and, though intended as a temporary support for coffee, valorisation was successfully tried again in 1917–18 and 1922 when, once more, bumper crops threatened to bring prices crashing down. As in 1908, sales from the 1922 valorisation were vested in a London committee (Bacha and Greenhill 1992: 36–42). By the 1920s, too, the São Paulo State Government began to further improve the market position of its coffee producers by direct intervention. It constructed officially regulated stores, primarily at the rail junctions in the interior. The value-added from stockholding would be retained in Brazil rather than in the consuming ports or remitted abroad as the profits of foreign-owned warehouse companies. Farmers increasingly used the official stores rather than those owned privately. Similarly, the São Paulo Government opened its own commodity exchange, the Caixa de Liquidação in the 1920s.

These successes strengthened pressure from coffee interests to establish price support on a more permanent basis and to avoid the heavy losses of short-term market fluctuations which seemed to profit exporters and importers given the stability of roasted coffee prices. Thus, the federal government decided to transfer all responsibility for the financing and control of the coffee policy to the state of São Paulo which could now exploit its investments in warehouses and exchange facilities. In 1924 the São Paulo Institute for the Permanent Defence of Coffee was created. The new defence scheme introduced innovations in support of its usual price support through direct intervention by regulating the entry of coffee from the producing areas to Rio and Santos. It retained coffee up-country in its newly-built warehouses to which all supplies went before being released to the ports in quantities determined by officials (Krasner 1973).

The new system differed radically from previous valorisations in that the authorities took no responsibility to purchase farmers' coffee. The price received by farmers from the actual sale of their coffee was the price ruling in Santos on the day of the sale. Farmers used warrants issued by the official warehouses against coffee deposited in them as collateral for an advance, normally 60 per cent of a crop's value, to finance their cash needs during the retention of the stocks. But it was now the farmer, as ultimate holder of the stocks, who bore the risks of the operation and could reap the profit from it. Officials were optimistic about the effectiveness of artificial price control following the earlier valorisations, and it was this perspective which appealed to *fazendeiros*.

In 1926 the floating of £10 million in London under a state of São Paulo guarantee financed the new Institute and strengthened the authorities' role in its work (Bacha and Greenhill 1992: 42–6). Together the state government and the Institute also acquired control of the Banco do Estado de São Paulo to manage the financial operations and lend the proceeds of the loan on the security of warehouse warrants. The Institute's greater financial strength enabled it to successfully manage the large 1927 crop as well as the smaller one in 1928 on terms favourable to planters. The policy of coffee defence was firmly established.

VALORISATION: INSTITUTIONS AND ORGANISATIONS

The success of São Paulo's coffee policy remains a matter of debate. Some of the arguments are well-known and need little elaboration. Fritsch (1988) contends that permanent valorisation was 'a clearly necessary and timely stabilisation policy ... [which] exerted a beneficial influence, avoiding major external disequilibria with damaging consequences for overall economic performance'. Similarly, even Keynes apparently argued (according to Fritsch) that 'the coffee valorisation of the Brazilian government ... brought into existence by the post-war troubles and the slump of 1920–1 were fully justified' (quoted in Bacha and Greenhill 1992: 47). On the other hand, Delfim Netto (1979: 185–90) suggests that Brazil's industrial development was retarded because factors of production which would have been released from the coffee sector were retained there as a consequence of the extra profits provided by the valorisation policies. He goes on to argue that the 'efficiency losses' of such resource allocation should be measured against 'the terms of trade gains' from valorisation. The net result, from a social point of view, was not necessarily positive.

Moreover, successful valorisation had to overcome real difficulties. It inevitably found little favour with contemporaries committed to the virtues of *laissez-faire* and the free market. Even in Brazil opinion remained divided. Minas Gerais and Rio de Janeiro needed safeguards for their low-grade coffee and other commodity producers (cocoa, sugar and rubber) demanded equal treatment. The costs of valorisation were enormous, forcing the federal authorities to raise huge loans in New York and Europe. Consolidated in 1908, the loans were used to pay planters for the surplus coffee and to cover storage and administrative costs and were serviced by means of a tax on each bag of coffee shipped. In the consuming markets, especially the United States, opinion hardened against government interference which had the appearance of raising coffee to a level above the equilibrium price. Furthermore, in the absence of suitable warehouses, Brazil could not hold the coffee internally but had to seek stores abroad. Most problematic was the fact that Brazil lost control over the management of sales to a committee of bankers in London until the stocks were liquidated (Greenhill 1977: 221–5).

Even worse in the long term was valorisation's effect on world coffee supplies. Although price stability is sensible for farmers and consumers, it may send the wrong signals to producers, particularly if the indicator price is set too high. The policy of higher and more stable prices during the 1920s contained the seeds of its own destruction. Despite assurances to the contrary, farmers inside and outside Brazil were effectively encouraged to produce more. Colombia, Central America, Indonesia and East Africa, for example, gained under the classic free-rider principle (UN/FAO 1961). They expanded their acreage under coffee, storing up trouble for the future. They did not contribute to or bear the costs of São Paulo's coffee policy but benefited from its effects on prices and greater market certainty.

Nor did the valorisation policy solve the problem of foreign participation in Brazil's coffee trade. The response of foreign capitalists in the coffee trade to Brazilian policy, given that policy was partly designed to reduce the power of this group, has not been greatly explored. How did expatriate coffee firms react to the authorities' intervention? How much market influence did they continue to exert? Did policy offer new business opportunities?

From 1920 the development of Brazilian coffee policy put foreign investments in warehousing and exporting at risk. According to one British company, official bonded stores in the interior, which farmers now used, represented 'a great blow to the public warehouse companies' in Santos (*The Times* 8 May 1925: 21e). Similarly, there was a substantial loss of business for the Companhia Registradora de Santos (also British-owned) when the state government established its own *caixa* since the firm could not offer the same guarantees to traders and farmers to match those of the government's exchange. The officially regulated flow of coffee into the ports was a blow to the transportation companies and the transfer of the stockholding risk to the farmer reduced the profits merchants had customarily received from price changes.

One British company in the coffee trade, Brazilian Warrant, responded in four ways to the changing market. First, it tendered for (and in 1922 gained) the contract for the marketing of valorised coffee through the London committee of bankers.[14] In 1908 the German House, Theodor Wille, an arch-rival, obtained the contract. The bankers who financed the loans in 1908 and 1922 needed to use the marketing expertise of one the main Brazilian shippers and in the latter year Brazilian Warrant profited enormously from this role.[15]

A second response was to develop backward linkages into coffee plantations and estate management in which, hitherto, exporters had been generally un-willing to invest. It now appeared logical to acquire plantations and ship the company's coffee in a fully integrated operation from the farm to the consumer. The permanent coffee *defesa*, which raised prices and protected the *fazendeiro*, suggested that production was more likely to be profitable than either warehousing or exporting coffee. In 1920 the Companhia Agricola Fazendas Paulistas was incorporated as a wholly owned subsidiary of Brazilian Warrant (*The Times* 12 May 1920: 46). In 1924 they purchased the Cambuhy estate, a model *fazenda* (Little 1960), a deal, the shareholders were told, which was 'the result of the deliberate policy of the Board to lean more upon coffee growing and less upon trading in the article, which has become year by year a more and more difficult operation' (*The Times* 8 May 1925: 21e-f). These developments also gave the company greater control over the quality of its coffee for export. In 1926 Brazilian Warrant paid for a third major estate, which it managed through a local flotation, the Companhia do Rio Tibirica (*The Times* 24 June 1927: 23c, 1 June 1928: 23b).

Estate management offered a third way forward. For all three of its estates Brazilian Warrant acted as agents, drawing commission upon its services, and bankers. Agency work had long been a feature of its operations but now it went beyond arranging shipping space and insurance facilities. In addition, Brazilian Warrant also acted as agents for several other coffee estate companies formed in the 1920s, no doubt also exploiting the favourable pricing prospects for coffee growers. Managing agencies were arranged for the São Paulo Coffee Estates Company and for the São Paulo Land Company.[16]

Finally, Brazilian Warrant considerably developed another of its complementary services. Like all merchant firms it had supplied credit to clients in Brazil but now the need to finance planters' coffee in the official warehouses offered more business. Farmers would present their warrants, as proof of deposit, and collect an advance on their coffee. Once the coffee was sold they would use the receipts to repay the loan and keep the remainder. This provided Brazilian Warrant with substantial business during the 1920s when such advances represented a large part of the company's assets on its balance sheet. Using its access to cheap funds in London, and past profits in Brazil, the company developed a wide-ranging crop financing role.[17]

INSTITUTIONS AND EXPORT PERFORMANCE

This chapter touches upon a particular political process as a critical factor in the performance of Brazil's coffee policy. It is probable that a degree of market influence, at least in the short run, was achieved and that the price of coffee was stabilised for a time at a higher level than market forces alone might have achieved. Moreover, the discretion for foreigners to manipulate prices in their own interests was also curtailed. But the policy may well have had unwelcome side-effects as foreign merchants, like Brazilian Warrant, and non-Brazilian producers responded to the *defesa*. The increased corporate ownership of plantations and the provision of credit allowed greater British penetration of the Brazilian coffee trade. Similarly, overseas planters exploited the favourable market conditions with which they were unexpectedly presented.

But of greater interest may be the light which new institutional economics can shed on the question of Brazilian valorisation policies. Institutions, notes Douglass North (Ch. 2, this volume), are set up to be efficient by reducing uncertainty in human exchange but reflect also social and political power. Brazilian coffee planters, who were politically and socially influential and whose manipulation of policy reflected their dominance seem to fit neatly into this approach. The extent to which São Paulo's coffee *defesa* represented successful market intervention remains unclear. But, as Bates (Ch. 3, this volume) suggests, it as possible to have government and institutional failure as it is market failure, while Toye (Ch. 4, this volume) asks whether imperfect governments should correct imperfect markets. Certainly, the work of Manuel Font (1990) indicates the differences of view between Brazilian planters in the 1920s so that policy was not necessarily with the agreement of all planters but merely with a group of them, later overthrown in the Vargas revolution.

It might also be possible to apply simple game theory to the issue of Brazil's coffee policy (see Bates, Ch. 3, this volume). Undoubtedly, both domestic and non-Brazilian producers had much to gain from cooperation, that is from stable and higher prices. But, in fact, given the pay-off, non-Brazilian producers gained more by not cooperating, that is the avoidance of the costs of valorisations while enjoying its benefits. Brazil, on the other hand, bore the costs without necessarily enjoying long-term advantages. As Brazil manipulated prices for its farmers so outside producers simply planted more coffee which later on made market conditions worse. Cooperative solutions in game theory are, argues North (Ch. 2, this volume), 'most likely when the play is repeated, when the players have complete information about the other players' past performance'. And, the game was repeated, not only in the 1920s but throughout the inter-war years. Faced with the known response of outside farmers it might make more sense for Brazilians not to engage in price stabilisation policies but rather to allow competitive forces to operate in the market place from which Brazil ought to be able to expel many of its rivals. But Brazil continued the policy of *defesa*. Why?

Again, new institutional economics might help supply the answer through two of its ideas, the issue of mental models and path dependence. Choice of policy is based upon the mental models of its formulators. Individuals may learn and change their modes of thinking, especially when observed outcomes are inconsistent with their expectations. But, if fluctuations or declines in coffee prices are laid at the door of foreign merchants, as many planters believed, then they are unlikely quickly to reverse their valorisation policy which is expected to offset foreign price manipulation. Individuals and organisations with bargaining power have a crucial stake in perpetuating the system which may be hard to reverse.

In this way an economy like Brazil's can become locked into a pattern of path dependence. In the short run Brazilian intervention in the coffee business may have solved some problems but it created others. In the long run, however, it set the pattern for intervention which the Vargas Government continued in a different form during the 1930s – as a Federal policy rather than a state initiative – and which assumed international dimensions during the Second World War when both the main consuming country (the United States) and other Latin American producers reached a coordinated agreement about prices and markets (Gordon-Ashworth 1984). From the 1950s, of course, intervention took the form of successive international coffee agreements under the International Coffee Organisation, an approach with which policy-makers are still grappling today.

NOTES

I am particularly grateful to Dr W.G. Clarence-Smith (School of Oriental and African Studies) for commenting on an earlier draft of this paper. I am, of course, responsible for any errors which remain.

1 Consular Reports (Rio de Janeiro), Parliamentary Papers, XCIV (1898: 267) and XCVIII (1899: 278).
2 Commonwealth Secretariat, *Plantation Crops* (1970: 29), makes the point that 'this delayed adjustment of supply to demand is the prime cause of the periodic crises which afflict the world's coffee industry'.
3 The story of the development of direct purchasing by one coffee exporter is well-explained in the letter books (2 volumes, henceforth, EG I and II) of Edward Greene, the Santos manager of and later a partner in E. Johnston & Co. (London). The letter books are contained in a small archive in University College London (henceforth, UCL). See, for example, Greene's out letters of 18 April and 12 September 1899, and 13 July 1903.
4 Calculated from data in *Jornal do Comércio, Boletins Mensais do Centro de Comércio de Café de Rio de Janeiro* and *Exportação de Café Pelo Porto de Santos.*
5 João Luso, in *The United States of Brasil* (c. 1919), explains the origins of the major American houses in the Brazilian coffee trade. For a history of the leading German shipper, see Zimmermann (1969).
6 Edward Greene out letters (mainly to Reginald Johnston) 6 and 27 April 1896, 21 July 1897, 10 December 1900 and 25 August 1901, UCL, EG I contain information on the milling investments of E. Johnston & Co.
7 Brazilian Warrant, which took over E. Johnston in 1909, formed the União de Transportes in 1912 as the amalgamation of a number of transport firms.
8 *Jornal do Comércio* produced comprehensive annual lists of the various prices – on an *ex post* basis.
9 Edward Greene to Reginald Johnston 1 November 1899, UCL, EG II, pp. 3–4.
10 *Brazilian Review* (28 May 1901: 379) reported the view of Dr Neiva in the Brazilian Congress who argued that 'exporters ... in combination with the big roasting houses monopolise the markets and persistently and systematically "bear" coffee'. Such views are further explained in Greenhill (1977, see also Ridings 1989).
11 These arguments are particularly taken up with regard to the cocoa trade by Peter

Bauer but might equally well be applied to coffee (see Bauer 1963; Bauer and Yamey 1968).

12 United States Monthly Consular Reports (July 1903: 343–5, November 1907: 158–60); *South American Journal* (24 January 1903: 89, 7 March 1903: 230).

13 The *Jornal do Comércio*'s annual *Retrospecto* for 1906 and other years contains details of the *Convenção de Taubate*. A good recent analysis of Brazil's valorisation policy is Krasner (1973).

14 Brazilian Warrant's participation in the 1922 Valorisation Scheme is fully documented in the archives of Baring Brothers & Co. Ltd, Partners Files, Nos 147 and 153.

15 See Balance Sheets of Brazilian Warrant for the years 1922–4, Guildhall Library, London.

16 See Annual Reports and Balance Sheets of the Cambuhy Coffee and Cotton Estates and the São Paulo Coffee Estates Companies, Guildhall Library, London.

17 Brazilian Warrant Balance Sheets, Guildhall Library, London.

12

INSTITUTIONAL THEORY AND SOCIAL CHANGE IN UGANDA

E. A. Brett

INSTITUTIONAL DECLINE AND ECONOMIC FAILURE IN AFRICA

Economic and political failure in Africa has reduced most countries to foreign dependence and many to civil war. Millions have been killed, tortured, displaced or dispossessed. Economic policy is made in Washington then inefficiently implemented by unaccountable national governments. Little now remains of the vision of an autonomous and prosperous democratic state system which legitimated the decolonisation process in the 1950s and 1960s.

The causes of failure are clearly structural rather than contingent, since breakdown is almost universal and cannot simply be attributed to particular national circumstances. Instead they must stem from the nature of the institutional arrangements developed under colonialism and hastily modified during the political transition of the 1950s and 1960s. The crisis confirms North's claim that 'it is the successes and failures in human organisation that account for the progress and retrogression of societies' (North 1981: 59). Institutional arrangements which encourage mismanagement and waste must now be replaced by others which force their managers to serve the public interest rather than their own.

This chapter approaches the problem by developing a theoretical framework for the analysis of social change in the real conditions which apply in disturbed African countries. It does so using the experience of a single country which has undergone a major process of social transformation over the past thirty years. Uganda has been a model colony, 'modernising state', then political autocracy. It is now managing a process of growth and reconstruction which is unique in the region. The experiences of success as well as failure outlined in the second part of the paper therefore provide a wide range of evidence against which to test the logic of the theory developed in the first.

INSTITUTIONAL THEORIES AND SOCIAL CHANGE

Institutions facilitate social integration by allowing individuals to cooperate to achieve common purposes. They are the 'rules of the game in a society' which 'structure incentives in human exchange' to ensure individual compliance with collective decisions through appropriate incentives or sanctions (North 1990a: 3). While institutional arrangements create this framework, collective action takes place within organisations which operate within their limits to produce services for their own members or outsiders. Social change is a function of variations in the terms on which institutional and organisational arrangements are governed to provide essential services in any society. Institutional arrangements structure the opportunities available to individuals, so the form taken by key structures – the family, production unit, state and religion – determines the attitudes which individuals will develop towards gender roles, systems of social and political control, theories of knowledge, and supernatural authority. At any point in time these arrangements will be more or less stable, and serve as the basis for the persistence of social structure.

The orthodox social sciences have emerged to explain the logic of the dominant institutions which constitute the modern state system. They focus on the conditions which ensure their successful survival and adaptation and thus need only identify the functions performed by key structures and the corresponding value systems required to sustain them. However, explaining progressive or regressive structural change raises different problems – the need to deal with conflicts of value, and tendencies to disequilibrium which disrupt the agreements which sustain the status quo.

Orthodox theorists assume that 'social institutions evolve to meet a society's functional needs ... [and] persist because they continue to satisfy our needs' (Knight 1992: 94). These evolutionary assumptions contribute to an explanation of the functioning of institutions in modern societies which operate as they do because their members have at least partially internalised the appropriate value and behavioural systems. However, theories which assume that institutions exist to maximise collective benefits and that individuals will habitually recognise the obligations required to sustain them cannot explain social change driven by distributional conflict in contexts where people can ignore collective obligations because of competing value systems which justify opportunistic and predatory behaviour. Here individual and social rationality need not correspond, creating situations where power can be systematically used for private gain, and dominant social groups will support autocratic or predatory institutional arrangements. Progressive change will depend on the actions of groups and strata which do have an interest in creating open and accountable structures, and we will need to discover how they can be assisted to do so and thus create the arrangements which orthodox theorists simply take for granted.

Second, orthodox models focus upon equilibrium rather than change, and cooperation rather than conflict, while development presupposes an inherently conflictual evolutionary process in which more advanced institutions displace less advanced ones in some areas, and are then adapted and adopted elsewhere by groups which recognise the benefits they bring. Less efficient must give way to more efficient structures, with a corresponding denial of the rights of power-holders and of the credibility of existing belief systems. Thus explanations of change-oriented social action require a *critical* theory of existing institutions which shows why they produce sub-optimal results for at least some groups, and thus generate opposition and demands for new forms of organisation. No such possibilities exist if we assume a system, as orthodox theorists do, already based on individual freedom and voluntary exchange.

Nevertheless, orthodox theories are essential for development as they can provide the ideal-typical institutional models which demonstrate what must be done in LDCs that wish to 'catch up'. However theories which assume that equitable property rights already exist and that pre-capitalist structures and values are no longer salient, cannot explain the dynamic processes which are changing the face of contemporary Africa. This requires a normative theory of institutional transformation which not only recognises the rationale for the conservative or predatory behaviour which inhibits reform, but also for altruistic attempts to replace it by building progressive structures in these inhospitable environments. This theory cannot be developed in the abstract but must be related directly to the arrangements which prevailed in African countries at independence, and to the nature of the change process which they have undergone since then.

The development problem: reforming regressive capitalist structures

Theories of development assume that welfare can be increased by creating institutions which operate on the basis of more efficient principles than those which already exist. With the collapse of state socialism this process is now dominated by attempts to produce progressive modern capitalist structures – the liberal democratic state, merit-based bureaucratic management, autonomous scientific research and the competitive market economy – in countries where they have been suppressed or only partially introduced. These structures emerged in their countries of origin out of a long and violent process strongly resisted by those with a vested interest in the old order. However, their superiority to existing forms was such that they were forced into existence by previously excluded social groups – notably the modern bourgeoisie – and then came to be accepted by the majority of the population.

An understanding of orthodox theory facilitates the management of social systems already based on these principles, but not those where they have yet to be consolidated, as in Africa. While the development process there has long been driven by the forces unleashed by the Western capitalist revolution, its evolution as a dependent offshoot of external interests produced institutional distortions which have yet to be overcome. Capitalism was not taken to Africa by disinterested social scientists, but by slave traders, merchants, planters, soldiers and missionaries who maximised their own interests with little reference to those of local people. The colonial state was created to consolidate the new situation and introduced a distorted set of capitalist structures which blocked indigenous opportunities for autonomous growth and reinforced many of the regressive characteristics of traditional institutions. Monopolistic arrangements safeguarded the interests of private expatriate firms and the bureaucratic apparatus excluded the African elite from the higher levels of the capitalist economy.

At independence, therefore, the institutional arrangements in most African states were dominated by dualism and monopoly. Traditional values and structures survived at the societal level, distorted by their coexistence with the dominant modern system. Modern political and economic institutions were based on monopolistic principles which guaranteed the power of those who controlled the state and marginalised the interests of the great majority. The attempt to democratise the state shortly before independence then failed because of the non-existence of autonomous political and social structures in civil society. This produced closed and hierarchical capitalist systems dominated by institutions which bore little resemblance to the liberal and competitive models described in the orthodox texts.

Explaining institutional decline: bounded rationality and malfeasance

Thus institutional failure in Africa cannot be understood as the outcome of orthodox capitalist principles, but of the contradictory tendencies generated by their partial integration into less complex systems. Orthodox theories assume a world of self-interested but law abiding and socially responsible individuals who choose freely between competing alternatives on the basis of perfect information. These conditions are imperfectly met even in advanced countries, as those who use new institutional economics recognise. In Africa, however, choices are constrained by political and economic monopolies, limited information and mistrust. The result is levels of bounded rationality and opportunism which produce instability and inefficiency.

Complex information is required to manage modern institutions which exploit economies of scale by extending social control over wide areas of time and space. They can only be effectively managed by executives who understand the technical and organisational challenges which they present, and are accountable to stakeholders who understand and can enforce their rights over them. This in turn presupposes an educational system which provides correspondingly complex skills, and an autonomous system of social investigation and diffusion which will provide both managers and stakeholders with reliable evidence on which to base their judgements about institutional performance.

The dominant institutions in post-colonial Africa were modelled on those created in developed societies and had been managed by an expatriate political and economic class educated in and accountable to principals in their countries of origin. They were run on monopolistic principles which distanced them

203

from their beneficiaries and allowed managers to conceal information about their activities from the public. At independence an African managerial and entrepreneurial class hardly existed because they had been excluded from higher education and economic opportunities, the public as a whole was largely illiterate, there were no mass circulation newspapers, and radio and television were directly controlled by the state. Neither effective management nor democratic control is possible in such circumstances.

The survival of free institutions also depends on a general willingness to honour contracts and refrain from corrupt or criminal behaviour. Both rulers and citizens can only have 'rights in so far as [they have] duties, and duties in so far as [they have] rights', if they are to create a legitimated political and economic order (Hegel 1967: 109). Where many fail to do so a culture based on malfeasance will develop and undermine the basis for effective cooperation and institutional survival.

However, the conditions created during the colonial transition discouraged the development of universalistic value systems which would support a nationally oriented political and economic order. The values developed in traditional African societies had emerged in response to the demands of small-scale face to face systems. Individuals drawn into the new system quickly assimilated new values, but these were distorted by the coercive and exclusivistic nature of the modern world created for them in Africa. Colonialism did not offer Africans democratic, open and merit-based structures, but racist discrimination and exclusion. It is not surprising that those who inherited power did not adopt principles which their mentors espoused in theory but ignored in practice.

Explaining institutional reform: altruism and reciprocity

Recognising negative motivations explains many destructive tendencies in institutional change, but not progressive movements which require self-sacrifice to achieve a collective good. If all behaviour was motivated by self-interest and opportunism, as economic theorists assume, people would never risk their lives to oppose an oppressive government, refuse a bribe, or work voluntarily to save the rain forest. In fact few of our day-to-day actions are actually motivated by the expectation of immediate personal gain. Most – in personal relations, politics, culture, leisure and social provision – are based on long-term normative and emotional commitments to others rather than the expectation of an equivalent payment of a directly calculable kind. Further, most individuals do not exploit every opportunity to maximise their own benefit at the expense of others even in markets based on pure self-interest. Thus, while decline occurs when people behave worse than neo-classical theorists assume, reform is only possible when they behave much better.

The survival of a modern state and property rights system which allows individuals to maximise their personal gain through exchange depends on what

Hegel (1967) calls a 'fundamental sense of order' which causes people to respect the rights of others. However, while he sees this as an attribute which everybody possesses, the African crisis suggests that it cannot be taken for granted but depends upon the development of a more appropriate fit between institutional arrangements and cultural values than now exists. Not only must individuals learn to behave better than they now do in their public lives, but they must also make major personal sacrifices to create progressive movements if they are to reform regressive structures.

However, reform not only requires changes in values, but also the establishment of an appropriate relationship between the incentive and accountability systems which govern the key institutions in society, and the collective value systems which sustain the system of political and property rights on which they depend. Culture is not simply a given derived from individually chosen preferences, but an outcome of the interaction between values and institutional and organisational rules and structures. Neither slaves nor their masters are likely to believe in liberty, equality or fraternity. For as long as oppressive conditions prevail, individual behaviour will be dominated by opportunism. However, the creation of progressive structures should produce a virtuous circle in which people recognise their social obligations because they can reliably expect others to do the same.

Thus the stability of a modern social order depends upon the establishment of a just balance between managerial privilege and public accountability. But this does not explain progressive behaviour in a regressive system where most people's immediate self-interest is best served by malfeasance or quietism. Here orthodox theory shows that pure self-interest will produce a 'free-rider problem' which will preclude collective organisation where the chances of success are small (Olson 1965). Yet revolutionary movements do occur and can only be explained by transcending the individualistic and equilibrium assumptions of orthodox theory. Such movements emerge when the breakdown of an existing framework is so costly that key groups recognise that an investment in political activism designed to replace it with another will produce a higher rate of return in the long run than a continued willingness to allow predation to continue.

Here rational self-interest must transcend the short-term calculations of market theory, and recognise the collective obligations and self-sacrifice required to create the social movements which will campaign for institutions based on freedom and competition. Such systems emerged only recently and have yet to be fully implemented anywhere, so they will not be easy to create in societies dominated by competing religious, cultural and economic interests. There is no necessary link between individual self-interest, group solidarity and a realistic policy programme around which a political movement can be organised. Only where these very exacting conditions are met will the Hegelian 'historic subject' emerge – the group or class able to act consciously to transform a social system for the better.

Marx assumed that this role would first be played by the national bourgeoisie, then by the working class. The first prediction has been confirmed in the developed world, the second only partially. However the capitalist revolution is still far from complete in Africa where the process of institutional decay and transformation in Africa must be understood in relation to the contradictory needs and objectives of a weak bourgeois class struggling to consolidate its position by building modern capitalistic institutions in a highly competitive and anarchic situation. The next section will attempt to provide the empirical substantiation for this assertion.

INSTITUTIONAL TRANSFORMATION IN PRACTICE: THE UGANDA CASE

Institutional change in twentieth-century Uganda can be broadly divided into four stages – the creation of a modern state and economic system under direct foreign control; the Africanisation of these structures in the 1940s and 1950s; the dissolution of the post-colonial state structure between 1964 and 1986; and the subsequent attempt to create a democratic, open and rule governed system through the structural adjustment programme. Each period has involved significant changes in the relationship between control and accountability in the dominant institutional structures. This chapter concentrates on the last two of these, and only deals with the most central aspects of the earlier periods.

The colonial legacy

Recent institutional change in Uganda is the outcome of a dynamic process involving a conflictual relationship between external and domestic groups and classes involving a continuous struggle for control over the state and productive assets. The discontinuity and speed of this process has been a function of the technological gap between foreign and domestic systems which existed at the end of the nineteenth century. The new expatriate ruling class – officials, soldiers, traders and missionaries – based their claim to rule on their capacity to introduce more efficient institutional structures than those which existed already. Their control was initiated by force, but depended on local recognition of the limitations of indigenous technological capacity and their need to learn from the West. This recognition was formalised in the Uganda Agreement of 1900 in which the Baganda, the dominant tribe in the south, accepted British authority in exchange for recognition of the rights of the traditional political hierarchy. Thus external authority was initially hegemonic rather than coercive, and contact initiated a process of rapid social change based on the transfer of external knowledge and institutional forms.

The transformation process presupposed that Uganda would become an independent democratic, capitalist and Christian country of the kind which had already emerged in colonies of settlement when local groups had acquired the skills and resources required to manage the modern structures. Colonialism was thus a radical force for institutional change, but one which marginalised indigenous structures and excluded local people from the management or regulation of the new ones. Good governance and accountability in this context therefore depended on the technical competence of the expatriate elites and the adequacy of the external controls to which they were subjected.

Great controversy surrounds the relationship between colonialism and development in Uganda, but the close links it created with Britain did produce some positive results. State authority was not challenged for the first sixty years, so law and order was maintained with a minimal investment in force. An externally viable currency, taxation, transport and administrative systems were created which, together with the activities of an innovative Asian entrepreneurial class, produced a rapid growth in agricultural exports. While the colonial state did not answer directly to the local population, a public service ethic among officials and political supervision from Britain with its long colonial tradition, excluded the worst forms of inefficiency and predation.

However, the dominance of expatriate interests led to the suppression of African opportunities. Rapid education and economic advancement would have produced early demands for political rights in the modern system, so higher education was neglected and African capitalism suppressed. The weakness of the entrepreneurial class forced the state to take a dominant role in building the economic system, while expatriate economic interests used their political influence to create monopoly privileges which constrained African opportunities and reduced economic efficiency.

The positive aspects of British rule stemmed from the progressive nature of the institutional framework which it introduced; the negative aspects from the monopolistic power which opportunistic expatriate interests were able to exercise before Africans had acquired the information and skills to challenge them.

The transition to independence was driven by African demands for higher positions in and then control over the new institutional structures. It was the logical culmination of the colonial commitment to self-government, and the outcome of an indigenous struggle against external control. The dynamic nature of the new colonial institutional structures had generated a demand for competent indigenous labour in all sectors, and thus for formal and informal educational arrangements to speed up the transfer of imported skills. Where these new skills created a capacity for local management in areas monopolised by expatriates (higher administration, the 'modern' economy) they were increasingly associated with demands for political and economic rights and more equitable access to market opportunities. This culminated in the nationalist demand for political independence and an end to external economic exploitation.

Nationalism was not a rejection of foreign institutions, but a demand to Africanise them as fast as possible. Indeed, once sovereignty had been ceded

in 1962, the new incumbents did not attempt to introduce specifically indigenous values or structures, but to speed up the process of institutional transfer
and development. Everyone assumed that localising managerial control and
accountability would expedite the transition to a modern institutional system
based on democracy and secure private property rights of the kind which
North sees as the prerequisite for economic efficiency and long-term progress.
However independence was followed by a period of political conflict and civil
war which reduced welfare to levels which are probably still little better than
they were in 1962.

The dynamic of institutional decline

Post-colonial decline can be understood using the assumptions of opportunism, bounded rationality and market and state failure detailed earlier. These
have to be seen as the outcome of inappropriate institutional arrangements
involving perverse incentives and weak accountability mechanisms. The modern capitalist state presupposes an organic relationship between a political
system which regulates the economic system and guarantees individual property rights, and a private sphere in which firms offer goods and services in
response to consumer demand. Accountability is based on competitive elections and market competition.

These relationships will only hold where a number of restrictive conditions
are met – these include the existence of autonomous groups in society with a
vested interest in supporting a socially responsible state system, an informed
population, and an entrepreneurial class able to provide essential goods and
services without the need for subsidies, force or fraud. This class should not
only provide economic services, but also intervene at the political level to
guarantee the integrity and rationality of the system as a whole. These conditions hardly existed in Uganda in 1962, making it impossible to create either a
coherent system of property rights or political accountability.

The emergence of a national bourgeoisie in Uganda was inhibited by
conflicts over property rights between traditional and modern systems, and
foreign and domestic interests. These inhibited the development of a free
market in land, led to demands for monopolies and subsidies from politically
influential groups, and legitimated direct state management and control. Traditional land rights inhibited market transfers and thus the development of a
capitalistic farming system, monopolies favoured foreign buyers and proces-
sors of crops in the inter-war period, and state and cooperative agencies from
the 1940s.

The elite which took power in 1962 did so in the name of a predominantly
peasant population but was composed of lower level civil servants, cooperative
officials, small businessmen and rich farmers. They had been marginalised by
the privileges accorded to expatriate capital, had no commitment to free
markets and depended on a capacity to extract surpluses from direct producers.

The latter were illiterate, atomised and subject to the constraints on collective action identified by the rational choice theorists (Bates 1981). They had little capacity to organise politically, inform themselves about policy and bring their representatives to account. The national commitment to large-scale state projects was reinforced by the interests of large foreign companies and the official donors which supported them, since the projects they assisted also depended on monopoly rights and subsidies. Thus the monopolies inherited by the new elite offered ample opportunities for rent extraction while limited democratic accountability, poor educational and public information services, and the search for rents by the new elite encouraged opportunism and bounded rationality. The process has many parallels with Marx's description of 'primitive accumulation' (Marx 1974: vol. I, part 8).

Fully fledged predation took some time to emerge since the threat of elections and the influence of external donors initially imposed some limits on the new elite. World prices were high and foreign aid flowed, so growth continued. However the leadership immediately began to marginalise political opposition and use state power to advance the interests of its own clients. The state and parastatal bureaucracies were rapidly Africanised, the rights of the Asian commercial and industrial elite were eroded and most of their agricultural processing facilities were expropriated. Foreign aid went almost exclusively to the state sector, usually into economically irrational projects (like tractor hire services) motivated by the needs of industries in donor countries rather than those of local entrepreneurs. By 1967 the regime had dismantled the 1962 constitution and thereafter ruled by force.

In 1971 Idi Amin took over and government became little more than a system of organised crime. In 1972 all Asian properties were expropriated and rented out to local entrepreneurs. The state sector, expanded to include the large Asian enterprises, was handed to political cronies and used to extract rents from the public. Export prices to farmers were savagely cut through direct controls, inflation and currency depreciation; state contracts became a source of kick-backs and theft; essential imports were controlled by parastatals which inflated prices and constrained supply. Military spending escalated and the government liquidated or drove out many of the best educated and most committed people. The Amin regime was defeated by the Tanzanians in 1979 and a new regime elected in 1980, but predation continued. By 1986 services and productive capacity had been reduced to virtual ruin.

The dynamic of institutional reform

By the mid-1970s Uganda appeared to have no future since opposition was ruthlessly repressed. In 1986, however, a new regime took power after a civil war, which is managing a reform programme which has involved the emergence of broad reform-oriented political movements, and a search for appropriate and accountable institutional alternatives. To explain this it is

necessary to understand the social dynamics that have generated the opposi-
tional political movements which have marginalised the predatory state system
and prepared the ground for new kinds of institutions to emerge. Similarly, it
is necessary to ask why many Ugandans have been prepared to risk their lives
to overthrow a predatory regime, why the state was unable to contain opposition, and why widespread support now exists for institutional arrangements
to control abuse and support collective activities on a voluntary basis?

State predation arose out of the contradictory needs of a domestic and
foreign elite made up of donor-funded foreign firms, the political and bureaucratic class, and well-connected members of the indigenous petty bourgeoisie,
all of whom benefited from the rents derived from state monopolies. The
policies which made these rents possible were based on widely accepted
interventionist economic theories which had served as the basis for post-war
recovery in Europe and were strongly supported by external advisers (Brett
1985: part 3). Their success in Europe depended on the existence of relatively
accountable political systems. In Uganda, where democracy hardly existed,
they gave the elite many opportunities for predatory surplus extraction,
allowing particular families, firms and regions to accumulate assets at the
expense of others. This ensured that the policies were inconsistently applied,
producing direct transfers from some groups to others and an overall loss of
welfare. An effective opposition was to emerge when the changes which they
generated altered the balance of influence between winners and losers, reduced
the state's capacity to manage the system effectively, and exposed the iration-
ality of the policies themselves.

Opposition to predatory policies is likely to be concentrated in an independent bourgeois class capable of generating its own resources in the market
and concerned to minimise state exactions and controls. In the 1960s no
African bourgeoisie had yet developed with these capacities because of their
exclusion during the colonial period and their inability to compete on equal
terms with expatriate firms. Established expatriate capitalists, on the other
hand, had relatively weak political links. State intervention offered some
groups very visible benefits which many participants could attempt to capture
for their businesses or regions. On the other hand losses were much less visible
and widely distributed. Thus beneficiaries were conscious and organised,
losers (consumers, small producers and Asian capitalists) were dispersed and
unorganised. Growth suffered, but the losses could never be quantified, while
well-placed minorities were making enough gains to ensure that the process
continued.

As the irrationalities intensified, however, it soon became plain that losers
would greatly outnumber winners, and that the latter were not being selected
on merit but on the basis of ethnic identity, political connections or corrupt
payments. The losses were compounded by increasing levels of direct extortion
based on state power which undermined the services on which 'legitimate'
businesses came to depend; the monopoly powers, border controls and licens-

ing regulations imposed by the state also excluded private firms from profitable sectors and imposed heavy costs on their day-to-day activities. Companies which obeyed the law and paid their taxes found it almost impossible to operate profitably. The result was a rapid decline in support for the state and the emergence of countervailing tendencies which were to undermine the system from within and without.

These regressive tendencies had both practical and ideological effects – they weakened the state's ability to control resources and thus to resist pressures for change, and also exposed the irrationality of interventionist theory and generated new social groups with a vested interest in promoting policies based on commitments to market competition and pluralistic democracy. The nature of the reform process can only be understood by looking at the connection between these structural and ideological changes.

Recent Ugandan history demonstrates that a state which relies on predation and perverse incentives undermines its own capacity to act. Individual resistance to state controls led to an expansion of the black economy to the point where it dominated the production of goods and services. This process included a *de facto* privatisation of the operation of state enterprises themselves – patients and students had to pay for notionally free or subsidised services, while Marketing Board, Cooperative and parastatal officials traded official assets for private profit. This process of class formation was accelerated by the transfer of Asian assets in 1972 to many thousands of local people who were suddenly given new market opportunities. The results were contradictory – the loss of skills and international support reduced economic activity and welfare, but it strengthened a local class long excluded by state monopolies and established foreign firms. The collapse of state services also led to an expansion in private not-for-profit structures involved in education, social insurance, health and income-generating activities. These latter activities were directly supported by a rapid expansion in not-for-profit provision by international NGOs funded by foreign donors.

These structures operated in the private sphere and were governed by mechanisms which made them directly accountable to their beneficiaries. Private producers operated in an open and highly competitive market system; NGOs had to perform if they were to retain the support of donors or members. Exclusion from effective social regulation increased the transaction costs and reduced the economic potential of these agencies, but as private organisations they could not be used as a basis for systematic extortion, except where (as was sometimes the case) they were backed by Mafia-type protection services, with covert support from the state. This unplanned and unacknowledged process thus produced a major social transformation – the development of a weak domestic bourgeoisie, but one with a collective interest in reducing the transaction costs imposed upon it by the predatory state system.

Its development went hand in hand with a reduction in the regulatory and coercive capacity of the state, since predation undermines its own beneficiaries.

211

The growth of the black economy reduced the state's access to foreign exchange and taxes, and this was compounded by the corruption of its own banking, customs and tax officials. This produced a balance of payments and fiscal crisis which reduced its capacity to pay and service its staff and undermined its regulative, extractive and coercive capacity even further. Many of the services which it provided were taken over by the not-for-profit sector which included international NGOs with million dollar budgets, the major Churches, and small community groups which also strengthened the associational basis of civil society.

These changes had dramatic political and ideological effects. While a minority continued to benefit from monopoly rents, the majority suffered losses which became increasingly visible as services collapsed, crime and extortion increased, and the behaviour of power-holders became more and more cynical and repressive. In 1982 the National Resistance Army went into the bush and was able to mobilise enough popular support to build and supply an army and create an associated political movement committed to democratisation and economic reform (Museveni). They depended on voluntary support for fighters and money, so they had to take account of the needs and interests of their stakeholders. Predation had undermined the state's capacity to respond and the civil war weakened it further by requiring greater extortion and coercion. By the end of 1985 it had lost the war and the NRM took power.

The National Resistance Movement based its campaign on a critique of the predatory state system and made a commitment to democratisation and economic reconstruction. The new regime has appointed a 'broad based' government which is clearly responding to new social forces which are deeply concerned to avoid the political and economic errors of the past. The reform process, initiated in 1986 and strongly influenced by donor pressures, has involved a general commitment to liberalisation, privatisation and the consolidation of private property rights. Asian assets have been restored, the foreign exchange market deregulated, most parastatals are being sold off, and the monopoly powers of those that remain have been eliminated. The restoration of law and order and reduction in state controls has produced a dramatic growth in private sector activity with average growth rates of nearly 5 per cent since 1986, and the virtual elimination of inflation. A democratic local government system is being created, a new national constitution drawn up and civil war in the north and northeast almost ended. All of these initiatives have strong public support, and the political leadership as well as the donors are now fully committed to a development process based upon local and foreign capitalist enterprise.

However, many regressive interests remain, so progress could easily be reversed. The new regime inherited a demoralised state apparatus and has had to continue to depend on an underpaid official class which has long earned its income from predation or moonlighting rather than bureaucratic performance. The civil war imposed heavy costs, while donor dependence has produced many projects whose rationale and cost effectiveness leave much to be desired. The new business class has great energy but it has limited capital and skills, so its capacity to produce sustained export growth is limited. State managed services are equally deficient, and their limitations are being further exposed by an explosion in HIV-related illnesses and mortality. The initiation of full-scale democratic competition for high office could revive earlier sectarian and ethnic rivalries and precipitate another period of adversarial winner-takes-all political conflict (Brett 1994).

CONCLUSIONS

This chapter has been concerned to identify the dynamic processes involved in the attempt to create open, efficient and rule governed institutional arrangements in African countries now dominated by instability and autocracy. It accepts that orthodox Western theories provide ideal-typical models which recognise the principles on which such institutions must operate if they are to function effectively. However it also recognises that they only provide an effective basis for the day-to-day management of existing institutional arrangements in societies where progressive structures already exist and people have already internalised the value systems required to sustain them. They focus mainly on systems maintenance rather than change and fail to recognise the salience of patterns of motivation which exist in contexts where value-systems have been shaped by the very different socio-economic and cultural conditions which were created by the coexistence of a variety of traditional and modern institutional arrangements in the colonial and post-colonial situations.

Adjustment policy in LDCs is not designed to maintain existing arrangements but to restructure them in fundamental ways, so interventions are driven by the need for change oriented to institutional and ideological transformation which creates continuous conflict over structures and values. This commonly produces opportunistic behaviour which can systematically undermine the reform process, and this is reinforced by poor levels of education and information which limit people's capacity to respond rationally to the requirements of modern structures. Here institutional change can never be managed with certainty because the contingent nature of individual behaviour makes it impossible to predict or control the long-term consequences of short-term decisions. The structural change created by black and informal markets in Uganda in response to state monopolies is one example of this effect.

This disproves crude evolutionary theories which assume an automatic and linear transition from underdevelopment to development. However, our evidence also suggests that progressive change is not random, but a response to a widespread willingness among people to set aside self-interest and demonstrate high levels of altruism where they can be made to recognise the need for and possibilities of collective solutions to problems of social breakdown through institutional reform. The amount of support which can be mobilised for new arrangements in these circumstances will depend on the extent to which they do increase the range of freedom among the various social forces in the society. Since all new arrangements allocate benefits unequally, progress will be resisted by groups which have benefited from past arrangements or are marginalised by new ones. While stability in all systems depends in some measure on force and ignorance, the main obstacle to change consists in the non-availability of more progressive alternatives.

Change in advanced societies occurs incrementally, but institutional transformations occur when more advanced systems developed in one society are transferred as theory to another. Until a new option emerges existing structures, however oppressive, are likely to survive for lack of alternatives. Once a more progressive alternative does emerge – as with capitalism in the seventeenth and eighteenth century – it will spread into new areas, but will offer very unequal advantages and impose very unequal costs on different groups in the indigenous society. To the extent that new structures really do offer greater options to a wider range of people, and that revolutionary activity has at least some chance of success, the human potential for altruism can generate an immense capacity for solidaristic action and self-sacrifice, and corresponding processes of progressive social change. Perhaps this explains the influence of liberal and socialist revolutions since the seventeenth century, and attempts by Africans in many countries to create free and democratic systems.

NOTE

I am grateful for assistance from the British ODA ESCOR programme which funded my research, and from the Institute of Development Studies, Sussex University for supporting the time required for writing.

13

THE WORLD BANK AND THE ANALYSIS OF THE INTERNATIONAL DEBT CRISIS

Beatriz Armendariz de Aghion and Francisco Ferreira

INTRODUCTION

Many Less Developed Countries (LDCs) were devastated by the debt crisis of the early 1980s. Economic growth rates declined sharply and the living standards of the poor in some countries did not improve for at least a decade.[1] Developed countries were also affected, as the stability of the international financial system itself was under threat in the early years of the crisis. Now that the crisis is nearly over – especially from the standpoint of most Latin American countries, where economic recovery has started – it seems appropriate to take stock of the experience, and learn its lessons for the future.

This chapter focuses on the role played by the World Bank in generating, absorbing, disseminating and applying ideas on two main areas: the macroeconomic management of developing countries in the run up to the crisis in the 1970s ('the origins'), and the proposals of mechanisms to address the problem of chronic indebtedness in the 1980s ('the solutions'). It is about the internal intellectual dynamics of an important international institution, as it struggled to respond to a serious crisis. Other chapters in this volume have stressed that the new institutional economics sees non-market institutions and organisations arising where they can efficiently correct market failures or, as Bates (Ch. 3, this volume) puts it, 'transcend social dilemmas'.

But institutions may also adapt sluggishly, and we illustrate the importance of changing ideas, views and perceptions of a problem within a large organisation – the World Bank – in shaping its overall policy response to that problem – in this case the international debt crisis of the 1980s. In assessing the intellectual contribution of the Bank and comparing the evolution of its views with those of outside analysts – mostly academics – we demonstrate, in a case study, that 'ideas and ideologies play a major role in choices', as North suggests (Ch. 2, this volume).

It is worth emphasising that, in focusing on the Bank's intellectual contributions, we deliberately leave outside our scope most of the more applied aspects of operational work with specific countries. Those are perhaps the Bank's principal concern, and our comments should therefore not be taken as

215

an overall assessment of the Bank's performance *vis-à-vis* the debt crisis, but as remarks specific to its intellectual and research activities. A further cautionary note regards the complementarity between the Bank and the IMF. It has generally been the case that, whereas the Bank specialises in internal – often project or sectoral – micro-economic work, the Fund concentrates on balance of payments difficulties and, by implication, on issues of macro-economic management. In the 1980s, therefore, division of labour between the two institutions might entail the Bank dedicating itself to internal problems of structural adjustment, while the Fund focused more firmly on the international aspects of managing the debt problem.

Nevertheless, as has been argued elsewhere (see Ferreira 1992; Stern and Ferreira forthcoming), structural adjustment and stabilisation are so closely related to the debt crisis, that an international institution of the size and importance of the World Bank can not afford to rely entirely on others to respond to events and ideas, or indeed to generate those ideas, on debt. There are two major tasks one might reasonably have expected the World Bank to fulfil in its role as the leading international development agency with respect to the LDC debt crisis. First, during the run up to the crisis in the 1970s, one would have expected the Bank to have monitored the LDCs' debt build-up and macro-economic policy as part of its role in country policy assessment. We will argue that more cautious advice on the magnitude of borrowing in the late 1970s and up to 1982 might have helped avoid – or at least alleviate the severity of – the belated adjustment process that followed in most LDCs.

The second task relates to the period since 1982, when the search for mechanisms to resolve the crisis became crucial to determine how and when growth, poverty alleviation and development in general might resume in a large number of LDCs. The evidence we will discuss suggests that the Bank was over-optimistic before 1982, sometimes disseminating assessments and advice which it would directly contradict later, with the benefit of hindsight. And it also seems that during the crisis, it was a slow follower in the debate on possible remedies.

The remainder of the chapter is divided into sections: the first discusses the origins of the crisis and the second looks at proposed solutions. In both these sections an attempt is made to compare and contrast the views expressed by academics with those of the Bank. In the final section, some conclusions are drawn.

ORIGINS

Historically we have come to mark the onset of the debt crisis in August 1982, when Mexico declared a moratorium on the servicing of its external obligations. This announcement was only the beginning of a decade of crisis, the causes of which are now well understood.[2] These fall into three categories: the oil shocks of the 1970s, the sudden changes in the world macro-economy in the early 1980s and inappropriate policies in borrowing countries, often in the context of an import-substitution development strategy.

The link between the oil shocks and the debt accumulation of the 1970s has demand and supply side explanations (in the international capital markets). On the supply side, the oil price rises in 1973 and 1979 created large current account surpluses in oil-producing countries (the so-called petrodollars) which were made available for financial intermediation through the industrialised countries' commercial banks. On the demand side, among others, were the low interest rates, and the consumption-smoothing behaviour by oil importing LDCs which had been adversely affected by the oil shocks.

The sudden changes in the international macro-economy in the early 1980s precipitated the crisis. On the one hand, there was the very rapid increase in the world real interest rates, due to tight monetary policies in the industrialised countries;[3] and on the other was the sharp fall in export revenues by LDCs due to the world recession.[4] These two effects combined had a drastic impact on the cost of servicing LDC debts, and on LDCs' ability to do so.

Finally, recent studies (see, notably, Berg and Sachs, 1988) have suggested that the crisis had (deeper) structural explanations. In particular, import-substitution development strategies followed by many LDCs considerably lessened their ability to service their (foreign currency denominated) debts, by reducing their flexibility to respond to balance of payments crises through a sufficiently rapid export expansion.

Academics

The large build-up of external debt in the 1970s did not appear to trouble most academic economists at the time. The consensus, according to Cohen (1993), reflected the view that foreign borrowing by LDCs to finance current account deficits was an equilibrium phenomenon, in the sense that such deficits would allow LDCs to augment productive capacity and repay their debts. It was not until the early 1980s that the predominance of this view came to be questioned.

The distinctive feature of international debt contracts is that they cannot be legally enforced, and in 1981 the *Review of Economic Studies* published a paper by Eaton and Gersovitz which highlights this point and pioneers what later came to be known as the 'willingness to pay' approach.[5] They present a theoretical model and an empirical analysis for the case of sovereign debt contracted abroad by poor countries. They argue that since such debt cannot be legally enforced, the default penalty from the country's standpoint is the impossibility of re-accessing the international capital markets.

For our purposes, this paper provides an example of early academic work that could have encouraged a more cautious attitude towards very high levels of borrowing, in the Bank or elsewhere, prior to the collapse of voluntary lending in 1982. Eaton and Gersovitz (1981: 291) note, in their Theorem 1, that: 'the probability of default in period t increases monotonically with debt service obligations $d(t)$ in period t'. Now, since:

$$d(t+1) = R b(t)$$

it would follow that very sharp increases in the effective interest rate (R), combined with an explosion of new lending ($b(t)$), such as was observed from 1979 to 1981, should cause the default risk to be increasing quite rapidly.[6] In their framework, this increase in risk leads to a tightening of credit constraints. This suggestion is in fact borne out by their empirical analysis, where 65 countries in a sample of 81 appeared to have – already in the mid-1970s – a limited access to the international capital market.

This is not to claim that Eaton and Gersovitz 'predicted' the debt crisis, as it came to pass. But we do think that it provides an interesting benchmark for comparison with the general tone and some specific statements emanating from the Bank around the same time – and later. They will be the subject of the next sub-section.

The Bank

Between 1974 and 1982, the Bank's view of LDC borrowing was influenced by the need of the global economy to respond to the large current account imbalances which originated with the vast terms of trade changes of the oil price rise of 1973/4, and were exacerbated by the second shock, in 1979: '*the world* faces the need to adjust – to payments imbalance and expensive energy – on a scale comparable to 1974–75' (*World Development Report* (*WDR*) 1980: 3, our emphasis).

The scale of the subsequent adjustment was, of course, to be much greater than that of 1974–5, but such optimism was partially based on the perception that the large payments imbalances of the late 1970s were something the world had to respond to globally. This was to take place through recycling funds from current account surplus countries to those in deficit. It would allow adjustment to proceed with relatively little reduction in absorption (as compared to the alternative without borrowing), and thus with a lower cost in terms of 'human development'.[7] It is thus that the *WDR* (1981: 54) states that: 'There is nothing inherently undesirable about external deficits, since deficits implied resource transfer. These effects ... provide a rationale for external borrowing to contribute to structural adjustment.' The *WDRs* of the day advocated a 'high growth' mode of adjustment; of central importance to this was the availability of external finance to allow a smoothing of import reduction over time and cushion its impact on both consumption and investment.

In his 1975 Presidential Address, McNamara regarded the need of middle-income countries for greater access to external capital as the 'most immediate and pressing problem in the global development scene' (McNamara 1981: 297). Two years later, he felt 'even more confident ... than we were a year ago that the debt problem is indeed manageable, and need not stand in the way of desirable rates of growth for the developing countries' (McNamara 1981: 456; see also Gazdar 1990).

The main factors conspiring to make many borrowers' positions unsustainable by 1982 were clearly identified by the *WDR* of 1981: the tightening of monetary conditions globally in 1979, the contemporaneous fall in the terms of trade for most LDCs, the world recession, the rising proportion of debt owed to commercial lenders, the rising proportion of loans contracted in variable interest rate (VIR) agreements, and the rise in commercial bank exposure to LDCs (measured in terms of outstanding loans to LDC customers as share of total portfolio) from 49.6 per cent in 1975 to 61.5 per cent in 1978. In light of the Bank's awareness of these phenomena, it is remarkable that they continued to make the optimistic predictions about the availability of voluntary capital flows in the 1980s which can be seen in Table 13.1. We believe that

Table 13.1 A comparison of World Bank predictions[a] and actual data for a number of variables in the 1980s

	Low case prediction	High case prediction	Actual figure
Average annual % growth of GDP per capita, 1980-90 in			
Industrial countries	2.3	3.1	2.5
All developing countries	2.2	3.3	1.2
Low-income countries	1.5	2.6	4.1 (1.3)[b]
Middle-income countries	2.2	3.4	0.5
Latin America and Caribbean	2.3	3.2	−0.5
Oil-exporting countries[c]	2.9	4.0	−2.5
Average annual % growth in exports for all LDCs, 1980-90	3.9	7.6	4.1
Official development assistance receipts (all LDCs) 1985[d]	35.5	40.9	25.6
Official development assistance receipts (all LDCs) 1990[d]	53.6	65.7	47.2
Direct private investment (all LDCs) 1985[d]	13.6	15.7	4.5
Aggregate net transfers (all LDCs) 1985[d,e]	36.3	54.3	−0.7
Aggregate net transfers (all LDCs) 1990[d,e]	56.7	96	−9.8[p]

Notes: [a] Both low case and high case predictions made in the *WDR* 1981
    [b] figure in brackets excludes China and India
    [c] excludes the former USSR
    [d] in US$ billions at current prices
    [e] defined, as in *World Debt Tables 1989/90*, as the difference between aggregate net flows and interest payments on all debt.
    [p] actual figure for 1988.
Sources: *World Development Report*, 1981, 1991, 1992.
    World Debt Tables (World Bank 1990)

the generally over-optimistic nature of their predictions about the performance of LDCs in the 1980s was strongly related to the assumption that voluntary capital flows would be sustained throughout the decade – in other words, to their failure to foresee, to any extent whatsoever, the coming debt crisis.

So, while the *WDR* of 1981 predicted middle-income oil-importers to grow by 5–6 per cent p.a. in the 1980s, their actual average growth between 1980 and 1989 was 2.9 per cent p.a. (*WDR* 1991). Latin America, which had been expected to grow from in the region of 2.3 per cent to 3.2 per cent, had by 1990 averaged negative 0.5 per cent p.a. since 1980. This is clearly not unrelated to the fact that whilst they had predicted net capital transfers to developing countries to have reached US$177.9 billion in 1990 (*WDR* 1980), the *World Debt Tables 1989/90* (World Bank 1990) registered a net capital *outflow* of US$9.8 billion from all developing countries in 1988 (see Table 13.1). Their unwillingness to read the signs that they themselves had just laid out, or at least to publicly acknowledge their implications, is made quite plain in the same *WDR* (1981: 61): 'While [the above] trends indicate that the developing countries will face more serious debt-management difficulties in the future, *they do not signal a generalised debt problem for the developing countries*' (our emphasis).

The importance of external finance to enable most of these countries to manage the high-growth mode of adjustment advocated in this *WDR* – and generally by the Bank at this stage – was obvious, so any vestige of doubt as regards its availability was quite uncomfortable:

> However, given the profitability of lending to developing countries, their exemplary records (with few exceptions) in meeting their obligations and their continuing need for foreign finance, it seems unlikely that financial intermediaries will discriminate against developing countries as a group.

Hence:

> Summing up these various influences on commercial banks, it seems highly probable that both borrowers and lenders will adapt to changing conditions without precipitating any general crisis of confidence.
>
> (*WDR* 1981: 61)

These quotes and predictions reveal an institution publicly unable or unwilling to foresee the impending collapse of voluntary lending, or any of its severe consequences to developing countries. In this chapter, we have not claimed that there was, anywhere outside the Bank, a crystal ball predicting the debt crisis either. We have presented some evidence, however, of academic work which should have been taken more seriously by the Bank.

SOLUTIONS
Academics

The debate among academics after 1982 turned to the best ways to remedy the crisis in the LDCs and to prevent the world financial system from collapsing. In the first three years (1982–5), the debate centred on whether LDCs were experiencing a liquidity or a solvency problem. A debtor country was defined as illiquid if the expected present discounted value of its trade surpluses in the short run was not high enough to service its external debt, but when such surpluses in the longer run were.

Advocates of the liquidity view argued that the crisis was a short-run phenomenon. In particular, Sachs (1984) suggested that the amount of money borrowed was decided by an LDC government so as to maximise the growth rate, with investment as the control variable. He admitted the possibility that some of the external borrowing did not materialise in higher capital accumulation, particularly because of political reasons, but he did not perceive that as a danger to the ability of LDCs to repay, albeit after some 'adjustment period'. The policy implications of this view were clear: countries should be granted greater access to external financing until they adjusted to the sudden changes in the international macro-economy.

Advocates of the solvency view, on the other hand, emphasised that, first, the debt accumulation of the 1970s came about as a result of LDCs wanting to maintain consumption levels, at the expense of investment, after a negative terms of trade shock and, second, the way consumption was being maintained in the short run was through an overvaluation of the real exchange rate (see, in particular, Dornbusch, 1985). Both the framework and the empirical evidence Dornbusch presented suggest the possibility that highly indebted countries were not going to repay their debts, at least not out of the returns on investment, because a large portion of the money borrowed had not been invested but consumed. Moreover, a large volume of such debt had taken the form of capital flight, as in Argentina and Venezuela.[8] Dornbusch's paper suggested that the whole financial strategy of the 1970s had been a failure and that ways should be found to share the costs, as had been the case in the aftermath of the defaults of the 1930s.[9]

This view seems to have been shared by Peter Kenen who, as early as 1983, suggested the creation of an 'International Debt Discount Corporation' which would buy the debt from the commercial banks at a 10 per cent discount. It would then be able, because of the discount from which it benefited on purchase, to lower the interest rate charged to debtors. He further envisaged it to extend loan maturities, in another concessional element.[10]

But those early proposals containing a debt-relief element, although important from a historical viewpoint, were not very influential at the time. The predominant view among academics in the first half of the 1980s appears to have had two distictive features: first, countries are illiquid and, second, countries may be unwilling to repay if they are not given the 'right incentives'; i.e. if creditors fail to implement an appropriate carrot-stick mix. Accordingly, the provision of increased access for LDCs to lending (or debt rescheduling) was perceived as the key to solving the crisis.

Sachs (1984) sees the relationship between a debtor country and its foreign creditors as a Repeated Prisoners' Dilemma. In particular, he argues that, as long as both parties value positively their future relationship, it is in their own interest to play cooperatively. Accordingly, we should expect creditors to be willing to extend new lending to a debtor experiencing financial distress. New lending, or more specifically, the re-lending of the due interest, principal, or both, was seen as the strategy that would prevent widespread defaults and keep the international financial system alive. The problem with such a strategy, however, is that there was a multiplicity of creditors involved, leading to a free-rider – or 'moral hazard in team' – problem. This could threaten the whole approach by severely reducing voluntary lending levels, as anticipated by Cline (1983), Sachs (1984) and Krugman (1985, 1988).

Sachs (1986) and Krugman (1988), on the other hand, were first to suggest that some LDCs had accumulated so much debt that creditors no longer expected it to be repaid in full. Hence the high discounts in the secondary market. At such high levels of debt, it was no longer possible for indebted LDCs to obtain voluntary lending. Therefore, existing creditors faced the following trade-off (see Krugman 1988): new lending (or rescheduling) could avert defaults, but would at the same time trigger disincentives to invest in adjustment, as LDCs at such high levels of indebtedness would be discouraged by the awareness that future benefits from investment (or economic adjustment) would accrue largely to their creditors. One way out of this dilemma, Krugman argued, was by forgiving portions of the debt instead. This trade-off is didactically captured in Figure 13.1 (see Krugman 1989).

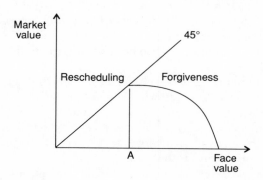

Figure 13.1 The debt relief Laffer curve

As we move from left to right on the Laffer curve in the above figure, we are first on the 45° line. The market value of the debt is then identical to its face value. As the face value of the debt continues growing, say, through rescheduling repayments, the disincentives to invest (or to undertake adjustment policies) come into play. Such disincentive effects will be reflected in the market value of the debt, which will rise less than proportionally as the face value increases. After a point (to the right of A) the market value of the debt will actually start declining. Creditors may then find it in their interest to forgive portions of their claims.

The above incentive argument, known as the debt overhang hypothesis, stands as the most widely accepted rationale for forgiveness. It gained official support from the US Treasury in March 1989, with the so-called Brady Plan, which called for debt write-downs in the case of heavily indebted middle-income countries. Its counterpart for low-income countries is the Toronto Agreement.[11]

In practice, the adoption of the Brady Plan by the US, and its subsequent acceptance by most other creditor governments, meant that debt reduction became a feasible option, albeit generally in fairly restricted conditions. Due to the large discounts in the secondary market, some LDCs began to engage in a number of transactions involving debt retirement. The simplest of all was straightforward buy-backs. However, because debtors were generally officially banned from undertaking buy-backs,[12] more sophisticated ways of taking advantage of low market prices for debt were found. Among the most common types of market transactions were the debt for equity swaps, debt securitisation, and debt for nature swaps. Because debt retirement triggers positive incentive effects, these market transactions are generally viewed as a mutually beneficial way out of the crisis. In reality, such transactions have not been substantial.[13]

The Bank's approaches to solving the crisis

Having traced the principal ideas in the debate on solutions to the debt crisis since 1982, we now attempt to place the Bank's views and contributions into that context. At the onset of the crisis, the Bank, now under Clausen and Krueger,[14] took a very cautious line, changing the focus from macro-economic concerns with the availability of foreign finance, so prominent under McNamara and Chenery, to micro-economic advice on 'getting prices right'. External causes were de-emphasised, and blame for the crisis was laid predominantly on domestic policy errors, notably the use of borrowed funds for consumption or inadequate investment purposes, due to distorted prices. In 1986, an Operations Evaluation Department report stated that: 'The flexibility provided by access to foreign borrowing will have been lost because of past policy errors' (World Bank 1986).

The Bank adhered closely to the view, espoused publicly by the governments of its major shareholders, that a 'solution' to the crisis must be based on a 'restoration of creditworthiness', and that the way for countries to achieve this was to maintain debt service up to date and avoid the need for rescheduling loans as long as possible. These objectives could best be secured through prompt efforts at internal adjustment aimed at switching production toward tradables, through the familiar combination of expenditure-reduction and expenditure-switching policies:

> Despite the many problems they have had recently, developing countries need a continuing flow of bank lending to regain their growth momentum. For this to happen, however, developing countries must restore their creditworthiness – and that depends on their own policies and on the strength and stability of world economic growth.
>
> *(WDR* 1985: 124)

The role envisaged for the international financial system was merely to provide some rescheduling when there were no other alternatives. In other words, the Bank adhered firmly to the liquidity view of the debt problem, and gave little serious consideration to the more radical early proposals mentioned above, such as that by Kenen.

The liquidity view was the prevalent one at the 'International Debt and the Developing Countries' conference, held by the Economics Research Staff of the Bank in April 1984.[15] The papers presented there were compiled in a volume edited by Cuddington and Smith (1985), and included contributions by Cooper and Sachs, Gersovitz, Krugman, Simonsen, Dornbusch and Harberger.

Generally, they emphasised two shortcomings of the current strategy. It was felt that the 'public good' nature of involuntary sovereign lending by a private bank and the ensuing free-rider problem provided scope for greater coordination of the process by the IMF, the Bank and even creditor governments. As already suggested, the lead here had clearly been taken by the academics, as in Cline (1983) and Sachs (1984). Second, short-term reschedulings (generally of one year) which were then the rule, were seen as collectively inefficient, even if a single lender had an incentive to keep a problem debtor on a 'short leash'.

Thus, whilst there were indeed suggestions that some due interest should be capitalised, and the loan maturities extended (Simonsen), as well as that banks ought perhaps to charge interest rates below market rates on some of their loans (Krugman) – justifying the organisers' claim that debt relief was suggested – this was on a very modest scale. This was in contrast to the more radical proposals mentioned earlier, as well as to the tone of the academic debate a few years down the road, and to the views expressed in the Bank's own subsequent conference in 1989. In short, the 1984 Conference brought the current state of the academic debate to the Bank. Most of the participants were key academics, and their conclusions were broadly in line with the predominance of the liquidity view in the debate which had been taking place outside the Bank for at least two years.

In terms of policy implementation, there was some response to the concerns expressed most vocally at the 1984 conference, notably with the short-term nature of rescheduling and the need for greater coordination of involuntary lending, to combat the free-rider problem. The Baker Strategy, proposed by the then US Treasury Secretary in March 1985, was intended to address exactly these issues. Longer periods for rescheduling became more common, starting with a $49 billion multi-year package for Mexico. In light of the prominence of these ideas in the public debate for some time, however, it would clearly be incautious to claim that the driving force behind the Baker Strategy was the aforementioned conference.

But if the Bank's official positions were not radical or innovative in the 1982–5 period, from 1986 to 1988 they appeared to lag further behind the rapidly evolving debate. In a paper written before joining the Bank, Fischer (1989) emphasises the severe decline in income per capita in the Baker fifteen heavily indebted countries, the massive resource transfers from these countries and the resulting collapse in their domestic investment rates. The focus had changed substantially from the liquidity view, towards a concern with the seriousness of the effects of the crisis on the debtor countries, and the proposed solutions reflect that change. In this, as well as in most other papers devoted to possible solutions to the crisis in Sachs (1989), the possible desirability of debt relief and a variety of mechanisms through which to achieve it efficiently are discussed. There is no contention over Sachs's claim that 'partial debt relief can therefore be Pareto improving (i.e. to the benefit of both creditors and debtors)' (1989: 28). Yet, years after the debt overhang hypothesis had been proposed, the role of the Bank continued to be that of a supporter of the Baker Strategy, with its response to the concerns so widely voiced in 1984/5 still based on concerted lending and loan rescheduling.

An indictment of this role appears in the paper by Diwan and Husain (1989)[16] which introduces their volume on *Dealing with the Debt Crisis*, a report on the Bank's 1989 Conference on Debt. There they acknowledge, in so many words, that the strategy was unsuccessful, that it had modest targets for new money ($13 billion annually), that even those targets were never achieved (net annual flow was only about $4 billion), that 'the official sector had only moral suasion to ensure that the private sector met the plan's targets' and, fundamentally, that: 'controversies, even of a few billion dollars, miss the point: the transfer of resources from the highly indebted countries to the industrial countries for external debt was more than $100 billion during 1986–88' (1989: 4).

An admission of the reasons behind the Bank's behaviour was given by the Chief Economist in 1989:

the record shows that frank and open debate does not take place in official and banking circles. It was clear to the participants in this conference at the beginning of 1989, as it had been clear to many much earlier, that growth in the debtor countries would not return without debt relief. But the official agencies operate on the basis of an agreed upon strategy, and none of them could openly confront the existing strategy without having an alternative to put in place. And to propose such an alternative would have required agreement among the major shareholders of these institutions. So long as the United States was not willing to move, the IFIs were not free to speak...

(Fischer, in Diwan and Husain 1989: v)[17]

In 1988, a willingness to contemplate some debt reduction began to manifest itself among those 'major shareholders'. K. Miyazawa, then Japan's finance minister, used the IMF–World Bank meetings in Berlin that year to propose officially sponsored debt reduction schemes. Mitterrand of France followed suit later that year, in Toronto, where official creditors agreed on a set of guidelines for concessional relief for low-income severely indebted countries, thereafter known as the Toronto terms. The *WDR* of 1988, the first entirely under Fischer as Chief Economist, marks the Bank's official jump from the Baker bandwagon, by including suggestions that some debt relief, and 'reduction of the debt overhang' could be important elements to facilitate the transition from adjustment to growth.[18] It was just in time to claim marginal precedence to the change in the US official position, which came with the Brady Plan in 1989, aimed at middle-income severely indebted countries, but considerably later than Dornbusch (1985) and Sachs (1986), which we suggested marked the rise of the solvency view and the debt overhang argument.

From then on, there appears to have been an increase in the liveliness of the debate on debt in the Bank, as well as in its sponsorship of research on the topic. The Debt and International Finance Department issued papers quite frequently, often focusing on issues connected with voluntary, market-based debt reduction schemes and the related incentive problems (e.g. Claessens 1988).

To this improvement in the Bank's record as a follower of the theoretical debate since 1988, it must be added that one sphere of intellectual activity where the Bank had long been making a significant contribution to the study of LDC debt was the publication of comprehensive data on the direction, magnitude and effects of the debt flows. This was mostly through the *World Debt Tables* which, complemented by the World Development Indicators, provided the basis for much academic and policy work on the subject. Within the framework of the Brady Initiative, furthermore, the Bank's role in helping countries to design and negotiate the menus for debt reduction with their creditors provided new scope for application of the ideas being researched and debated throughout the profession. By the end of 1990, Brady deals had been concluded with Costa Rica, Mexico and the Philippines, and other countries were negotiating their own packages. The Mexican example, besides being the earliest, is also probably the most studied (see van Wijnbergen 1991; Armendariz de Aghion and Armendariz de Hinestrosa 1994).

CONCLUSIONS

As Fischer's quote (pp. 225–6) suggests, a comparative review of the academic writings on LDC debt and of the evolution of opinion at the Bank in the 1980s must lead us to conclude that this was not an area of strong intellectual performance by the World Bank. There are, as we indicated in the introduction, a number of alleviating circumstances, notably the justifiable perception that this subject fell more naturally within the realm of responsibility of the IMF, and the political pressures and constraints that clearly hampered free enquiry and debate into some aspects of the problem in official circles. Nevertheless, given the wealth of advice and predictions which the *WDRs*, among other vehicles for dissemination of Bank thinking, published on managing the current account deficits, and later the debt itself, it is clear that the issue was understood to be important.

There are three main conclusions which can be drawn from the evidence discussed above. First, it appears to us that the Bank's attitude towards the rapid growth in the level of the external obligations of many developing countries in the late 1970s was misguided. Their view that deficits implied resource transfers, whilst definitionally correct, could very well be taken as an endorsement of the high borrowing strategy which led so many countries to be viewed as financial pariahs in the 1980s. Second, from 1982 to their Conference on Debt in 1984 and the advent of the Baker Strategy in March 1985, the Bank was unoriginal in terms of proposing solutions to what had by then become the greatest immediate obstruction to a resumption of growth and development in a large number of countries. It shared the concerns of most of the profession with insufficient levels of lending due to free riding in a multi-lender framework.

Finally, from 1985 to around 1988, there was a further worsening of the Bank's record as a follower of the debate. This was a time when the balance of academic opinion was changing towards recognising the necessity of some debt relief, or forgiveness. This was heavily influenced by Dornbusch's (1985) suggestion that the crisis did, in a sense, reflect a solvency problem, and even more so by Sachs (1986), which contained an early discussion of the debt overhang hypothesis. That was a time of growing recognition that the early proposals to create institutional mechanisms aimed to reduce the present value of LDC external obligations might at least have been pointing in the right direction. Not so at the Bank, however. As we have seen, very senior officers at the Bank were quite prepared to recognise, at the 1989 Conference, that the institution had been confined to the role of supporting the Baker Strategy at a time when it was becoming abundantly clear to the informed public that debt reduction was an urgent necessity.

This urgency was only recognised at the Bank from 1988/89, following Japanese, French and finally American policy changes which culminated in the Brady Plan. From 1989 onwards, as we briefly suggested above, the Bank was free to follow the academic debate more closely, and to contribute to it through what it does best: applied country work, this time mostly advising countries in the design and negotiation of their debt reduction menus with commercial creditors.

On the whole, however, it is not possible to claim that the Bank displayed intellectual leadership on issues relating to the debt crisis of the 1980s. As Fischer admits from the Bank:

> academic research, writing and opinion have been far more influential on the debt issue than the academics may believe, or than officials like to pretend, for the academics are unencumbered by the official need to support the official strategy. It was academics who were first to point out that the stabilization focus of the programs imposed on debtors to deal with the debt crisis from 1982 to 1985, while necessary, was not sufficient for growth.
>
> (Fischer, in Diwan and Husain 1989)

NOTES

1 Average GDP per capita growth in LDCs fell from 2.7 per cent in 1970–80 to 1.2 per cent in 1980–90. In the fifteen most heavily indebted countries the 1980s actually saw a 0.4 per cent fall in GDP per capita (from data in the *World Development Reports* 1981 and 1992). The percentage of the population living below the poverty line in, for example, Mexico, was 17 per cent higher in 1984 than in 1970 (see Cardoso and Helwege, 1992).
2 See for example, Cuddington and Smith (1985), Dornbusch and Fischer (1987) and Sachs (1989) for detailed expositions of the origins of the crisis.
3 The real US prime rate rose from – 0.6 per cent in 1977 to 12.8 per cent in 1981 (Dornbusch and Fischer 1987).
4 A weighted index of non-oil commodity prices fell from 121 in 1977 to 81 in 1982 (1980 = 100) (see Dornbusch and Fischer 1987).
5 A first version of the paper was received by the RES in April 1978 (see also Eaton *et al.* 1986).
6 Eaton and Gersovitz (1981) have one period maturities; $b(t)$ denotes new lending and $d(t)$ denotes repayment obligations at period t.
7 Human development, broadly understood to mean poverty reduction and an improvement in the social indicators and living standards of all – but principally the poorest – segments of developing country populations, was then, and had been since McNamara's Nairobi speech in 1973, the paramount articulated policy objective of the Bank.
8 On evidence of capital flight from Latin America in the 1980s, see also Pastor (1990).
9 Dornbusch often emphasised that in the aftermath of the defaults of the 1930s the creditors had negotiated substantial write downs in the face value of their claims

with the LDCs. For more on historical experiences of debt settlements, see Eichengreen and Portes (1989).

10 Kenen was not the only person to have anticipated in the early 1980s the direction of the debate among academics. Felix Rohatyn proposed to the US Senate that LDC debt could be stretched out to longer maturities (15 to 30 years) and interest reduced to something like 6 per cent. Norman Bailey, of the US National Security Council suggested that the debt be swapped for a form of equity asset that would entitle the holder to a fraction of the country's export earnings (see Cline 1983, for a more complete survey of these early proposals).

11 The terms of the Toronto Agreement apply to official debt (Paris Club debt), owed by low-income, predominantly African, countries. See p. 226 for more on Toronto.

12 The reasons are twofold. First because they reward the least reliable, and second because of moral hazard reasons, i.e. countries will be encouraged to default in order to lower the price of their debt to then undertake the buy-back (see Krugman 1988).

13 One exception is Chile, where the debt-for-equity swaps have been substantial (see Armendariz de Aghion 1991).

14 As President and Vice-President for the Economics Research Staff, respectively.

15 We find this to be the case despite the fact that Dornbusch, an early advocate of the solvency view as discussed above, was present at the Conference (see Dornbusch 1985).

16 Both were economists at the Debt and International Finance Division of the International Economics Department of the World Bank.

17 It is quite likely that the reasons for the Bank's lack of enthusiasm for debt forgiveness are not entirely political. It has been privately suggested by a senior Bank official that, as an intermediary that raises finance from the market, and whose ability to do so is affected by its credit rating, the Bank was naturally hesitant to propose policies which, if applied to its own loans to developing countries, might lead to asset write-offs.

18 The *World Debt Tables 1987–88* (World Bank 1988) contained some consideration of the need for partial forgiveness, but still pledged official allegiance to the rationale of the Baker Strategy. We are grateful to Ishrat Husain for bringing this to our attention.

Part IV

NIE: INSTITUTIONS, ORGANISATIONS AND THE STATE

14

THE POLITICS OF MONEY IN MID-NINETEENTH-CENTURY ARGENTINA[1]

Jeremy Adelman

INTRODUCTION

Between 1852 and 1865, Argentina's monetary affairs changed dramatically. An anarchic montary regime gave way to centralised and highly concentrated powers over the regulation of money. From a fragmented and unstable system was created a fiduciary regime willing and able to defend private property rights in an emerging commercial order. This transition, however, implied a broader transformation in the composition of state powers. In the case of Argentina in the nineteenth century, conflicts over monetary regulation quickly escalated into civil war between competing notions of sovereignty and political power bases of rival rulers. Control over money was first and foremost a political proposition. This was only too evident to nineteenth-century statesmen.

Little is known of the monetary aspects of statebuilding in Argentina (but see Burgin 1946; Halperín Donghi 1982; Scobie 1954; Cortés Conde 1989). By the 1840s, a growing number of businessmen and political economists clamoured for monetary stability and a new spirit of economic policy. Their opportunity came with the defeat of the Buenos Aires *caudillo* Juan Manuel de Rosas in early 1852. As the process of institution-making intensified in Argentina after 1852, money politics was central to the creation of the state.

Focusing on these 'formative' years raises a host of problems presented by public-choice theorists. According to this view, states exist to defend and uphold property rights. This they do by lowering the costs of obtaining information and settling accounts – in a word, easing the costs of making contracts, otherwise known as transaction costs.[2] For the moment I am not concerned with this formulation of state theory as a set of ground rules by which individual actors bargain rationally. But this chapter raises questions about how the rules themselves become encoded. The crisis of the Argentine political economy in the mid-nineteenth century exposed the rules of transacting to perpetual contestation, threat, and hence insecurity. No single agent or party of agents wielded sufficient strength to impose their juridical will. In sum, contestation meant that the rules governing entitlements and duties of property rights cannot be treated as a departure point of economic behaviour. The purpose of drawing attention to this 'formative' period is precisely to explore the manner in which property rights and relations became encoded through a struggle over political power – a process glossed over by public choice theorists.

The concern here with money allows historians to explore the role of policies governing a public good – the open use of money as a medium of exchange and store of value – over which the state may or may not exercise a monopoly.[3] Monopoly power over the issue of legal tender is one clear example of the way in which states shape property rights. Rampant emissions can lead to inflation and thereby imperil stable contracts and enhance the position of debtors; likewise tight money, by increasing borrowing costs, shifts bargaining power in favour of creditors. Yet, no-one could live without money. Argentina is a good example of this dilemma since public authorities had a grip over monetary powers. The problem was, no-one had a firm grip over public authority – at least until the 1860s.

Resolving these monetary issues were the institutional problems which occupy the core of this chapter. While it was not the term they used, political economists and a clutch of statesmen argued that stable money alleviated transaction costs and allocated property rights in favour of creditors. After decades of turmoil, the construction of a fiduciary base in turn required creating mechanisms to monopolise and regulate the issue of legal tender. The power of money was both a magnet for competing claims to control state resources, and at the same time a vehicle for allocating proprietary rights within civil society.

CONSTITUTIONS AND MONEY: 1852–9

A provincial alliance led by General Urquiza and backed by Brazil toppled the Buenos Aires strongman General Rosas, but it inherited a monetary mess. Unstable inconvertible paper was accepted as a medium of exchange throughout Buenos Aires, somewhat in the Littoral region, and even as far as the Andes. In the words of an agent dispatched by Buenos Aires's London financiers,

> this wretched currency is in every respect injurious to the community being based upon no tangible security and having only a fictitious and conventional value; the fluctuations are enormous and trade is thus to a considerable extent reduced to the level of a mere speculation.[4]

Faced with this state of affairs, merchants conducted their business in alternative forms of exchange. The most common was the *letra de cambio* (bill of exchange or lading) which through redrafts and multiple endorsements circulated in limited fashion through commercial sinews as an alternative instrument to settle accounts. Limited to inter-mercantile transactions, the bill of exchange shared only some features of a circulating medium.

If merchants greeted the fall of Rosas with optimism, hoping that the vexing problem of Argentine unity and constitutional order could now be solved, their hopes were dashed.[5] Rosas's fall unleashed a decade of conflict within and between the provinces. Each side used money, or their own notes as a weapon to wage war, as a cudgel to force rivals into submission. To the extent that each side sought to vanquish the other, they also brought their own economies to near-ruin through rampant emissions. By 1859, the spectre of catastrophe forced them to reconsider the grounds of their feuds.

Political conflict took the guise of constitutional discord. These squabbles had monetary underpinnings. Constitutional wranglers faced the following Gordian knot: as long as Buenos Aires enjoyed some measure of sovereignty over issuing fiduciary rights, jurisdictional transfers from Buenos Aires to the incipient National Government implied forfeiting control over the power to back local currency. Buenos Aires, wanting no part of any curb on its autonomy, unilaterally left the Confederation, and for the next decade managed an independent existence. The Confederation's capital moved to Paraná in the province of Entre Ríos, where provinces of the Interior and Littoral struggled on their own to cobble together the legal foundations of statehood (see Gorostegui de Torres 1972: Ch. 4, Scobie 1964).

Any early signs of cooperation between Buenos Aires and the Confederation soon withered. Secessionist battles in the countryside forced the Buenos Aires provincial government to print 87 million pesos between July 1852 and June 1853 — increasing the supply of pesos by 50 per cent in less than a year. To this were added another 8–10 million pesos in 'gratuities' to victorious officers.[6] The interim Provincial Finance Minister José Benjamín Gorostiaga, named by Urquiza, strove to shore up the peso, first by removing controls on specie flows (specie exports had been banned in 1837), and then gathered the city's most prominent merchants for their advice and help.[7] He admitted that the Province's unfunded debt surpassed 73 million pesos (33 million left from Rosas's last battles, and another 40 million from this administration). But merchants recoiled from extending even the most usurious loan. As an emergency measure and in an effort to undermine Gorostiaga's credibility, Casa de Moneda authorities, following orders of localist leaders, set aside 10 million pesos to the credit of a sinking fund to cover current expenditures. To the Minister, struggling to restore the confidence of merchants, this came as a slap in the face: he resigned. Shortly thereafter, *porteños* flocked behind the 11 September 1852 Revolution. With the provinces now in full civil war, Casa emissions intensified and the peso plummeted.[8]

Buenos Aires fared better than its neighbours. But it did not succeed in establishing solid monetary foundations on its own. Part of the Buenos Aires problem was inherited; and part was created out of policy decisions. The first challenge was redrafting the powers of the Provincial Bank to loosen its ties to 'political' authorities, provide it with a greater measure of autonomy, and ascribe it means for latitude in open market operations and rediscounting: to make it less an instrument of deficit financing and more a tool for maintaining monetary stability. After some debate over the new charter, the renamed Banco de la Provincia y Casa de Moneda opened its doors on 1 January 1855. Assuming responsibility for old Bank notes (between 204 and 212 million pesos in circulation), the new bank was supposed to receive deposits, make easier commercial loans and, most importantly, issue discounts at the discretion of the Directors. By executive order, the Bank was also required to honour diligently all bills of exchange which it had discounted, thereby reversing arbitrary payments on bills depending on the Bank's accounts.[9] In the first four years of its existence, the new Bank desisted from any emissions and appeared to be well on track to stabilising the peso.[10]

Several factors undermined Buenos Aires's unilateral efforts at monetary stability. First, the Bank succeeded only in raising 4,112 in metal pesos and 5.3 million in inconvertible paper. One observer wrote years later that this amount of capital 'could never serve as base of an organisation capable of restoring notes to their old value' (Pedro Agote (1881) cited in Prebisch 1921: 291; see also Lamas 1886). The tight capital shortage was evident to the Directors. One Director appealed to the Ministry to allow greater incentives to depositors. But increasing interest rates and lowering charges on accounts to augment savings did not offset persistent lack of confidence.[11] There was also concern about speculation and liberal credit. The Finance Minister exerted constant pressure on Bank Directors to keep interest rates over 10 per cent, fearing that 'speculators' were responsible for the peso's tremors. In mid-1855, he reminded Bank President Jaime Llavallol that rates must remain high, and that the Bank should call in all dubious rediscounted notes from agents involved in 'demoralizing and prejudicial traffic; and to whom we must deny all the credit they have thus far enjoyed, thus ending all types of transactions with them'.[12] The conundrum of raising Bank capital through the open market, maintaining a tight reign on dubious notes, while at the same time offering credit to merchants in a bid to raise the institution's profile, stemmed from a common source: merchants were expected to be both patrons and clients. Under the circumstances, merchants declined to sponsor the government's bid to create a sounder monetary authority, even if it meant merchants would have to endure more years of fiduciary turbulence.

Any collaboration between merchants and officials had to wait for the government to address the disorder in its own house. In February 1855, Norberto de la Riestra took over the Provincial Finance Ministry. He brought extensive experience as a commercial agent in London and Buenos Aires, and enjoyed contacts among merchants which other officials simply lacked. For the first time, this Ministry was in the hands of a businessman. More than any other individual, Riestra shaped the basis for monetary and fiscal stability in Argentina.

First, he sought to replace short-term deficit financing with longer-term public credit — reversing Rosas's own preference to issue money over public credit. Doing so helped alleviate the pressure on the Bank to print pesos. In September 1856, the Provincial legislature approved a law creating a sinking fund of 10 million pesos bearing 6 per cent interest, which would assign 100,000 pesos yearly to amortise existing debt, and into which the government could dip to cover current expenses. The same law ordered the Bank to issue bonds on the open market for sale at not less than 75 per cent of their face value.[13] According to one observer, 'even private persons came forward offering to take it at a more favourable rate than that proposed to the Bank, shewing the facility with which the government can raise means whenever their own requirements oblige them'.[14] Bit by bit, the government turned to this new fund to take the pressure off Bank emissions. Two years later, the government created another 12 million pesos in public funds for the same purposes. By all accounts this modest initial effort succeeded, and set the stage for a much more dramatic programme of debt reconsolidation and amortisation after reunification.

The second prong of Riestra's strategy aimed at the peso's volatility in relation to gold. Many, including Riestra himself, were impatient to impose some discipline on the unruly peso by making it convertible to specie. Riestra wrote a grim but revealing report to the Directors of the new Bank, urging the Bank to limit emissions to metal coins so that 'they may circulate and be received without depreciation outside the country'. In July 1857, the Legislature endorsed several foreign currencies as legal tender. But convertibility was a long-term goal. Riestra must have known that such immediate efforts were futile, for the rest of the earlier report was a long disquisition on why convertibility was impossible at the moment. The underlying problem, according to the Minister, was chronic trade imbalances which drained Buenos Aires (and perforce its neighbours) of precious metals. Without stable reserves, civilians fled from paper whenever the peso's security was questioned. Getting reserves required positive trade balances.[15] Riestra made the accumulation of reserves a cornerstone of financial policy. While his policies took time to bite, they signify an important change in priorities — neither Rivadavians in the 1820s nor the *rosistas* paid much attention to bank reserves, and preferred to leave the peso exposed to civilian flight.

If immediate convertibility was a dead letter, the diagnosis was right, and herein lay the main obstacle to monetary stability. Under normal circumstances, Buenos Aires realised trade deficits with the rest of the world while enjoying surpluses with other provinces, while some interior provinces enjoyed trade surpluses with the healthier Chilean and Bolivian economies, earning them valuable specie which was then used to pay for manufactured imports shipped from Buenos Aires. Buenos Aires trade deficits with foreign trading partners could only be offset by surpluses with neighbouring provinces — a precarious balance in the context of civil war. With Buenos Aires finances still wobbly, in July 1856 the Confederation imposed strict differential tariffs on trans-shipped cargo through Buenos Aires to redirect traffic to Confederation ports such as Rosario (Scobie 1964: 159–64; *El Nacional* 8 January 1857).

To this was added the international crisis of 1857 and a slump in exports (see Amaral and Adelman, forthcoming). These shocks simply complicated the underlying problem facing *porteño* authorities. Without a constitutional arena in which to settle inter-regional accounts and funnel money to Buenos Aires, efforts to stabilise financial reserves always faced the threat of non-cooperation by other provinces, and just as often, outright war. As a result, chronic constitutional turmoil stood squarely in the way of sound money and hence a regime of stable fiduciary rights.

CONFEDERATION FINANCE: 1852–9

As for the Confederation, policy-makers struggled to create parallel institutions to Buenos Aires's Bank and private market for funds. Their efforts failed for the same reasons that Buenos Aires's institutions remained suspended in a tense equilibrium: Confederation exports simply could not match imports, and the bulk of customs receipts were siphoned off by Buenos Aires. This ultimately drove the Confederation to re-ignite the war with the port in 1859.

Urquiza, without a Bank (and hence unable to print his way through the wars with Buenos Aires), and without an indigenous capital market (from which to borrow), turned to the Spanish merchant José de Buschenthal who was fast becoming the Confederation's informal agent. Buschenthal raised 225,000 silver pesos in Montevideo, charging 16 per cent (Scobie 1954: 61). Meanwhile, the Confederation's first Finance Minister, Mariano Fragueiro, presented a financial blueprint for the regime to establish its own monetary authority and slash public sector borrowing.[16] On the day of the statute's promulgation, Fragueiro also sent a circular to the Provinces advising them of the new Confederate peso (worth 20 Buenos Aires pesos — the initial issue being worth some 6 million silver pesos). These moves aimed to staunch the drainage of money from the region to Buenos Aires, and to start re-importing silver.

By decree, in February 1854 the National Bank of Rosario opened its doors and in March the new offices of the General Administration of Finance and Credit began operations. The Bank was supposed to act as the national Treasury, receive deposits, offer credit, and monopolise the handling of legal tender. But without stipulations on reserve levels, guidelines on the exact convertibility of notes, nor a nascent capital market in which to introduce securities it is hard to imagine how the statute might work. To make matters worse, bonds were to be denominated in national pesos, obligatory legal tender in all transactions. The first essay was a complete disaster: Chilean gold, Bolivian silver, old Spanish doubloons, and even *porteño* paper were preferable to Confederation scrip; the Rosario bank never got off the ground. The 1.7 million pesos in notes were withdrawn from circulation, and Fragueiro himself resigned from the Cabinet in September 1855 (Quintero Ramos 1965: 38–9).

By the end of that year, the Confederation was demonetising at an alarming rate.

Confederation statesmen turned to foreign financiers. Buschenthal lined up meetings with the French financial group Trouvé-Chauvel & Dubois in April 1855, to finance public works and lend the government money for current expenditures. After a brief *tripotage* the French lost interest. In 1855 Juan Bautista Alberdi left for Europe to help raise funds directly, to little avail.[17] In May 1856, the Spaniard Esteban Rams y Rubert floated government bonds valued at 300,000 silver pesos (which raised 250,000 Bolivian pesos). At the end of 1857, Brazilian Baron Mauá set up a branch of his bank in Rosario, which closed two years later. Wanting to help cripple their rivals in Buenos Aires, even the Brazilian government lent 300,000 silver pesos to Paraná (Scobie 1954: 61; Gorostegui de Torres 1972: 54–5).

As the Confederation stumbled, it attacked the source of its problem: a chronic trade deficit with Buenos Aires. Indeed, only the provinces bordering on Chile and Bolivia could boast stable accounts due to trade with their neighbours; the rest faced imbalances until the 1856 Differential Duty Act designed to promote direct trade to the port of Rosario. This Act slapped extra charges on goods shipped via Buenos Aires and Montevideo in an effort to redirect ships which conventionally stopped off at the larger ports to load and unload, thereby allowing Buenos Aires to exact its levies at the expense of the Confederation. This move increased the level of uncertainty and opposition more than it did revenues, provoking a wave of complaints among merchants.[18]

Financial collapse loomed. Hit with the international downturn in 1857, the Confederation was in full economic crisis by 1858–9. Foreign merchants in Rosario who had been accepting government bills began jostling with each other over claims for redemption from the customs house.[19] As relations with Buenos Aires deteriorated, even the Confederation invasion of the city had to be postponed to raise money. Finally, Confederation forces met the Buenos Aires army and cavalry at the battle of Cepeda on 23 October 1859. Urquiza soundly beat Mitre in the field, but Buenos Aires had won the economic war. The armistice agreement of 11 November was the first step to national reintegration, and its terms set the stage for drastic centralisation of economic regulation.

FAILED CONVERGENCE: 1859–61

From the ruins of 1859, Buenos Aires and the Confederation converged – out of necessity more than out of conviction. Since neither side held the other in high regard, any talk of reconciliation was treated with a fair measure of suspicion and not a bit of duplicity. This was especially evident in talks over monetary controls, for here state-builders reopened the debate over political sovereignty. Who would control money, the national government, or Buenos

Aires and the *porteño* merchant class? The dispute, in the end, led to war again, in 1861, by which time, the Confederation was a shadow of its former self.

In the months leading to Cepeda, both Buenos Aires and the Confederation resorted to measures which would burden the political apparatus emerging from the armistice. The Confederation leased the rights on Santa Fe customs houses for two years in return for a special monthly credit of 12,000 silver pesos; Buenos Aires opened another fund created out of a 10 per cent surcharge on imports, and in mid-July 1859, returned to monetary emissions (by October, the Bank had printed 60 million pesos).[20] Across the country real money was becoming scarce as civilians fled from worthless paper and scrambled to hoard metal. Llavallol warned Riestra that 'a million and a half [metal] pesos is very exiguous in proportion to the amount of paper in circulation, as the daily supply rises in our market'.[21] The problem was, any enforcement of the Armistice necessarily involved dealing with an even greater mess.

The Pacto de Unión of 11 November provided the terms for economic stabilisation. There were two essential components to the deal. First, Buenos Aires was to elect a slate of delegates for an *ad hoc* Constitutional Convention to amend the 1853 magna carta to the liking of *porteños* (they were finally chosen in August 1860, but were in the end refused admission to the Convention – providing the pretext for a return to war in 1861). Second, a financial deal allowed Buenos Aires to retain control over customs while 'nationalisation' talks took place, but since the national regime was bereft of funds, the province agreed to subsidise the national Treasury at a rate of 1.5 million pesos per month.

Meanwhile, national economic public institutions cried out for reform. The new President Derqui offered the Finance Ministry to Norberto de la Riestra who began sorting out the Confederation's obligations, settling accounts with Buschenthal and reclaiming authority over the nation's customhouses. Re-monetising the economy proved more difficult. Using an expedient tried in Buenos Aires years earlier, Riestra declared foreign currency legal tender to try to stymie fluctuations among metal and paper notes. He then negotiated an arrangement to declare the Buenos Aires paper peso legal tender, with the idea that the Provincial Bank would open branches across the Confederation.[22] Eventually, the Bank would become a national institution, and no longer a Buenos Aires provincial preserve. This is important since it would have implied the creation of the first semblance of national monetary authority – which, if approved would have enhanced the sovereign powers of the national government. In the end, however, opposition in both the national and Buenos Aires legislatures scuppered Riestra's plans.[23] The Minister resigned from the National Government in January 1861.

Riestra was caught in a cul-de-sac: the Confederation had to make some overtures to Buenos Aires to assure currency stability, and approval of the customs law. Both of these would save Riestra from having to turn to Buenos Aires every time the Confederation needed money.[24] At the same time, without these legal victories, the national monetary base remained delicate at best. The slightest political tremor provoked a flight back to metal and liquidity shortages. As the provinces de-monetised, Confederation politicians blamed Buenos Aires for all their troubles.

If weak national finances, constitutional wrangling over the status of revenue machinery, and the inability to restore fiscal balance provided the context, war was the proximate cause for monetary instability. Tensions mounted between Paraná and Buenos Aires. With Buenos Aires' Treasury unable to balance the books, in September 1861 and in January 1862 the Provincial Bank allocated 50 million pesos to pay for rearmament. In total, from 1859 to 1861, the Bank issued 185 million pesos – nearly as much as the 202 million issued from 1836 to 1859. By May 1862, the price of gold peaked at 426 (Quintero Ramos 1965: 41). The Bank's metal stock vanished, and in April 1861, Directors voted to honour metal-denominated bills only in inconvertible paper, causing a storm within the Board. One Director claimed that gold reserves should be increased by increasing interest rates, for 'it is cruel to give paper pesos to debtors so that they consume their own sacrifice buying gold at a time of rising premiums, with great damage to the credit of our currency'.[25]

War appeared increasingly inevitable. As Buenos Aires Governor Mitre mustered his cavalry, Confederation forces swept into Buenos Aires and began plundering livestock herds. Colonel Saa alone rounded up some 60,000 cattle, and rather than engage his enemy, began to drive his booty back up to San Luís. Confederation forces fanned out across the pampas to take advantage of the anarchy and compensate for a decade of tough austerity – all of which probably weakened the national cause and prolonged the war further. Urquiza re-emerged from Entre Ríos to assume command over his acephalous forces, using his own personal fortunes to finance this last campaign. On 17 September, armies clashed at Pavón along the banks of the Arroyo del Medio. The battle, however, was indecisive: Urquiza, rather than engage his superior cavalry, withdrew; Mitre took the most losses, but retained the field. Urquiza's motives remain shrouded in controversy, but it is possible that he recognised that another armed victory could not compensate for the nation's crippled finances. The news from his vice-president was sobering:

> We resorted to the emission of one hundred thousand pesos in treasury notes ... and because of the poverty, lack of patriotism or bad faith of these capitalists, or for other reasons, despite the backing of that paper, it suffered a loss of value of some seventy per cent before fifteen days had passed .... Our penury is absolute and complete. Our credit amounts to nothing.[26]

By the end of 1861, most of Argentina was convulsed by insurrection. From Córdoba to Corrientes, the heads of governors began to roll, and one by one, northern provinces fell to Mitre's forces led by General Paunero.

What would have happened if the combination of Riestra's customs reforms, reconsolidation of Confederation debt, and curbing of peso emissions had been passed or worked? Certainly the national government would not have been driven to the brink that it would reach, which in the end hobbled its bargaining power with Buenos Aires. This in turn would have ensured that a greater measure of sovereign powers over economic policy-making passed to national authorities when a constitutional deal was finally struck in 1862 – after the collapse of Urquiza's last armed attempt to bring Buenos Aires to heel at Pavón. Second, the opportunity to broaden the base of the national money market was lost: hereafter Buenos Aires would be the exclusive source of private finance, and would be able to dictate terms of interprovincial relations in a way only dreamed by central state-builders since the 1820s. Third, the basic monetary instruments remained in the hands of Buenos Aires authorities, so that policy governing national legal tender was centralised in *porteño* hands. While this counterfactual cannot be tested, it is likely that a solution in 1860 would have yielded greater national sovereignty (possibly alongside more 'federalisation') over economic policy than the deal struck in 1862.

RECONSTRUCTION AND THE QUEST FOR STABILITY: 1862–5

After 1862, Buenos Aires and the rest of the provinces slowly resolved their differences. The Confederate state was incorporated into the new national regime, while Buenos Aires began to forfeit some of its jurisdictions. Two aspects in particular capture some of the problems faced by money-managers during these years of consolidation. First, they enforced dramatic stabilisation in an effort to check the turbulence of the war years and restore confidence in the peso. Second, they had to resolve the vexing issue of who would control money. Not surprisingly Mitre's victory ensured that in fact Buenos Aires would retain its authority over monetary affairs, and therefore vested fiduciary power in the hands of a tight *porteño* clique. Furthermore, the nature of stabilisation tightened even more Buenos Aires' monetary reins over the rest of the country – imposing, as it did, its own authority over the far-flung union. In a word, these were years of dramatic centralisation of monetary authority.

As the morphology of national authority began to take shape in 1862, the dire situation became clearer. By the end of the war, Buenos Aires had resorted to direct borrowing from merchants to keep their operations afloat: the peso was worth so little, emissions were pointless. By early 1862, the market was awash with 378 million pesos – more than triple the supply when Rosas was overthrown a decade earlier. Some relief came on 7 December 1861, with the arrival of the news that Urquiza had left the battlefield. For a moment, the peso spiral halted – temporarily.

Authorities faced several challenges, most immediate and important being re-monetisation. To save the Confederation, Buenos Aires leaders created an emergency 50 million peso fund, issuing bonds bearing 9 per cent. The Buenos

Aires government lobbied hard to encourage the use of pesos in all official transactions. Riestra personally met with the owners of rural slaughterhouses (the region's largest economic enterprises), urging them to adopt paper in their own transactions. In June, Riestra presented a proposal to restore confidence by gradually withdrawing pesos from the market by selling 6 per cent bonds. Here, provincial legislators proved as uncooperative as their national counterparts a year earlier, and rejected the scheme. Riestra responded in kind by resigning from the Cabinet, claiming that immediate withdrawal of banknotes and stabilising the currency were the 'basis of all my financial plans'.[27] Riestra did continue, informally, to be now-President Mitre's principal adviser on economic matters, and would soon rejoin the administration. But the conflict foreshadowed a stormy relationship between the executive branch and the legislature over the direction of economic reconstruction over the ensuing two years.

Re-monetisation depended on a settlement of the country's enormous debts. In the context of such an under-monetised economy (and like the recent experience of hyper-inflation under Presidents Alfonsín and Menem), deficit financing by printing money had sharp and unmediated effects on inflation and foreign exchange rates. In the long run, acceptability of pesos as legal tender rested on reconversion of short-term obligations to longer-term debt, and of course, amortisation. National authorities faced a daunting task: theoretically they inherited not only the previous state's debts, but those of the provinces, Buenos Aires included. But the real problem was a lack of an independent revenue network: in the fallout of Pavón, customs reverted to provincial jurisdiction until a new Constitutional framework could be worked out. In the meantime, officials directed efforts to reconsolidating the mess of obligations: old Treasury bills, promissory notes and a thicket of 'extraordinary' loans. It was estimated that by December 1861, the Confederation's consolidated and floating debt reached 3.7 million silver pesos, with Buenos Aires's over 11 million silver pesos. The total public debt amounted to 16 million silver pesos (320 million in paper).

One of the first acts of the provisional national government was to create in January 1862, a public fund of 50 million pesos to be raised with 9 per cent bonds and amortised at 3 per cent, to be administered by an *ad hoc* Junta de Administración, and covered by a special tariff of 2.5 per cent on exports and imports (which remained in place until the extinction of the bonds in 1878).[28] Furthermore, and in a display of one advantage to settling constitutional discord, the Provincial Bank handled 45 million pesos worth of the national issues. Hitherto, as long as the Bank remained an exclusively Buenos Aires provincial device, the national government had always lacked an instrument with which to negotiate public borrowing of any term. This was the first step in consolidating the accumulated debts incurred by the wars. To consolidate the Confederation's floating debt generated from April 1861 and the collapse in December of 1861, in November 1863 the national government created an additional public fund of 7 million pesos bearing 6 per cent and amortised at 1 per cent (Agote 1881: 33–8).[29] Finally, open market transactions became devices for handling national debt.

But the main problem was Buenos Aires' enormous debt and the promise to cover the province's budgetary needs (which already outstripped its own resources) as customs transferred to the national domain. Scobie (1954: 73) estimated the provincial expenditures, including interest and amortisation charges on the old foreign debt, and promises to transfer funds to withdraw old paper from circulation, at 54 million pesos per annum (1859 revenues were 10 million).[30] Final reconsolidation and formalisation of an amortisation plan for Buenos Aires came in October 1866, by which time the nation was already making payments on an *ad hoc* basis to defend its own creditworthiness. According to Cortés Conde (1989: 24–5), annual interest payments alone reached 6 million pesos fuertes. The form and scale of these payments burdened the national government and made the issue one of burning concern – most of all because persistent uncertainty depressed the value of the peso. Faced precisely with this problem, the Finance Minister admitted that

> after everything, I confess, that in such a grave matter, I am improvising, and we are all learning. All of us who have come to the world since the year 1820 until now, we cannot know much of these matters .... For my part, I say that we are in the dark.[31]

Stabilising the peso was a difficult process and required some severe but delicate currency withdrawal. The peso continued to sink from an annual average of 344 pesos per ounce of gold in 1860, reaching a nadir in February 1863 at 449. In December 1862, Riestra reminded the President of his proposal, now eight years old, of moving toward convertibility,

> of fixing an exchange value relative to circulating paper money, with the objective of avoiding great oscillations which cause such great unrest for commerce ... not only to maintain morale and public faith, but also to prevent the demonetization of paper itself ...[32]

A week later Mitre invited Riestra to meet in the Presidential Palace with Finance Minister (since October) Dalmacio Vélez Sarsfield to discuss immediate Bank policy governing note supply.

The Executive presented Congress with two important steps toward currency reform. First, in October 1863 the paper peso became national legal tender and established a preliminary schedule of exchange rates. A year later, in November 1864, Congress created a sort of dual exchange standard, declaring paper fixed at 25 per silver peso (400 per gold ounce), and banning all future unbacked emissions. The former measure really made *de jure* what was accepted *de facto*, that paper be the dominant means to settle accounts beyond the boundaries of Buenos Aires. As for gold, full convertibility had to wait for the 1880s and the deluge of foreign loans, but wild peso oscillations began to calm down (Ascote 1881: 105–7; Cortés Conde 1989: 22).[33] In practice, the Bank accelerated the withdrawal of notes in circulation. From a stock of 378 million paper pesos in circulation in early 1862, the Directors managed to slash supply by 150 million by early 1865.[34] Liquidity shortage, combined with new borrowing to cover budget deficits, brought howls from commercial and rural sectors about the shortage of credit and usurious interest rates.

There remained a pressing 'constitutional' problem involving the sources of sovereignty governing monetary affairs. As the nascent national regime struggled to assert control over currency, the principal instrument of issuances and redemptions remained in the hands of the province of Buenos Aires: the Provincial Bank (this split being a clear violation of the 1853 Constitution which vested all monetary authority in the hands of the federal government). All roads led to banking reform as the key to monetary stability. Several schemes were debated, but none accepted. Simply put, Buenos Aires politicians did not want to forfeit their grip on monetary affairs (Scobie 1954: 75–6).[35]

The financial situation, despite earlier interim measures, worsened as 1863 unfolded. Bank Directors staunched the falling peso by accepting foreign currency deposits, raising interest rates and accelerating the withdrawal of paper from the market. Merchants gathered in the Colón Theatre to express their concern, and struck a committee to pressure provincial and national governments to adopt one of several schemes. Meanwhile, budget cuts left the administration bereft of operating funds, and the Minister of the Interior cancelled all transfers to provinces, restoring penury to the interior and aggravating civil strife. Unilaterally, the provincial government of Buenos Aires initiated talks with Baring Brothers to raise a loan.[36] Matters worsened when 'El Chacho' Peñaloza revolted in La Rioja, followed by General Flores's invasion of Uruguay; the peso resumed its tumble. With rumours that Urquiza would join Peñaloza in a pincer movement on Buenos Aires and a return to civil war, the flight to metal became a stampede, and merchants complained loudly of liquidity shortages. Still, with the Buenos Aires legislature refusing to entertain any loss of monetary sovereignty, Vélez Sarsfield abandoned Mitre's national cabinet.[37]

Federal forces eventually overwhelmed the rebels in the Interior. Financially, a combination of desperate appeals by provincial governments, emergency loans by *porteño* merchants and the new London and River Plate Bank, and a trade boom based on wool exports to Europe and the United States, brought relief (Amaral and Adelman, forthcoming). By now, also, earlier measures began to bite. The fiscal deficit halved; the government created a 5 million silver peso fund, and authorised the Provincial Bank to withdraw 2 million paper pesos a month on this fund. To afford this, Riestra devised a scheme to raise extraordinary funds, to sell the Western Railway, to auction frontier land to bidders, and finally to muster a large internal loan.[38] In due course, the peso's wild fluctuations ended.

The Provincial Bank's capital stock would likely have improved as a result of the re-monetisation and debt-consolidation measures, but prudence and caution by the Directors helped bolster confidence. By 1864, reserves rose to 4.7 million silver pesos and 12 million paper pesos (up from 704,000 and 9.7 million respectively in 1860). Personal interest-bearing deposits rose from practically nothing to 2.3 million silver and 292 million paper pesos (Agote 1881: 121).[39] If we include bank deposits and capitalisation as part of a generic monetary base (and not just notes in circulation), this suggests a rapid process of re-monetisation of the Argentine economy. Moreover, it might suggest that the complaints of liquidity shortage prompted by note cancellations, may have exaggerated the real effects of austerity – though the overall tightness of monetary stabilization should not be belittled (Cortés Conde 1989: 58). This time, liquidity shortage was by design, not default.

CONCLUSION

Argentina faced two principal challenges. First, the country needed a secure and stable currency to provide acceptable legal tender for commercial transactions. Legal uncertainty surrounding the value and juridical status of the many instruments of exchange at the disposal of traders and producers posed immense risks. By the end of the Rosas era, this was a clear source of grievance, especially among the merchant class. It was in their name that Urquiza first toppled Rosas, Riestra struggled to bring order to the circulation of paper pesos and Mitre oversaw strict austerity from 1862 to 1865. Stabilisation was, in this sense, a process by which fiduciary rights became more easily defined and enforced.

The second main challenge, often cast by political and legal historians as the 'constitutional' impasse, involved the creation of delineated sovereign powers over monetary policy. This involved two sources of monetary power: first control and direction of bank (money emission) policy which was centralised in the Provincial Bank of Buenos Aires; and second, the terms of public credit. The conflict over these sources of sovereignty found regional expression. For some regions, like Buenos Aires and its hinterland, rising exports and the control over customs revenues provided the basis for printing pesos and for handling public obligations. For other regions, like the Cuyo and Córdoba, exports to Bolivia and Chile brought in enough specie to afford imported manufactures from Buenos Aires, and thus some local sovereignty. But other regions, like the Littoral, found themselves pinched by their utter reliance on Buenos Aires. So long as there existed no national regime for settling inter-regional accounts through the nationalisation of debt and currency, these imbalances of sovereignty led to war.

These two developments, the creation of a stable medium for commercial transaction in a nationally unified market and the formation of a constitutional authority able to govern monetary policies, were clearly interdependent. Without stable money, political factions enjoyed greater incentives to assault adversaries since inflation and monetary oscillations undermined confidence in authority. Moreover, economic hardship accompanied instability, creating likely constituencies for armed opposition. This helps explain the cycles of civil war throughout the post-colonial era. Conversely, without constitutional authority, currencies became easy vehicles for short-term political gains by warring parties. Constitutional authorities, by definition concerned with more than local and immediate advantage over adversaries, were thus less tempted to use fiduciary emissions to wage war.

The very interrelatedness of the these developments means that sorting out cause and effect sequences in monetisation of economic relations and the formation of states and institutions is, to say the least, complex. If nothing else, this chapter draws attention to the often contradictory and circular paths toward the constitution of property rights – that is, the contingencies presented by collective action when the rules of behaviour are still in their formative stage. In this sense, *encoding* new notions of property and the rights and duties which they entailed, was above all a *political* process.

It is worth exploring the relationship between encoding powers to create and regulate property rights, and state-formation. The very political nature of this process riddled it with contigencies and paths-not-taken. As such, it was not free of ambiguity. Two aspects of the power to issue and retire currencies bear mentioning. First, it assured a more universal basis for extracting fungible assets from society as a means to solve fiscal deficits usually brought on by war. Hitherto, the state was too weak to rely on direct extraction through taxation or forced loans. This weakness meant that short-term debt (like emissions) was often the only expedient. Emissions, inflation and instability narrowed the scope of market activity. On the other hand, stabilisation, by restoring confidence to the circulating medium, bolstered open market activity. This meant that the state could more easily adapt to society's productive structure, tapping into pools of capital and men where and when these resources accumulated. Monetisation – through the spread of acceptable legal tender – allowed the revenue machinery of the state to put a levy on the most visible and easily monitored parts of the Argentine commercial system. Over the long run, it was this advantage that tipped the scales in the civil wars, in favour of secessionist Buenos Aires at the expense of the Confederation.

Second, monetisation reinforced state-consolidation indirectly by making public notes, once and for all, the dominant medium of exchange. From the point of view of the producing and commercial classes this meant a reduction in the risk of using legal tender, the final eclipse of the colonial tradition of using merchant-money, and the emergence of an incipient private credit system. As civil society increasingly accepted paper pesos, that is, exploited money as a public good, the costs of withdrawing from open market relations – or exercising the 'exit' option in the words of Albert Hirschman (1970: 1–15) – rose. In other words, the opportunity costs of insurrection increased. This was not the language of General Urquiza, but it was the problem he faced, and which prompted him to withdraw from the battlefield at Pavón, and to support General Mitre's efforts to galvanise a new national state on terms dictated by the *porteño* elite. Monetisation and commercialisation of civil society placed severe limits on the autonomy of dissenting political groups, forcing them to accept minimal rules of political conduct. Increasingly, the promise of issuing and regulating public goods such as money bought societal respect for state power and forced political rivalries to be directed through constitutional channels.

NOTES

1 This essay is a compressed and early formulation of material forthcoming in my *Law, Property and Revolution: the Origins of the Modern State in Argentina*.
2 The literature on this theme is now voluminous, and largely redundant. For recent surveys of rational choice theories which tackle unequal exchange and transition periods, see Buchanan (1993), Smith (1988) and March and Olsen (1984). For useful reviews of basic principles, see North (1981, 1990a), Libecap (1986) and Machina (1987).
3 See Kindleberger (1978: 9). This is not the place for an extended discussion of fiduciary rights and relations except to note – in agreeement with Roberto Manga-beira Unger – that they exemplify the problematic of market and contractarian structures. They are, as it were, the culminating point of abstract universalism (see Unger 1983: 83–4).
4 George White to Baring Brothers (1852), quoted in Reber (1979: 31).
5 *Asambleas Constituyentes Argentinas seguidas de los textos constitucionales legis-lativos y pactos interprovinciales que organisaron políticamente la nación* (Buenos Aires, 1937) t. IV, p. 304. (Henceforth *Asambleas Constituyentes Argentinas.*)
6 Baring Brothers Archive, House Correspondence (BBA, HC) 4.1/24.4, 'Buenos Ayres Paper Money', nd; *Registro Oficial de Buenos Aires*, 32: 1 (abril 1853: 30).
7 *Registro Oficial de Buenos Aires*, 32: 6 (julio 1852: 156).
8 Public Record Office, Foreign Office 6 (hereafter FO 6)/170–171/Gore to Mal-colmson, 25 December 1852; 176/Gore to Russell, 1 April 1853.
9 *Registro Oficial de Buenos Aires* (1854: 104–5).
10 Quintero Ramos (1965: 40–1). For a strong dissenting remark on the reforms, see *El Nacional*, 12 agosto 1853.
11 *Registro Oficial de Buenos Aires* (1856: 3); Archivo del Banco de la Provincia de Buenos Aires (henceforth ABPBA) *Libros de Actas*, t. IX, p. 1144.
12 ABPBA, *Libros de Actas*, t. IX, Riestra to Llavallol, 26 junio 1855; ABPBA, Ministerio de Hacienda, *Correspondencia*, 023–1–3, p. 1207.
13 *Registro Oficial de Buenos Aires* (1856: 106, 1857: 30, 186, 321); ABPBA, Ministerio de Hacienda, *Correspondencia*, 023–1–4, p. 1276.
14 FO 6/196/Parish to Clarendon, 20 October 1856.
15 ABPBA, *Libros de Actas*, t. VIII, Riestra to Directors, 31 marzo 1854, p. 435. An amended version can be found in Archivo del General Mitre (henceforth AGM) t. XV, *Cartas confidenciales de varios sobre diversos asuntos*, Norberto de la Riestra to Junta de Administración de la Casa de Moneda, 5 julio 1854, pp. 37–41.
16 Cited in Díaz (1973: 119). The British delegate to the region claimed the statute would eliminate 'an evil which was the cause of great dissatisfaction', paper notes, FO 6/186/184/Parish to Clarendon, 29 November 1854.

17 With Alberdi's support, Buschenthal even returned to the House of Baring for money. See BBA HC 4.1/38/Buschenthal to Barings, 19 August 1858.
18 FO 6/201/343/Christie to Clarendon, 2 December 1857.
19 FO 6/218/126, Fagan to Malcolmson, 20 April 1859; 219/100, Fagan to Malcolmson, 24 August 1859.
20 ABPBA, *Documentación*, 017–1–14, No. 4, 'Emisiones sucesivas desde la creación del papel moneda' (nd).
21 Archivo Histórico de la Provincia de Buenos Aires (henceforth AHPBA) *Papeles de Hacienda*, 50b/A3/L30 (1859) Documento sin número, Llavallol to Riestra 25 June 1859.
22 AGM, t. VII, Derqui to Mitre, 23 junio 1860, pp. 13–14.
23 *Registro Oficial de Buenos Aires* (1860: 156–7); FO 6, 226/109/Thornton to Russell, 19 June 1860; Museo Mitre, *Archivo del General Mitre*, Archivo Intimo (hereafter MM-AI) 8/13/42/12.332, Mitre to Riestra, 22 octubre 1860.
24 Transfers began in August 1859, and were deposited in a national Colecturía General. ABPBA, *Libros de Actas*, t. X, p. 77. For an instance in which Riestra's patience wears thin, see AHPBA, Papeles de Hacienda, 50B.A4.L4 (1860–61), Riestra to Finance Ministry in Buenos Aires, 14 enero 1861.
25 ABPBA, *Libros de Actas*, t. XI, p. 69.
26 Pedernera to Urquiza, 25 November 1861, cited in Scobie (1954: 68–9).
27 *Archivo del General Mitre*, t. VIII, Riestra to Mitre, 24 julio 1862, p. 198; FO 6, 240/101, Doria to Russell, 28 July 1862.
28 ABPBA, Ministerio de Hacienda, *Correspondencia*, 023–1–6; Province of Buenos Aires, *Memoria sobre la organisación de la Oficina del Crédito Público de la Provincia de Buenos Aires* (Buenos Aires, 1882) pp. 49–51. Plans for reconsolidation began months before the Battle of Pavón. See *Archivo del General Mitre*, t. VIII, Riestra to Mitre, 29 noviembre 1861, pp. 190–91.
29 See Agote (1881, t. I: 33–8). On Mitre's own doubts about this plan, see AGM-AI, 8/13/42/12. 358, Mitre to Riestra, agosto 1863.
30 See also *Asambleas Constituyentes Argentinas*, t. V, p. 191.
31 *Asambleas Constituyentes Argentinas* t. V, p. 195.
32 AGM-AI, 8/13/42/12.352, Mitre to Riestra, 9 diciembre 1862.
33 See also FO 6, 251/249, Thornton to Russell, 22 November 1864. On the convertibility debate in 1863–64, see Rosa (1909: 15–24).
34 Burning began in earnest in December 1862, ABPBA, *Libros de Actas*, t. XII, p. 24.
35 On the debate over the US model, see *Asambleas Constituyentes Argentinas*, t. V, pp. 209, 244, 252–60.
36 BBA, HC. 41/43, Luís Domínguez to Barings, 27 January 1863.
37 *Archivo del General Mitre*, t. XXIII, Vélez Sarsfield to Mitre, 19 septiembre 1863, pp. 47–49: FO 6, 245/273, Doria to Russell, 26 June 1863. Mitre then turned to former Finance Minister Juan Bautista Peña, who after the example of Riestra and Vélez Sarsfield, turned down the offer.
38 See Riestra, 'Informe sobre los proyectos de redención del papel moneda y bancos particulares de emision', AGM-A1/8/9/29/11, 789.
39 It is worth noting that there is some discrepancy in the numbers: for the sake of caution, I am using the lower estimates. For the internal discussion on how the bank might augment operations, see *Registro Oficial de Buenos Aires* (1862–63: pp. v-xxi).

15

POLITICAL FACTORS
SHAPING THE ROLE OF
FOREIGN FINANCE
The case of Greece, 1832–1932

Ioanna Pepelasis Minoglou

INTRODUCTION

During the century following independence the gap in economic performance between Greece and the industrial nations widened. Greek historiography has blamed the foreign factor for this persisting economic backwardness, arguing that Greece – a small open economy with a limited number of exportables, almost no coal and a permanent grain deficit – was sensitive to fluctuations in the world market, was dependent on large foreign capital flows and was subject to various forms of economic coercion, ranging from trade blockades and financial embargoes, to the imposition of international supervision over public finances (Samaras 1982; Simopoulos 1990; Pizanias 1987). Undoubtedly, Greece was in a vulnerable position, namely a market of minor importance in the international economy, heavily dependent on Britain, its major trading partner and source of supply of capital (Dertilis 1984). Nevertheless, traditional analyses of Greek underdevelopment are myopic. They fail to observe that the root cause of late industrialisation was not mere foreign exploitation (as backwardness essentially invited exploitation), but the existence of a melange of diverse internal blockages which accounted for a low accumulation and misuse of capital.

This chapter challenges conventional historiographical practices. Instead of treating foreign capital as an independent variable – that is as a chisel sculpting the country's economic performance – it explores the ways in which political factors shaped the role of foreign finance. Hence, the analysis concentrates on Greek politics and, in particular, the strategy of the Greek state towards international finance. The tentative conclusion reached is that the political system, the legal framework and cultural factors, trapped Greece in an inefficient path regarding the flow and utilisation of foreign finance. A vicious circle of 'non-productive' borrowing was established whereby loans were raised largely to cover current government expenditure and to pay off old debts. The shift towards borrowing for productive purposes occurred at too late a date to have a decisive impact on productivity and the course of economic development. In essence, the story of foreign finance is one of missed opportunities.

The period studied begins in 1832, the year Greek independence was declared, and closes in 1932, which marks the third and last foreign loan default of the Greek government. The first section sets the background by briefly outlining the impediments to industrialisation and the problem of capital shortage. The second section examines how property relations in agriculture and industry, and the ideological opposition of the state towards concession granting in public works acted as a 'brake' on Foreign Direct Investment. The third section sketches the origins, size, allocation and fluctuations in foreign borrowing and shows how financial insolvency undermined the internal sovereignty of the state. The fourth section explains the reasons why foreign portfolio investment failed to act as a demand 'pull' force or to enlarge the country's capital base. Finally, the last section examines the nature of the relationship between foreign finance and domestic institutions, arguing that heavy foreign borrowing and the concomitant foreign control should be seen as the natural outcome of the internal arrangements – the system of property rights – devised by the state in order to promote political democratisation. This final argument suggests a revised interpretation of how the Greek state came to maturity.

INTERNAL BLOCKAGES TO INDUSTRIALISATION AND CAPITAL FORMATION

Early propensities for growth were manifested in the industrial spurt of the late 1860s, the export boom of the 1880s, and the growth of Greek shipping associated with transition from sail to steam in the early 1900s. However, these tentative moves were too weak to put the country on the path of self-sustained development (Agriantoni 1978: 116; Zolotas 1964; Lampe and Jackson 1982: 192; Dritsas 1990). As a result, the rise in the standard of living was feeble and Greece remained entangled in poverty, a mercantile economy with a dominant subsistence sector.

In part, late industrialisation can be attributed to environmental factors and the institutional make-up of agriculture. A mountainous and largely barren country, Greece was endowed with a comparative advantage in the cultivation of Mediterranean goods such as currants, oil and tobacco (Spulber 1963: 355). This was a blessing in disguise. The labour-intensive nature of these crops, the share-cropping system (large estate owners were effectively absentee urban dwellers little interested in the employment of modern methods of production) and land fragmentation of peasant holdings (in Greece primogeniture never existed) did not leave much scope for mechanisation (Mouzelis 1978: 19, 98). The commercialisation of farming did not trigger sustained growth and the twenty-year boom in currant exports in the late nineteenth century proved to be a missed opportunity. There was no spillover into other areas which would have enhanced the industrial character of the economy. Currant production and the currant trade had no substantial forward linkages and the extra profits reaped from the boom were either ploughed back to extend the area under vines or were 'consumed' by the moneylenders of Patras and the Ionian islands and the local commercial houses (Dertilis 1980: 169). Apparently, this was not an unusual pattern of behaviour. Merchants had established a long tradition of appropriating surplus capital from agriculture and finance and were also unwilling to invest in industry (Mouzelis 1978: 15–16, 106). To put it simply, Greek merchants were 'rent seekers' and distorted the capital market, raising opportunity costs associated with capital improvement in industry (Jones 1988). The banking sector was underdeveloped, especially prior to the 1870s, and interest rates were usurious: rates of from 20–24 per cent for mortgage loans and 36 to 50 per cent for personal loans were usual (Stavrianos 1958: 297; Zolotas 1964: 107, 119, 508). It could be argued that the comparative advantage Greeks acquired in mercantile activities worked at cross purposes. This 'innate' talent to perform exceptionally well in commerce and shipping was not a new or transient phenomenon. By the eighteenth century Greek merchants controlled the trade of the Balkans and the Levant, making Greece a merchant empire before it became a nation (Pepelasis 1969; Mouzelis 1978: 6–12).

Industry failed to attract or create capital and the growth of manufacturing was constrained by a number of environmental, demographic and institutional factors. Raw materials were to a large degree imported. Although there was surplus population in agriculture, the attachment of the peasants to the land in combination with mass emigration to the USA, provoked by the currant crisis of 1892, did not permit the formation of a cheap pool of urban labour. As a result industrial wages were relatively high. In addition, the heavy emphasis placed by the state on classical education and a neglect of the applied sciences and vocational training made for a lack of skilled labour. Furthermore, the domestic market for industrial goods was limited as a result of the small size of the population in absolute terms (particularly prior to the 1920s), the highly unequal income distribution and the tenacity of subsistence farming which survived unscathed. Also, the national network of local toll stations divided the country in regional protected markets (Sakellaropoulos 1991; Pepelasis 1958). Finally, it should be added that the legal framework was inimical to industrial development. The 1835 commercial law, inspired by the Napoleonic Code, was of little relevance to the needs of a backward economy and remained unrevised for too long. A 'modern' framework for joint stock companies was not introduced until 1920 (Pepelasis 1959). Family and private law, and the 'code of obligations', also posed problems, particularly in areas such as inheritance: they were a complex and confusing collection of anachronistic laws derived from Byzantine Law (Triandaphyllopoulos 1924). These legal arrangements immobilised capital and stifled any initiative for long-term investment.

The problem, then, was not simply one of an absolute lack of capital but of relative shortage. Two sectors suffered most: agriculture and industry. It can be argued that the predominance of merchant capital in the Greek economy, in combination with legal factors and an inadequate banking system, worked against the attainment of an agricultural or industrial revolution. Under these circumstances, with the given level and composition of local capital creation it was not possible for Greece to take off into self-sustained growth. Ironically, backwardness – or to put it otherwise – the 'peculiarity' of the Greek economic formation had negative repercussions not only on domestic capital accumulation but also on foreign financial flows.

INSTITUTIONAL BLOCKAGES TO FOREIGN DIRECT INVESTMENT

If the Greek state had not sought loans in the world capital market, international finance would have played but a limited role in the Greek economy. Compared to other countries such as Spain, Greece remained in the backwaters of the concession hunting game throughout the nineteenth century. Foreign direct investment (FDI) was equivalent to roughly 5 per cent of total foreign capital inflows and only became relatively prominent during the financial embargo (see p. 254). Institutional factors explain why, with the opening of the international capital market in 1879, direct investment did not become pronounced in agriculture, industry and public works.

The absence of FDI in agriculture was a Balkan trait. The lack of a national land registry was an important deterrent. Moreover, farming could not be organised under modern conditions as there was a scarcity of wage labour. In addition, escalating pressure for land reform made it difficult to sell state lands to foreigners. The only major agricultural enterprise to attract foreign investment in Greece (and in fact the Balkans as a whole) was the British-backed Lake Copais Company established in 1887 (Hill 1939). In return for undertaking drainage work, the company was granted a concession to cultivate 190,000 stremmas (one stremma equals a quarter of an acre). But, due to a scarcity of wage labour, the company was obliged to limit the introduction of high yield crops and modern methods of cultivation only to one quarter of the concession, the remaining land was leased to share-croppers (Freris 1976). The traditional literature asserts that foreign capital dominated the Greek industrial sector. This view cannot be substantiated for the period under review (Pepelasis Minoglou 1984). Industry failed to attract foreign interest in part for reasons cited above and also because of insufficient state incentives by government to draw foreign investment to manufacturing (Lampe and Jackson 1982: 90, 106; Spulber 1963: 351). Moreover, as a rule, foreign capital was only prepared to invest in industry in association with leading local firms (Papayiannakis 1982; Pepelasis Minoglou 1984). Neither was FDI common in the area of public works. Initially, major public work projects such as the Corinth canal and the first railways were built by foreign companies within a concessionary framework. This pattern did not continue for long for a number of reasons. In the case of the Corinth canal, the original investors quickly withdrew as the project became financially unprofitable (Papayiannopoulos 1989). The set of factors affecting the demise of foreign direct investment in the railways was more complicated, though, again, profits were lower than anticipated. But the critical factor was the strategic decision of the Greek government, following the naval blockade of Piraeus in 1885 by the Great Powers, to expand the state railway network. This was done by borrowing abroad, thereby confirming the trend towards portfolio investment (Papayiannakis 1982: 102–3). Subsequently, the government sought to extend its control of the railway system. By the inter-war period granting concessions to foreign companies for public utilities came to be viewed as generally unacceptable by the political body. Repeatedly, negotiations with foreign interests were unsuccessful because, as illustrated by the case of the railway concession, the state was unwilling to forgo the right to intervene in the management of public utilities or to guarantee an acceptable level of profit (National Bank of Greece, Historical Archive, Public Works, B Railways, files 28–30). It was no coincidence that only one large public utility concession awarded to a foreign company materialised during the infrastructure boom of the 1920s. This was granted in 1925 under the short-lived Pangalos dictatorship and subsequently it was revised upon the return to parliamentarism (Pandelakis 1991; Stephanides 1930).

In conclusion, FDI did not acquire a position of pre-eminence in the Greek economy (Yiannitsis 1977; Hill 1939). The system of property relations in agriculture, the small size of the rural labour market, the legal framework for foreign investments in industry, and the refusal of the state to grant public work concessions under terms acceptable to potential investors acted as a brake on direct foreign capital flows. These factors combined with the limited supply of local capital, arrested development. The state was poor, and prior to the 1920s, apart from building railways, was not interested in borrowing foreign capital to improve the physical infrastructure. Instead, as will be demonstrated below, access to the international capital market was used to fund current – largely political – and not developmental needs.

Before moving on to consider foreign portfolio investment, a few words on capital shortage in the public sector are required. The budget was in state of near permanent deficit and fiscal problems escalated after 1868 following constitutional reform and an extension of the franchise (Lazaretou 1993: 305–6; *Ikonomiki Epetiris tis Ellados* 1939: II, 170). At the time there was an international embargo on Greek loans and the government sharply increased note circulation in order to cover rising expenditure, a practice that continued even after the embargo was lifted in 1879. These conditions prevailed until 1898 when the International Financial Commission (IFC) was established and imposed on Greece by foreign creditors. For the next twenty years the Commission enforced a policy of deflation. (The link between democratisation and the fiscal gap, the international embargo and the imposition of international financial supervision are discussed below.) Recourse to deficit financing would not occur again until 1920 during the Asia Minor military campaign (1919–22) when the Greek government was prepared to confront the IFC. For the first two decades of the twentieth century the Commission imposed a rigid fiscal discipline upon successive Greek governments. During this period several loans were raised overseas. Access to domestic credit was limited by the small size of the market. Indeed, forced loans accounted for 40 per cent of local funds acquired by the Greek state during this period and internal borrowing provided only a partial answer to the needs of the government to cover capital investment and current expenditure (Pepelasis Minoglou 1993).

THE HISTORY OF THE FOREIGN LOANS: ORIGINS, DISTRIBUTION AND POLITICS

Historically, foreign capital inflows took the form of portfolio investment (see Table 15.1), a situation dating from the national uprising against Turkey. The financial insolvency of the Greek state was systematically exploited by the Powers. National sovereignty was thus undermined in military and constitutional matters. Upon the formal declaration of independence with the 1832 Treaty of London, the three protecting powers – the United Kingdom, France and Russia – arranged for Rothschilds to provide a 60 million gold franc loan. In spite of the ample safeguards offered, the bank withheld 60 per cent of the nominal value of the loan to cover initial interest and amortisation payments (Andreadis 1904: II, 82–3). Instead of being used to improve the condition of the war-ravaged economy, the balance of the loan was dissipated on salaries to the highly paid foreign troops of the Bavarian regency and other war-related expenses such as the purchase of the province of Fthiotida from the Porte (Campbell and Sherrard 1969: 90; Andreadis 1904: II, 82–3). Unable to service this loan or obtain additional funds overseas, Greece defaulted in 1843 and for the next forty-seven years was excluded from the international capital market. Default placed the country in a vulnerable position as bondholders had first claim on government revenue. The guarantor powers did not immediately

Table 15.1 Breakdown of the foreign public debt in 1932 (%)

Foreign loans of the state	74
Foreign loans of public bodies*	6
Foreign loans to banks	3
Foreign loans to merchants and industry	8.5
Foreign investments in foreign enterprises	3.5
Foreign participation in Greek enterprises	3
Miscellaneous	2

Note: *By public bodies is meant non-central government institutions such as municipalities, port funds, the National Mortgage Bank and the state monopolies.
Source: Bank of Greece, Tsouderos Archive, file 23: League of Nations, Financial Committee, Report to the Council on Greece, Extraordinary Session held in London, 6-14 June 1933.

Table 15.2 Foreign loans raised by the state

	1832–1914 (G. francs)	1922–1932 (£)
(I) Target nominal value*	1,766,000	49,500,000
(II) Actual nominal value**	1,311,000	39,300,000
(III) Real value	116,000 36,100,000	
(II) as % of (I)	74%	79%

Notes: *By target nominal value is meant the amount which the underwriters had agreed to raise for the state. (In the 1920s by target value is meant the amount the state demanded to be raised but for which the underwriters did not give their final assent.)
**The bank commission and stamp duty has not been taken into consideration.
Source: Compiled from Haritakis (1933).

oblige Greece to resume repayments as they might have done according to the 1832 Treaty of London (Kaltchas 1940: 91). However, in 1854, under the pretext of seeking redress for mounting debt arrears, an Anglo-French naval force blockaded the port of Piraeus for three years. The real motive behind this action was to penalise Greece for invading Thessaly during the Crimean war (Dertilis 1988: 46). Wishing to maintain the Ottoman Empire intact as a check against Russian expansionism in the Balkans, Britain disapproved of Greek irredentism and repeatedly castigated governments in Athens for military adventurism. London argued against lavish military expenditure on political and economic grounds: as Greece enjoyed the protection of the Powers, there was little justification for such expenditure which served only to deplete the meagre resources available to the Greek government (Campbell and Sherrard 1969: 66).

Greece wanted to raise a foreign loan in the 1860s but international borrowing was not possible until 1879 after a debt settlement was reached with Rothschilds. The conjuncture was favourable to Greece. On the political front an important factor was the temporary convergence between Athens and London on the issue of Greek territorial expansion. During the Russian Turkish war of 1875–8 Greek acceded to a British request to limit territorial claims to Thessaly (Dertilis 1983). Funds were available in the world money market as a result of the depression in the advanced countries (Stavrianos 1958: 415–16). Furthermore, the flourishing banking and commercial communities of the Greek Diaspora in Central Europe, France, Russia and the Mediterranean basin decided to act as unofficial 'international' agents of the government. Threatened by rising nationalism in the various outposts of the Ottoman Empire, these communities were eager to diversify their economic activities by marketing Greek government loans (Hristopoulos 1977/8: vol. 13, 315, vol. 14, 79).

In a span of fifteen years Greece borrowed about 640 million gold francs, an amount equivalent to about 60 per cent of the value of Greek exports for the same period (Dertilis 1936: 131–3). This extensive flow of funds took the form of syndicated issues. Rothschilds was not among the underwriters. Its interest in Greece had waned by the 1880s. New actors appeared on the scene and the bulk of the funds was raised by three institutions: Hambros of London, the Comptoir d'Escompte de Paris in which a Greek expatriate financier, Andreas Vlastos, held a prominent position, and the Bank of Constantinople controlled by French interests and another expatriate Greek, Andreas Syngros (Haritakis 1933; Hristopoulos 1977/8: vol. 14, 78; Papayiannopoulos 1989). In addition to marketing and organising these issues, Greek financiers of the Diaspora actually purchased approximately 15 per cent of the bonds (Tsoukalas 1977: 249).

The post-1879 stream of foreign capital did not lift the economy from its quasi-mercantile, pre-industrial level. The net inflow was substantially lower than the face value of the bonds. The nominal value of the loans was roughly 640 million gold francs and the real value 468 million gold francs but only 359 million gold francs reached the hands of the Greek government (Tsoukalas 1977: 249; Svoronos 1976: 103; Stephanides 1930: 183). Apart from a small amount spent on building railways (about 6.6. per cent of total foreign portfolio investment) funds were applied to current consumption needs. As a result of this borrowing spree, by the end of the 1880s 33 per cent of the budget was allocated to the foreign debt and more than half of the state revenues were mortgaged to loan repayment (Stavrianos 1958: 472).

In 1893 Greece defaulted once again under the pressure of mounting debt charges and a sudden drop in the price of currants, the main export commodity (Campbell and Sherrard 1969: 97; Stavrianos 1958: 47, 477–8). Amortisation payments were suspended and only 30 per cent of the interest charges were met (Lazaretou 1993: 298). By 1896 foreign bondholders assented to a settlement which was advantageous for Greece in that it did not provide for foreign control. However, this agreement was not signed because of the imminence of hostilities with Turkey over the Cretan question. One year later Greece went to war with Turkey and was defeated. In order to secure funds to pay a war indemnity to the Ottoman state, Greece was forced by Britain, France, Germany, Italy, Austria and Russia to accept control over its public finances. Hence, in 1898 the International Financial Commission was set up (Kalliavas 1929). The terms were harsher than those applied to the Egyptian and the Ottoman Public Debt Administrations set up in the late nineteenth century. No rescheduling agreement was made for the existing debt and although at the time 17 per cent of the foreign debt was in Greek hands no provision was made for Greek representation on the IFC (Kalliavas 1929: 360; Levandis 1944: 107). Arguably, the Commission enhanced the country's position in the world capital market. Certainly, the issue price of Greek loans rose and the spurt in the flow of funds that had begun in 1879 was more or less maintained up to the outbreak of WWI (see Table 15.3).

Table 15.3 Nominal and real capital of the foreign loans raised by the state

	(I) Nominal capital	(II) Real capital	(II) as a % of (I)
1879-93	639,739,000 G. Francs	468,358,500 G. Francs	73%
1898-1914	671,916,000 G. Francs	603,846,345 G. Francs	89%
1922-32	£39,300,000	£ 36,100,000	92%

Source: Compiled from Dertilis (1936: 131-3).

Several factors conspired to halt new borrowing overseas between 1914 and 1924. These included the Allied reaction to the pro-German position adopted by the Greek government during the First World War, the Asia Minor campaign and domestic instability. Foreign borrowing was resumed in late 1924 and in a span of six and a half years loans valued at 950 million gold francs were obtained (*Ikonomiki Epetiris tis Ellados* 1932: 493–536). This amount was equivalent to around one-third of the value of Greek exports for the period (*Ikonomiki Epetiris tis Ellados* 1929: 198, 1939: 2,14: Freris 1976: 105). A distinct feature of this new wave of foreign portfolio investment was that it was vested with the type of control normally associated with FDI. These new loans were tied and were either managed by private business interests or supervised by the League of Nations. This state of affairs had repercussions regarding the nature and extent of foreign control. In 1923 the League of Nations stepped into Greece, appointing an 'autonomous' organisation which settled almost half a million refugees from Asia Minor in the sparsely populated Northern Regions (Howland 1939; Ladas 1932). Four years later, upon securing political stabilisation (namely, a curtailment of the role of the military in politics) the League introduced a financial stabilisation scheme designed by the Bank of England (Pepelasis Minoglou 1993: 142–50, 174–94). British control over macro-economic policy became more pronounced and the IFC literally became an appendage of the British Treasury.

Another distinct feature of the flow of funds in the 1920s was that loans were directed at improving agricultural productive capacity, expanding the physical infrastructure and reforming the banking system. Only 2 per cent of the loans were expended on current consumption. This shift in the use of foreign borrowing reflected a discontinuity in modern Greek history brought about by the Asia Minor debacle of August 1922. Irredentism (the driving force

258

of Greek politics since 1832) suffered a fatal blow. In addition, the influx of 1.2 million largely destitute refugees brought about a sudden net population increase of about 13 per cent (Pentzopoulos 1962). Never before in Greek history had the tension between population and resources (capital and land) been so pronounced. It could be argued that the combination of population pressure and military defeat acted as a catalyst forcing the state at last to employ foreign capital for the modernisation of the country's infrastructure (North 1981: 3–12, 59–68.)

WHY FOREIGN PORTFOLIO INVESTMENT DID NOT TRIGGER SELF-SUSTAINED DEVELOPMENT

As already explained, foreign capital inflows did not create take-off conditions as the bulk of the funds were not channelled towards developing the country's resources. Even the small proportion of foreign portfolio investment sunk in railways, flood control projects, land improvement and other public works had a limited impact due to institutional and organisational constraints which underscored the low capital absorptive capacity of the economy. Actual costs invariably exceeded original estimates. The state often undertook projects without adequate feasibility studies which resulted in substantial changes to technical specification part way through construction. More importantly all projects were undertaken on an agency (cost-plus) basis. No upper limit was placed on construction costs and contractors were given no incentive to economise. On the contrary, the larger the project spend, the greater the agency fee (Stephanides 1930: 101–3). This arrangement also led to considerable delays in completion, particularly to schemes initiated in the 1920s. Bloated costs quickly ate up the funds available and the drying up of foreign loans in 1931 left many public works incomplete, further inflating final costs. A classic example was land reclamation in the Vardar and Struma valleys of northern Greece which took not seven years as planned, but twenty-five (Pepelasis Minoglou 1993: 267–303, 378–86). Similarly, the scheme for the construction of a national network of roads was abandoned due to shortage of funds in the early 1930s and, when restarted in the 1950s, required the rebuilding of those sections completed before the crash. These difficulties suggest a massive organisational failure at state level and hint, too, at the weakness of the market.

The indirect effects of foreign portfolio investment were also limited. Theoretically, capital inflow should have increased the level of aggregate demand but it did not. The explanation is simple. From the moment that the embargo on loans to Greece was lifted in 1879, the net annual inflow of new foreign funds was slightly smaller than the amounts paid in debt service (see Table 15.4). The low issue price of the loans combined with high bank commissions, tight repayment schedule and large sinking fund provision, led to inflated amortisation and interest payments. Domestic backward linkages were also reduced as a significant portion of general purpose loans was spent

Table 15.4 Real value of the foreign loans issued and the service of the debt

	(I) Real value of the foreign loans issued*	(II) Service of debt
1879–93	468,358,500 G. Francs	470,400,000 G. Francs
1898–1922	603,846,345 G. Francs	880,179,193 G. Francs
1922–32	18,155,000,000 Drs.	24,610,000,000 Drs

Note: *By real value of the loans is meant the amount made available to the state taking into consideration the issue price. Actually the net inflow was smaller for these figures do not take account of the bank commissions nor do they take account of the fact that often the underwriters – when public issues went poorly – bought the bonds 3 to 10 points below the issue price.

Source: compiled from Dertilis (1936: 131, 132, 139) and Hristopoulos (1978: XV, 337).

abroad, for example on armaments or war indemnities (Dertilis 1936: 131–2). Even in the case of the public works loans, the multiplier effect was low. The projects were built by foreign contractors with foreign machinery and mostly imported construction materials. Even material readily available in Greece, such as timber for railway construction, was imported (Dertilis 1977: 170; Papayiannakis 1982: 78; Pandelakis 1991). Finally, and paradoxically, foreign finance accentuated domestic capital shortage. This was especially the case for manufacturing. Overseas borrowing crowded out local saving instead of widening the amount available for productive investment. In 1933 it was established that over half of the foreign debt was held by Greeks living at home and abroad (League of Nations 1933). It could be argued that the popularity which foreign bonds enjoyed with the Greek public starved industry of funds.

But the story of how foreign portfolio investment affected the supply of domestically available capital does not stop here. The administration of around half of total fiscal revenue by the IFC and financial reconstruction schemes applied by it and the League of Nations exacerbated capital shortage. In the case of the Commission, financial reconstruction entailed a policy of budgetary and monetary contraction to restore the drachma to its official gold parity. As a result of the austere regime imposed by the IFC, the paper drachma regained its gold parity in 1910. Currency appreciation encouraged the inflow of emigrant and shipping remittances and helped make Greek bonds more popular with investors thereby distorting the capital market. Finance and commerce were favoured by investors rather than agriculture or industry. Furthermore, IFC supervision of state finances immobilised a substantial volume of local capital and entailed a significant involuntary transfer of funds abroad. In seeking to restore confidence in Greek bonds, the Commission held large cash reserves (in Greece and overseas) and paid bondholders a rate of interest higher than that specified on the coupons of 'old' gold loans issued between 1881 and

1896 before the IFC was established (Kalliavas 1929). This policy also implied reduced domestic access to foreign exchange (Pepelasis Minoglou 1993: 181–84). Only with financial reconstruction and banking reforms implemented under the auspices of the League of Nations in the 1920s was there a significant monetisation of the economy and discernible flow of finance to industry (Dertilis 1988; Kostis 1987).

While it is not possible to give exact figures, it may be argued with confidence that foreign investment did not trigger economic growth in Greece. Rather, the country remained trapped on an inefficient path dependent course. Perhaps missed opportunities, in both a chronological and structural sense, are the most important feature of the history of foreign investment in Greece during the century following independence. Accidental and exogenous factors were not the sole or original causes of this phenomenon. In addition to the long embargoes, the limited impact of foreign capital on the economy was a repercussion of domestic political factors. On the one hand, the slow moving bureaucracy and the absence of any notion of planning limited the absorptive capacity of the economy. On the other hand, foreign capital was acquired in order to serve a political and not an economic function.

THE SYSTEM OF PROPERTY RIGHTS AND FOREIGN CAPITAL: INVESTMENT AND DEMOCRACY

An evaluation of the role of foreign investment in Greek development which focuses exclusively on the economic misses the central objective of state strategy. Prior to the mid-1920s, the primary concern of successive administrations was not the development of the economy *per se* but national unification and the consolidation of democracy (Dakin 1972: 261). Seen from this perspective it is clear that foreign portfolio investment assisted the process of state building. This is a novel concept which challenges three prevalent notions in Greece. The first is that foreign finance served no useful function from the point of view of the nation at large. The second is that the state was a passive tool of foreign interests. The third is that the state was grasping, corrupt and inefficient, extracting high taxes from the populace and squandering resources on an expanding, parasitic bureaucracy and war adventures (Tsoukalas 1981; Dakin 1972: 320–21). Recent research, however, has shown that deficit financing was largely a result of the adoption of a Western system of parliamentary rule prior to industrialisation and not of political backwardness or greed (Dertilis 1993: 51–2).

Parliamentarism was not implanted in Greece by its Protecting Powers but emerged from the national project of those groups struggling for independence. The three powers which guaranteed Greek independence in the Protocols of 1832 had vested Greece with a monarchy that had no constitutional limitations. Soon after independence Greece began to acquire a series of progressive institutions, some of which were found to be too radical by its protectors. Free education was introduced in 1844 (Kaltchas 1940: 103–7). In spite of British protests, the franchise was extended in 1843 and universal male suffrage adopted in 1864. The ideological inspiration for the libertarian bent in the realm of public law came from such sources as the dissemination of the principles of the French Revolution by the Greek intellectuals of the Diaspora, the populist nature of the Greek War of Independence (liberty from alien rule and domestic autocracy being its basic axiom) and the absence of a Western type feudal past with its related established economic orders (Kaltchas 1940: 33; Tsoukalas 1981: 45–6). In fact the constitutions drafted during the War of Independence were considered to be the most democratic and liberal of the time in Europe. Overall, the liberalism of the state in combination with its policy of deficit financing probably helps to explain why Greece experienced fewer military coups and was politically more stable than its neighbours, the only drawback of Greek politics perhaps being the frequency of short-lived administrations (Dertilis 1993: 41).

Deficit financing thus became an instrument of policy. The political system rested on an institutional arrangement in which all social strata expected some specific privilege or concession from the weak yet modern state. The need to secure political stability and consensus for parliamentarism induced governments to enforce a system of property rights that was economically inefficient in that it promoted fiscal disequilibrium. Parliamentary rule was staked on the low taxation of the higher classes and the peasantry. Regarding the under-taxation of the higher classes it is notable that Greece was amongst the last countries in Europe to apply income and inheritance taxes. The first was introduced in 1910 and the latter in 1898. Tax evasion being widespread amongst the rich, income tax did not surpass 6 per cent of state revenues (Dertilis 1993: 62). The under-taxation of the peasantry started progressively from 1864. A landmark was the abolition of tithe and tax farming in 1880, a fiscal innovation was made possible by the confidence which the 60 million gold franc loan, raised abroad the previous year, inspired in government circles (Sakellaropoulos 1991: 303). Peasants constituted the largest voting group of Greek society, at first because of their numerical preponderance and in the twentieth century as a result of the electoral system. Apart from political considerations, the under-taxation of the peasants had an economic basis. They lived at the margin of subsistence and thus had little if any surplus that might be extracted.

The fiscal burden – both direct and indirect taxation – which fell on the middle class and the urban dwellers was heavy. Peasants effectively escaped the burden of indirect taxes as they operated basically within the confines of subsistence farming and barter trade. The state stifled urban unrest by becoming the largest employer in the country and absorbing the surplus labour that could not be assimilated elsewhere. What is more, urban dwellers were those who probably benefited most from the welfare policy of a state which gave large handouts such as war pensions and compensation to the urban refugees.

By 1907 the number of civil servants per 10,000 of population was roughly seven times higher in Greece than in Britain (Mouzelis 1978: 17). Seen from this perspective, the country's disproportionately large civil service was not a by-product of its Ottoman past but instead a consequence of the fragile equilibrium on which the political framework rested.

The perceived need to establish a solid democratic system precluded the productive utilisation of foreign finance. To put it otherwise, the system of property rights set up to accommodate political modernisation did not change over time. A constant feature of the Greek formation, it as it were dictated an economically inefficient utilisation of foreign loans. Foreign capital was not seen by the state as a tool for promoting economic growth, but rather as a means of enabling the central government to enhance its position in Greek society. This was the case even with the banking reform and the transportation projects of the 1920s. These schemes were viewed as useful not because they were regarded as intrinsically developmental but because they contributed to the monetisation of the economy and the creation of a unified national market, processes that were necessary for a more democratic form of government. It is clear, then, that the Greek state was not a predatory state. It was a lethargic, inefficient state (Jones 1988: 1–9). The Greek state did not seek to maximise revenue but chose a set of property rights regardless of the negative effect on economic efficiency. On the contrary, the objective was political stability and social cohesion rather than a system of law which would promote economic efficiency and thus tax revenue. North has argued that societies that adopt the formal rules of another society will have very different performance characteristics than the original country (North, in this volume). This was the case with the enforcement of political Westernisation in Greece. Interestingly, the state departed from the Western 'model' in that the political leaders of Greece were not budget balancers. Hence the fiscal arrangement on which political Westernisation rested brought the Greek authorities into conflict with the country's international supervisors, first the IFC and subsequently the League of Nations. Both organisations were staunch supporters of the gold-standard-currency school of thought which placed a high priority on monetary stability. But Greek governments only accepted the principles of 'sound finance' under duress when it was absolutely essential to do so in order to contract foreign loans. This was the case between 1898 and the First World War and again from 1927 to 1932.

In conclusion, socio-political factors prevented foreign finance – predominantly portfolio investment – from triggering economic development. The state lacked a growth ethic and, due to institutional factors, the capital absorptive capacity of the Greek economy was low. As a result of the Westernisation of the political system, Greece had to live with a fundamental dichotomy. The need to attain social equilibrium led to an internal institutional arrangement that fostered external intervention and dependence. But exogenous factors such as foreign capital proved less important than internal factors in determining the development process in Greece. Foreign finance and control, as it was played out in the Greek context, perpetuated and enhanced the country's underdevelopment but did not cause it, as has been asserted in the orthodox historiography.

NOTE

I wish to thank Professor G. Dertilis, Dr S. Ioannides, Professor A. Lazaris, Professor A. Pepelasis and Dr M. Psalidopoulos for commenting on earlier drafts of this chapter.

16

REGULATORY REGIMES, CAPITAL MARKETS AND INDUSTRIAL DEVELOPMENT

A comparative study of Brazil, Mexico and the United States, 1840–1930

Stephen Haber

Economists have long debated the effects of government regulation in LDCs. One group, dominant in US economics departments in the 1970s and 1980s, has held that government regulatory policies are neutral with respect to economic efficiency. In this view, largely derived from the historical experiences of Great Britain and the USA, the private sector can easily mitigate any attempts to constrain its activities. Institutional innovations to get around government regulation are therefore relatively costless. The other group in this debate has held that regulatory policies in LDCs exert powerful and enduring effects on economic efficiency. In this view, the response of the private sector to government regulation is not flexible and automatic because the high costs of coordination and cooperation in LDCs exceed the *ex ante* benefits to any individual agent.

Which of these two views is the more accurate description of the effects of government regulation is an empirical question. The only way to answer it is by careful analysis of the historical record of government regulation and economic performance in a number of countries over long periods of time. This chapter therefore offers an empirical contribution to the literature through an analysis of the impact of regulatory environments on the development of the intermediaries responsible for the financing of industry. It briefly examines the histories of government regulation of banks and securities exchanges in three countries, assesses their roles in the financing of industry, and then measures the impact of access to institutional sources of capital on the cotton textile manufacture.

I focus on the cotton textile industry for two reasons. First, cotton goods manufacture was the most important manufacturing industry in the underdeveloped economies to be studied and there are compelling theoretical reasons to consider cotton textiles. In underdeveloped economies numerous factors, such as large economies of scale or technological barriers to entry, can condition the development of many industries. Separating the effects of access to impersonal sources of capital from among these other factors is difficult across the entire industrial sector. In the cotton textile industry, however, these other factors did not come into play: the capital equipment was easily divisible, the minimum efficient scale of production was small, and non-financial barriers to entry were largely absent. The only important barrier to entry was access to finance. The textile industry therefore provides an excellent test case of the relationship between the development of the financial markets that provide capital to an industry, and the development of the industry itself.[1]

The cases selected for study were chosen in order to test the hypotheses that the regulatory environment has a profound effect on the structure and size of financial markets, and that the structure and size of financial markets has a significant effect on the size and structure of industry. I therefore searched for cases which had notably different histories of financial market regulation.

The United States was chosen because it is the touchstone case: it was an international leader in financial market development and industrial growth during the period under study.[2] Brazil and Mexico were chosen because they were the most industrialised countries in Latin America. More importantly, these two cases provide a counterfactual test of the central hypotheses. Throughout the nineteenth century, Brazil and Mexico both followed highly repressive regulatory polices. In 1889, however, Brazil drastically changed its financial market regulations to a liberal, relatively non-repressive environment, while Mexico held to its old repressive policies. Moreover, the costs of obtaining information were lowered in Brazil because its financial market regulations required all publicly held joint stock companies to publish balance sheets and lists of shareholders twice a year. Brazil thus provides a relevant test for understanding the opportunity lost by Mexico when it failed to enact less repressive policies and failed to lower the costs of obtaining information.

The argument advanced runs in the following terms. The size and structure of capital markets played a crucial role in determining the size and structure of the textile industry. In Mexico, where the banking system was small and concentrated, the distribution of bank loans among potential textile industrialists was narrow. Differential access to loans from banks or from the informal network of large, Mexico City merchants, in turn, gave rise to differential access to equity capital: entrepreneurs with the proven ability to obtain loans for working capital had a significant advantage over their competitors when it came to selling equity in the securities markets. In short, a small group of powerful financiers was able to obtain all they capital they needed, while everyone else was starved for funds. The result was slow rates of industrial growth and high levels of industrial concentration.

In countries where the institutional rules of the game created larger and less concentrated capital markets, such as the USA or post-1889 Brazil, the distribution of funds among potential textile industrialists was broader. Access to institutional sources of finance did not, therefore, serve as a barrier to entry, which in turn meant that the textile industry in those countries tended to grow faster and be relatively less concentrated.

CAPITAL MARKETS AND TEXTILE FINANCE

The United States

Beginning in the 1820s the USA started to develop a modern, mechanised cotton goods industry. From the very beginning, this industry drew on institutional sources of capital. Moreover, the institutional rules of the game were such that many entrepreneurs could tap into these impersonal sources of equity finance and credit.

There were basically two sources of impersonal sources of capital available to textile industrialists in nineteenth-century New England. The first was the Boston Stock Exchange. As early as 1835, 14 textile issues were traded on the Boston Stock Exchange. This grew to 32 by 1850 and to 40 in 1865. Although not yet a well-developed securities market it provided for a wider distribution of ownership than more traditional forms of business organisation would have. Indeed, one of the striking aspects of the large, Massachusetts-type companies was the pattern of widely dispersed ownership of shares among individuals and institutions (Davis 1958: 207–14; Martin 1898: 126–31; Navin and Sears 1955: 110).

As important as the sale of equity in the capitalisation of the early textile mills was the ability of manufacturers, especially small- and medium-sized ones, to obtain loans from banks and other institutions. This kind of institutional lending to manufacturers appears to have been confined to the US northeast, which quickly developed a large banking system. As early as 1819 New England had 84 banks with a capital of $16.5 million. By 1860 the region boasted 505 banks with $123.6 million in capital (Davis and Stettler 1966: 2, 5; Davis 1957: 192; Lamoreaux 1985: 651).

The large number of bank loans to textile manufacturers is not surprising when it is recollected that the owners of mills tended to be the same people that owned the banks. Basically, kinship groups tapped the local supply of investable funds by founding a bank and selling its equity to both individual and institutional investors. The founding kinship groups then lent those funds to the various enterprises under their control, including their own textile mills (Lamoreaux 1985).

Had legal restrictions been placed on the founding of banks, these insider arrangements would have concentrated capital in the hands of a small number of kinship groups, which, in turn would have led to concentration in textile manufacturing. The fact that entry into banking was essentially free, however, meant that it was difficult to restrict entry into the textile industry by controlling access to capital. In the USA, the chartering of banks was left up to the states, which competed against one another as locales for new business. The result was chartering provisions that could easily be met by any medium-sized entrepreneur. The US system did not provide for a completely equal distribution of investable funds, but it did allow a large number of players to enter the game.

This regionally based capital market was gradually transformed into a national capital market in the second half of the century, thanks to the passage of the National Banking Act, which created a network of nationally chartered banks, and the widespread sale of government bonds to the public. By the end of the First World War, the textile industry was awash in finance and many companies took advantage of the swollen credit markets to float numerous securities issues (Temporary National Economic Committee 1941: 255; Kennedy 1940: Chs 2, 10).

In short, it was not the case that all American textile industrialists had equal access to impersonal sources of capital. Indeed, one of the primary reasons that the textile industry concentrated for so long in New England was because of inter-regional capital immobilities. But relative to the underdeveloped countries discussed below, large numbers of US industrialists were able to tap into the capital markets quite early in the country's industrial history.

Mexico

Mexico's experience stands in stark contrast to that of the USA. While Mexico began the transition to a mechanised textile industry as early as the 1830s, it was not until the 1890s that the industry underwent sustained growth. By this point, however, technological changes had raised the cost of entry into textile manufacturing. Thus, unlike US textile manufacturers, who were able to finance a significant part of their expansion and modernisation through an extended process of the reinvestment of profits, most Mexican textile firms had to purchase their equipment all at once, increasing the importance of impersonal sources of capital.

The institutions that could mobilise impersonal sources of capital, however, were very poorly developed in Mexico. Institutional lending to industry was largely absent in Mexico until the 1880s. As late as 1884 there were only 8 banks in operation, and as late as 1911 Mexico had but 47 banks, only 10 of which were legally able to lend for terms of more than a year.[3] Not only were there few banks, but the level of concentration within this small sector was very high. In 1895, three banks – the Banco Nacional de México, the Banco de Londres y México and the Banco Internacional Hipotecario – accounted for two-thirds of the capital invested in the banking system. Even as late as 1910 the same banks dominated the credit market, accounting for 75 per cent of the deposits in Mexico's nine largest banks and roughly one-half of all bank notes in circulation (Sánchez Martínez 1983: 81–2, 19: 258). If anything, the years after 1910 saw an increase in concentration, as the Mexican Revolution in that year threw capital markets into disarray, destroyed the public's faith in paper money, and put a brake on the development of the banking sector until the late 1920s (Cárdenas and Manns 1989).

The result of Mexico's slow and unequal development of credit intermediaries was that most manufacturers could not obtain bank financing. Even those that could only succeeded in getting short-term loans to cover working capital costs. Thus, Mexico's largest bank, the Banco Nacional de México, provided credit to a number of large industrial establishments in which its directors had interests. But even these insider loans constituted a small part of the total capital of those manufacturing firms. An analysis of the balance sheets of three of the country's largest cotton textile producers during the period from 1907 to 1913 indicates debt–equity ratios averaging 0.20:1.00. Virtually all of this debt was short term, most of it consisting of trade credits provided by suppliers (Sánchez Martínez 1983; Haber 1989: 65–7).

Equity financing through the creation of a publicly held, joint stock company was also unknown in the Mexican textile industry until the late 1880s. Even after the first industrial companies appeared on the Mexico City stock exchange, however, the use of the exchange to raise equity capital remained limited. By 1908 only fourteen industrials were traded on the exchange: no new firms joined their ranks until the late 1930s. Of those industrial companies only four were cotton manufacturers. These were the Compañía Industrial de Orizaba (CIDOSA), the Compañía Industrial Veracruzana (CIVSA), the Compañía Industrial de Atlixco (CIASA), and the Compañía Industrial de San Antonio Abad. Thus, of Mexico's 100 cotton textile firms in 1912 (controlling 148 mills), only 4 per cent represented publicly traded joint stock companies.[4] These four firms, however, took a disproportionate share of total capital invested in the industry, accounting for 27 per cent of all active spindles.

The reason that capital markets were so late in developing in Mexico and then grew in such a limited way was largely owing to two factors. The first was the loose enforcement of financial reporting requirements. In fact, publicly traded manufacturing companies often failed to publish balance sheets in public organs (such as the *Diario Oficial* or the financial press) even though the law required them to do so. The result was that individuals tended to invest only in those enterprises controlled by important financial capitalists. In this sense, Mexico's major financiers played the same role as individuals like JP Morgan in the financing of US heavy industry. Their presence on the boards of companies signalled to the investment community that a particular enterprise was a safe bet (on the US case see Davis 1963; De Long 1991). Two characteristics of the Mexico City stock exchange are particularly striking in this regard. First, almost all of the publicly traded industrials had well known, politically well-connected financial capitalists like Antonio Basagoiti, Hugo Scherer or León Signoret as directors. Second, there was very little entry and exit in the stock exchange. It was not the case that small firms tried to float issues and failed, nor that small firms succeeded in selling equity and then went out of business. Rather, the pattern was for a few large firms to be capitalised through the sale of equity. These firms then dominated their respective product lines well into the 1920s and 1930s.[5]

The second factor slowing the development of impersonal sources of finance was Mexico's regulatory environment. Throughout the early and mid-nineteenth century, the lack of modern commercial and incorporation laws retarded the development of banks and joint stock companies. No body of mortgage credit laws was written until 1884, and it was not until 1889 that a general incorporation law was established. Even when those laws were in place, however, new restrictive banking regulations prevented the widespread development of credit institutions. The Mexican government favoured the nation's largest bank, the Banco Nacional de México, with all kinds of special rights and privileges. These included reserve requirements that were half those demanded of other banks, the sole right to serve as the government's intermediary in all its financial transactions, a monopoly for its notes for the payment of taxes or other fees to the government, an exemption from taxes, and the sole right to establish branch banks. At the same time that the government created this privileged, semi-official institution, it erected significant barriers to entry for competing banks, including extremely high minimum capital requirements (originally 500,000 pesos, later raised to 1,000,000), high reserve requirements (banks were required to hold one-third the value of their bank notes in metallic currency in their vaults and an additional third in the Treasury), a prohibition on creating new banks without the authorisation of the secretary of the treasury *and* the Congress, a prohibition on foreign branch banks from issuing bank notes, a 5 per cent tax on the issue of bank notes, and the restriction of bank notes to the region in which the bank operated.[6]

The motivation behind these restrictive banking policies was essentially twofold. First, the Mexican government was more concerned about establishing a secure, stable source of finance for itself than creating large numbers of institutions designed to funnel credit to manufacturers. Second, the group of financiers who controlled the Banco Nacional de México also happened to belong to the inner clique of the Díaz regime. They used their political influence to obtain a special concession that restricted market entry.

The tight regulation of banking had two important ramifications. The first was that the number of banks and the extent of their operations remained small: industrial companies could not therefore generally rely on them as a source of finance. The second was that the credit market could not serve as a source of finance for speculation on the stock exchange as it had in the USA (and as it would in Brazil). This served to further impede the growth of the Mexico City stock exchange.

One might think that foreign capital could have made up for the lack of a well-developed Mexican capital market. After all, foreign investors were pumping billions of dollars into Mexican oil wells, mines, railroads, utilities and export agriculture. There was in fact some foreign portfolio investment in Mexico's cotton textile industry, but the phenomenon was not widespread. In any event, to the extent that foreigners invested in the textile industry they invested in the large, well-established firms that already had privileged access to the Mexico City stock exchange, thereby reinforcing the problem of differential access to capital. The reason for this lack of foreign investment in textiles was that manufacturing enterprises sold their output domestically, and thus earned their incomes in Mexican silver pesos. But silver lost 50 per cent of its value against gold during the 1890–1902 period and this meant that the rate of return in foreign, gold-backed currency was halved once an investor converted his Mexican dividend payments back into sterling, dollars or francs. In fact, the one foreign company that specialised in Mexican manufacturing investments, the Société Financière pour l'industrie au Mexique, fared very poorly for precisely this reason.[7] Hence, foreign investors tended to focus on enterprises in which income was earned in foreign, gold-backed currencies, like oil extraction, mining and export agriculture, or where the Mexican government offered sizable subsidies, like railroading.

In short, throughout its first hundred years of existence, the Mexican cotton textile industry had to rely on informal networks for its financing. When institutional innovations in the capital market created new opportunities for firms to obtain impersonal sources of finance, only a small group of entrepreneurs was able to benefit.

Brazil

Until the last decade of the nineteenth century, Brazilian textile entrepreneurs faced a capital market similar to their Mexican counterparts. Beginning in the 1890s, however, Brazil's capital markets, prompted by government regulatory reforms, underwent a long process of expansion and maturation. The result was that impersonal sources of finance became widely available to textile manufacturers.

Throughout most of the nineteenth century, institutions designed to mobilise impersonal sources of capital were largely absent in Brazil. An organised stock exchange had functioned in Rio de Janeiro since early in the century, but it was seldom used to finance industrial companies. During the period from 1850 to 1885 only one manufacturing company was listed on the exchange, and its shares changed hands in only three years during this period. Neither could Brazil's mill owners appeal to the banking system to provide them with capital. In fact, formal banks were so scarce as to be virtually non-existent. As late as 1888 Brazil had but 26 banks, whose combined capital totalled only 145,000 *contos* – roughly US$48 million. Only 7 of the country's 20 states had any banks at all, and half of all deposits were held by a few banks in Rio de Janeiro (Topik 1987: 28; Peláez and Suzigan 1976: Chs 2–5; Saes 1986: 73; Levy 1977: 109–12; Stein 1957b: 25–7). The slow development of these institutions can be traced in large part to public policies much like Mexico's. Bank regulations were designed to restrict entry into banking in order to favour a single, large super-bank that could serve as a source of government finance. The absence of banks not only restricted the amount of credit available to textile entrepreneurs, but it also meant that banks could not underwrite securities trading or finance securities speculation, the way they did in the USA and Western Europe (Sylla 1975: 52, 209). Finally, a system of special permits made the formation of a limited liability company an extraordinarily difficult affair (Levy 1977: 117, 245; Peláez and Suzigan 1976: 143; Saes 1986: 22, 86).

The last decade of the nineteenth century, however, witnessed a dramatic and sustained transformation of Brazil's capital markets. In the wake of the Revolution of 1889 that deposed the monarchy and established Brazil's First Republic came public policies that deregulated the banking industry and securities markets. As of 1889, legal barriers to entry into banking were removed and banks could engage in whatever kind of financial transactions they wished. Other reforms eased the formation of limited liability joint stock companies and encouraged securities trading by permitting purchases on margin.

Also of importance were financial reporting requirements that made managers more accountable to stockholders. Brazil's publicly traded corporations were required to produce financial statements twice a year and reprint them in public documents (such as the *Diario Official* or the *Jornal do Comércio*). In addition, their biannual reports had to list the names of all stockholders and the numbers of shares they controlled. Investors could thus obtain reasonably good information on the health of firms and the identities of their major shareholders.[8]

For textile industrialists these reforms produced dramatic results (Topik 1987: 28–31; Peláez and Suzigan 1976; Stein 1957b: 86). Over the short term, the *Encilhamento*, as the investment boom came to be called, created large numbers of banks, which both directly lent funds to manufacturers as well as financed stock market speculation (Levy 1977: 117, 245). The second and more important effect of the *Encilhamento* was that it financed the creation of large numbers of joint stock manufacturing companies. In 1888 only three cotton textile enterprises were listed on the Rio stock exchange; by 1894 there were 18, which grew to 25 in 1904 and to 57 in 1915, when growth began to level off. Thus, in 1915, 57 of Brazil's 180 cotton textile companies (32 per cent) were publicly traded, joint stock limited-liability corporations.[9] These firms with access to the equities markets accounted for 43 per cent of all invested capital in the industry. Recall that in Mexico only 4 per cent of cotton textile firms were publicly traded, but that these firms took up a relatively more disproportionate share of invested capital (27 per cent).

The *Encilhamento* also created a market for publicly traded corporate debt. As early as 1905, 31 of Brazil's 98 textile firms (32 per cent) were raising capital through the sale of debt. By 1915, 50 of the country's 180 firms (28 per cent) reported bond debt in their census returns. In fact, a comparison of the 1905 and 1915 censuses indicates that new debt issues accounted for 32 per cent of all new investment during that ten-year period.

The development of the bond market appears to have been slowed by the First World War. Between 1915 and 1924, the nominal value of outstanding long-term debt actually declined. The most important source of new investment capital was retained earnings, which accounted for 62 per cent of new additions to capital. The remainder of new capital spending was made up of new equity issues by already established companies and the founding of new firms, particularly in the state of São Paulo.[10] In the latter part of the 1920s the debt market began to recover, though it appears that much of the debt issued was used to fund operating losses during the Great Depression.

In short, Brazilian textile industrialists were limited in their sources of finance throughout most of the nineteenth century. Beginning in the late 1880s, however, regulatory reforms brought about important innovations in financial intermediation that made access to institutional sources of finance relatively easy for many entrepreneurs. Even though the development of these new sources of finance was slowed by the First World War, it still produced an extraordinarily large and well-integrated capital market by the standards of developing economies at the time.

FINANCE AND THE STRUCTURE AND GROWTH OF THE TEXTILE INDUSTRY

What effects did these differences in the development of capital have on the development of the textile industry in these countries? Logically, three consequences might have been anticipated. First, Mexico's textile industry should have grown much more slowly than that of Brazil. Second, privileged access to capital should have served as a barrier to entry: capital immobilities should have resulted in high levels of industrial concentration. Industry should have been most concentrated in Mexico and least concentrated in the USA, with Brazil falling between the two. Third, different trajectories of concentration might have been expected. Concentration should have fallen the fastest in Brazil, after the opening of its capital markets in the 1890s, and most slowly in Mexico.

An examination of the data on the development of the textile industry in the three countries bears out these hypotheses. With regard to the rate of growth of the textile industry, the Brazilian textile industry, which had been virtually non-existent in the first half of nineteenth century, quickly outgrew Mexico's after the capital markets opened up. From 1895 to 1905 the Brazilian cotton textile industry, flush with funds from the Rio de Janeiro stock and bond markets, outgrew Mexican industry by a factor of five, producing for the first time an absolute size difference in favour of Brazil. By the outbreak of the First World War, Brazil's industry was roughly twice the size of Mexico's, a gap which grew to three to one by the onset of the Great Depression (see Tables

16.1 and 16.2). These size differences, it should be pointed out, cannot be explained as a function of differences in national incomes or population sizes. In fact, during the period 1877 to 1910, when Brazil witnessed the most dramatic growth, Mexican income per capita outgrew Brazilian income per capita by a factor of ten.[11] As for the effects of capital immobilities on industrial concentration, the data are unequivocal: access to capital had a significant effect on the level of concentration. Tables 16.1, 16.2, and 16.3 and Figures 16.1 and 16.2 present estimates of four-firm concentration ratios (the percentage of the market controlled by the four largest firms) for all three countries and Herfindahl Indices (the sum of the squares of the market shares of all firms in an industry) for Mexico and Brazil.[12] There are a number of striking features of the data.

The first is the low, and continually declining, level of concentration in the United States, a result we would expect given the absence of barriers to entry in the industry (see Table 16.3).

The second is that the opening of Mexico's capital markets actually produced an increase in concentration. The trend in Mexico from the 1850s to the late 1880s was a gradual decrease in concentration: exactly the trend that could be expect in an expanding industry characterised by constant returns to scale technology. As Table 16.2 and Figures 16.1 and 16.2 indicate, Mexico's

Table 16.1 Size and structure of the Brazilian cotton textile industry

Year	Active firms	Firms with useful data	Active spindles	Four-firm ratio*	Herfindahl index*
1866	9	9	14,875	.766	.1773
1882	41	30	70,188	.376	.0631
1883	44	33	65,937	.371	.0582
1895	43	27	169,451	.349	.0585
1905	98	80	734,928	.207	.0279
1907	117	115		.203	.0250
1914	227	210		.143	.0144
1915	180	168	1,492,822	.161	.0165
1924	202	162	2,161,080	.212	.0222
1925	226	186	2,469,247	.179	.0182
1926	272	213	2,504,339	.166	.0155
1927	273	231	2,634,293	.162	.0141
1934	266	247	2,700,228	.173	.0168

Note: * Concentration measured at the firm level.
Sources: Borja Castro (1869: 3-73); Commissão de Inquerito Industrial (1882); Ministerio da Indústria, Viação e Obras Públicas, Relatorio, 1896; Vasco (1905); Centro Industrial do Brasil (1909, 1917); Centro Industrial de Fiação e Tecelagem de Algodão (1928); Stein, (1957b: Appendix 1).

Table 16.2 Size and structure of the Mexican cotton textile industry, 1843-1929

Year	Firms listed	Firms with useful data	Active spindles	Four-firm ratio*	Mexico Herfindahl Index*
1843	52	51	95,208	0.376	0.0524
1850	51	51	135,538	0.449	0.0686
1853	36	36	121,714	0.430	0.0677
1862	40	40	129,991	0.319	0.0490
1865	52	52	151,722	0.342	0.0501
1878	81	81	249,294	0.160	0.0209
1883	83	83		0.189	0.0225
1888	110	91	249,561	0.217	0.0249
1891	80	78		0.228	0.0268
1893	89	83	351,568	0.284	0.0355
1895	85	85	411,090	0.363	0.0480
1896	97	83	397,767	0.371	0.0513
1902	109	109	595,728	0.381	0.0637
1906	106	106	688,217	0.338	0.0486
1912	100	100	749,949	0.271	0.0343
1919	88	88	735,308	0.374	0.0592
1929	123	123	839,109	0.278	0.0335

Note: * Concentration measured at the firm level.
Sources: Secretaría de Hacienda y Crédito Público (1977: 81); Ministerio de Fomento (1854: Table 2); Ministerio de Fomento (1857: docs. 18-1, 18-2); Dirección de Colonización e Industria (1851); Pérez Hernández (1862); Ministerio de Fomento (1865: 438-40); Secretaría de Fomento (1890); Secretaría de Fomento (1894); Secretaría de Fomento (1896); Secretaría de Hacienda (1896); Archivo General de la Nación, Ramo de Trabajo, caja 5, legajo 4; Secretaría de Hacienda, *Boletín*, second semester 1919, first semester 1920, Jan. 1930; *La Semana Mercantil*, 23 June 1902, 25 June 1906; Haber (1989: 125, 158).

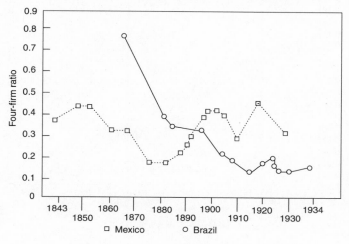

Figure 16.1   Four-firm ratios

275

four-firm ratio fell from a high of 0.449 in 1850 to a low of 0.160 in 1878, while the Herfindahl dropped from a 0.0686 to 0.0209 over the same period. Beginning in the late 1880s, the trend reversed, even though the industry was witnessing rapid growth. By 1902, both the four-firm ratio and the Herfindahl had nearly regained their 1853 levels. Concentration then began to decrease again to 1912, when the Revolution intervened and again reversed the trend.

Table 16.3 Size and structure of the US cotton textile industry

Year	Active mills	Spindles	Four-firm ratio*
1850	1,094		.100
1860	1,091		.126
1870	956		.107
1880	756	10,653,435	.087
1890	905	14,384,180	.077
1900	1,055	19,463,984	.070
1910	1,324	28,178,862	.075
1920	1,496	34,603,471	.066
1930	1,281	33,009,323	.095

Note: * Concentration measured at the firm level.
Sources: Calculated from US Bureau of the Census, *Census of Manufactures*, 1849-1929; Bateman and Weiss Large Firm Sample for 1840-1860; *Davison's Blue Book*; *Official American Textile Directory*; *The Textile Manufacturer's Directory*; and *Dockham's American Report*.

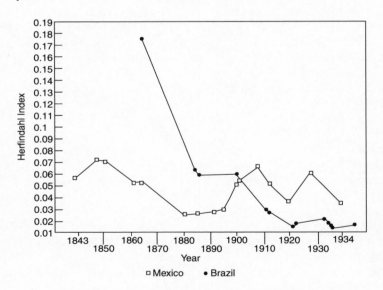

Figure 16.2 Herfindahl Indices, Brazil and Mexico

The final striking feature of the data is that it indicates that the more profound opening of Brazil's capital markets produced exactly the opposite result than that obtained in Mexico (see Table 16.1 and Figures 16.1 and 16.2). The sharp drop in concentration from 1866 to 1882 is clearly a mathematical identity, having to do with the small size of the industry in 1866 when there were only nine firms. What is more relevant for our purposes is that this rapid rate of decrease in concentration took off again during the years from 1895 to 1907, and then slowed only slightly to 1914, when it began to gently level off. By 1914, the estimated Herfindahl index for Brazil stood at less than one-quarter of its 1882 value.[13]

Compared to Mexico, Brazil's textile industry was surprisingly unconcentrated, and became increasingly less so over time. Prior to the 1890s, Brazil's relatively small textile industry displayed higher levels of concentration than Mexico's. By 1905, however, relatively widespread access to institutional sources of capital in Brazil drove concentration down to roughly 60 per cent of that in Mexico. Just prior to the onset of the Great Depression, the level of concentration in Brazil was only 58 per cent of that in Mexico measured by the four-firm ratio and only 42 per cent of that in Mexico measured by the Herfindahl Index.

One might argue that Mexico's higher concentration ratios had little to do with capital immobilities: high levels of concentration were produced by demand, not supply factors. Mexico had higher levels of concentration and a different trajectory of concentration because it had a smaller textile industry than Brazil or the United States. This view contains a number of implications that are testable in the light of the empirical record.

First, the view that differences in concentration were a function of industry size assumes that Mexico's high levels of concentration were a function of the fact that only a small number of large firms could operate at the minimum efficient scale of production in Mexico. According to this view, it should be possible to observe statistically significant differences in total factor productivity between the industry leaders that dominated the market and their smaller competitors. But total factor productivity estimates at the firm level for both 1896 and 1912 show that, regardless of the specification of the production function, the minimum efficient scale of production was reached at surprisingly small firm sizes. The large firms financed by the capital market were no more productive per input of capital and labour than their competitors.

Second, the view that differences in concentration were a function of differences in industry size assumes that there is a direct link between industry size and industry structure: the larger a country's industry, the less concentrated it should be. This implication is easy to test. This hypothesis was tested by the construction of a simple OLS regression that measures the elasticity of concentration with respect to industry size. The logic behind the estimation is the following: in an industry characterised by modest returns to scale, with no significant technological changes that would raise the minimum efficient scale

277

of production in a discontinuous way, we should be able to predict the level of concentration simply by knowing the size of the industry. Similar regression results for Brazil and Mexico would indicate that concentration was simply a function of industry size. If, however, similar specifications of the regression for each country yield different results, then some intervening variable (like an imperfection in a factor market) must have been at work.[14]

Table 16.4 presents various regression specifications. All values are converted to natural logs in order to capture how changes in the size of the industry effect the change in concentration. Concentration is measured as the Herfindahl Index. All three specifications of the regression indicate that concentration in Brazil was a function of industry size, but in Mexico it was not. A glance at Tables 16.1 and 16.2 and Figures 16.1 and 16.2 quickly indicates why it was not: in many years in post-1890 Mexico concentration actually increased as industry size grew.

What would Mexican industry have looked like, in terms of its structure, had differential access to capital not served as a barrier to entry in Mexico's cotton goods industry? Assuming that in the absence of this barrier to entry the same relationship between industry size and industry structure would have held for both Brazil and Mexico, estimating Mexico's predicted level of concentration is a straightforward operation. It simply entails estimating a predicted Herfindahl series using the Brazilian coefficients from the first specification of the regression (see Table 16.4) and the actual Mexican data on numbers of firms.[15]

Table 16.5 and Figure 16.3 present these predicted Herfindahl values for Mexico, as well as the actual Mexican and Brazilian series. There are two

Table 16.4 Alternate specifications of industrial concentration regressions: Mexico (1843-1929) and Brazil (1866-1934)

	Mexico			Brazil		
	Spec. 1	Spec. 2	Spec. 3	Spec. 1	Spec. 2	Spec. 3
Intercept	−1.28	−1.92	−3.83	−.31	2.09	−.08
(ln)firms	−.44		−1.29	−.72		−.60
	(−1.73)		(−2.58)	(−22.66)		(−3.12)
(ln)spindles		−.09	.50		−.42	−.07
		(−0.74)	(1.97)		(−13.80)	(−.59)
R²	.17	.04	.38	.98	.95	.98
N	17	15	15	13	11	11

Note: Dependent variable: (ln)Herfindahl Index; T statistics in parentheses.
Source: See Tables 16.1 and 16.2.

Table 16.5 Actual and predicted Herfindahl Indices, Mexico and Brazil 1843–1934

	Actual Mexico	Predicted Mexico	Actual Brazil
1843	.0524	.0432	
1850	.0686	.0432	
1853	.0677	.0556	
1862	.0490	.0515	
1865	.0501	.0426	
1866			.1773
1878	.0209	.0310	
1882			.0631
1883	.0225	.0305	.0582
1888	.0249	.0285	
1891	.0268	.0318	
1893	.0355	.0305	
1895	.0480	.0299	.0585
1896	.0513	.0305	
1902	.0637	.0250	
1905			.0279
1906	.0486	.0255	
1907			.0250
1912	.0343	.0266	
1914			.0144
1915			.0165
1919	.0592	.0292	
1924			.0222
1925			.0182
1926			.0155
1927			.0141
1929	.0335	.0229	
1934			.0168

Source: Actual data from Tables 16.1 and 16.2. Predicted Mexico series uses the parameter estimates for Brazil from specification one in Table 16.4 and the actual Mexican data on number of firms with useful data. It predicts Mexico's level of concentration had the same relationship held between industry size and industry structure as in Brazil.

features about the predicted series that are notable. The first is that until the early 1890s the fitted series does a reasonably good job of predicting the movement of concentration in Mexico, indicating that the statistical relationship between industry size and concentration observed in Brazil held in Mexico as well until its capital markets opened up. The second is that after 1893 Mexico's actual and predicted Herfindahl values moved in entirely different directions. By 1902, the actual level of concentration in Mexico was more than twice its predicted value.

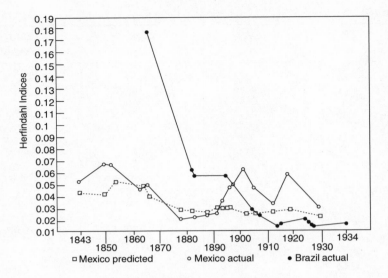

Figure 16.3 Herfindahl Indices, actual and predicted

CONCLUSIONS

What lessons can be drawn from this story about government regulation, capital market development, and the growth and structure of industry?

The first is that government regulatory policies had a significant effect on the growth of capital markets. Capital market development in the three countries was not completely endogenous to the process of economic growth: different histories of government regulation in each of the cases gave rise to very different sizes and structures of capital markets.

Second, capital immobilities appear to have been in large part the product of the inability of investors to obtain information and monitor managers. In Mexico, information was difficult to obtain, as a result well-known financiers with established reputations had privileged access to the capital markets. This was a very different outcome from that which obtained in Brazil where the costs of information appear to have been much lower.

Third, differences in capital market development had a significant impact on the rate of growth of industry. Mexico's financial system, in which a small group of entrepreneurs could get access to impersonal sources of capital while most entrepreneurs could not, gave rise to a small textile industry relative to Brazil. The rapid expansion of the Brazilian textile industry after the opening up of the capital markets in the late 1880s underlines the important role played by access to finance in industrial growth.

Fourth, imperfections in capital markets also had a significant effect on the structure of industry. The much more limited opening of the capital markets in Mexico gave rise to higher levels of concentration than in Brazil and the United States. Analysis of the data indicates that these differences existed independent of industry size.

NOTES

This research was made possible through support provided by the US Agency for International Development under Cooperative Agreement No. DHR–0015–A–00–0031–00 to the Centre on Institutional Reform and the Informal Sector (IRIS) and administered by the Office of Economic and Institutional Reform, Center for Economic Growth, Bureau for Global Programs, Field Support and Research. Financial support was also provided by the Social Science Research Council, the Center for US–Mexican Studies at the University of California, San Diego, and Stanford University's Institute for International Studies.

1 This does not mean that scale economies were insignificant in cotton textile production. Indeed, had economies of scale been negligible, access to capital could not have served as a barrier to entry. It does mean, however, that scale economies were exhausted in textiles at relatively small firm sizes compared to such industries as steel, cement and chemicals.
2 This is not to suggest that problems of capital mobilisation did not exist in the United States. The market for industrial securities was regional in nature until the late nineteenth century. Similarly, banks tended not to make loans outside their region. It is to suggest, however, that capital mobilisation problems were significantly less severe in the United States than in the underdeveloped world and that the regulation of financial markets was far less repressive in the US case than in the underdeveloped world.
3 By 1910 the United States had some 25,000 commercial banks alone. This does not include the thousands of trust companies, savings banks, and savings and loan associations.
4 The activity of the Mexico City stock exchange was followed by Mexico's major financial weeklies: *La Semana Mercantil*, 1894–1914; *El Economista Mexicano*, 1896–1914; *Boletín Financiero y Minero*, 1916–1938. The behaviour of the shares of these firms is analysed in Haber (1989: Ch. 7). The total number of firms is from textile manuscript censuses in Archivo General de la Nación, Ramo de Trabajo, caja 5, legajo 4 (also see caja 31, legajo 2).
5 Examples can be found in the steel, beer, soap, dynamite, cigarette, wool textile, and paper industries, in addition to cotton textiles. See Haber (1989: Chs 4, 5).
6 When the first minimum was established in 1897, it was equal to $233, 973 US. The increase in 1908 brought the minimum capital requirement up to $497,265, roughly five times the minimum for nationally chartered banks in the United States. For a discussion of these various privileges and barriers to entry, as well as changes in banking laws, see Sánchez Martínez (1983: 43, 61–2, 67); Ludlow (1986: 334–6); Bátiz (1986: 286, 287, 293).
7 The annual reports of the Société Financière pour l'industrie au Mexique can be found in *La Semana Mercantil*, 8 Aug. 1903; *El Economista Mexicano*, 11 Oct. 1902, 6 July 1904, 4 Aug. 1904, 21 Oct. 1905, 18 Aug. 1906.
8 Shareholder lists were not published in the abbreviated reports reprinted in the *Jornal do Comércio* or the *Diario Official*, but they were published in the original annual reports.
9 Calculated from: Centro Industrial do Brasil (1917); Levy (1977: 245, 385). The

peak number of publicly traded textile firms was reached in 1922, when 64 textile issues traded on the Rio exchange. By 1927 this had fallen to 52 firms, as the slow growth of the Brazilian economy in the early 1920s forced out weak firms.

10 Calculated from Vasco (1905); Centro Industrial (1917, 1927). All averages are weighted by the value of capital.

11 Estimates constructed from Coatsworth (1978: 82); Instituto Nacional de Estadística, Geografía, e Informática (1985: 9); Instituto Brasileiro de Geografía e Estatística (1990: 33).

12 These estimates of concentration are all calculated at the firm level. For the US, Mexican and Brazilian data, this involved combining the market shares of all mills held by a single corporation, partnership or sole proprietor. Market shares for Mexico and Brazil were calculated from estimates of the actual sales or value of output of mills. Market shares for the United States had to be estimated from information on installed spindles. Econometric work on the United States indicates that there was a 25 per cent difference in output per spindle between average and best practice techniques. I therefore assumed that the largest firms in the United States were 25 per cent more productive than the average, and adjusted their market shares upwards accordingly. On average and best practice techniques see Davis and Stettler (1966: 231).

13 One might argue that these differences in concentration would disappear if imports of foreign textiles were accounted for, but that argument does not stand up to the empirical evidence on textile imports. Indeed, both Brazil and Mexico followed highly protectionist policies after 1890, virtually eliminating imported cloth except for fine weave, high value goods.

14 The model makes the reasonable assumption that there were no discontinuous jumps in minimum efficient scales in either country, though it does allow for a gradual increase in minimum efficient scales. For this reason, it is unlikely that the elasticities of the size variables will sum to unity. Observations by contemporaries indicate that there were no discontinuous jumps in textile manufacturing technology during the period that affected the Brazilian or Mexican industries. The only major innovation was the Northrup automatic loom, which was developed in the 1890s. But the Northrup loom was not widely adopted in either country (there were only twenty-five of them in service in Mexico as late as 1910). Moreover, to the extent that there were technological jumps, these would be more pronounced in the Brazilian regressions than in those for Mexico, because of Brazil's faster purchase of new capacity. This would tend to bias the results against the hypothesis advanced here.

15 This is an upper bound prediction. The model assumes that Mexico's industry size would have been the same in the presence of a better developed capital market, which is highly unlikely. Had the size of the industry been larger, the predicted concentration ratios would be even lower than those estimated here. The first specification of the regression was used because it provided the best fit for both the Mexican and Brazilian data.

17

THE STATE AND THE ECONOMY IN INDONESIA IN THE NINETEENTH AND TWENTIETH CENTURIES[1]

Anne Booth

ANALYSING THE STATE IN ASIAN ECONOMIC HISTORY

A central concern of Douglass North's work has been an examination of the way in which institutions interact with, and influence, long-run economic change. As he has recently written, 'the polity and economy are inextricably interlinked in any understanding of the performance of an economy and therefore we must develop a true political economy discipline' (North 1990a: 112). If economic historians want to evolve a satisfactory explanation about why the Industrial Revolution has taken so long to become a universal phenomenon and why so many parts of the world are still economically backward and undeveloped, it is necessary to look not just at the way particular polities have specified and enforced property rights, but also at the larger issue of the way governments intervene to regulate private and public enterprises, and raise and spend resources. In short, it is essential to examine the economic role of governments, how that role has changed over time in the context of a specific economy, and how it varies across countries at a particular point in time.

In a paper originally published in 1979, North pointed out that, while the existence of some form of government is essential for economic growth, economic historians had paid little attention to the role of the state when considering secular patterns of economic change. He argued that 'while the long path of historical research is strewn with the bones of theories of the state developed by historians and political scientists, economists traditionally have given little attention to the issue' (North 1981: 20). For North, 'two general types of explanation for the state exist: a contract theory and a predatory or exploitation theory' (1981: 21). The contract theory is inherently appealing to neo-classical economists because it rests on an assumption that the role of the state is to ensure that individuals can maximise their individual wealth holdings without damaging the chances of other citizens to do likewise; contract theories thus offer plausible reasons for the emergence of an efficient regime of growth-promoting property rights, although they have little to say about why such regimes have historically been so rare.

Predatory or exploitation theories of the state, on the other hand, have attracted a much wider range of adherents. Essentially, these view the state as controlled by ruling cliques or classes, and its main function is thus to maximise the incomes accruing to the rulers, almost regardless of the impact on the rest of the citizenry. Such theories have been propounded by both Marxist and neo-classical economists, especially those seeking to explain the failure of particular countries or empires to achieve self-sustaining economic growth. A good example of this approach, explaining the failure of Asian countries to develop their economies between 1400 and 1800, can be found in the work of Mokyr:

> Almost any area between Constantinople and Peking was ruled by greedy and incompetent parasites, who subjected their hapless peasantry to indescribable misery to satisfy their own lust and gluttony. Taxation was arbitrary and total. Investment was consequently negligible and possibly negative if we take into account the ecological destructions caused by deforestation. Asia ... was an Arthur Laffer nightmare come true; inept and confiscatory government had condemned the population to perpetual poverty by thwarting individual initiative.
>
> (Mokyr 1984: 176)

Whether this is an historically accurate picture of economic conditions in a large part of the world over a period of almost half a millennium is open to question, but some sort of predatory theory would seem to be needed to explain long periods of stagnation in economies such as China, or parts of the Middle East, which had earlier showed a remarkable capacity for technological innovation. More generally, North (1981: 25) has drawn attention to the 'persistent tension between the ownership structure which maximised the rents to the ruler (and his group) and an efficient system that reduced transaction costs and encouraged economic growth'. Rulers usually resist changes in property rights regimes which adversely affect either their own wealth or that of key supporters, even if they might increase revenues for the state as a whole, and permit more rapid development of infrastructure and economic institutions which are in turn supportive of rapid economic growth. In short, rulers usually have had no concept of a wider national interest, beyond that of their immediate circle, and certainly no concept of economic growth as a legitimate national objective. Why then does sustained economic growth ever occur?

> Changes in information costs, technology and population (or relative factor prices in general) are all obvious destabilising influences. Also significant is the fact that the ruler is mortal.

A change in relative prices that improves the bargaining power of a group of constituents can lead to alteration of the rules to give that group more income or, alternatively, the constituents can force the ruler to give up some of his rule-making powers. Sometimes the emergence of 'representative' government has come in the face of an external threat to the ruler .... While changes in military technology were a major (though certainly not the sole) source of the growth of pluralist or representative government in the ancient and medieval world, the modern alterations in control of the state have been associated with the radical change in relative prices stemming from the Second Economic Revolution.

(North 1981: 29–30)

The rapid structural transformation of economies that began with the industrialisation of northwest Europe and North America in the nineteenth century gave rise to new social classes who, over time, were able to secure political power commensurate with their growing economic dominance.[2] The old landed gentry declined as a political force as the new commercial bourgeoisie became dominant. By the end of the century political parties which drew their support from trade unions and which were often Marxist in their philosophy were also becoming more powerful in the industrialised nations. Marxists believed that capitalism would eventually collapse under the weight of its recurrent crises, and that a socialist political and economic system would prevail which in turn would bring about a fairer distribution of income and wealth. Such ideas became influential in other parts of the world as well, especially in those countries which had not industrialised but which were closely linked to the major industrial nations through colonial domination.

At first glance, it might appear that theories of the predatory state could serve to explain the phenomenon of the growth of Western colonial control over other parts of the world in the nineteenth century. As the countries of northern Europe developed industrially, they acquired both the need for new markets for their rapidly growing output, and the superior military and transport technologies which made large colonial empires strategically feasible. By the turn of the century, radical critics of Western colonialism indeed attributed it at least partly to the need of industrial capitalism for ever larger markets. Certainly, the major late nineteenth-century European colonial powers behaved as if they thought the chief function of colonies was to bring wealth to the metropolitan powers and were reluctant to see their European rivals acquire more overseas possessions.

But by the early twentieth century, several colonial powers in Asia had begun to adopt policies which were much more overtly 'developmental' in their aims. While the main emphasis of colonial administrations continued to be on the maintenance of law and order and the collection of taxes, there was growing recognition that there was also a responsibility to improve the living standards of the indigenous population. These goals partly reflected changing views on the role of government in the metropolitan countries, but partly also a growing realisation that poverty-stricken colonial populations were unlikely to provide a growing market for manufactures from the metropolitan country, and in the long-run might become a costly burden to metropolitan tax-payers. An additional concern was, of course, the growing power of nationalist movements, especially among the educated indigenous elites, and the perennial threat that, in the event of instability, hostile foreign powers might intervene. In South East Asia such hostile foreign powers were not just other European powers hungry for colonies, such as Germany, but also a rapidly industrialising Japan.

Probably nowhere in Asia did the reformist or developmental aspects of Western colonialism have such a dramatic impact on policy as in Indonesia in the final four decades of Dutch colonial rule. The so-called 'Ethical Policy' led to a substantial growth in the government budget and also to a considerable redirection of government policies and expenditures. The nature of these changes will be examined in greater detail below but it should be noted here that their occurrence would appear to confirm an important conclusion reached by North (1981: 31–2) in propounding his neo-classical theory of the state. The main reason that individuals do not rebel against repressive regimes is that the perceived costs are extremely high, and while the potential benefits may also be very high, the chances of success are assumed to be very low. For the individual, the cost of acts of rebellion was either imprisonment for long periods in remote and inhospitable places, or death.

Reforms initiated by the colonial government can also be interpreted as designed to make Indonesia safe for Western, and especially Dutch, capitalism, in the context of an economy where labour was increasingly abundant due to population growth and financial capital was in short supply. In the event reforms failed in their aim, mainly because of two exogenous events which the colonial government was powerless to affect: the depression of the 1930s and the Japanese invasion in 1942. When peace was restored in 1945, the balance of power in East Asia was changed irrevocably. The European colonial powers were greatly weakened at home as a result of the devastation of the war while the USA, which was in a position to dictate to other Allies, saw its interests in Asia best served by the emergence of strong, non-communist independent states.

But the newly independent state of Indonesia which emerged after protracted negotiations with the Dutch in 1949, although benefiting from overseas support, was internally weak and divided. From an economic point of view, these weaknesses manifested themselves in a chronic inability to widen the fiscal base beyond a narrow range of taxes, primarily on foreign trade. As demands for increased public expenditures grew inexorably and revenues stagnated, the budget deficit widened and inflation increased. As will be argued in greater detail below, the Indonesian government essentially failed in the implementation of its development objectives between 1950 and 1965 because of an inability either to reimpose the colonial fiscal system or to evolve a new regime capable of funding public expenditure growth in a non-inflationary way.

The coup which brought President Suharto to power in 1965 ushered in a long era of 'developmental authoritarianism' which continues to this day. The rise of this phenomenon in Indonesia and a number of other economically successful East Asian states has given rise to a large literature to which both economists and political scientists have contributed (Haggard 1990; Deyo 1987; Appelbaum and Henderson 1992). According to this literature, sustained economic growth in South Korea, Taiwan and Singapore has been due in each case to state autonomy from sectoral and societal interests, and hence its ability not only to reconcile differences and maintain order but to map out a strategy for improving the position of the country in the world capitalist system (McVey 1992: 13). According to this view, these states have succeeded because they have been able to insulate themselves from pressures from powerful vested interests and pursue policies which give top priority to the achievement of rapid rates of economic growth. They have managed to overcome what a distinguished development economist of an earlier generation termed the soft-state syndrome in developing countries, where officials widely ignored or perverted government rules and directives, and colluded for personal gain with the very groups whose behaviour they were supposed to regulate (Myrdal 1970: 211).

Whether or not Indonesia is a successful developmental authoritarian regime in this sense will be discussed below. But first it is necessary to address the issue of how the rise of these developmental 'hard states' in East Asia fits North's description of the processes through which states evolve away from the predatory model to produce an efficient, growth-promoting regime of property rights. It is not difficult to explain why countries like South Korea, Taiwan and Singapore gave such high priority to accelerated economic growth in the 1960s and 1970s; all faced threats from hostile neighbours and all realised that only accelerated growth could both increase their own self-defence capability and win support within the domestic population. All these countries were influenced by the growing international debate on economic development as a policy goal, and Western-educated technocrats held key posts in government and the bureaucracy. And in addition, all benefited from the liberal world trade environment of the time; once the decision was taken to promote export-oriented industries, capital and technological expertise were provided through direct foreign investment and market opportunities were available in the industrial world.

Several recent writers have stressed that the success of these states has been due in considerable measure to the very active guidance provided by government agencies. The argument is not that these economies have had a large government sector (in fact they have tended to have smaller ratios of public expenditure to GDP than other, slower growing economies in both the developed and the developing world) (Kuznets 1988). Rather it is that they have developed sophisticated economic bureaucracies which have become extremely astute in assisting those industries with export potential to grow rapidly through penetration of foreign markets. An important message of this literature is that the economic bureaucracies have managed to insulate themselves from pressures exerted by special interest groups and have thus been able, for example, to withdraw support from those industries which have not met export performance targets (Johnson 1982; Amsden 1989; Wade 1990). As with the changes made by colonial regimes, the experience of policy reform in the East Asia developmental states would seem to support North's argument that institutional innovation will come from rulers rather than constituents.

In South East Asia by contrast a rather different process of policy reform has been underway in the 1980s. In Thailand, Malaysia and Indonesia, in spite of their tradition of rather authoritarian, and in the case of Thailand and Indonesia, military-supported, regimes, successive governments have found the process of policy reform hampered by the need to appease different constituencies based on different regional, religious or ethnic groups. It has been argued that in these countries institutional change has come about more as the result of skilful lobbying by particular interest groups such as business associations rather than being imposition from above via 'insulated' government bureaucracies (Macintyre and Jayasuriya 1992). Such an argument does not necessarily refute North's hypothesis, but it does suggest that the processes of adjustment to perceived threats to regime survival and to changing domestic and international economic opportunities is complex and unpredictable.

THE CHANGING ECONOMIC ROLE OF THE STATE IN INDONESIA

By the end of the nineteenth century, virtually the whole of South and South East Asia had been colonised by one or other of the major industrial powers. But the motivations of the various colonial powers in Asia differed considerably. The British saw their South East Asian dependencies largely as adjuncts to more important possessions in the Indian sub-continent and in Australia and Oceania. The British were quick to appreciate the strategic importance of the Straits of Malacca, and especially of Singapore, and secured in a treaty with the Dutch in 1824 (the Dutch in return gained control of most of the island of Sumatra) (Ricklefs 1993: 143). After the end of the Napoleonic Wars, Britain returned the island of Java to the Dutch mainly in order to strengthen the rather weak and unstable Dutch state against its more powerful neighbours.

On return to Dutch rule, Java experienced a period of maladministration. By 1829 accumulated colonial government deficits came to 38 million guilders, rather more than twice the level of imports in that year (Creutzberg 1976: 17). Most of this expenditure had been for military purposes. After 1830, experimentation gave way to systematic exploitation, the main aim of which was to secure as large a surplus as possible for remittance to the Netherlands (Booth *et al*. 1990; Fasseur 1991). Indigenous cultivators were forced to grow specified export products which were then collected by government agents. While the cultivators, and domestic middlemen did receive payments, these were well below the amount derived by the government from the sale of crops. Further revenue was extracted from state monopolies, and land and trade taxes. The net outcome was a colonial budget that was almost continually in surplus from 1835 to 1875, facilitating large transfers to the exchequer in the Netherlands. There can be little doubt that this fiscal 'drain' ensured that the domestic economy of Java captured few of the potential benefits of export growth in the half century before 1870.[3] A considerable part of the gains from Javanese trade went on providing the citizens of metropolitan Holland with the infrastructure and education which were denied the colonial population (Griffiths 1979: 4ff; Fasseur 1991: 43). While critics of the system may have exaggerated its deleterious impact on native living standards, there can be no doubt that, had government expenditure policies been directed more towards providing infrastructure and services in Java, their living standards could have been considerably higher by the turn of the century. But extracting revenue for remittance to the metropolitan exchequer, rather than improving the condition of the indigenous majority, was the main aim of colonial policy at that point. Judged by this criterion, colonial fiscal policy was a considerable success.

Day (1900) regards the outbreak of the Aceh War in 1873, and the greater expenditure which that conflict entailed, as the major factor in bringing to an end the long era of colonial fiscal surpluses, a view which has been confirmed by more recent scholars (Fasseur 1991: 43). In addition, as Fasseur (1991: 49–50) has argued, business aversion to government intervention in economic activities was an important reason for the adoption of a more liberal policy after 1870. The opening of the Suez Canal ushered in a period of rapid expansion of Asian trade with Europe and entrepreneurial elements within the colony wanting to exploit new commercial opportunities. From the government perspective, a revenue regime based on the enforced cultivation and sale of crops was increasingly cumbersome and inefficient. Taxes were clearly a much 'cheaper' source of revenue in terms of collection costs than monies yielded from sales of produce. Moreover, labour was becoming increasingly abundant and willing to work for low wages while Western entrepreneurs were now more prepared to invest in export-oriented agricultural enterprises if labour supplies could be guaranteed (Booth 1988a: 70; Blusse 1984). Far better to let the private sector produce export crops, allowing the government to tax corporate and personal incomes to finance essential expenditure within the colony. In order to facilitate the growth of both indigenous and foreign agricultural enterprises, new land legislation was passed which conferred freehold on the indigenous owners while at the same time allowing foreign companies to obtain long leases for the development of commercial estates.[4]

International comparisons indicate that between 1860 and 1885, public expenditures per capita in Indonesia were low in comparison with British India

ANNE BOOTH

and other British dependent colonies, although there was little difference in per capita expenditure between India and Indonesia from 1885 to 1910 (Table 17.1). On the other hand, total government revenues per capita (in sterling) were higher than in British India for the entire period from 1860 to 1912, even though they fell after 1875–9. This indicates the conservative nature of Dutch colonial fiscal policy for most of the nineteenth century. Total revenues in Indonesia were high relative to expenditures and when deficits occurred they were much smaller in per capita terms than in either India or other dependent British colonies. After the turn of the century, the cessation of hostilities in Aceh permitted the government to reduce military spending. It might have been expected that this in turn would have led to a considerable reduction in taxation, and a smaller budget. But this was not the option taken by the colonial officials charged with the implementation of the new Ethical Policies after 1901. Instead they embarked on a programme of rapid growth in public expenditures, oriented increasingly towards development activities.

Table 17.1 Government revenues and expenditures per capita in Indonesia, India, and other British dependent colonies, 1860–1912 (pounds sterling per capita)

| Year | Indonesia | | India | | Other British colonies | |
	R	E	R	E	R	E
1860–64	.39	.28	.31	.38	.66	.64
1865–69	.36	.29	.31	.44	.65	.68
1870–74	.37	.31	.29	.46	.62	.65
1875–79	.37	.38	.31	.49	.61	.65
1880–84	.34	.36	.33	.51	.67	.78
1885–89	.30	.29	.23	.33	.76	.89
1890–94	.28	.29	.18	.25	.72	.99
1895–99	.27	.29	.20	.29	.57	.81
1900–04	.28	.29	.23	.33	.42	.61
1905–09	.31	.31	.23	.36	.38	.55
1910–12	.40	.41	.22	.34	.39	.64

Notes: R = Total government revenues
E = Total government expenitures
Sources: Davis and Huttenback (1986): 123, 222. Indian data exclude the princely states and refer to the national government only. Dependent colonies include all British colonies in Asia, the Pacific, Africa, the Caribbean and Latin America, excluding those which were self-governing. Indonesian data: Creutzberg (1976).

The changing role of government in the colonial economy in the last four decades of the colonial era was manifested in the growth of government expenditure on a range of development activities (Boomgaard 1986). There was, too, increasing intervention in order to attain objectives which would not have been achieved had product and factor markets been left to their own devices. Indeed, the last generation of colonial civil servants foreshadowed many of the policies which would be enthusiastically adopted by newly industrialising countries in many parts of the world after 1945. Much has been written about the change in government policies towards colonial industrial development in the 1930s in the colony (Shepherd 1941: Ch. 3; Sitsen 1943; Segers 1987). But government intervention and regulation was not restricted to the industrial sector. Boeke (1953: Ch. 23) discusses the regulation of rice exports necessitated by shrinking world markets and the growth of intervention in markets for basic foodstuffs. In the 1930s the colonial government participated in a number of international commodity stabilisation programmes and attempted, with varying degress of success, to regulate output of rubber, tea and tin (van Gelderen 1939: Ch. 4).

By the late 1930s the Department of Economic Affairs was behaving much like a planning agency (Barber 1939). While to some, not least the officials themselves, this may have seemed a desirable development, to others it smacked of 'administrative tyranny' (Bousquet 1940: 51). There can be no doubting Higgins' assertion that an important effect of the 1930s depression was 'a shift from a relatively free to a highly regulated economy' (1968: 693). But the free economy was itself very much a creation of the Dutch colonial system after the gradual retreat from the *dirigisme* of the years from 1830 to 1870. And the impact of the Ethical Policy after 1900 had been a slow, rather than a dramatic, shift in the pattern of official expenditure over the first two decades of the twentieth century. Public expenditures had begun to grow in real terms, and relative to an expanding GDP and by 1920 had reached 14 per cent of GDP (see Figure 17.1). There was also a considerable redirection of expenditure away from military and defence and towards salaries and perquisites of the civilian bureaucracy, public works, and to a lesser extent health and education (Booth 1990: Table 10.5). By 1921 public works accounted for almost 40 per cent of the total budget.

Revenues did not keep pace with expenditure growth and, by the 1910s, the budget deficit averaged more than 78 million guilders per annum, reaching 3.4 per cent of GDP in 1920 (van der Eng 1992). These deficits were met by increased government borrowing, and by 1923 the accumulated stock of public debt amounted to over 21 per cent of national income, and debt service payments to around 6 per cent of commodity exports (see Table 17.2). Although these ratios were low compared with what they were to become later in the century, they were sufficient to attract adverse attention in the Netherlands, and the advent of a more conservative Governor-General in 1921 brought considerable changes. Although government expenditures continued to grow in real terms, they fell as a proportion of GDP, from the peak of 14 per cent in 1921 to around 10 per cent by the mid-1920s (Figure 17.2). The budget deficit was reined in and the debt stock fell somewhat compared with the early part of the decade.

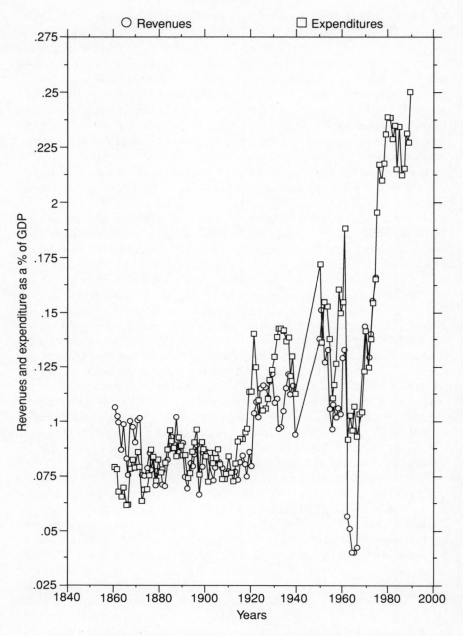

Figure 17.1 Government revenues and expenditures as a percentage of GDP

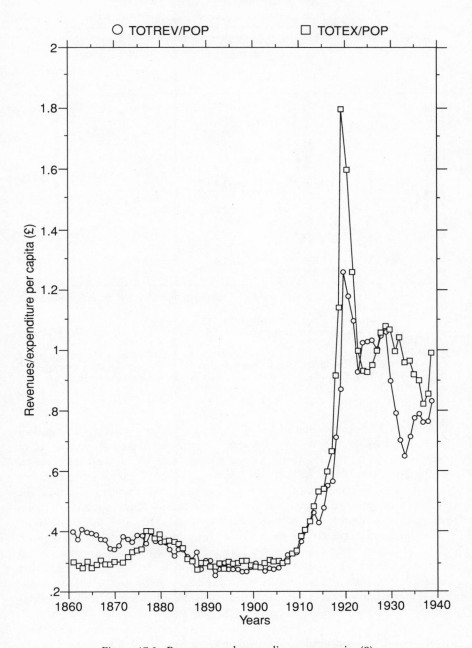

Figure 17.2 Revenues and expenditures per capita (£)

Table 17.2 Trends in public debt and debt service payments in Indonesia, 1911–90

Year	Public debt as a percentage of:		Debt service as a percentage of:	
	GDP	Exports	Exports	Total public expenditure
1911	2.9	17.5	0.8	1.8
1914	4.8	25.0	0.8	1.7
1919	8.8	24.8	1.1	3.6
1923	21.3	93.9	5.7	11.9
1928	15.8	63.2	6.2	13.1
1933	43.0	290.0	20.0	20.8
1938	34.2	199.7	11.0	14.6
1952	a	63.5	n.a	n.a
1958	a	77.8	n.a	n.a
1965	a	333.2	n.a	n.a
1970[b]	25.3	206.3	13.9	5.6
1980[c]	23.8	80.1	13.9	6.7
1985[c]	36.3	150.8	28.8	14.6
1990[c]	55.9	190.1	31.1	27.1

Notes: [a] The overvalued exchange rates makes comparisons with GDP difficult, especially in 1958 and 1965.

[b] 1970 data refer to long-term public debt only.

[c] In these years debt service payments include private as well as public debt payments. GNP is used rather than GDP.

Sources: 1911–38: Creutzberg (1976); Korthals Altes (1991); GDP data from van der Eng (1992); 1952 and 1958: Bank Indonesia, *Annual Reports*; 1965: Panglaykim and Arndt (1966): 5 1970–90: World Bank, *World Debt Tables* and *Indikator Ekonomi,* various issues.

Given the sophistication of the late colonial administrative apparatus, it is perhaps surprising that more effort was not made to reduce the public sector borrowing requirement during the inter-war years by increasing revenues, particularly tax yields. In fact these two decades witnessed a considerable change in the relative importance of tax and non-tax revenues. Although the ratio of total revenues to national income did not alter much, the share of total revenues accounted for by taxes grew fairly steadily (Booth 1990: Table 10.7). This was mainly due to the growing importance of taxes on incomes (both personal and corporate), taxes on foreign trade and specific excises. This increase occurred in spite of the fact that prominent civil servants argued that in Java in the early the people were already being taxed 'to the utmost limit' and that further increases in the tax burden would adversely affect indigenous welfare (Penders 1977: 91–6).

Certainly there was an attempt to increase government revenues from taxes which would fall on upper income groups, rather than from the land tax or from other sources such as the government monopolies whose incidence was probably more regressive. But despite a diversification in revenue sources, taxation of the indigenous population increased over these two decades. At the same time powerful business interests objected to the growing burden of personal and corporate income tax which was claimed to be adversely affecting the international competitiveness of export industries, especially the agricultural estates. Although, with the improvement in the business climate, revenues rose after 1934 as personal and corporate incomes recovered, increased rates of direct taxation were ruled out during the 1930s. Taxes on foreign trade, which had risen to 25 per cent of total government revenues in the years from 1920 to 1936, fell back again in the latter part of the 1930s (Table 17.3).

Turning to examine the role of the government in the economy in the immediate post-independence years, from 1950 to 1965, a paradox immediately presents itself. As in many newly independent Asian countries in the 1950s, the leaders of the Indonesian independence movement were greatly

Table 17.3 Foreign trade taxes as a percentage of total government revenues and as a percentage of commodity exports and imports, 1900–90

Year	Foreign trade taxes as a percentage of:	
	Total government revenues[a]	Commodity export and import receipts[b]
1900	8.1	2.7
1910	8.5	2.3
1913	8.5	2.3
1920	9.4	1.9
1925	12.5	3.3
1929	14.1	4.2
1933	14.5	5.8
1936	25.1	11.7
1939	16.8	6.2
1951	57.8	82.3
1954	23.1	15.9
1958	36.4	55.6
1961	16.2	14.1
1965	5.6	81.9
1969/70	38.6 (28.3)	24.3 (20.0)[c]
1973/74	50.5 (29.9)	21.2 (13.1)
1980/81	68.0 (20.2)	33.9 (9.3)
1986/87	33.7 (6.7)	19.8 (4.4)
1990/91	40.9 (8.0)	21.2 (3.9)

Notes: [a] Figures in brackets show foreign trade taxes excluding the oil company tax as a percentage of total government revenues excluding the oil company tax.
[b] Figures in brackets show foreign trade taxes excluding the oil company tax as a percentage of non-oil exports and imports, converted at the prevailing exchange rates.
[c] Export and import data refer to calendar year 1969.
Sources: 1900–39: *Jaarcijfers* and *Indisch Verslag*, various issues; 1951–65: Bank Indonesia, *Annual Reports*, various issues; 1969/70–1990/91: Bank Indonesia, *Indonesian Financial Statistics*, various issues.

influenced by European socialist thought, including its Marxist-Leninist derivatives, when formulating economic policy. In fact, reviewing developments in the last phase of the Guided Economy era, Castles (1965: 13) argues that the 'rejection of capitalism and espousal of socialism as the preferred pattern of economic organisation has been an almost universal element in Indonesian political thinking since independence'. But in spite of this pronounced ideological inclination to the left, the entire period from 1950 to 1965 can be viewed as one of gradual attenuation of government control of the economy. As stated above, the inter-war years – particularly the 1930s – witnessed a considerable growth in government economic management, measured in terms of increased expenditure and regulation. In contrast, the 1950s and early 1960s saw a gradual decline in the ratios of government expenditure and revenue to GDP (Figure 17.1), mounting inflation, and increasing economic dislocation as the authority of the central government collapsed and with it the capacity to direct the course of economic events.

Here indeed is an intriguing paradox. Why was a newly independent nation, apparently committed to planned economic development along Indian – if not Russian – lines, apparently incapable of substantially increasing the share of government expenditure in national income? (In India the share of government expenditures in national income more than doubled in the first fifteen years after independence.) Why, in spite of drawing up several ambitious development plans predicated on substantial government investment on infrastructure and productive activities, did the newly independent government allow its share of GDP and of total capital formation to fall even below that which was achieved by a conservative colonial regime three decades earlier? Yet another paradox arises from data on the government deficit. Almost all students of the Indonesian economy in the years between 1950 and 1965 claim that it was persistent government deficits which fuelled the almost continual inflation which by the mid-1960s had reached triple digit figures (Sundrum 1973: 77). But these deficits never exceeded 7 per cent of GDP, which meant that they were relatively not much different to those of the early 1930s. Yet the 1930s were characterised by deflation rather than inflation. Why was the effect of budget deficits on monetary stability so different in the immediate post-independence period from the inter-war years?

An investigation of revenue policy provides a partial answer to these questions. The failure of revenue policy was ultimately responsible for the problems with fiscal strategy in these years. By the end of the colonial period, tax revenues accounted for about 60 per cent of total government revenues, the rest comprising income from state monopolies and utilities. About one-third of all tax revenues accrued from personal and corporate income taxes, a further one third from import and export taxes, and the remainder comprising land and property taxes and excise duties (Booth 1980: Tables 1 and 2). In short it was a fairly diversified revenue system, with revenues amounting to between 10 and 12 per cent of GDP (Figure 17.1). Taxes on foreign trade never accounted for more than 25 per cent of total government revenues and in most years were between 15 and 20 per cent. In India, by contrast, customs duties accounted for a third of central government revenue in 1924/5 and about 43 per cent a decade later (Lal 1988: 200–2). In the early 1950s the ratio of revenue to GDP was rather higher than in the late 1930s, but the structure of revenues had changed considerably. Direct taxes had contracted while revenues from foreign trade accounted for over one half of total government income in 1951 (Table 17.3). These revenues came from a mixture of 'orthodox' export and import taxes, from the so-called 'inducement certificates' and from import surcharges. By the early 1950s income from surcharges exceeded revenues from regular trade taxes. Corden and Mackie (1962: 39ff) have described the working of these certificates and surcharges in detail; in effect they amounted to a subsidy to exporters, allowing exporters to convert their export earnings into rupiah at a more favourable rate than the official exchange while imposing a heavy 'exchange tax' on importers. The profits from these exchange dealings were retained by the government.

With the collapse of the Korean War boom and the subsequent slump in export prices, revenues from taxes and levies on trade fell, both as a percentage of total revenues and as a percentage of total export and import earnings (Table 17.3). Although there were several attempts at reform between 1952 and 1957, reforming finance ministers lacked the authority to make new measures stick. By the early 1960s the gap between revenues and expenditures was widening rapidly (Figure 17.1) and the deficit funded largely by government borrowing from the central bank, thereby stoking inflation. Civil service salaries fell sharply in real terms, revenue officials were demoralised and easily corrupted. By 1962 the government was caught in a vicious spiral of inflation leading to deteriorating revenue performance leading to larger deficits and further inflation from which it seemed impossible to break free. One of the most damaging consequences of this failure of the fiscal system was that successive governments were incapable of implementing planned investment projects. At the end of the 1950s, Indonesia ranked lowest among major Asian countries in terms of the ratio of government investment to GNP, and in terms of the percentage share of government in total investment (ECAFE 1961: 36). The situation deteriorated further in the 1960s, to the point where the government could not even maintain existing infrastructure, let alone begin new projects. Although other countries, such as Burma, Pakistan and Thailand were devoting an even higher proportion of total government expenditures to defence than Indonesia, they also managed to spend more on economic services and infrastructure, both as a proportion of GDP and as a proportion of the total budget (Anspach 1960: 41).

The attempted coup in September 1965 resulted in the murder of six army generals and ushered in a period of bloody conflict between the army and the Communist Party. In March 1966 a triumvirate, consisting of General Suharto, the Sultan of Yogyakarta and Adam Malik took power and immediately embarked on a programme of stabilisation with the advice and support of the International Monetary Fund (IMF). This programme has come to be regarded as one of the most successful in the world (Sutton 1984). The government was able to reduce the rate of inflation virtually to zero within the space of three years without a rise of unemployment, deteriorating living standards and falling production which have characterised IMF stabilisation programmes in many other countries. The paramount importance of balancing the budget as a means of reducing inflation was stressed. This was to be achieved through more intensive collection of taxes and 'severe austerity' on the expenditure side. Because most of the expenditure cuts fell on sectors such as the military, the public at large was not greatly affected. Deregulation, reform of the banking sector, credit liberalisation and the realistic pricing of foreign exchange were other policy measures stressed at the time (Arndt 1966: 4).

By 1969, the success of the stabilisation programme was clear and the government felt sufficiently confident to shift the focus of economic policy from stabilisation to the promotion of long-run economic development and structural change. While balanced budgets and monetary discipline were an essential prerequisite for sustained growth, the government was convinced that some medium-term direction of the economy through indicative planning was essential to reassure foreign investors, aid donors and domestic public opinion that economic development was now to be accorded top priority. Under the Old Order there had been two attempts at implementing a development plan. The first five-year plan was scheduled to run from 1956 to 1960 and aimed to enhance investment, especially in agriculture, transmigration, irrigation, energy, transport and education. Until 1958, when the plan was abandoned, implementation was reasonably successful (Pond 1964: 96). The same could not be said for the subsequent attempt. The eight-year plan, drawn up after the return to the 1945 constitution in 1959, set government investment targets for the 1960–68 period. Although most observers agreed that the choice of projects was sensible (many were carry-overs from the 1956–60 plan), political and economic circumstances were hardly propitious and little was achieved after 1961 (Paauw 1963: 222–31).

No doubt partly because of the conspicuous lack of success of the two Old Order development plans, the first five-year plan (Repelita I) of the New Order was quite modest in aims and content. The tone of the new plan was pragmatic rather than ideological and technically unsophisticated; there was no reliance on planning models of the Indian variety. Agriculture was accorded priority in the allocation of investment funds, particularly rice production, which was projected to grow by almost 50 per cent. The focus on agriculture was explained by the fact that

> the greater part of the Indonesian people lives in this sector, working either as farmer producers or as farm labourers ... the development of the agricultural sector is expected to open up growth possibilities in other

sectors so that an opportunity will be created to combat the backward-ness of the Indonesian economy on many fronts.

(Department of Information 1969: 13)

The government devoted 30 per cent of its development budget to agriculture and irrigation, and a further 20 per cent to the rehabilitation and upgrading of the road system which would facilitate access to agricultural inputs (especially fertiliser) and marketing of output. Although rice production did not grow as fast as the plan predicted (the actual increase was almost 3 million tons between 1968 and 1973, representing an annual growth of 4.6 per cent) there was a considerable improvement over the performance of the 1960s. There was also an ambitious programme of infrastructure grants to lower levels of government intended to rehabilitate and extend roads, irrigation facilities and so forth, using labour-intensive construction techniques (De Wit 1973).

The dramatic jump in oil prices between 1974 and 1980 triggered a set of adjustment problems characteristic of economies with booming export sectors. These problems were due to the so-called 'Dutch disease' effects on other tradable goods, both exports and import substitutes. The Indonesian government chose to absorb a substantial part of the increase in oil revenues into the domestic economy via the budget, thus aggravating domestic inflationary pressures. The rupiah, which remained pegged to the dollar in nominal terms, experienced a substantial real appreciation relative to the currencies of its major trading partners, as during the 1930s, due to the determination of the Dutch government to stay on the gold standard. As a result the 'competitiveness index' fell from 100 in 1971 to 67 in 1977 (Warr 1984: 67). This made it difficult for Indonesian producers of (non-oil) traded goods to compete with foreign suppliers in either domestic or international markets.

The government reacted to this problem in a number of ways. On the import side, considerable protection was given to domestic producers through tariffs, quotas and input subsidies. In the manufacturing sector, domestic producers of a range of consumer durables were given almost total protection through tariffs and quota restrictions. In the crucially important food-crop sector, the government controlled rice imports to allow domestic prices to rise slightly above declining world levels while at the same time giving considerable assistance to producers through subsidies on irrigation and fertiliser. Under these conditions, manufacturing output boomed although much production was of lower quality and higher price than potential imports. Rice output increased, but at a slower pace than during the Repelita I planning period. Non-oil export production languished. Paauw (1978: 208) estimates that the volume of the eleven leading non-extractive export commodities, all agricultural, stagnated between 1971 and 1976 and there was virtually no increase in manufactured exports. This contrasted sharply with the situation in other parts of Asia where traditional and new export industries grew rapidly. Devaluation in 1978 gave some encouragement to non-oil exports, but the price effects of the devaluation were rapidly eroded by subsequent inflation.

Medium-term planning was complicated by extreme and unpredictable fluctuations in oil revenues from 1974 to 1981 and the second and third five-year plans of the New Order were overtaken by events in the world oil market almost as soon as they appeared. But there can be little doubt that the two oil shocks together led to a considerable growth in government expenditure as a percentage of GDP. In 1980/81, total government expenditures accounted for about 24 per cent of GDP, an historic high (see Figure 17.1). At the same time most commentators agreed that the oil boom years saw a marked retreat from the liberal economic policies of the early New Order period. This was most obvious in the growth of restrictions on foreign investment and international trade. In a survey of manufacturing protection policy, Pangestu and Boediono (1986: 9ff) argue that after 1972 a range of protective devices were adopted that were additional to measures like tariffs, import restrictions and licences applied since the 1950s. They listed twenty-two different policy instruments including at least one devaluation (1978) which was scarcely justified on balance of payments grounds, government monopolies and procurement policies, preferential credit policies and compulsory use of domestic components by domestic manufacturers which conferred considerable protection on certain industries in addition to the tax and tariff regimes.

The oil boom was thus characterised by rather conflicting tendencies in the role of government in the Indonesian economy. The public sector increased its share of GDP. Intervention increased as did the regulation of private markets for goods, services and factors of production. But there was a pronounced weakness in the capacity of government to control either the economy's longer-term development in the face of unstable world economic conditions, or those domestic institutions, including state enterprises, which were only partially under the control of economic technocrats in the Finance Ministry, the National Planning Board and the central bank. These circumstances contributed to adjustment problems after the boom.

In several respects 1982 was a watershed for New Order economic policy. Although world oil prices held at 1981 levels for much of the year, Indonesia followed the OPEC-mandated production cuts and both petroleum export earnings and revenues began to fall in absolute and relative terms. The balance of payments deficit in 1982/83 increased sharply as a percentage of GDP and there was growing awareness of a burgeoning resource constraint, particularly for the public sector. The government was faced with a stark choice: it could retreat from the partial liberalisation of commodity trade which had occurred after 1968, returning to the regime of quantitative controls which had prevailed prior to 1965 in the hope of restricting imports, or it could remove the disincentives to export production in the hope of encouraging a dramatic acceleration in non-oil exports.

From 1982 until 1985 the government appeared to favour adopting the former option, applying additional quantitative controls on imports while at the same time applying measures to reinforce import substitution rather than export promotion. But 1983 also saw several new initiatives in monetary, fiscal and exchange rate policy as well as the 'rescheduling' of several large public sector industrial projects about which concern had been expressed in the previous year. The rupiah was devalued in March 1983 and a number of deregulation initiatives were announced in the financial sector (Arndt 1983). In December 1983, parliament approved three tax reform laws which were implemented over the following eighteen months. But while these liberalisation measures were being applied, quantitative restrictions on imports were increasing. By early 1985, a lively debate was under way involving academic economists and the media about the causes of the 'high-cost economy' and the need for liberalisation of the 'real' economy. Many observers argued that financial deregulation and fiscal reform were not in themselves sufficient to make Indonesia an internationally competitive producer of non-oil export goods and services. Excessive protection from tariff and non-tariff barriers were depicted as a major cause of the high-cost economy: these would have to be removed (Dick 1985: 19).

The first intimation that the government was heeding calls for a more export-oriented trade regime came in March and April 1985. The tariff system was rationalised in March of that year: the number of rates was streamlined and the maximum *ad valorem* rate reduced from 225 per cent to 60 per cent. More dramatically, in April the notorious Directorate General of Customs was relieved of all responsibility for visible trade and customs surveillance was handed to a Swiss company: clearance procedures were greatly simplified and the time taken to complete formalities was greatly reduced. Inter-island trade also benefited from the long overdue elimination of customs controls and the introduction of more efficient trans-shipment procedures (Dick 1985: 11). The momentum for reform was maintained after 1986 with a further large devaluation of the rupiah and the implementation of a series of measures, including a duty drawback scheme, designed to encourage non-oil exports (Muir 1986). Incentives were also given to tourism. In October 1988, a long-awaited banking reform package was announced and in November further deregulation of inter-island shipping was announced. Additional financial sector reforms were implemented in 1989/90 and a start made on the complex issue of establishing performance criteria for state enterprises: the aim was to determine the form of ownership and control most suited to these enterprises (Booth 1988a; Mackie and Sjahrir 1989: 26–30).

Looking back on the changing role of government in the Indonesian economy between 1983 and 1990, it is obvious that much progress was made in terms of the goal of making the economy more internationally competitive and less reliant on exports of oil and gas. The government was extremely successful in controlling domestic inflation after two large devaluations, bringing about a large and sustained fall in the real effective exchange rate

(Asian Development Bank 1990: 246–7). This in turn was an important factor in the growth of non-oil exports. Arguably, changing the mental attitudes of government officials and the business community was a still greater achievement. Although many officials were hostile to the deregulation drive of the latter part of the 1980s which threatened their jobs, status and incomes, there is little doubt that by 1990 a sizeable constituency in favour of liberalisation had been built up within the government apparatus. This in turn built confidence amongst the foreign and domestic business community. Yet even as the government was winning foreign praise (especially from major bilateral and multilateral donors) for the speed and success of its economic reforms, there were worrying indications that the 'deregulation drive' was at best partial in its coverage, and often erratic in its implementation.

There are at least four reasons for thinking that regulatory overhang from the late colonial and post-colonial era, together with the legacy of extensive state intervention during the oil boom, will not be removed quickly.

First, at least in part, export growth results not from the classic market mechanism – comparative advantage – but rather from continuing government intervention: for example, selective bans on commodity exports designed to foster valued-added exports of semi-processed goods. More generally, the trade regime remains distorted with rates of effective protection varying considerably from industry to industry.

Second, extensive networks of political patronage are leading to the growth of large conglomerates, the majority of which are run by Chinese, and most of the rest by the children of President Suharto, or by other well-connected indigenous businessmen. In spite of much government rhetoric and some action to foster indigenous businessmen, very few large businesses controlled by non-political *pribumi* interests had emerged over the New Order period. Some conglomerates are using political connections to expand operations and drive out smaller competitors.

Third, there has been little attempt to privatise state enterprises, and only partial success in enforcing tougher performance standards on the less profitable ones. Some new state enterprises, especially those run by the ambitious Minister of Research, Dr Habibie, have been given extensive access to off-budget funding through bank loans. Attempts to make these operations more transparent and accountable to the State Audit Board or to parliament have so far been unsuccessful.

Fourth, generally there is still a widespread feeling that the government is failing to act as a facilitator of market-led development in what could be termed the World Bank mould. While good progress has been made with the provision of infrastructure, health care and education, much remains to be done, especially outside Java. The government is perceived as lacking a real commitment to strengthen the rule of law and to provide a robust system of individual rights, including property rights, enforced in politically independent courts.

FROM PREDATORY TO DEVELOPMENTAL STATE?

Successive Indonesian governments since the late nineteenth century can be depicted as struggling to redirect taxation, expenditure and regulatory policies away from essentially predatory concerns with revenue extraction, towards more broadly based development concerns. The first watershed occurred in 1901 with the inauguration of the Ethical Policy. This led to a change in the economic role of government, a change which was manifested in a considerable increase in expenditure in per capita terms and in a redirection of expenditures away from law and order and administration towards public works. The reasons for these changes are complex but the growth of political democracy in the Netherlands certainly led to changes in public opinion about the appropriate role of colonies. In addition, commercial interests in the Netherlands realised that Indonesia could not continue to increase exports without investment in infrastructure and that a poverty-stricken colony would not provide buoyant markets for Dutch manufactures. By the late colonial period (and especially in the 1930s), the colonial authorities had moved a considerable way towards the rational planning model and were beginning to experiment with a developmental state model, assuming responsibility for directing the growth of a modern manufacturing and commercial sector and for establishing a growth-promoting property rights regime.

It is fascinating to speculate on the course of Indonesian economic history had not the Dutch experiment in 'managed' colonial development been terminated by the arrival of the Japanese in 1942. After the Second World War the newly independent government undoubtedly wished to move further in the direction of comprehensive economic planning, following the prevailing ideology which viewed the state as the prime initiator of economic development. This move was frustrated by political instability which made rational economic management almost impossible. The result was a gradual decline in the tax base, a widening budgetary deficit, and inflation by the mid-1960s.

After 1965, the New Order government moved more firmly towards rational economic planning, with considerable encouragement and assistance from the international development agencies. Government bureaucracies, such as the National Planning Board (Bappenas), the Ministry of Finance and the central bank, often staffed by technocrats trained in the USA, assumed greater control over economic policy-making and embarked on ambitious development programmes in education, health care, family planning and the physical infrastructure. The more technocratic ministries tended to view the role of the state as that of facilitator of market-led economic development, although they also assumed that in the provision of infrastructure, education and public health the state should take the leading role, and consistently tried to curb other ministries and state enterprises that espoused ambitious plans to develop heavy industries producing traded goods at high cost, for example iron and steel and aeronautics. That they have been only partially successful in these endeavours testifies to the power of other parts of the bureaucracy who wish to see a more powerful developmental state emerging with government agencies assuming responsibility especially for high technology sectors of the economy. During this period, an authoritarian state has also sought to promote economic development in order to secure political support while suppressing critical political movements (Willner 1981; McVey 1982; Anderson 1983; Booth 1989).

Yet in the background lurks the ever-present shadow of the predatory state in the guise of powerful vested interests who wish to use the power of the state to build personal empires based on preferential access to government contracts, licences and bank credit. These vested interests have become more prominent in recent years, not least because many of them are closely connected with the President and his family. A crucial element in the success of the East Asian developmental states is that the 'bureaucratic guardians' have managed to keep themselves reasonably free from capture by special interest groups and are therefore able to deal firmly with those industries which have received preferential treatment but have been unable to measure up to the performance standards exacted in return. If a would-be developmental state does not have such a class of bureaucratic guardians it is probably well-advised to limit the function of government to provision of infrastructure, education and to the development of a legal system which supports a growth-promoting regime of property rights. In each of these areas Indonesia has made considerable progress since the 1960s. But there is still a real risk that the developmental state may in fact be simply a front for a predatory state. This has adverse implications for the country's economic prosperity in the medium term.

Indonesia has not yet reached the stage where the 'apathy and acceptance of the state's rules, no matter how repressive' which form the kernel of the free-rider problem as North (1981: 32) describes it, have given way in the face of challenges from new classes, whose demands will lead to a substantial erosion of the powers of the predatory state. However, outside pressures for policy change are growing and new interest groups are emerging which are pressing for change on the economic, if not the political front (Macintyre 1991). Suharto's remarkable durability has been in large part due to his ability to play off factions and interest groups against one another, without becoming wholly beholden to any of them. As a regime change becomes more imminent, it remains to be seen whether rules for the succession will be devised to minimise the opportunities for disruptive change or revolution upon the 'death of the ruler'. The alternative possibility is that the rapidly growing middle class, itself a product of the economic development of the past three decades, will demand a larger say in its political destiny. The consequences of such demands are difficult to predict but they could involve far-reaching changes in the present political system.

NOTES

1 This chapter draws heavily on my forthcoming book *The Economic History of Indonesia in the Nineteenth and Twentieth Centuries*.

2 Most economic historians seem to agree that north west Europe was unique in that a state system emerged there after the Renaissance which encouraged the development of an efficient regime of private property rights. On the one hand the states were sufficiently large and powerful that they were not prone to endemic baronial warfare or foreign invasion, but on the other hand there was always sufficient threat of a challenge to the rulers that they did not dare to extract the maximum feasible revenue from their citizenry. For a more formal model of the predatory state along these lines see Lal (1988: 297–306).

3 Between 1825 and 1840 cash-crop production in Java grew very rapidly at over 10 per cent per annum. But after 1840 the rate of growth slowed to around 1 per cent per annum. See van Ark (1986) for data on production and export volume indexes.

4 For a more extended discussion of the evolution of land, labour and credit markets in Indonesia in the nineteenth and twentieth centuries see Booth (forthcoming).

18

EXPLAINING THE ECONOMIC AND POLITICAL SUCCESSES OF RAWLINGS

The strengths and limitations of public choice theories

E. Gyimah-Boadi

INTRODUCTION

Public choice theories, especially the Batesian variant (see Bates 1981, 1983), offered a very powerful explanation of the economic (and political) failures of successive post-colonial African regimes in the 1960s and 1970s. Widespread economic stagnation and accompanying social dislocations as well as political decay were blamed on the persistent pursuit of ruinous economic policies. With minor differences in emphasis, the list of such economically harmful policies have included the following: restrictions on the operations of product, factor and financial markets; a tendency to rely on parastatals as the chief instruments of industrial and agricultural development; and an urban bias in resource allocation. Such policies were deemed to have caused an erosion in production incentives, a precipitous drop in export earnings, an exacerbation of fiscal crises, and in turn, the dramatic social and political upheavals of the continent.[1]

Reform of ruinous economic policies was held to be more or less impossible, or at best extremely difficult. Reform was seen to run counter to the narrow political and economic interest of the dominant/ruling coalition of post-colonial cum bureaucratic elites and urban workers. The interests of this coalition were seen to coincide with statist and interventionist policies and the accompanying distortions. Distortions such as over-valued currency, an over-manned public sector, predatory marketing boards, stringent price controls, etc. provided short-term rentier advantages and patronage resources for the 'deleterious coalition' of political-bureaucratic elites and their urban working-class allies. Thus, the narrow and short-term interests of this coalition were deemed to guarantee the persistence of status quo economic policies and to preclude the likelihood of meaningful reforms.

With the adoption of the World Bank/IMF structural adjustment (SAP) reforms (in the 1980s and 1990s), some African governments appear to be executing a retreat from the anti-market and statist economic policies (said to be economically ruinous but politically prudent) in favour of pro-market and neo-liberal policies (said to be politically dangerous but economically correct). That some of them, like Ghana's Provisional National Defence Council (PNDC), led by J. J. Rawlings, have managed to implement such reforms in a sustained manner and with a significant degree of success, would seem to challenge the validity of the public choice approaches that offered apparently convincing explanations of the causes of the crisis confronting the pre-reform political economies of such countries. Having gone admirably beyond the simplistic neo-classical economists'emphasis on 'getting prices wrong' as the leading cause of economic and political crises (see Bauer 1954, 1972), the ability of public choice theories to explain the political economy of 'getting prices right' (despite all the reasons for 'keeping them wrong'), has yet to be seen.

This chapter examines how the public choice thesis and some of its central ideas concerning the political and economic origins of the African development crisis, and on solutions to it, hold up in the light of the Ghanaian experience with relatively successful economic reform in the 1980s and early 1990s. It highlights the limitations of the public choice/new institutional economics explanations, and raises questions about whether they offer any great explanatory power over and above that provided by conventional explanations, such as authoritarianism, luck, pluck and other idiosyncratic factors. It concludes that, at best, public choice explanations must be combined with conventional ones in order fully to understand the complex politico-economic circumstances under which change and continuity occurs, in Ghana in particular and sub-Saharan Africa in general.

The chapter begins with an outline of the pre-adjustment Ghanaian economy, highlighting its 'non-liberal' and anti-market features. The second part summarises the distance travelled towards economic liberalism/free market from a non-liberal base within roughly one decade, and the economic and political successes enjoyed therefrom. The third section reviews some of the explanations given for the successes, and relates them to the public choice explanations of the same events. It concludes with a suggestion that it takes a combination of public choice and non-public choice explanations to gain a comprehensive picture of change and continuity in the political economy of sub-Saharan African countries such as Ghana.

THE PRE-ADJUSTMENT GHANAIAN ECONOMY

The economic regime prevailing in Ghana at the time of independence was relatively liberal. However, from the early 1960s, the country began to move steadily away from economic liberalism to statism. By the time the structural adjustment programme was initiated in 1983, the economy bore all the marks of a non-liberal economy and its corresponding distortions.[2] Some of its leading features were as follows:

1 An inflexible foreign exchange policy which pegged the local currency (the cedi) to the dollar at fixed rates of 1.15 from 1973 to 1977 and 2.75 from 1978 to 1982 – leaving the cedi over-valued by 816 per cent, according to World Bank estimates for that year, and the disparity between the official and black market rates at 20:1.

2 A system of foreign exchange rationing and administered import licences intended to conserve foreign exchange and to improve allocative efficiency.

3 Stringent and energetically (if episodically) enforced controls on the prices of hundreds of imported and locally produced foods, and on other common consumer items (staples, soaps, matches, petroleum products etc.), transport fares, rents, etc.

4 A system of industrial protectionism that depended on an increasing array of bans, quotas, and import tariffs, reaching its highest level in the 1970s with the enactment of decrees that allowed the state to take a majority shareholding in foreign-owned enterprises or compelled the sale of foreign-owned assets to nationals.

5 A proliferating network of state-owned enterprises established to promote the goals of socialism (in the Nkrumah era), social welfare and general economic development – with the number of SOEs growing from a handful in the 1950s to over 230 by 1982. These had grown exponentially in the socialist phase of the Nkrumah era, the economic nationalist era of I. K. Acheampong/National Redemption Council/Supreme Military Council in the 1970s and during the Rawlings/Armed Forces Revolutionary Council inter-regnum of 1979, and operated in all areas of the economy – from industry, agriculture and commerce to finance. They persisted despite overwhelming evidence of failure, an inability to break even, a chronic dependence on government subventions (reaching 10 per cent of government expenditures by 1982), and a combined operating deficit amounting again by 1982 to 3 per cent of GDP.

6 A system of monopolistic marketing boards, typified by the Cocoa Marketing Board, which handled both the internal and external marketing of cocoa, and under which real producer prices had declined precipitously. The share of cocoa revenue paid to the Ghanaian farmer had dropped from 69 per cent in 1965 to 26 per cent in 1981, supply of inputs had been erratic, the smuggling of cocoa to neighbouring countries had been rampant, and farmers had been abandoning cocoa farming altogether.

Predictably, such policies combined to create acute shortages of foreign exchange, and of consumer and capital goods, as well as massive economic distortions reflected in an escalating black market, the erosion of producer incentives, and also other speculative activities which provided enormous rentier profits to strategically placed elites.

ECONOMIC LIBERALISATION SINCE 1983

After 1983, Ghana's PNDC, led by Flight Lieutenant J. J. Rawlings, embarked on a massive and comprehensive programme of economic recovery and structural adjustment (ERP/SAP), with the heavy involvement of the World Bank, the IMF and various Western multilateral and bilateral agencies. The reforms included economic stabilisation and retrenchment measures such as cost recovery, the withdrawal of government subsidies and introduction of fees with respect to social services such as health, education, water, electricity, etc., wage restraint and the control of inflation.[3] It also included job retrenchment, in which the Cocoa Marketing Board, renamed COCOBOD, reduced its staff from about 100,000 in 1983 to roughly 30,000 by 1992, and at least 30,000 people were 'redeployed' from the civil service between 1987 and 1990. There was also an energetic effort to mobilise external resources through the regular, but revamped revenue collection agencies and extra-legal ones such as the National Investigation Committee. Additionally, attempts were made to rehabilitate the export sector – cocoa, timber and mining, along with the economic infrastructure of harbours, railways, roads, etc.

The clear thrust of the economic reform programme was liberalisation, and the measures undertaken in pursuit of this included the following:

1   Movement from a fixed exchange rate regime to a more flexible one, beginning in 1983 with a series of large, both disguised and open devaluations of the local currency. This, in conjunction with other measures, nearly unified the official and unofficial rates at which the dollar was exchanged for the cedi. Foreign exchange transactions were decriminalised through the institution of privately operated foreign exchange bureaux from 1988 onwards. Thus by 1992, very few restrictions remained on currency trading in Ghana.

2   Removal of price controls, so that by 1991 only eight goods (imported rice, sugar, baby food, cement, textiles, drugs, matches and soap) were subject to price regulations, and even then such regulation was administered jointly by the statutory Prices and Incomes Board on the one hand, and traders/producers on the other, using guidelines established by a tripartite committee of government, employers and trade unions.

3   Liberalisation of imports through the abolition of the previous system of import licensing and its replacement by import declaration, in addition to a significant simplification of tariff structure and some reduction in tariff rates, as well as a moderating of the level of protection.

4   Liberalisation of exports, including schemes under which exporters of timber and the so-called non-traditional goods (fruits, craft items, foods, etc.) were allowed to retain part of their external earnings, in addition to tax concessions.

5   A marked retreat by the state from some of the advanced positions it had taken in the economy. The PNDC embarked on a programme of

privatisation, in which a number of state-provided services were sub-contracted to private operators and most of Ghana's more than 300 parastatals were earmarked for divestiture. A total of 93 had been divested by early 1993, and the remainder ordered to operate according to market guidelines.

6 Enactment of relatively liberal investment and trading codes, aimed at attracting private investors.

By 1991, the PNDC had managed to bring about a degree of economic liberalisation unprecedented in Ghana's post-colonial history, although severe restrictions remained.

ECONOMIC GAINS

Thanks largely to the neo-liberal reform, the Ghanaian economy recorded undeniable gains, especially in macro-economic terms. Ghana's Gross Domestic Product (GDP) registered a positive growth rate for the first time in many years as GDP increased by an annual average of over 5 per cent from 1984 to 1990. Real GDP grew at 8.6 per cent in 1984 and averaged 5.3 per cent from 1985 to 1988. (By contrast real GDP had fallen on average by 5 per cent in each of the three years preceding the ERP/SAP.) Gross Domestic Investment as a percentage of GDP also rose significantly during the period. From a low of 4 per cent of GDP in 1982/83, it rose to 12.5 per cent in 1988. The government deficit was reduced from 47 per cent of GDP in 1983 to 0.3 per cent in 1987, and from 1986 to 1990, a surplus of $12 million was recorded. The overall balance of payment recorded a surplus of $139 million in 1987, $125 million in 1988, $127 million in 1989 and $85 million in 1990. Arrears on external debts were reduced from $171 million in 1986 to $17.3 million in 1989 and completely eliminated in 1990. There was also a moderation in the rate of inflation, though the rates prevailing under ERP/SAP remained somewhat high. The average annual rate of inflation decelerated from about 123 per cent in 1983 to 25 per cent in 1989, though it rose to 37.7 per cent in 1990, and then fell to a historically low 15 per cent in 1991–2.

Production declines in the export sector were also reversed in the ERP/SAP period. Cocoa production rose from a low of 159,565 metric tonnes in 1983 to 247,470 in 1990; timber exports went up from 103,000 cubic metres in 1983 to 538,000 in 1988; gold production went up from 282,646 ounces in 1983, to 541,408 ounces in 1990. During the same period, bauxite production rose from 82,310 to 388,859 metric tonnes, manganese from 131,344 to 254,710 metric tonnes and diamonds from 450,000 to 636,000 carats. Consequently, overall export earnings rose from roughly US$400 million (FOB) in 1983 to about US$620 million (FOB) in 1990, despite drastically reduced export prices for most of these commodities.

Additionally, there were modest but noticeable increases in the production and export earnings from non-traditional exports of pineapples, fish, shrimps/lobsters, aluminium products, processed natural rubber and handicrafts. Local export earnings of US$1.9 million in 1984 rose to US$62.34 million in 1992, amounting to 4–5 per cent of total export earnings. Thus it could be said that under economic liberalisation, a long overdue start was being made under ERP/SAP on diversifying Ghana's exports.

Perhaps the most visible aspect of ERP/SAP macro-economic improvements has been the massive rehabilitation of the country's long decaying economic and social infrastructure. This includes the Ghana Railway Corporation (especially the western line), the deep water ports of Tema and Takoradi, and the resurfacing and upgrading of major roads such as the one connecting Accra and Kumasi and the northern regions of Ghana. The projects to extend electricity to the Brong Ahafo and the Northern Regions of the country may stand as the greatest achievement of the PNDC government in this regard. Improvements in telecommunications include the introduction of a direct dial service between Ghana and Europe and the United States in 1988, and the rehabilitation of telephone lines in many parts of the country. Radio and television networks were fitted with new transmitters and the spatial coverage of the latter extended. Additionally, public organisations were better provisioned in the ERP/SAP era. Key parastatals such as Water and Electricity Corporations received new equipment and operational vehicles, and some government buildings received fresh paint for the first time in decades.[4]

Finally, there was a noticeable increase in the supply and distribution of consumer goods and services. This is partly reflected in the increase in the value of imports from $593 million in 1983 to $1,025 million in 1987.

To be sure, very severe limitations remained on Rawlings's economic liberalisation, the related reforms and associated improvements. After nearly a decade of economic growth, real GNP had not regained the level of 1974, and per capita income had not regained the level of 1981. Moreover, the sustainability of the ERP/SAP was dramatically called into question in 1990 when Ghana's growth rate fell sharply to 2.7 per cent per annum, and output in both agriculture and manufacturing declined. Furthermore, the response of the private sector to the economic reforms was rather lukewarm. Despite the steps taken to liberalise the economy and to improve the general climate for business, private investment did not rise significantly. After an initial increase from 2 per cent in 1982 to 4.4 per cent in 1984, the share of private investment (most of it in mining) accounted for a dismal 3 per cent of total private investment by 1992. And although Ghana did not enter the ERP/SAP with a debt problem, it came to have one. The country's total foreign debt which stood at about US$1.6 billion in 1980, reached $US3.6 billion in 1988, and debt service ratios were running at an average of over 50 per cent, reaching an astronomical 75 per cent in 1988.

Furthermore, there were, and continued to be, widespread public complaints over the rising cost of living arising from the withdrawal of subsidies, the introduction of and increase in user fees, the decontrol of prices, the steep devaluations, wage restraint policies, etc., as well as rising unemployment due to job retrenchment, the freeze on hiring and other measures intended to reduce public spending and control demand.

Studies undertaken in the mid- to late 1980s indicated that there was a rising incidence of malnutrition among segments of the Ghanaian population, especially among children. The percentage of children immunised against the six childhood diseases was low (about 50 per cent) and was suspected to be falling. Some people were rumoured to avoid hospitals when they were sick. In the area of education, primary school enrolment fell by 3.4 per cent between 1983/4 and 1986/7, in contrast to a rising trend in the 1970s. Although these negative socio-economic indicators may reflect a more complex set of causes, there was a least a prima facie basis for speculating that they were linked with the ERP/SAP. For instance, there had been an immediate 25 per cent drop in the number of visits to Korle Bu Hospital (Ghana's premier hospital) and a 50 per cent drop in visits to Korle Bu Polyclinic after the government had introduced a range of fees for hospital attendance. Reported outbreaks in some parts of the country of diseases previously thought to have been eradicated, such as guinea-worm infection in 1988 and 1989, and buruli ulcer in 1993, also appeared to be related to the imposition and increase in user fees for utilities; and the drop off in school enrolment may have resulted from the decision to charge fees in elementary school.[5]

THE POLITICAL SUCCESS OF RAWLINGS

The political import of Rawlings' success may be seen not only in the magnitude of the economic reforms undertaken, but also in the implied psychological and ideological breakthrough, as well as the ability of the regime politically to survive despite implementing such harsh economic measures. The neo-liberal reforms undertaken by J. J. Rawlings represented a major ideological/psychological shift from the state-socialist and social welfarist orientation of public policy prevalent in Ghanaian regimes from Nkrumah to the early Rawlings period (see Killick 1978; Roemer 1984; Botchway 1993). In the past, when such an orientation had prevailed, partial attempts at neo-liberal economic reforms by the regimes of the National Liberation Council (1966–69), the Busia-Progress Party and Limann-Peoples' National Party had been effectively denigrated as 'reactionary' by Ghana's articulate public. It may be a measure of the ideological shift of the Rawlings-PNDC era that none of the manifestos and economic programmes of the parties competing against Rawlings in the 1992 presidential elections were markedly different from the pro-market thrust of the Rawlings-National Democratic Congress manifesto.[6] The reforms may have been deeply resented for the austerity they entailed, but they were not denigrated as reactionary, even for the purpose of scoring political points.

Second, the Rawlings government was able politically to survive economic reforms of a kind that had been a leading factor in the overthrow of previous regimes which had only expressed an intention to implement such reforms (the Limann government), or had only partially attempted to do so (the Busia and Akuffo governments). Under the military-cum-political National Liberation Council, only about twelve state enterprises had been sold as compared to over ninety under the Rawlings-PNDC regime (by 1992),[7] and a devaluation of 48 per cent and a small development levy on public servants had provided the pretext for the military coup of 13 January 1972 which overthrew the Busia government (see Goldsworthy 1973; Bennet 1975; Gyimah-Boadi 1993). Indeed previous military governments with the same potential to engage in political repression shied away from neo-liberal reforms not only for ideological reasons, but also because they were not sure they could survive such measures politically. Economic retrenchment measures, including a minor devaluation under the Akuffo (military) regime, had been a factor in the first Rawlings coup in 1979. Moreover, the presence of foreign experts within strategic places in the public service, such as the Ministry of Finance and the Bank of Ghana, had always been a sore issue in Ghanaian politics,[8] and yet under Rawlings, numerous World Bank and IMF missions visited Ghana every year and hundreds of expatriate technical advisors were posted to the ministries, the banks and key parastatals (see Callaghy 1989).

In the 1990s, Rawlings could boast of a decade of development, but that was largely an acknowledgement of the benefits of neo-liberal reforms, which others would not or could not undertake for ideological and political reasons. In return for his commitment to neo-liberal economic reforms, donors had poured over $5 billion into Ghana between 1983 and 1992, helped to underwrite the reforms, and thereby ensured the economic success and political survival of J. J. Rawlings. Indeed, some have seen Rawlings's victory in the 1992 multi-party presidential election in Ghana as a translation of his economic success into political success.[9]

CONVENTIONAL EXPLANATIONS OF RAWLINGS'S SUCCESS

Explanations of the success of J. J. Rawlings and his government fall into four broad categories. One set of explanations emphasises a combination of external factors leading to the ascendancy of the ideology of economic liberalism. These factors include:

1　The demise of the allegedly bankrupt neo-Marxist/dependency socialist ideology of development which had inspired the ruinous economic policies of the past (see Ahiakpor 1985; Herbst 1993).
2　The coming to the fore of the neo-conservatism and supply side economic philosophies of the Reagan–Bush and Thatcher era in the early to mid-1980s.
3　The appearance of an intellectually solid diagnosis and prescription for the

maladies afflicting African political economies – in the form of the Elliot Berg Report of 1981 and Robert Bates's 1981 and 1983 publications (Herbst 1993: 34).

A second group of explanations sees the successes of Rawlings as, above all, a vindication of the technical superiority and efficacy of market versus non-market strategies of economic growth and development. Here, the simple explanation of why Rawlings was successful is that he had the good sense and 'pragmatism' to abandon unworkable anti-market for 'sound' pro-market policies, and especially that he managed to 'get prices right' (Ahiakpor 1991; Kapur *et al.* 1991). In these explanations, some credit is also accorded to the availability of stable and apparently superior technocratic support from external and internal sources (Callaghy 1989). The rendering of reform (policies) into sophisticated technical packages, the eagle-eyed monitoring of implementation by the resident IMF and World Bank missions, backed by visiting teams of technical experts/consultants, in combination with the politically suave presentation of those programmes, and their effective management/implementation by the local team of technocrats (notably, Finance Minister Botchway, and economic advisor J.L.S. Abbey backed by a cadre of 'patriotic' professionals) are held to be critical elements in the success.[10]

However, critics of the World Bank, the IMF and Rawlings's structural adjustment propound a rather cynical version of the ideological/technocratic explanations. In this view, success is explained *not* by the inherent technical superiority of neo-liberal economic reforms, but by the fact that they are the only reform packages that 'donors' would finance. Success, it is argued, only reflected a 'temporary' boom made possible by the pumping of over $5 billion into Ghana by the World Bank/IMF and Western donors, who were anxious to serve Ghana up as a 'success story' and to advertise the benefits of adjustment (Hutchful 1989). Alternatively, it was contended that the success was largely the product of post-drought weather. Success is thus dismissed as either ephemeral and/or the outcome of a conspiracy by neo-colonial powers to lure poor countries back into the trap of underdevelopment.

The third set of explanations focuses on the successful imposition of relatively thoroughgoing authoritarian rule on Ghana by Rawlings and his regime, and the key role played by authoritarianism in inducing compliance with difficult reforms.[11] The key elements of the Rawlings-era authoritarian syndrome are given as follows:

1 The lack of public participation in the making of important national decisions, notably the decision to become involved with the IMF and the World Bank and accept the accompanying 'harsh conditionalities', such as currency devaluation and job retrenchment.
2 Wanton disregard for due process, epitomised by the public tribunals in which prosecution and judgeship had been fused, and where kangaroo trials had been organised, with opponents of the regime as its chief victims.

3 A ubiquitous and proliferating security network, supported by pro-government vigilantes and enforcers (Bureau of National Investigations, People's Militia, Commandos, Panthers, etc.).

4 A pattern of physical and psychological violence inflicted on political opponents – notably the kidnap and murder of three judges and a retired army officer in June 1982 by agents of the government, and the numerous executions of alleged 'subversive' elements.

5 The tight control over the media and its use in propagandising for the regime and intimidating its adversaries, complemented by neo-corporatist arrangements involving the so-called 'organs of the revolution' (31st December Women's Movement, June 4th Movement, the National Mobilisation Programme), some unions (e.g. the Ghana Private Road Transport Union) and the Armed Forces.

In the above explanation, these non-democratic arrangements are regarded as having provided the political means by which Rawlings and his regime have managed to survive the imposition of harsh economic reform and sustained their implementation.

The final set of explanations emphasises the personal qualities and leadership style of J. J. Rawlings. It focuses on Rawlings's 'charisma', which is said to have made Ghanaians believe in themselves again; his willingness to get his hands dirty, which made people believe in him; and his personal integrity (Shillington 1992: 129–44). Such explanations also highlight the strength of Rawlings's character and his determination, which enabled him to push through and to stick with difficult economic reforms, especially after he had come to perceive reforms as consistent with his 'Robin Hood' world-view (see Jeffries 1992b; Ahiakpor 1991). On the other hand, the detractors of Rawlings are likely to emphasize 'opportunism' and 'lack of principle' as the underlying explanation for his survival and perhaps his prosperity. They point out that, instead of admitting that he had been wrong about his previous opposition to neo-liberal economic recipes or confessing his philosophical discomfort with neo-capitalist solutions, Rawlings has acquiesced in their imposition by neo-colonial interests for the sake of his political survival.[12]

PUBLIC CHOICE EXPLANATIONS OF SUCCESS

Commendably, the public choice explanations of Rawlings's success attempt to go beyond the neo-classical economists' ahistorical emphasis on good outcomes being simply the result of pursuing good policies, and especially of 'getting prices right'. They attempt to provide a historical context to the explanation of why good policies had not been chosen before, and in particular, why good policies came to be chosen at the time they did. In these explanations, conjunctural factors are presented as, at least, intermediate variables in the adoption of neo-liberal economic reforms. These include the 'trough factor' in

Ghana's political and economic history immediately before (in 1982 and 1983 when drought, bush fires and famine were compounded by the sudden expulsion of 1.2 million Ghanaians from Nigeria); the reluctance of the Soviet Union and the other socialist countries to provide the funds to underwrite the incipient radical/socialist reform programme in 1982; and the disappearance of competing ideologies of economic development and 'bankable' options combined with the availability of ideologically and technically superior strategies and technocratic support.

The problem with such explanations is that they imply a degree of social learning and consensus over economic policy within the Rawlings government (and perhaps among the general public) as well as the emergence of an identifiable coalition for such a policy change, both of which are empirically difficult to sustain. The record does not show that Rawlings, his government and key supporters had become persuaded that neo-liberal reforms would bring better economic or political outcomes. On the contrary, the record suggests that the degree of social learning, the diffusion of neo-liberal ideology, and consensus over the new economic policy was relatively low. There were intense disagreements within the regime and among its supporters over the political, ideological and technical 'correctness' of switching to neo-liberal economic policies. This had been a leading factor in the resignation of key left-wing elements of the regime between 1982 and 1984, and at least two attempted coups in late 1982 and 1983.[13] Moreover, although internal opposition to neo-liberal reforms subsided over time, there is evidence that it never died down completely, nor disappeared to a point where the existence of a consensus could be inferred. By late 1986, when the neo-liberal reforms were arguably yielding somewhat positive results, a leading official of the government was describing some of IMF/World Bank prescriptions for economic reforms as 'bizarre', and warning of their negative impact on the 'constituency of the Revolution'.[14] The constituency of the revolution, comprising mainly urban workers, students and radical intellectuals, could surely be counted among the segments of Ghanaian society worst affected (subjectively and objectively) by the austerity measures entailed in the economic stabilisation and liberalisation reforms, such as cost recovery, withdrawal of government subsidy and job retrenchments.[15]

Public choice explanations of the Rawlings era policy change, incorporating political and institutional development variables, such as the state and policy coalitions, are thus not fully convincing. They point to the emergence in the early 1980s of a somewhat new and 'virtuous' coalition initiating, implementing and supporting neo-liberal economic reforms. Among the main reasons for the adoption and successful implementation of the new economic policies, they count the emergence of a 'pragmatic political leadership', especially J. J. Rawlings, and 'patriotic professionals and bureaucrats' fed up with ruinous economic policies and accompanying ravages, as well as the 'technocratic change teams', notably Finance Minister Botchway and economic advisor

Abbey. However, that hardly provides enlightenment on/whether or how this group was any different from the group of politicians, technocrats/ bureaucrats and economic advisors who had tried to initiate and sustain the implementation of neo-liberal economic reforms under previous regimes (the National Liberation Council, 1966–68; Progress Party-Kofi Busia, 1969–72; Supreme Military Council-General Fred Akuffo, 1978; and Peoples' National Party-Hilla Limann, 1979–81), and had been unsuccessful. The questions as to why Rawlings succeeded in 1982–92 in moving the Ghanaian economy along neo-liberal lines, where Busia had failed in 1969–72, or why, as Finance Minister, Kwesi Botchway had succeeded in 1982–92 where his predessesor J. H. Mensah had failed in 1969–72, or why, as economic advisor, Joe Abbey was successful in 1982–92 when he himself had failed in 1978 and 1979–81 in a similar capacity, are hardly answered in these explanations.

Public choice explanations of the success of J. J. Rawlings do not receive much help from coalition analysis. They are unable to assert positively that a coalition supporting the change in policy towards neo-liberalism had been formed between the 'change' professionals and politicians initiating and implementing the new policies and the assumed beneficiaries of such policies – rural farmers and export interests.[16] The principle of 'transaction costs'[17] is invoked to explain the absence of a strong pro-reform coalition among the actual and potential beneficiaries of the economic liberalisation reforms, by pointing out that the beneficiaries were too diffused and/or ethnic-minded, and that start-up costs had been high (see Herbst 1993: 76–94). Such beneficiaries would include farmers enjoying increased producer prices and other incentives arising from the lifting of controls on food prices, and others benefiting from the improvements in the supply of consumer goods.

Most significantly, a coalition analysis of the Rawlings success does not receive much help from the results of elections held during the tenure of the reforming Rawlings-PNDC government. The district level elections held in late 1988 and early 1989 failed to yield an unequivocal indication that the regime was able to capture political gains in the rural areas from its putatively pro-rural economic programmes.[18] Moreover, any expectation that the 1992 presidential elections would produce a majority reflecting a 'new' pro-reform coalition in Ghanaian politics did not materialise either. There were very few differences to be discerned in the manifestos of the various parties and candidates contesting the presidential election. All of them had expressed a commitment to economic and political liberalism, rural development and social justice (Ephson 1992). At any rate the election results did not deviate much from the Ghanaian norm. The incumbent won, having manipulated the electoral system somewhat.[19]

Second, there was an ethnic and regional pattern of voting as in previous elections.[20] The two leading presidential candidates scored heavily in their home regions. While Rawlings secured 93.3 per cent of the votes in the Volta Region (where his Ghanaian mother comes from), Adu Boahen received 60.5

Table 18.1 Presidential candidates and votes received in their 'home' regions (percentages)

	Adu Boahen	Hilla Limann	J.J. Rawlings
Akan (speaking) regions			
Western	22.8	8.2	60.7
Central	26.0	1.9	66.5
Eastern	37.7	1.9	57.3
Ashanti	60.5	2.5	32.9
Brong Ahafo	29.5	5.3	61.9
Ewe (speaking) region			
Volta	3.6	0.7	93.2
Mole/Dagbani regions			
Northern	16.3	11.0	63.0
Upper West	8.9	37.1	51.0
Upper East	10.5	32.5	54.0

Source: Interim National Electoral Commission, Accra, 14 December 1992.

Table 18.2 The pro-Rawlings votes in the 1992 presidential elections by region

Region	Percentage
Volta	93.2
Central	66.5
Northern	63.0
Brong Ahafo	61.9
Western	60.7
Eastern	57.3
Upper East	54.0
Upper West	51.0
Ashanti	32.9

Source: Interim National Electoral Commission, Accra, 4 December 1992.

per cent of votes in the Ashanti Region. In fact Rawlings received his highest vote in the Volta Region, which had benefited least from the neo-liberal reforms and associated macro-economic gains, and his lowest vote in Ashanti, which counts among the leading beneficiaries of the same reforms (Tables 18.1 and 18.2). That there has been an ethnic and regional pattern to voting that disregarded the ethno-regional benefits accruing from neo-liberal economic reforms and recovery would appear to cast doubt on any notion that national political coalitions in Ghana necessarily reflect economic interests. To be sure, the pro-Rawlings vote was strong in the rural areas, but that could be attributed as much to campaign advantages on the part of the incumbent Rawlings and his party as to the lack of opportunity for the oppositon to penetrate such areas within the rather short period allowed for the election campaign. On the other hand, the urban working class did not appear to penalise Rawlings at the polls in reaction to perceived 'policy betrayal'. Though the votes for Rawlings in the urban centres were lower than the national average, he did quite well among voters in some constituencies with high concentrations of urban workers. For instance, he got 63 per cent of the votes in the heavily working-class constituency of Ashiaman in the Greater Accra Region, 59.8 per cent in Bimbila in Northern Region and 52.9 in Ayawaso East in Accra (see Table 18.3).

Unable unambiguously to assert that there has been a coalition for policy change, and to describe its size and composition (in order to differentiate it from the previous 'vicious' coalition) public choice explanations have turned to an analysis of why there was *not* a strong anti-reform coalition. Factors such as disunity and demoralisation among the trade unions and their leadership, the nebulous character and/or weakness of civil society and the intellectual and/or financial bankruptcy of the left-wing supporters of the regime have been cited to explain away the 'curious' fact that an anti-reform coalition failed to materialise (Ahiakpor 1991; Jeffries 1992b).

Once more the principle of 'transaction costs' is invoked to explain why a strong anti-reform coalition has not emerged from the ranks of the many direct losers from the neo-liberal economic policies, such as the urban workers who have suffered from job retrenchment, increased prices for food and other

Table 18.3 The pro-Rawlings vote in selected urban constituencies

Region	Constituency	Percentage
Western Region	Sekondi	33.8
	Takoradi	33.5
Central Region	Cape Coast	45.9
Greater Accra	Ayawaso East	52.9
	Ayawaso West	41.1
	Ayawaso Central	46.5
	Ashiaman	63.0
Volta	Ho Central	94.1
Ashanti	Bantama	16.8
	Manhyia	13.2
	Old Tafo Suame	16.7
Eastern	Koforidua	41.5
Brong Ahafo	Sunyani West	47.9
	Sunyani East	40.3
Northern	Yendi	41.2
	Bimbila	59.8
Upper West	Wa East	55.9
	Wa West	64.0
Upper East	Bolgatanga	39.4
	Navrongo	41.2

Source: Interim National Electoral Commission, Accra, 14 December 1993.

consumer goods and services and wage restraints; the business community, who have been made to pay more taxes and higher interest on loans and lost industrial protection; and students and others who have paid more fees under cost recovery measures.

However, a transaction costs explanation of why a strong anti-reform coalition has failed to emerge seems to assign considerable weight to elements of political repression and political authoritarianism, such as the insulation of politicians and their technocratic allies from particularistic interests and group constraints, which is mainly a function of non-democratic politics (Herbst 1993: 68). In such explanations, political repression and the skilful deployment of the national security apparatus – in other words, the literally high physical and political (transaction) cost attached to opposition to neo-liberal economic reforms – become the key factors that have kept the opposition at bay and the politically difficult economic reforms on track. However, that also begs the empirically troubling questions of whether the Rawlings-era authoritarianism has been the most intense in post-colonial Ghanaian history, and also why other military/non democratic governments, with the aid of good advice, would not or could not muster the necessary authoritarian control and political power to initiate and implement similar reforms. After all, the neo-liberal economic reforms of the military regimes of the National Liberation Council (1966–68) and the Akuffo-Supreme Military Council II (1978) had been frustrated, and ultimately abandoned, in the face of intense public pressure, and the *coup d'états* of Colonel Acheampong in 1972 and Flight Lieutenant Rawlings in 1979 and 1981 had been staged, in part, to forestall the initiation and/or abort the implementation of such reforms.

CONCLUSION

Under the rule of J. J. Rawlings, the Ghanaian economy has made significant strides away from statism and towards neo-liberalism. As might be expected, many of the bottlenecks and distortions in such areas as the import–export trade, foreign currency transactions, the distribution of consumer items and the pricing of producer crops have been considerably reduced.

There is very little doubt that the neo-liberal economic reforms, pursued with such single-mindedness by J. J. Rawlings and his government for about a decade, have been responsible for the undeniable macro-economic improvements in the economy. It is also very likely that relative economic success has been a major factor in the political clout that Rawlings and his government have enjoyed with external and internal forces. While the issue of the role played by 'good' – i.e. neo-liberal – economic policies in relative economic and political success is well explained by neo-classical economics, the equally important issues of why Rawlings was able to do it (while others failed), and why or how he managed to sustain these difficult reforms where others did not dare to try, are not so easily explained. Public choice theories do provide

interesting hypotheses, and point to directions of potentially rewarding research into the roles played by history, politics and institutional development
in successful economic reform. However, the available public choice influenced analyses of the success of J. J. Rawlings with pro-market economic
reforms hardly live up to that potential. They mainly go only so far as to explain
how sound policies have been transformed into proficient technical packages,
and to assert that the anti-reform coalition has been too weak to sabotage the
programme. They attempt to bring history and the state back into the explanation of change, but do not succeed in doing so.[21] They thus hardly make a
convincing case for neglecting conventional explanations of the success of J. J.
Rawlings – such as authoritarianism, luck, courage and good timing. For now,
an eclectic approach to the analysis of the political economy of change and
continuity in African development remains the best option.

NOTES

1 The World Bank's influential study, *Accelerated Development in Sub-Saharan Africa: Agenda for Change* (1981) stands as one of the best statements of the perspectives on the African economic crises emphasising internal policy variables. Also, see Bates (1981).

2 The World Bank's *World Development Report* (1983: 62) described the Ghanaian economy as one of the most distorted in the world. For a comprehensive descrip-tion of the pre-structural adjustment Ghanaian economy, see Killick (1978) and Huq (1989).

3 For a detailed account of the measures taken under Ghana's economic recovery and structural adjustment, see Ewusi (1986), Loxley (1988) and Anyemedu (1993).

4 I discuss the state and infrastructural rehabilitation aspects of Ghana's structural adjustment programme in 'Ghana: Adjustment, State Rehabilitation and Democ-ratisation' (forthcoming).

5 Recognition of the negative social impact of the reforms apparently led the gov-ernment of Ghana and the donor community to design the programme of Actions to Mitigate the Social Cost of Adjustment (PAMSCAD). See UNICEF (1986) *Programmes to Protect Children and other Vulnerable Groups*; UNICEF/Govern-ment of Ghana (1990) and Kraus (1990).

6 For the manifestos of the parties that contested the 1992 presidential elections, see Ephson (1992).

7 The best indicator of the Rawlings era divestiture of public enterprises may be the planned sale of half of the shares owned by the government of Ghana in the Ashanti Goldfields Corporation, which produces over 70 per cent of the country's gold output, and which is now the country's leading export and foreign exchange earner.

8 The Ghanaian nationalist intelligentsia held the presence of the Harvard Group advising the Busia government as major evidence of the pro-imperialist leanings of that government.

9 This is the position taken, albeit with qualifications, by Richard Jeffries (1992a); see also Jeffries and Thomas (1993).

10 Callaghy makes this point in his 'Lost between State and Market: the Politics of Economic Adjustment in Ghana, Zambia, and Nigeria' (1990) and in 'Toward State Capability' (1989).

11 Nearly all analysts of the Rawlings success recognise this factor, but they have not

necessarily considered it crucial. The evaluations emphasising the linkage between the economic reform programme and the pronounced authoritarianism of the PNDC era include my 'Economic Recovery and Politics in the PNDC's Ghana' (1990) and Adu-Boahen, *The Ghanaian Sphinx* (1988).

12 This view is most prominent among the legions of former Rawlings comrades who became disaffected and are living in exile. See for example Zaya Yeebo's *Ghana: the Struggle for Popular Power* (1991).

13 For details of attempted coups and other threats to the stability of the Rawlings-PNDC government in the early to mid-1980s, see Ray, *Ghana: Politics, Economics and Society* (1986: 99–117).

14 Colonel J.Y. Assassie in his 'CDRs and the National Economy' (1986). It is instructive to note that Colonel Assassie was not only a leading official of the regime, but was also in charge of the economic education of the populist Committee for the Defence of the Revolution.

15 For the hostile reaction of the popular classes to the neo-orthodox economic reforms and entailed hardships in the early 1980s, see Rothchild and Gyimah-Boadi (1986); for the continuing labour opposition to the reforms, see Gyimah-Boadi and Essuman-Johnson (1993).

16 The outline of a model of a 'pro-development coalition' may be developed out of Bates (1980), especially the concluding chapter.

17 Both North's and Williamson's conceptualisation of transaction costs are employed in this analysis. See, for example, North (1989a) and Williamson (1985).

18 Claims of a rural support base for the regime have been largely based on the steady increases in the nominal prices of export crops and deregulation of food prices, and assumed improvements in rural incomes and living standards. These claims lack empirical validation. They also fail to balance the rural gains against the losses associated with the withdrawal of input subsidy, introduction of user fees for elementary school education, primary health care and other social services, as well as the retrenchment of their urban-based sons and daughters from public sector jobs. Admittedly, it is extremely difficult to make such evaluations in a situation where there is so little reliable data. However, it is instructive to note that the PNDC government itself was likely to emphasise the equity in the fact that the urban workers and not the rural dweller had borne the brunt of the reform programme.

19 Most independent assessments of the 1992 presidential elections concede that there had been a degree of manipulation by the incumbent regime. They have, however, disagreed on the almost unprovable point of whether or not Rawlings could have won without rigging (see Commonwealth Secretariat 1992). For a balanced assessment of the election and the victory of Rawlings, see Haynes (1993), also my 'Issues and Problems in Africa's Transition to Democratic Rule: Lessons and Insights from the Ghanaian Experience' (1994).

20 On the ethnic and regional patterns of voting in Ghanaian elections see Chazan (1987: 61–86).

21 John Toye also, in Chapter 4 in this volume, criticises the failure of new institutionalist approaches adequately to incorporate history into their analysis.

BIBLIOGRAPHY

Abdel Fadil, M. (1980) *The Political Economy of Nasserism*, Cambridge: Cambridge University Press.

Abdel Khalek, G. (ed.) (1982) *The Open Door Policy: The Roots, the Harvest and the Future*, Cairo: Al Markaz al Arabi Lil Bohouth wal Nashr.

Abel, C. (1985) 'Politics and the Economy of the Dominican Republic', in C. Abel and C.M. Lewis (eds) *Latin America: Economic Imperialism and the State*, London: Athlone Press.

Acheson, J. (ed.) (1994) *The New Institutionalism and Modern Anthropology*, Boston: University Press of America.

Adams, D.W. and Nehman, G.I. (1979) 'Borrowing Costs and the Demand for Rural Credit', *Journal of Development Studies* 15, 2.

Adelman, J. (forthcoming) *Constitutionalism and Economy: The Formation of the State in Nineteenth-century Argentina*.

Adu-Boahen, A. (1988) *The Ghanaian Sphinx*, Accra: Ghana Academy of Arts and Sciences.

Africa-Guinea, Alcala de Henares, Archivo General de Administración, 104–3, F. Sabater 'Ensayo', 1906.

Africa-Guinea, Alcala de Henares, Archivo General de Administración, 152–1, 'Bases para la reorganisación del registro de la propriedad', 1926.

Agote, P. (1881) *Informe del Presidente del Crédito Público sobre la deuda pública, bancos y emisiones del papel moneda y acuñación de monedas de la República Argentina*, Buenos Aires.

Agrawal, A. (1992) 'Community Safeguards for Natural Resources: A Study of Village India', unpublished Ph D thesis, Duke University. Durham, NC.

Agriantoni, C. (1978) 'Fisikes Sinthikes, Kinonikes: I Elia, I Mouria ke to Ambeli tin Ora tis Viomihanias', *Deltio tis Eterias Spoudon tou Neoellinikou Politismou ke Genikis Pedias* 2.

Ahiakpor, J. (1985) 'The Success and Failure of Dependency Theory: The Experience of Ghana', *International Organisation* 35: 532–55.

Ahiakpor, J. (1991) 'Rawlings, Economic Policy Reform, and the Poor: Consistency or Betrayal?', *Journal of Modern African Studies* 29, 4: 583–600.

Ahvenainen, J. (1986) 'Telegraphs, Trade and Policy: The Role of International Telegraphs in the Years 1870–1914', in W. Fischer, R. McInnis and J. Schneider (eds) *The Emergence of a World Economy*, Bamberg.

Akerlof, G.A. (1970) 'The Market for "Lemons": Quality Uncertainty and the Market Mechanism', *The Quarterly Journal of Economics* 84: 488–500.

Akerlof, G.A. (1984) *An Economic Theorist's Book of Tales*, Cambridge: Cambridge University Press.

323

Alvater, E. (1993) *The Future of the Market*, London: Verso.

Amaral, S. and Adelman, J. (forthcoming) 'River Plate Exports through the Port of Buenos Aires, 1810–1865'.

Amsden, A. (1989) *Asia's Next Giant: South Korea and Late Industrialisation*, Oxford: Oxford University Press.

Anderson, B.R.O'G. (1983) 'Old State, New Society: Indonesia's New Order in Comparative Perspective', *Journal of Asian Studies* 42, 3: 477–96.

Andreadis, A. (1904) *Istoria ton Ethnikon Danion*, Athens.

Anspach, R. (1960) 'Monetary Aspects of Indonesia's Economic Reorganisation in 1959', *Ekonomi dan Keuangan Indonesia* 13, 1–2: 2–47.

Anyemedu, K. (1993) 'The Economic Policies of the PNDC', in E. Gyimah-Boadi (ed.), *Ghana Under PNDC Rule*, Dakar: Codesria Book Series.

Appelbaum, R. and Henderson, J. (eds) (1992) *States and Development in the Asian Pacific Rim*, Newbury Park: Sage.

Aranha Corrêa do Lago, L. (1978) 'The Transition from Slave to Free Labour in Agriculture in the Southern Coffee Regions of Brazil: a Global and a Theoretical Approach and Regional Case Studies', unpublished PhD thesis, Harvard University.

Armendariz de Aghion, B. (1991) 'On the Pricing of LDC Debt: An Analysis Based on Historical Evidence from Latin America', LSE mimeo.

Armendariz de Aghion, B. and Armendariz de Hinestrosa, P. (1994) 'Debt Relief, Growth and Price Stability: The Case of Mexico', LSE mimeo.

Arndt, H.W. (1966) 'Survey of Recent Developments', *Bulletin of Indonesian Economic Studies* 5: 1–21.

Arndt, H.W. (1983) 'Oil and the Indonesian Economy', *Southeast Asian Affairs*.

Arrow, K. (1951) 'An Extension of the Basic Theorems of Classical Welfare Economics', in J. Neyman (ed.) *Proceedings of the Second Berkeley Symposium on Mathematical Statistics and Probability*, Berkeley: University of California Press.

Arrow, K. (1971a) *Essays on the Theory of Risk Bearing*, Amsterdam: North Holland Press.

Arrow, K. (1971b) 'Political and Economic Evaluations, Social Effects, and Externalities', in M. D. Intriligator (ed.) *Frontiers of Quantitative Economics*, Amsterdam: North Holland Press.

Arrow, K. and Hahn, F.H. (1971) *General Competitive Analysis*, San Francisco: Holden-Day.

Asian Development Bank (1990) *Asian Development Report*, Manila: Asian Development Bank.

Assassie, J. Y. (1986) 'CDRs and the National Economy', *The CDR Eagle* 1, 1.

Assoumou, J. (1977) *L'économie du cacao: agriculture tropicale et bataille du développement en Afrique tropicale*, Paris.

Atkins, R. (1977) *Combinatorial Connectivities in Social Systems*, Basel: Birkhauser Verlag.

Austin, G. (1984) 'Rural Capitalism and the Growth of Cocoa Farming in South Ashanti to 1914', unpublished PhD thesis, Birmingham University.

Austin, G. (1995) 'The Political Economy of Small and Big Farmers in Ghanaian Cocoa Cultivation, c. 1890–1992', in W. G. Clarence-Smith (ed.), *Cocoa Pioneer Fronts since c. 1800: The Role of Smallholders, Planters and Merchants*, London: Macmillan.

Ayala, E. (1982) *Lucha política y origen de los partidos en Ecuador*, Quito.

Bacha, E. and Greenhill, R. G. (1992) *150 anos de café*, Rio de Janeiro.

Bain, J. S. (1959) *Industrial Organisation*, New York: Wiley.

Baker, C. J. (1984) *An Indian Rural Economy, 1880–1935: The Tamilnad Countryside*, Oxford: Clarendon Press.

Barber, A. (1939) 'Six Years of Economic Planning in Netherlands India', *Far Eastern Survey* 8, 17: 195–203.

Bardhan, P. (1989) 'The New Institutional Economics and Development Theory: A Brief Critical Assessment', *World Development* 17, 9: 1389–95.

Bardhan, P. (ed.) (1989) *The Economic Theory of Agrarian Institutions*, Oxford: Clarendon Press.

Barro, R. (1993) 'Pushing Democracy is No Key to Prosperity', *Wall Street Journal* 14 December.

Barrows, R. and Roth, M. (1990) 'Land Tenure and Investment in African Agriculture: Theory and Evidence', *Journal of Modern African Studies* 28, 2.

Barzel, Y. (1989) *Economic Analysis of Property Rights*, Cambridge: Cambridge University Press.

Basu, K. (1985) 'Markets, Power and Social Norms', *Economic and Political Weekly* 21, 43: 1893–6.

Basu, K. (1990) *Agrarian Structure and Economic Development*, London: Harwood Academic Press.

Bates, R.H. (1980) 'Pressure Groups, Public Policy and Agricultural Development: A Study in Divergent Outcomes', in R.H. Bates and M. Lofchie (eds) *Agricultural Development in Africa: Issues of Public Policy*, New York: Praeger.

Bates, R.H. (1981) *Markets and States in Tropical Africa: The Political Basis of Agricultural Policies*, Berkeley and Los Angeles: University of California Press.

Bates, R.H. (1983) *Essays on the Political Economy of Rural Africa*, Berkeley and Los Angeles: University of California Press.

Bates, R.H. (1988) 'Contra-contractarianism: Some Reflections on the New Institutionalism', *Politics and Society* 16: 387–401.

Bates, R.H. (1989) *Beyond the Miracle of the Market: The Political Economy of Agrarian Development in Rural Kenya*, Cambridge: Cambridge University Press.

Bates, R. H. (1990) 'Capital, Kinship and Conflict: The Structuring Influence of Capital in Kinship Societies', *Canadian Journal of African Studies* 2: 151–64.

Bates, R. H., Brock, P. and Tiefenthaler, J. (1991) 'Risk and Trade Regimes', *International Organisation* 1.

Bates, R.H., Mudimbe, V. Y. and O'Barr, J. (eds) (1993) *Africa and the Disciplines*, Chicago: University of Chicago Press.

Bátiz V., J. A. (1986) 'Trayectoria de la banca en México hasta 1910', in L. Ludlow and C. Marichal (eds) *Banca y poder en México, 1800–1925*, Mexico.

Bauer, P. (1963) *West African Trade: A Study of Competition, Oligopoly and Monopoly in a Changing Economy*, Cambridge: Cambridge University Press.

Bauer, P. (1972) 'The Operation and Consequences of the State Export Monopolies of West Africa', in P. Bauer (ed.) *Dissent on Development*, Cambridge, MA: Harvard University Press.

Bauer, P. T. and Yamey, B. S. (1969) *Markets, Market Control and Marketing Reform*, London: Weidenfeld & Nicolson.

Beattie, H. J. (1979) *Land and Lineage in China: A Study of T'ung-Ch'eng County, Anhwei in the Ming and Ch'ing Dynasties*, Cambridge: Cambridge University Press.

Becker, G. S. (1981) *A Treatise on the Family*, Cambridge, MA: Harvard University Press.

Beckerman, W. (1990) 'How Large a Public Sector?' in D. Helm (ed.) *The Economic Borders of the State*, Oxford: Oxford University Press.

Beckford, G. L. (1983) *Persistent Poverty, Underdevelopment in Plantation Economies of the Third World*, London: Zed Press.

Bennet, V. P. (1975) 'Epilogue: Malcontents in Uniform', in D. Austin and R. Lockham (eds) *Politicians and Soldiers in Ghana*, London: Frank Cass.

Berg, A. and Sachs, J. (1988) 'The Debt Crisis: Structural Explanations of Country Performance', *Journal of Development Economics* 29: 271–309.

Berry, S. (1975) *Cocoa, Custom and Socio-economic Change in Rural Western Nigeria*, Oxford: Clarendon Press.

Best, Michael H. (1990) *The New Competition*, Cambridge: Polity Press.

Bhaduri, A. (1983) *The Economic Structure of Backward Agriculture*, London: Academic Press.

Bhaduri, A. (1986) 'Forced Commerce and Agrarian Growth', *World Development* 14, 2: 267–72.

Bhagwati, J.N. (1982) 'Directly Unproductive, Profit-seeking (DUP) Activities', *Journal of Political Economy* 90.

Bharadwaj, K. (1974) *Production Conditions in Indian Agriculture*, Cambridge: Cambridge University Press.

Bharadwaj, K. (1985) 'A View on Commercialisation in Indian Agriculture and the Development of Capitalism', *Journal of Peasant Studies* 12, 1: 7–25.

Bhattacharya, A. and Page, J. (1992) 'Adjustment, Investment and Growth in High Performing Asian Economies', paper presented at the Conference on 'The New Development Economies in Global Context', The American University in Cairo, Cairo: in press.

Bhattacharya, N. (1985) 'Agricultural Labour and Production: Central and South-East Punjab, 1870–1940', in K. N. Raj, N. Bhattacharya, S. Guha and S. Padhi (eds) *Essays on the Commercialisation of Indian Agriculture*, Delhi, pp. 105–62.

Biblawi, H. (1989) *The Predicament of the Economy and Economists*, Cairo: Dar al-Shorouk Press.

Biblawi, H. (1992) *Change for the Sake of Stability*, Cairo: Dar al-Shorouk Press.

Binswanger, H.P. and Rosenzweig, M.R. (1984) 'Behavioral and Material Determinants of Production Relations in Agriculture', World Bank, Research Unit, Agriculture and Rural Development Department, Report No. ARU 5.

Blaikie, P. M., Cameron, J. and Seddon, D. (1981) *Nepal in Crisis*, New York: Oxford University Press.

Blanc-Pamard, C. and Ruf, F. (1992) *La transition caféière, côte est de Madagascar*, Montpellier.

Blink, H. (1905/1907) *Nederlandsch Oost- en West-Indie, geographisch, ethnographisch en economisch beschreven*, Leiden.

Blusse, L. (1984) 'Labour Takes Root: Mobilisation and Immobilisation of Javanese Rural Society under the Cultivation System', *Itinerario* 8, 1: 77–117.

Boeke, J. H. (1953) *Economics and Economic Policy of Dual Societies: As Exemplified by Indonesia*, Haarlem: H. D. Tjeenk Willink & Zoon.

Bohle, H. G. (1992) 'Real Markets and Food Security with Evidence from Fish Marketing in South India', in L. Cammann (ed.) *Traditional Marketing Systems*, Munich: DSE.

Bohn-Young, K. (1982) 'The Role of Foreign Direct Investment in Recent Korean Economic Growth', Working Paper No. 8104, Korea Development Institute, Seoul.

Bohn-Young, K. (1984) 'Industrial Structure and Foreign Investment: A Case Study of their Interrelationship for Korea', Working Paper No. 8402, Korea Development Institute, Seoul.

Boomgaard, Peter (1986) 'The Welfare Services in Indonesia, 1900–42', *Itinerario* 10, 1: 57–82.

Booth, Anne (1980) 'The Burden of Taxation in Colonial Indonesia in the Twentieth Century', *Journal of Southeast Asian Studies* 11, 1: 91–109.

Booth, Anne (1988a) *Agricultural Development in Indonesia*, Sydney: Allen & Unwin.

Booth, Anne (1988b) 'Survey of Recent Developments', *Bulletin of Indonesian Economic Studies* 24, 1: 1–35.

Booth, Anne (1989) 'The State and Economic Development in Indonesia: The Ethical and New Order Eras Compared', in R. J. May and W. J. O'Malley (eds) *Observing Change in Asia: Essays in Honour of J.A.C. Mackie*, Bathurst: Crawford House Press.

Booth, Anne (1990) 'The Evolution of Fiscal Policy and the Role of Government in the Colonial Economy', in A. Booth, W.J. O'Malley and A. Weidemann (eds) *Indonesian Economic History in the Dutch Colonial Era*, New Haven: Yale University Press.

Booth, Anne (forthcoming) 'Markets, Entrepreneurs and the State in Southeast Asia', in *Festschrift in Honour of Professor Lim Chong Yah*, Singapore: Prentice Hall.

Booth, A., O'Malley, W. J. and Weidemann, A. (eds) (1990) *Indonesian Economic History in the Dutch Colonial Era*, New Haven: Yale University Press.

Borja Castro, A.V. de (1869) 'Relatório do segundo grupo', in A. J. de Souza Rego (ed.) *Relatório da segunda exposição nacional de 1866*, Rio de Janeiro.

Botchway, K. (1993) 'Deregulating the Foreign Exchange Market in Ghana', in D. Rimmer (ed.) *Action in Africa*, London: James Currey.

Boulding, K.E. (1950) *Reconstruction in Economics*, New York: Wiley.

Bourdet, I. (ed.) (1992) *Internationalisation, Market Power and Consumer Welfare*, London: Routledge.

Bousquet, G.H. (1940) *A French View of the Netherlands Indies*, London: Oxford University Press.

Boyce, James K. (1987) *Agrarian Impasse in Bengal: Institutional Constraints to Technological Change*, Oxford: Oxford University Press.

Boyd, R. and Richerson, P. J. (1985) *Culture and the Evolutionary Process*, Chicago: University of Chicago Press.

Brandt, L. (1989) *Commercialisation and Agricultural Development in East-Central China, 1870–1939*, Cambridge: Cambridge University Press.

Braudel, F. (1985) *Civilisation and Capitalism from the Fifteenth to the Eighteenth Centuries. Vol. II: The Wheels of Commerce*, London: Fontana.

Brett, E.A. (1985) *The World Economy since the War*, London, Macmillan.

Brett, E.A. (1994) 'Providing for the Rural Poor', *Journal of Modern African Studies* 32.

Buchanan, J.M. (1980) 'Rent-Seeking and Profit-Seeking', in J. Buchanan, R.D. Tollison and G. Tullock (eds) *Towards a Theory of the Rent-Seeking Society*, College Station: Texas A&M University Press.

Buchanan, J.M. (1991) 'The Minimal Politics of Market Order', *Cato Journal* 2: 215–26.

Buchanan, J.M. (1993) 'Asymmetrical Reciprocity in Market Exchange: Implications for Economies in Transition', *Social Philosophy and Policy* 10, 2: 51–64.

Buck, J.L. (1937/1982) *Land Utilization in China: Statistics*, New York: Garland.

Burgin, M. (1946) *Economic Aspects of Argentine Federalism, 1820–1852*, Cambridge, MA: Harvard University Press.

Byres, T.J. (1983) *Sharecropping and Sharecroppers*, London: Frank Cass.

Cain, P.J. and Hopkins, A.G. (1993) *British Imperialism: Innovation and Expansion, 1688–1914*, London: Longman.

Cairncross, A. (1993) *Austin Robinson: Life of an Economic Adviser*, London: Macmillan.

Caldeira, C. (1954) *Fazendas de cacau na Bahia*, Rio de Janeiro.

Callaghy, T.M. (1989) 'Toward State Capability and Embedded Liberalism in the Third World', in J. Nelson (ed.) *Fragile Coalitions: The Politics of Economic Adjustment*, Washington, DC : Overseas Development Council.

Callaghy, T.M. (1990) 'Lost Between State and Market: The Politics of Economic Adjustment in Ghana, Zambia and Nigeria', in J. Nelson (ed.) *The Politics of Adjustment in the Third World*, Princeton: Princeton University Press.

Cammann, L. (ed.) (1992) *Traditional Marketing Systems*, Munich: DSE.

Campbell, J. and Sherrard, P. (1969) *Modern Greece*, London.

Cárdenas, E. and Manns, C. (1989) 'Inflación y estabilización monetaria en México durante la Revolución', *El Trimestre Económico* 56: 57–80.

Cardoso, E. and Helwege, A. (1992) *Latin America's Economy: Diversity, Trends, and Conflicts*, Cambridge, MA: MIT Press.

Carter Center (1993) 'Executive Summary of the Report of the Observer Team for the Ghana Election', mimeo.

Cassen, R., Joshi, V. and Lipton, M. (1993) 'Stabilisation and Structural Reform in India', *Contemporary South Asia* 2, 2: 165–98.

Castles, L. (1965) 'Socialism and Private Business: The Latest Phase', *Bulletin of Indonesian Economic Studies* 1: 13–46.

Centro Industrial de Fiação e Tecelagem de Algodão (1928) *Estatísticas da indústria, commércio e lavoura de algodão relativos ao anno de 1927*, Rio de Janeiro.

Centro Industrial do Brasil (1909) *O Brasil: suas riquezas naturaes, suas indústrias*. Vol. 3: *indústria de transportes, indústria fabril*, Rio de Janeiro.

Centro Industrial do Brasil (1917) *O Centro Industrial na conferência algodoeira*, Rio de Janeiro.

Chalot, C. and Luc, M. (1906) *Le cacaoyer au Congo Français*, Paris.

Chandler, A.D. Jr (1977) *The Visible Hand: The ManagerialRevolution in American Business*, Cambridge, MA: Harvard University Press.

Chandler, A.D. Jr (1990) *Scale and Scope: The Dynamics of Industrial Capitalism*, Cambridge, MA: Belknap Press of Harvard University.

Chang, C.-L. (1955) *The Chinese Gentry: Studies on their Role in 19th-century Chinese Society*, Seattle: University of Washington Press.

Chang, H.-J. (1991) 'The Political Economy of Industrial Policy', unpublished PhD thesis, University of Cambridge.

Chang, H.-J. (1994) *The Political Economy of Industrial Policy*, London: Macmillan.

Chang, H.-J. and Rowthorn, B. (1993) 'The Role of the State in Economic Change: Entrepreneurship and Conflict Management', paper presented to the Cambridge WIDER Conference on the Role of the State in Economic Development.

Chao, K. (1986) *Man and Land in Chinese History*, Stanford: Stanford University Press.

Charlesworth, N. (1985) *Peasants and Imperial Rule: Agriculture and Agrarian Society in the Bombay Presidency, 1850–1935*, Cambridge: Cambridge University Press.

Chattopadhyay, B. (1969) 'Marx and India's Crisis', in P. C. Joshi (ed.) *Homage to Karl Marx*, New Delhi: People's Publishing House.

Chattopadhyay, B. and Spitz, P. (1987) *Food Systems and Society in Eastern India*, Geneva: UNRISD.

Chaudhuri, P. (1978) *The Indian Economy: Poverty and Development*, London: Crosby Lockwood Staples.

Chazan, N. (1987) 'The Anomalies of Continuity: Perspective on Ghanaian Elections since Independence', in F. Hayward (ed.) *Elections in Independent Africa*, Boulder, CO: Westview Press.

Chenery, H. (1979) *Structural Change and Development Policy*, New York: Oxford University Press.

Chenery H., Robinson, S. and Syrquin, M. (1986) *Industrialisation and Growth*, New York: Oxford University Press.

Cheung, S. N. (1987) 'Economic Organisation and Transactions Costs', in *The New Palgrave: A Dictionary of Economics*, London: Macmillan.

Chickering, A. and Salahdine, M. (eds) (1991) *The Silent Revolution*, San Francisco: International Center for Economic Growth.

Chiriboga, M. (1980) *Jornaleros y gran proprietarios en 135 anos de exportación cacaotera, 1790–1925*, Quito: Centro de Investigaciones y Estudos Socioeconomicos.

Church, R. (1993) 'The Family Firm in Industrial Capitalism: International Perspectives on Hypotheses and History', *Business History* 35: 17–43.

CIRAD (1990) *Economies et Filières en Régions Chaudes: Formation des Prix et Echange Agricole, Montpellier: CIRAD.*

Claessens, J. (1914) 'Note relative a la culture du cacaoyer au Mayumbe (Congo Belge)', *Bulletin Agricole du Congo Belge* 5, 2: 215–46.

Claessens, S. (1988) 'The Debt Laffer Curve: Some Estimates', World Bank, Debt and International Finance Department, Washington DC, mimeo.

Clarence-Smith, W.G. (1990) 'The Hidden Costs of Labour on the Cocoa Plantations of São Tomé and Principe, 1875–1914', *Portuguese Studies* 6: 152–72.

Clarence-Smith, W.G. (1993a) 'Labour Conditions in the Plantations of São Tomé and Principe, 1875–1914', *Slavery and Abolition* 14, 1: 149–67.

Clarence-Smith, W.G. (1993b) 'Plantation versus Smallholder Production of Cocoa: The Legacy of the German period in Cameroon', in P. Geschiere and P. Konings (eds) *Itinéraires d'accumulation au Cameroun*, Paris.

Clarence-Smith, W.G. (1993c) 'From Maluku to Manila: Cocoa Production and Trade in Maritime South East Asia from the 1820s to the 1880s', unpublished seminar paper.

Clarence-Smith, W.G. (1994) 'African and European Cocoa Producers on Fernando Póo, 1880s to 1910s', *Journal of African History* 35.

Clarke, S. (1982) *Marx, Marginalism and Modern Sociology*, London: Macmillan.

Cline, W. (1983) *International Debt and the Stability of the World Economy*, Washington, DC : Institute for International Economics.

Coase, R.H. (1937) 'The Nature of the Firm', *Economica* 4, 16 (NS): 386–405.

Coase, R.H. (1960) 'The Problem of Social Cost', *Journal of Law and Economics* 3, 1: 1-44.

Coase, R.H. (1992) 'The Institutional Structure of Production', *American Economic Review* 82, 4.

Coatsworth, John H. (1978) 'Obstacles to Economic Growth in Nineteenth-century Mexico', *American Historical Review* 83: 80–101.

Cohen, A. (1981) *Custom and Politics in Urban Africa*, Berkeley and Los Angeles: University of California Press.

Cohen, D. (1993) 'The Debt Crisis: A Post Mortem', CEPREMAP mimeo, Paris.

Collier, P. (1993) 'Africa and the Study of Economics', in R.H. Bates, V.Y. Mudimbe and J. O'Barr (eds) *Africa and the Disciplines*, Chicago: University of Chicago Press.

Commissão de Inquerito Industrial (1882) *Relatório ao Ministerio da Fazenda*, Rio de Janeiro.

Commonwealth Secretariat (1970) *Plantation Crops*, London: Commonwealth Secretariat.

Commonwealth Secretariat (1992) *Report of the Commonwealth Observer Group on the Presidential Elections in Ghana*, London: Commonwealth Secretariat.

Companhía da Ilha do Principe (1895ff) *Relatórios e contas da Companhía da Ilha do Principe*, Lisbon.

Congleton, R. (1980) 'Competitive Process, Competitive Waste, and Institutions', in J. Buchanan, R.D. Tollison and G. Tullock (eds) *Towards a Theory of the Rent-seeking Society*, College Station: Texas A & M University Press.

Conklin, J. (1993) 'Crown Debt, Credibility and Mechanisms of Commitment in the Reign of Philip II', Stanford University, mimeo.

Coquery-Vidrovitch, C. (1972) *Le Congo au temps des grandes compagnies concessionaires, 1898–1930*, Paris.

Corden, W.M. and Mackie, J.A.C. (1962) 'Development of the Indonesian Exchange Rate System', *Malayan Economic Review* 7.

Cortés Conde, R. (1989) *Dinero, deuda y crisis: evolución fiscal y monetaria en la Argentina*, Buenos Aires: Editorial Sudamericana.

Cowan, T. (ed.) (1992) *Public Goods and Market Failures*, New Jersey: Transaction Publishers.

Cowling, M. (1990) *Mill and Liberalism*, Cambridge: Cambridge University Press.

Crawford de Roberts, L. (1980) *El Ecuador en la epoca cacaotera: respuestas locales al auge y colapso en el ciclo monoexportador*, Quito.

Creutzberg, P. (ed.) (1976) *Changing Economy in Indonesia:* Vol 2: *Public Finance 1816–1939*, The Hague: M. Nijhoff.

Crow, B. and Murshid, F. (1991) *Foodgrains Markets in Bangladesh: Traders, Producers and Policy: Report to the ODA*, Milton Keynes: Open University Press.

Cuddington, J. and Smith, G. (eds) (1985) *International Debt and the Developing Countries*, Washington, DC: The World Bank.

Cummings, R.W. (1967) *Pricing Efficiency in the Indian Wheat Market*, New Delhi: Impex.

Dahl, D.C. (1979) 'Regulation Analysis as a Research Focus in Agricultural Economics', *American Journal of Agricultural Economics* 11, 2: 766–74.

Dahlman, C. J. (1979) 'The Problem of Externality', *Journal of Law and Economics* 22.

Dakin, D. (1972) *The Unification of Greece, 1770–1923*, New York: St Martin's Press.

Davidson's Textile Blue Book (1890–1930), New York.

Davis, J. (1992) *Exchange*, Milton Keynes: Open University Press.

Davis, L.E. (1957) 'Sources of Industrial Finance: The American Textile Industry, A Case Study', *Explorations in Entrepreneurial History* 9: 189–203.

Davis, L.E. (1958) 'Stock Ownership in the Early New England Textile Industry', *Business History Review* 32: 204–22.

Davis, L.E. (1963) 'Capital Immobilities and Finance Capitalism: A Study of Economic Evolution in the United States, 1820–1920', *Explorations in Economic History* 1: 88–105.

Davis, L.E. (1966) 'The Capital Markets and Industrial Concentration: The US and UK, A Comparative Study', *Economic History Review* 19: 255–72.

Davis, L.E. and Huttenback, R.A. (1986) *Mammon and the Pursuit of Empire: The Political Economy of British Imperialism, 1860–1912*, Cambridge: Cambridge University Press.

Davis, L.E. and North, D.C. (1971) *Institutional Change and American Economic Growth*, Cambridge: Cambridge University Press.

Davis, L. E. and Stettler, H. L. (1966) 'The New England Textile Industry, 1825–1860: Trends and Fluctuations', paper given at Conference on Research on Income and Wealth, Output, Employment, and Productivity in the United States after 1800, New York.

Day, C. (1900) 'The Dutch Colonial Fiscal System' in *Essays in Colonial Finance: Publications of the American Economics Association (3rd series)* 1, 3.

Debreu, G. (1951) *Theory of Value*, New York: John Wiley Sons.

Debreu, G. (1984) 'Economic Theory in the Mathematical Mode', *American Economic Review* 74, 3.

Deere, C.D. and de Janvry, A. (1979) 'An Empirical Framework for the Analysis of Peasant Production', *American Journal of Agricultural Economics* 61.

Deler, J-. P. (1981) *Genèse de l'espace Equatorien. Essai sur le territoire et la formation de l'état national*, Paris.

Delfim Netto, A. (1979) *O problema doe café no Brasil*, Rio de Janeiro.

De Long, J. B. (1991) 'Did J. P. Morgan's Men Add Value? An Economist's Perspective on Financial Capitalism', in P. Temin (ed.) *Inside the Business Enterprise: Historical Perspectives on the Use of Information*, Chicago: University of Chicago Press.

Demsetz, H. (1967) 'Towards a Theory of Property Rights', *American Economic Review* 57, 2: 347–59.

Department of Information (1969) *The Five-Year Development Plan 1969–74*, Jakarta: Department of Information.

Dertilis, P. (1936) *La Problème de la Dette Publique des Etats Balkaniques*, Athens.

Dertilis, G. (1977) *Kinonikos Metashimatismos ke Stratiotiki Epemvasi 1880–1909*, Athens.

Dertilis, G. (1980) *To Zitima ton Trapezon (1871–1873)*, Athens.

Dertilis, G. (1983) 'Diethnis Ikonomikes Shesis ke Politiki Exartissi: I Elliniki Periptossi, 1824–1878', *Historica* 1.

Dertilis, G. (1984) *Elliniki Ikonomia (1830–1910) ke Viomihaniki Epanastasi*, Athens.

Dertilis, G. (ed.) (1988) *Banquiers, Usuriers et Paysans Reseaux de Credit et Strategies du Capital en Grèce (1780–1930)*, Paris: Fondation des Treilles.

Dertilis, G. (1993) *Atelesfori i Telesfori, Fori ke Exousia sto Neoelliniko Kratos*, Athens.

Dervis, K., de Melo, J. and Robenson S. (1982) *General Equilibrium Models for Development Policy*, Cambridge: Cambridge University Press.

De Soto, H. (1990) *The Other Path*, New York: Harper & Row.

De Wit, Y. (1973) 'The Kabupaten Programme', *Bulletin of Indonesian Economic Studies* 9, 1: 65–85.

Deyo, F. C. (ed.) (1987) *The Political Economy of the New Asian Industrialism*, Ithaca: Cornell University Press.

Díaz, B. (1973) *Mariano Fraqueiro y la constitución de 1853*, Buenos Aires.

Dick, H.W. (1985) 'Survey of Recent Developments', *Bulletin of Indonesian Economic Studies* 21, 3: 1–29.

Dillard, D. (1980) 'A Monetary Theory of Production: Keynes and the Institutionalists', *Journal of Economic Issues* 14, 2.

Ding, C.-Q. (1992) 'Development of Capitalism in Modern Chinese Agriculture', in T. Wright (ed.) *The Chinese Economy in the Early Twentieth Century: Recent Chinese Studies*, London: Macmillan.

Dirección de Colonización e Industria (1851) *Memoria 1850*, Mexico.

Diwan, I. and Husain, I. (1989) *Dealing with the Debt Crisis*, Washington, DC: The World Bank.

Djurfeldt, G. and Lindberg, S. (1974) *Behind Poverty*, London: Curzon for the Scandinavian Institute for Asian Studies Series.

Dockham's American Report and Directory of the Textile Manufacture and Dry Goods Trade (1880–1900), Boston.

Dornbusch, R. (1985) 'External Debt, Budget Deficits, and Disequilibrium Exchange Rates', in J. Cuddington and G. Smith (eds) *International Debt and the Developing Countries*, Washington, DC: The World Bank.

Dornbusch, R. and Fischer, S. (1987) 'International Capital Flows and the World Debt Problem', in A. Razin and E. Sadka (eds) *Economic Policy in Theory and Practice*, London: Macmillan.

Dow, G.K. (1993) 'The Appropriability Critique of Transaction Cost Economics', in C. Pitelis (ed.) *Transaction Costs, Markets and Hierarchies*, Oxford: Basil Blackwell.

Dritsas, M. (1990) *Viomihania ke Trapezes stin Ellada tou Mesopolemou*, Athens.

Duffy, J. (1967) *A Question of Slavery: Labour Policies in Portuguese Africa and the British Protest, 1850–1920*, Cambridge, MA: Harvard University Press.

Dugger, W.M. (1992) 'An Evolutionary Theory of the State and the Market', in W.M. Dugger and W. Waller (eds) *The Stratified State*, New York: M. E. Sharpe (mimeo).

Dugger, W.M. (1993) 'Transaction Cost Economics and the State', in C. Pitelis (ed.)

Surveys in Transaction Costs, Markets and Hierarchies: A Critical Assessment, Oxford: Blackwells.

Eastman, L.E. (1988) *Family, Fields and Ancestors: Constancy and Change in China's Social and Economic History, 1550–1949*, Oxford: Oxford University Press.

Eaton, J. and Gersovitz, M. (1981) 'Debt with Potential Repudiation: Theoretical and Empirical Analysis', *Review of Economic Studies* 48, 2: 289–309.

Eaton, J., Gersovitz, M. and Stiglitz, J.E. (1986) 'The Pure Theory of Country Risk', *European Economic Review* 30: 481–513.

ECAFE (1961) *Economic Survey of Asia and the Far East, 1961*, Bangkok: United Nations Economic Commission for Asia and the Far East.

Eggertsson, T. (1990) *Economic Behaviour and Institutions*, Cambridge: Cambridge University Press.

Eichengreen B. and Portes, R. (1989) 'Dealing with Debt: The 1930s and the 1980s', The World Bank Working Paper No. 259, Washington, DC.

El-Shennawy, A. (1993) 'Financial Repression, Inflation and Growth in Egypt, 1974–1991', unpublished MA thesis, The American University in Cairo.

Ellis, F., Magrath, P. and Trotter, B. (1991) *Indonesia Rice Marketing Study, 1989–1991*, Jakarta: Bulog.

Elster, J. (1978) *Logic and Society*, Chichester: Wiley.

Elvin, M. (1970a) 'Early Communist Land Reform and the Kiangsi Rural Economy: A Review Article', *Modern Asian Studies* 4: 165–9.

Elvin, M. (1970b) 'The Last Thousand Years of Chinese History: Changing Patterns of Land Tenure', *Modern Asian Studies* 4: 97–114.

Ensminger, J. (1992) *Making a Market*, Cambridge: Cambridge University Press.

Ephson, B. (1992) *Elections Special*, Accra: Buck Press.

Esherick, J.W. (1981) 'Number Games: A Note on Land Distribution in Pre-revolutionary China', *Modern China* 7: 396–400.

Etzioni, A. (1988) *The Moral Dimension: Towards a New Economics*, New York: The Free Press.

Ewusi, K. (1986) *Structural Adjustment and Stabilization Policies in Developing Countries: A Case Study of Ghana's Experience in 1983–86*, Tema: Ghana Publishing Corp.

Fahmy, K.M. (1988) *Legislating Infitah: Investment, Currency, and Foreign Trade Laws*, Cairo: The American University in Cairo Press.

Fasseur, C. (1991) 'Purse or Principle: Dutch Colonial Policy in the 1860s and the Decline of the Cultivation System', *Modern Asian Studies*, 25, 1: 33–52.

Faure, D. (1989) *The Rural Economy of Pre-Liberation China*, Hong Kong: Oxford University Press.

Fergany, N. (1992) *Poverty and Unemployment Profiles on the Level of Administrative Units (Kism and Markaz): By Urban–Rural Classification and Implied Allocation of Funds*. Final Report, Second Phase of Targeting for the Social Fund, Cairo: Al Mishkat Center.

Ferguson, P.R. (1992) 'Privatization Options for Eastern Europe: the Irrelevance of Western Experience', *The World Economy* 15, 4: 487–504.

Ferreira, F.H.G. (1992) 'The World Bank and the Study of Stabilization and Structural Adjustment in LDCs', Development Economics Research Programme Discussion Paper No. 41, STICERD, London School of Economics.

Feuerwerker, A. (1980) 'Economic Trends in the late Ch'ing Empire, 1870–1911', in J.K. Fairbank and K.-C. Liu (eds) *The Cambridge History of China*. Vol. 11: *Late Ch'ing, 1800–1911, Part 2*, Cambridge, pp. 1–69.

Feuerwerker, A. (1983) 'Economic Trends, 1912–49', in J.K. Fairbank (ed.) *The Cambridge History of China*. Vol 12: *Republican China, 1912–1949, Part 1*, Cambridge: pp. 28–127.

Firmin, K. (1992) 'The Politics of Property Rights: State Creation and the Development of Markets in Historical Ghana', unpublished PhD thesis, Duke University, Durham, NC.

Fischer, S. (1989) 'Resolving the International Debt Crisis', in J. Sachs (ed.) *Developing Country Debt and the World Economy*, Chicago: University of Chicago Press.

Folbre, N. (1994) *Who Pays for the Kids? Gender and the Structures of Constraints*, New York: Routledge.

Font, M. (1990) *Coffee, Contention and Change in the Making of Modern Brazil*, Oxford: Blackwells.

Foreign Investment Advisory Service (1991) 'Egypt: Foreign Direct Investment Climate', Joint Service of International Finance Corporation (IFC) and Multilateral Investment Guarantee Agency (MIGA), Washington DC, mimeo.

Fourie, F.C. v. N. '(1991) A Structural Analysis of Markets', in G. Hodgson (ed.) *Rethinking Economics*, Cambridge: Cambridge University Press.

Fox, R.G. (1968) *From Zamindar to Ballot Box – Community Change in a North Indian Market Town*. Ithaca, NY: Cornell University Press.

Freris, A.F. (1976) 'To Xeno Kefaleo stin Ellada (1840–1940)', *Ikonomikos Tahydromos* 1134.

Friedman, M. (1953) *Essays on Positive Economics*, Chicago: University of Chicago Press.

Fritsch, W. (1988) *External Constraints on Economic Policy in Brazil, 1889–1930*, London: Macmillan.

Frohlich, N. and Oppenheimer, J.A. (1978) *Modern Political Economy*, Englewood Cliffs, NJ: Prentice-Hall.

Galal A., Jones, L., Tandom, P. and Vogelsang, I. (1992) 'Synthesis of Cases and Policy Summary, Welfare Consequences of Selling Public Enterprises: Case Studies from Chile, Malaysia, Mexico and the UK', World Bank Conference, 11–12 June, mimeo.

Gangnes, B. and Naya, S. (1992) 'Why East Asian Economies have been Successful: Some Lessons for Other Developing Countries', Paper presented at the Conference on The New Development Economics in Global Context, The American University in Cairo, 28–30 May.

García, R. (1984) *Food Systems and Society: a Conceptual and Methodological Challenge*, Geneva: UNRISD.

Gazdar, H. (1990) 'The Bretton Woods Institutions and the Debt Crisis', University of Sussex, IDS, mimeo.

General Agreement on Tariffs and Trade (GATT) (1992) 'Trade Policy Review Mechanism: The Arab Republic of Egypt', mimeo.

Gerschenkron, A. (1962) *Economic Backwardness in Historical Perspective: a Book of Essays*, Cambridge, MA: Harvard University Press.

Gibbons, R. (1992) *Game Theory for Applied Economists*, Princeton: Princeton University Press.

Giddens, A. (1992) *Sociology*, London: Polity Press.

Gilbert, E.H. (1969) 'Marketing of Staple Goods in Northern Nigeria: A Study of Staple Food Marketing Systems Serving Kano City', PhD thesis, Stanford University, California.

Goldsmith, A. (1985) 'The Private Sector and Rural Development: Can Agribusiness Help the Small Farmers?' *World Development* 13, 10–11: 1125–38.

Goldsworthy, D. (1973) 'Ghana's Second Republic: A Post-Mortem', *African Affairs* 62.

Gordon-Ashworth, F. (1984) *International Commodity Control: A Contemporary History and Appraisal*, London: Croom Helm.

Gorostegui de Torres, H. (1972) *Historia Argentina: la organisación nacional*, Buenos Aires: Paídos.

Goswami, O. (1984) 'Agriculture in Slump: The Peasant Economy of East and North Bengal in the 1930s', *Indian Economic and Social History Review* 21: 337–64.

Graham, E. and Floering, I. (1984) *The Modern Plantation in the Third World*, London: Croom Helm.

Graham, R. (ed.) (1969) *A Century of Brazilian History since 1865*, New York: Knopf.

Greenhill, R.G. (1977) 'The Brazilian Coffee Trade', in D.C.M. Platt (ed.) *Business Imperialism, 1840–1930: An Inquiry Based on British Experience in Latin America*, Oxford: Clarendon.

Greenhill, R.G. and Miller, R.M. (1973) 'The Peruvian Government and the Nitrate Trade, 1873–1879', *Journal of Latin American Studies* 5: 107–31.

Griffiths, R. T. (1979) *Industrial Retardation in the Netherlands, 1830–50*, The Hague: M. Nijhoff.

Griliches, Z. and Maitresse, J. (1990) 'R & D and Productivity Growth: Comparing Japanese and US Manufacturing Firms', in C. Hulten (ed.) *Productivity Growth in Japan and the United States*, NBER Studies in Income and Wealth, Chicago: Chicago University Press.

Groff, D. H. (1987) "Carrots, Sticks and Cocoa Pods": The Spread of Cocoa Production in Assikasso, Ivory Coast, 1908–1920', *International Journal of African Historical Studies* 20, 3: 401–16.

Guha, S. (1985) 'Rural Economy in the Deccan', in K.N. Raj *et al.* (eds) *Essays on the Commercialisation of Indian Agriculture*, Bombay: Oxford University Press.

Guislain, L. and Vincart, L. (1911) 'La Culture de cacaoyer du Venezuela et à l'Equateur', *L'Agronomie Tropicale* 3, 4: 65–73.

Gunnarsson, C. (1978) *The Gold Coast Cocoa Industry, 1900–1939: Production, Prices and Structural Change*, Lund.

Gyimah-Boadi, E. (1990) 'Economic Recovery and Politics in the PNDC's Ghana', *Journal of Commonwealth and Comparative Politics* 28, 3: 228–43.

Gyimah-Boadi, E. (1993) 'The Search for Economic Development and Democracy in Ghana: From Limann to Rawlings', in E. Gyimah-Boadi (ed.) *Ghana Under PNDC Rule*, Dakar: Codesria Book Series.

Gyimah-Boadi, E. (1994) 'Issues and Problems in Africa's Transition to Democratic Rule: Lessons and Insights from the Ghanaian Experience', *Journal of Democracy* 5, 2.

Gyimah-Boadi, E. (forthcoming) 'Ghana: Adjustment, State Rehabilitation and Democratization in Ghana', in T. Mkandawire and A. Olukoshi (eds) *Between Repression and Liberalisation: The Politics of Adjustment in Africa*, Dakar: Codesria Book Series.

Gyimah-Boadi, E. and Essuman-Johnson, A. (1993) 'The PNDC and Organised Labor: The Anatomy of Political Control', in E. Gyimah-Boadi (ed.) *Ghana Under PNDC Rule*, Dakar: Codesria Book Series.

Haber, S.H. (1989) *Industry and Underdevelopment: The Industrialisation of Mexico, 1890–1940*, Stanford: Stanford University Press.

Haggard, Stephan (1990) *Pathways from the Periphery: The Politics of Growth in the Newly Industrialising Countries*, Ithaca: Cornell University Press.

Hahn, F. (1987) 'Information, Dynamics and Equilibrium', *Scottish Journal of Economics*, 34: 321–34.

Haines, M. (1992) 'The Role of Government in the Regulation of Marketplaces', in L. Cammann (ed.) *Traditional Marketing Systems*, Munich: DSE.

Hall, C.J.J. van (1914) *Cocoa*, London.

Hall, C.J.J. van (1932) *Cacao*, London.

Hall, C.J.J. van (1946–50) 'Cacao', in C.J.J. van Hall and C. van de Koppel (eds) *De landbouw in de Indische Archipel*, vol. 28, The Hague: pp. 272–346.

334

BIBLIOGRAPHY

Halperín Donghi, T. (1982) *Guerra y finanzas en los orígenes del estado argentino (1791–1850)*, Buenos Aires: Editorial Sudamericana.

Handoussa, H. (1974) 'The Economics of the Pharmaceutical Industry in Egypt', unpublished PhD thesis, University of London.

Handoussa, H. (1979a) 'The Public Sector in Egyptian Industry, 1952–1977', in Société Egyptienne d'Economie Politique, de Statistique et de Legislation, *The Egyptian Economy in a Quarter Century*, Cairo: Al Haya Al Misriya Ama Lilkitab.

Handoussa, H. (1979b) 'Time for Reform: Egypt's Public Sector Industry', in H. Thompson (ed.) *The Political Economy of Egypt*, Cairo Papers in Social Science, Cairo: The American University in Cairo Press.

Handoussa, H. (1980) 'The Impact of Economic Liberalisation on the Performance of Egypt's Public Sector Industry', paper presented at Second BAPEG Conference, Boston: Boston University and Harvard Institute for International Development.

Handoussa, H. (1986) 'The South Korea Success Story: Comparisons and Contrasts with Egypt', *L'Egypte Contemporaine*, 77, 403.

Handoussa, H. (1989a) 'The Burden of Public Service Employment and Remuneration: The Case of Egypt', in W. van Ginneken (ed.) *Government and its Employees*, Geneva: International Labour Office.

Handoussa, H. (1989b) 'Egypt's Investment Strategy, Policies and Performance Since the Infitah', in S. El-Naggar (ed.) *Investment Policies in the Arab Countries*, Washington, DC: International Monetary Fund.

Handoussa, H. (1991) 'The Impact of Foreign Assistance on Egypt's Economic Development, 1952–1986', in U. Lele and I. Nabi (eds) *Transitions in Development: The Role of Aid and Commercial Flows*, San Francisco: International Center for Economic Growth Press.

Handoussa, H. and Kaldas, S. (1986) 'Efficiency Issues and the Allocation of Loans for Food Security Project', report prepared to the Ministry of Agriculture, mimeo.

Handoussa, H. and Potter, G. (1992) 'Egypt's Informal Sector: Engine of Growth?' paper presented at MESA Conference Portland, Oregon, 28–31 October.

Handoussa, H. and Shafik, N. (1991) 'The Economics of Peace: The Egyptian Case', paper presented at Conference on the Economics of Peace in the Middle East, Harvard University, Cambridge, MA, 15–16 November.

Handoussa, H. and Shafik, N. (1993a) 'Prospects for the Development of Export Oriented Industries in Egypt', study prepared for the Japanese Institute of Middle Eastern Economies, Tokyo.

Handoussa, H. and Shafik, N. (1993b) 'Egypt's Structural Adjustment Program and Prospects for Recovery', study prepared for the Workshop on Japanese Economic Cooperation with Developing Countries, 1–6 December 1992, Institute of Developing Economies, Tokyo.

Hanisch, R. (1991) 'Die politische Okonomie des Kakaoweltmarktes', in R. Hanisch and C. Jakobeit (eds) *Der Kakaoweltmarkt. Weltmarktinterierte Entwicklung und nationale Steuerungspolitik der Produzentenländer*, Hamburg.

Hansen, B. and Marzouk, G. (1965) *Development and Economic Policy in the UAR (Egypt)*, Amsterdam: North-Holland Publishing Company.

Hansen, B. and Nashashibi, K. (1975) *Foreign Trade Regimes and Economic Development: Egypt*, New York: National Bureau of Economic Research.

Haritakis, G. (ed.) (1933) *Ikonomiki Epitiris tis Ellados 1932*, Athens.

Harms, R. (1981) *River of Wealth, River of Sorrow, the Central Zaire Basin in the Era of the Slave and Ivory Trade*, New Haven: Yale University Press.

Harriss, B. (1979) 'There is Method in my Madness: Or is it Vice Versa? Measuring Agricultural Market Performance', *Food Research Institute Studies*, Stanford, 17: 197–218.

Harriss, B. (1981) *Transnational Trade and Rural Development*, New Delhi: Vikas Publishing Company.

Harriss, B. (1982) 'Food Systems and Society: The System of Circulation of Rice in West Bengal', *Cressida Transactions* 1–2, 1: 158–250.

Harriss, B. (1989) 'The Organised Power of Grain Merchants in the Dhaka Region of Bangladesh', *Economic and Political Weekly* 16, 10–12: 441–58.

Harriss, B. (1991a) 'Masters of the Countryside: Report to the Overseas Development Administration', Queen Elizabeth House, Oxford.

Harriss, B. (1991b) *Markets, Society and the State: Problems of Marketing Under Conditions of Small Holder Agriculture in West Bengal*, Report to WIDER, Helsinki, Queen Elizabeth House, Oxford, published as a Discussion Paper by the Open University Development Policy and Practice in 1993.

Harriss, B. *et al.* (1984) *Exchange Relations and Poverty in Dryland Agriculture*, New Delhi: Concept.

Harriss-White B. (1995) 'Order, Order ... Agrocommercial Microstructures and the State: The Experience of Regulation', in S. Subrahmanyam and B. Stein (eds) *Production Units in Micro and Macro Structural Perspective*, New Delhi: Oxford University Press.

Harwich, N. (1992) *Histoire du chocolat*, Paris.

Hausen, K. (1970) *Deutsche Kolonialherrschaft in Afrika. Wirtschaftsinteressen und Kolonialverwaltung in Kamerun vor 1914*, Zurich.

Hawkins, H.C.G. (1965) *Wholesale and Retail Trade in Tanganyika: A Study of Distribution in East Africa*, New York: Praeger.

Hayek, F.A. (1945) 'The Use of Knowledge in Society', *American Economic Review* 35, 4: 519–30.

Haynes, J. (1993) 'Sustainable Democracy in Ghana? Problems and Prospects', *Third World Quarterly* 14, 3: 451–67.

Hegel, G.W.F. (1837/1953) *Reason in History*, Indianapolis: Bobbs-Merrill, Library of the Liberal Arts.

Hegel, G.W.F. (1967) *Philosophy of Right*, London: Oxford University Press.

Heiner, R. (1983) 'The Origins of Predictable Behavior', *American Economic Review*, 73: 560–95.

Helm, D. (ed.) (1990) *The Economic Borders of the State*, Oxford: Oxford University Press.

Herbst, J. (1993) *The Politics of Reform in Ghana, 1982–1991*, Berkeley: University of California Press.

Heston, A. (1984) 'National Income', in D. Kumar with M. Desai (eds) *Cambridge Economic History of India.* Vol 2: *c. 1757–c. 1970*, Cambridge: pp. 376–442.

Hicks, J.R. (1946) *Value and Capital*, Oxford: Clarendon Press.

Higgins, B. (1968) 'Indonesia: The Chronic Dropout', in *Economic Development: Principles, Problems and Policies*, London: Constable.

Hill, H. (1939) *The Economy of Greece*, New York: Greek War Relief Association.

Hill, L.F. (ed.) (1947) *Brazil*, The United Nations Series, California University, Berkeley: University of California Press.

Hill, P. (1963) *Migrant Cocoa-farmers of Southern Ghana: A Study in Rural Capitalism*, Cambridge: Cambridge University Press.

Hirschman, A.O. (1970) *Exit, Voice and Loyalty: Responses to Decline in Firms, Organisations and States*, Cambridge, MA: Harvard University Press.

Hirschman, A.O. (1977) *The Passions and the Interests: Political Arguments for Capitalism before its Triumph*, Princeton: Princeton University Press.

Hjalmarsson, L. (1992) 'Competition Policy and Economic Efficiency: Efficiency Trade-offs in Industrial Policy', in I. Bourdet (ed.) *Internationalisation, Market Power and Consumer Welfare*, London: Routledge.

Ho, P.-T. (1959) *Studies in the Population of China*, Cambridge, MA: Harvard University Press.

Ho, P.-T. (1962) *The Ladder of Success in Imperial China*, New York: Columbia University Press.

Hodges, T. and Newitt, M. (1988) *São Tome and Principe: From Plantation Colony to Microstate*, Boulder, CO: Westview.

Hodgson, G. (1988) *Economics and Institutions*, Cambridge: Polity Press.

Hodgson, G. (1991) (ed.) *Rethinking Economics*, Cambridge: Cambridge University Press.

Hodgson, G. (1992) 'The Reconstruction of Economics: Is there Still a Place for Neoclassical Theory?' *Journal of Economic Issues* 3.

Hodgson, G.M. (1993) 'Institutional Economics: Surveying the "Old" and the "New"', *Metroeconomica* 44, 1: 1–28.

Hollander, S. (1985) *The Economics of John Stuart Mill* (2 vols.), Oxford: Blackwell.

Hopkins, A. (1973) *An Economic History of West Africa*, London: Longman.

Hopkins, N. S. (ed.) (1992) *Informal Sector in Egypt*, Cairo: The American University in Cairo Press.

Howland, C. (1926) *L'établissement de Réfugiés en Grèce*, Geneva: League of Nations.

Hristopoulos, G. (1977/8) *Istoria tou Ellenikou Ethnous*, Athens.

Huang, P.C.C. (1985) *The Peasant Economy and Social Change in North China*, Stanford: Stanford University Press.

Huang, P.C.C. (1990) *The Peasant Family and Rural Development in the Yangzi Delta, 1350–1988*, Stanford: Stanford University Press.

Huang, P.C.C. (1991) 'A Reply to Ramon Myers', *Journal of Asian Studies* 50: 629–33.

Hulten, C. (ed.) (1990) *Productivity Growth in Japan and the United States*, Chicago: University of Chicago Press.

Hulten, C. (ed.) (1992) *Arab Republic of Egypt – Staff Report for the 1992 Article IV Consultation*, 16 July.

Hunger, F.W.T. (1913) 'Cacao', in H.C. Prinsen Geerlings (ed.) *Dr K.W. van Gorkom's Oost-indische cultures, opnieuw uitgegeven*, Amsterdam: Vol. 2, pp. 357–458.

Huq, M.M. (1989) *The Economy of Ghana: The First 25 Years After Independence*, London: Macmillan.

Hutchful, E. (1989) 'From "Revolution" to Monetarism: The Economics and Politics of the Adjustment Programme in Ghana', in B. Campbell and J. Loxley (eds) *Structural Adjustment in Africa*, London: Macmillan.

Hyman, D.N. (1990) *Public Finance*, Chicago: Dryden Press.

Ikonomiki Epitiris tis Ellados 1929, 1932, 1933, 1939. Athens. (Haritakis, ed.)

Iliffe, J. (1983) *The Emergence of African Capitalism*, Minneapolis: The University of Minnesota Press.

Illori, C. (1968) 'An Economic Study of the Production and Distribution of Staple Foodcrops in Western Nigeria', unpublished PhD thesis, Stanford University.

Instituto Nacional de Estadística, Geografía e Informática (1985) *Estadísticas Históricas de México*, Mexico.

Instituto Brasileiro de Geografía e Estatística (1990) *Estatísticas Históricas do Brasil*, Rio de Janeiro.

Integrated Development Consultants (1989) *An Annotated Description of the Procedures for Establishing Small-scale Enterprises in Egypt*, prepared for the United States Agency for International Development, Cairo.

International Coffee Organisation (1978a) 'Coffee in Kenya, 1977', Document E.B. 1601/78 (E) 31 January.

International Coffee Organisation (1978b) 'Coffee in Tanzania, an Economic Report, 1978', Document E. B. 1642/78 (E) 25 September.

Issawy, C. (1990) 'Economic Evolution Since 1800', in I.M. Oweiss (ed.) *The Political*

Economy of Contemporary Egypt, Washington: Center for Contemporary Arab Studies, Georgetown University Press.

Jacobsson, S. (1993) 'The Length of the Infant Industry Period: Evidence from the Engineering Industry in South Korea', *World Development*, 21, 3: 407–19.

Jaffee, S. (1990) 'Alternative Marketing Institutions for Agricultural Exports in Sub-Saharan Africa with Special Reference to Kenyan Horticulture', unpublished D Phil thesis, University of Oxford.

Jagganathan, N.V. (1987) *Informal Markets in Developing Countries*, New York: Oxford University Press.

Janakarajan, S. (1986) 'Aspects of Market Interrelationships in a Changing Agrarian Economy: A Case Study from Tamil Nadu', unpublished PhD thesis, University of Madras.

Janakarajan, S. and Subramanian, S. (1991) 'Triadic Exchange Relations: An Illustration from South India', Queen Elizabeth House Working Paper, Oxford.

Jasdanwalla, Z.Y. (1966) *Marketing Efficiency in Indian Agriculture*, Bombay: Allied.

Jeffries, R. (1992a) 'Urban Popular Attitudes Towards the Economic Recovery Programme and the PNDC Government in Ghana', *African Affairs* 91: 207–26.

Jeffries, R. (1992b) 'Leadership Commitment and Political Opposition to Structural Adjustment', in D. Rothchild (ed.) *Ghana: The Political Economy of Recovery*, Boulder, CO: Lynne Rienner.

Jeffries, R. and Thomas, C. (1993) 'The Ghanaian Elections of 1992', *African Affairs* 92: 331–66.

Johnson, C. (1982) *MITI and the Japanese Miracle: The Growth of Industrial Policy, 1925–1975*, Stanford: Stanford University Press.

Johnson, J. (1990) 'The Rules of Q-Analysis', *Environment and Planning B Planning and Design* 17, 4: 475–86.

Jones, E. L. (1981) *The European Miracle*, Cambridge: Cambridge University Press.

Jones, E. L. (1988) *Growth Recurring: Economic Change in World History*, Oxford: The Clarendon Press.

Jones, W. O. (1972) *Marketing Staple Foodcrops in Tropical Africa*, Ithaca: Cornell University Press.

Jorion, P. (1988) 'Determinants sociaux de la formation des prix de marché', *Revue du Mauss* 9: 71–108.

Joseph, A. (1984) 'Transactions Governance in Marketing Structures: A Study in the Midwestern Hog Markets', unpublished PhD thesis, Illinois University.

Kalliavas, A. (1929) 'O Diethnis Ikonomikos Eleghos tis Ellados ke ta Apotelesmata Aftou', *Bulletin de la Chambre de Commerce et d'Industrie d'Athènes*, Athens.

Kalligas, P. (1930) *Systima Romaikou Dikeou*, Athens.

Kaltchas, N. (1940) *Introduction to the Constitutional History of Modern Greece*, New York: Columbia University Press.

Kapur, I., Hadjimichael, M.T., Hilbers, P., Schiff, J. and Szymczak, P. (1991) *Ghana: Adjustment and Growth*, Occasional Paper No. 86, Washington, DC: IMF.

Katz, E. and Lazarsfeld, P.F. (1964) *Personal Influence*, New York: The Freedom Press.

Kemner, W. (1937) *Kamerun, dargestellt in kolonialpolitischer, historischer, verkehrstechnischer, rassenkundlicher, und rohstoffwirtschaftlicher Hinsicht*, Berlin.

Kennedy, S. J. (1940) *Profits and Losses in Textiles: Cotton Textile Financing Since the War*, New York.

Keyes, C. (1983) 'Economic Action and Buddhist Morality in a Thai Village', *Journal of Asian Studies* 42, 4: 753–878.

Khan, M.H. (1989) 'Clientelism, Corruption and Capitalist Development', unpublished PhD Thesis, Faculty of Economics and Politics, University of Cambridge. (Forthcoming Oxford University Press)

Khan, M.S., Montiel, P. and Haque, N.U. (1990) 'Adjustment with Growth: Relating the Analytical Approaches of the IMF and the World Bank', *Journal of Development Economics* 32.

Kheir El-Din, H., El-Baradei, M. and El Sayed, H. (1989) *Evaluation of the Protection System in Egypt*, Center for Economic and Financial Research and Studies, Cairo University. Prepared for International Trade Center (UNCTAD/GATT).

Killick, T. (1978) *Development Economics in Action*, London: Heinemann.

Kindleberger, C.P. (1978) *Manias, Panics and Crashes: A History of Financial Crises*, New York: Basic Books.

Klitgaard, R. (1991) *Adjusting to Reality*, San Francisco: ICS Press.

Knight, J. (1992) *Institutions and Social Conflict*, Cambridge: Cambridge University Press.

Kornai, J. (1990a) *The Affinity between Ownership and Coordination Mechanisms: The Common Experience of Reform in Socialist Countries*, Helsinki: World Institute of Development Economics Research.

Kornai, J. (1990b) *The Road to a Free Economy*, New York: W. W. Norton & Co.

Korthals Altes, W.L. (ed.) (1987) *Changing Economy in Indonesia:* Vol 7: *Balance of Payments 1822–1939*, Amsterdam: Royal Tropical Institute.

Korthals Altes, W.L. (ed.) (1991) *Changing Economy in Indonesia:* Vol 12a: *General Trade Statistics 1822–1940*, Amsterdam: Royal Tropical Institute.

Koslowski, R. (1992) 'Market Institutions, East European Reform, and Economic Theory', *Journal of Economic Issues* 3.

Kostis, K. (1987) *Agrotiki Ikonomia ke Georgiki Trapeza (Opsis Ellinikis Kinonias ston Mesopolemo), 1919–1928*, Athens.

Krasner, S.D. (1973) 'Manipulating International Commodity Markets: Brazilian Coffee Policy, 1906–1962', *Public Policy* 21: 493–523.

Kraus, J. (1990) 'The Political Economy of Stabilisation and Structural Adjustment in Ghana', in D. Rothchild (ed.) *Ghana, the Political Economy of Recovery*, Boulder and London.

Kraus, J. (1991) 'The Struggle for Structural Adjustment in Ghana', *Africa Today* 38, 4: 19–39.

Krueger, A. (1974) 'The Political Economy of the Rent-seeking Society', *American Economic Review* 64.

Krugman, P. (1985) 'International Debt Strategies in an Uncertain World', in J. Cuddington and G. Smith (eds) *International Debt and the Developing Countries*, Washington, DC: The World Bank.

Krugman, P. (1988) 'Financing vs Forgiving a Debt Overhang: Some Analytical Notes', *Journal of Development Economics* 29: 253–71.

Krugman, P. (1989) 'Market-Based Debt Reduction Schemes', in M. Dooley and P. Wickham (eds) *Analytical Issues on Debt*, Washington, DC: International Monetary Fund.

Kurian, R. (1989) 'State, Capital and Labour in the Plantation Industy in Sri Lanka, 1834–1982', unpublished PhD thesis, University of Amsterdam.

Kuznets, P. (1988) 'An East Asian Model of Economic Development', *Economic Development and Cultural Change* 36, 3: S14–S43.

Ladas, S.P. (1932) *The Exchange of Minorities: Bulgaria, Greece and Turkey*, New York: Macmillan.

Lal, D. (1984) *The Poverty of Development Economics*, London: Institute of Economic Affairs.

Lal, D. (1988) *The Hindu Equilibrium*. Vol 1: Cultural Stability and Economic Stagnation, Oxford: Clarendon Press.

Lamas, A. (1886) *Estudio histórico y científico del Banco de la Provincia de Buenos Aires*, Buenos Aires.

Lamoreaux, N. (1985) 'Banks, Kinship, and Economic Development: The New England Case', *Journal of Economic History* 46: 647–67.

Lampe, J. R. and Jackson, M. (1982) *Balkan Economic History 1550–1950*, Bloomington: Indiana University Press.

Langlois, R. (ed.) (1986a) *Economics as a Process: Essays in the New Institutional Economics*, Cambridge: Cambridge University Press.

Langlois, S. (1986b) 'The New Institutional Economics: An Introductory Essay', in S. Langlois (ed.) *Economics as a Process*, Cambridge: Cambridge University Press.

Law, R. (1977) 'Royal Monopoly and Private Enterprise in the Atlantic Trade: The Case of Dahomey', *Journal of African History*,18, 4.

Law, R. (1992) 'Posthumous Questions for Karl Polanyi: Price Inflation in Pre-colonial Dahomey', *Journal of African History* 33.

Lazaretou S. (1993) 'Monetary and Fiscal Policies in Greece: 1833–1914', *Journal of European Economic History*, 22, 2.

Lazonick, W. (1991a) *Business Organisations and the Myth of the Market Economy*, Cambridge: Cambridge University Press.

Lazonick, W. (1991b) 'Organisations and Markets in Capitalist Development', in B. Gustavsson (ed.) *Power and Economic Institutions: Reinterpretations in Economic History*, Aldershot: Edward Elgar.

League of Nations, Financial Committee, Extra Session held in London, 6–14 June 1933, *Report to the Council on Greece*.

Lele, U. J. (1971) *Foodgrain Marketing in India: Private Performance and Public Policy*, Ithaca: Cornell University Press.

Leonard, D.K. (1991) 'Structural Reform of the Veterinary Profession in Africa and Theories of Organisational Choice', IDS, Sussex, draft mimeo.

Leplae, E. (1917) 'Notes au sujet du développement de l'agriculture au Congo Belge, No. 3', *Bulletin Agricole au Congo Belge* 8, 3–4: 177–8.

Leplaideur, A. (1992) 'Conflicts and Alliances between the International Marketing System and the Traditional Marketing System in Africa and Madagascar: The Results of Experience with Rice and Vegetables in Six Countries', in L. Cammann (ed.) *Traditional Marketing Systems*, Munich: DSE.

Levandis, J.A. (1944) *The Greek Foreign Debt and the Great Powers 1821–1891*, New York.

Levy, M.B. (1977) *História da Bolsa de Valores do Rio de Janeiro*, Rio de Janeiro.

Lewis, C.M. (1991) *Public Policy and Private Initiative: Railway Building in São Paulo*, London: Institute of Latin American Studies.

Lewis, W.A. (1976) 'The Diffusion of Development', in T.A. Wilson and A.S. Skinner (eds) *The Market and the State: Essays in Honour of Adam Smith*, Oxford: Clarendon Press.

Libecap, G.D. (1986) 'Property Rights in Economic History: Implications for Research', *Explorations in Economic History* 23, 3: 227–52.

Libecap, G.D. (1989) *Contracting for Property Rights*, Cambridge: Cambridge University Press.

Lippitt, V. (1978) 'The Development of Underdevelopment in China', *Modern China* 4: 251–328.

Little, D. (1989) *Understanding Peasant China: Case Studies in the Philosophy of Social Science*, New Haven: Yale University Press.

Little, G.F.G. (1960) 'Fazenda Cambuhy: A Case History of Social and Economic Development in the Interior of São Paulo', unpublished PhD thesis, University of Florida.

Little, I.M.D. (1982) *Economic Development*, New York: Basic Books.

Liverpool Central Libraries, John Holt Papers, 380 HOL-I, 9/1, Fernando Po letter, 9

April, 1907; Fernando Po letter, 21 January, 1910; Herschell Factory letter, 7 April, 1911.

Lopo, J. de Castro (1963) 'Para a história do cacau de Angola', *Actividade Econômica de Angola* 65: 33–56.

Lovejoy, P. (1974) 'Inter-regional Monetary Flows in the Precolonial Trade of Nigeria', *Journal of African History* 15, 4.

Lovejoy, P. (1982) 'Polanyi's "Ports of Trade": Salaga and Kano in the Nineteenth Century', *Canadian Journal of African Studies* 16, 2.

Loxley, J. (1988) *Ghana: Economic Crises and the Long Road to Recovery*, Ottawa: North-South Institute.

Ludlow, L. (1986) 'La construcción de un banco: el Banco Nacional de México, 1881–1884', in L. Ludlow and C. Marichal (eds) *Banca y poder en México, 1800–1925*, Mexico: Grijalbo.

Lundahl, M. (1979) *Peasants and Poverty: A Study of Haiti*, London.

Luso, J. (1919?) *The United States of Brazil*, Rio de Janeiro.

McAlpin, M.B. (1983) 'Famines, Epidemics and Population Growth: The Case of India', *Journal of Interdisciplinary History* 15: 351–66.

McCarthy, D.M.P. (1982) *Colonial Bureaucracy and Creating Underdevelopment 1919–1940*, Ames: Iowa State University Press.

Machina, M.J. (1987) 'Choice under Uncertainty: Problems Solved and Unsolved', *Journal of Economic Perspectives* 1, 1: 121–54.

Macintyre, A. (1991) *Business and Politics in Indonesia*, Sydney: Allen & Unwin.

Macintyre, A.J. and Jayasuriya, K. (1992) *The Dynamics of Economic Policy Reform in South-east Asia and the South-west Pacific*, Singapore: Oxford University Press.

Mackie, J.A.C. and Sjahrir, S. (1989) 'Survey of Recent Developments', *Bulletin of Indonesian Economic Studies* 25, 3: 3–35.

McNamara, R S. (1981) *The McNamara Years at the World Bank*, Baltimore: Johns Hopkins University Press.

McPhee, A. (1926) *The Economic Revolutioentífico del Banco de la Provincia de Buenos Aires*, Buenos Aires.

McVey, R. (1982) 'The Beamtenstaat in Indonesia', in B. Anderson and A. Kahin (eds) *Interpreting Indonesian Politics: Thirteen Contributions to the Debate*, Ithaca: Cornell Modern Indonesia Project.

McVey, R. (ed.) (1992) *Southeast Asian Capitalists*, Ithaca: Cornell Southeast Asia Program.

Madnick, S. E. (1991) 'The Information Technology Platform', in M. S. Scott Morton (ed.) *The Corporation of the 1990s: Information Technology and Organisational Transformation*, Oxford: Oxford University Press.

Mansfield, E. (1988) 'Industrial R and D in Japan and the United States: A Comparative Study', *American Economic Review*, 78, 5: 223–8.

Mantero, F. (1910) *A mão d'obra em S. Thomé e Principe*, Lisbon.

March, J.G. and Olsen, J.P. (1984) 'The New Institutionalism: Organisational Factors in Political Life', *American Political Science Review* 78, 3: 734–49.

Marichal, C. (1986) 'El nacimiento de la banca mexicana en el contexto latinoamericano: problemas de periodización', in L. Ludlow and C. Marichal (eds) *Banca y poder en México, 1800–1925*, Mexico.

Marion, B. W. and NC117 Committee (eds) (1986) *The Organisation and Performance of the US Food System*, Lexington, MA: D.C. Heath & Co.

Martin, Joseph G. (1898) *A Century of Finance: Martin's History of the Boston Stock and Money Markets. One Hundred Years, January 1798–to January 1898*. Boston.

Marx, K. (1971) *Grundrisse*, edited by D. McLellan, London: Harper.

Marx, K. (1974) *Capital*, vol. 1, London: Lawrence & Wishart.

Mathew, W.W. (1981) *The House of Gibbs and the Peruvian Guano Monopoly*, Royal Historical Society, Studies in History Monograph Series, No. 25, London.

Matthews, R.C.O. (1986) 'The Economics of Institutions and the Sources of Growth', *Economic Journal*, 96.

Mead, D.C. (1967) *Growth and Structural Change in the Egyptian Economy*, Illinois: Richard D. Irwin, Inc.

Michel, M. (1969) 'Les Plantations allemandes du Mont Cameroun, 1885–1914', *Revue Française d'Histoire d'Outremer* 57, 2: 183–213.

Mill, J.S. (1872/1987) *The Logic of the Moral Sciences*, London: Duckworth.

Ministerio da Indústria, Viação e Obras Publicas (Brasil) (1896) *Relatório, 1896*, Rio de Janeiro.

Ministerio de Fomento (México) (1854) *Estadística del Departamento de México*, Mexico.

Ministerio de Fomento (México) (1857) *Memoria del Ministerio de Fomento*, Mexico.

Ministerio de Fomento (México) (1865) *Memoria del Ministerio de Fomento*, Mexico.

Ministry of Industry (Egypt) (1990) *Industrial Public Sector: Overview of Reform Program and Performance over 1983/84 to 1988/89 Period*, Cairo.

Ministry of Industry (Egypt), (1991) Report on Performance Evaluation and Financial Statements for the Industrial Public Sector, 1989/90, Cairo.

Minister of Industry of Arab Republic of Egypt Engineer Mohamed Abdel Wahab (1992) 'Egypt's Program of Privatization and Structural Adjustment', Address to the Confederation of British Industry, Conference on Trade and Investment in Egypt, London.

Ministry of Planning (Egypt) (1982) *The General Detailed Framework for the Five-Year Plan for Socioeconomic Development, 1982/83 to 1986/87*, Cairo.

Ministry of Planning (Egypt) (1987) *Egypt's Second Five-Year Plan for Socioeconomic Development 1987/88 to 1991/92, with Plan for Year One, 1987/88*, Cairo.

Ministry of Planning (Egypt) (1992) *Egypt's Third Five-Year Plan for Socioeconomic Development, 1992/93 to 1996/97, with Plan for Year One, 1992/93*, Cairo.

Minot, N. (1986) 'Contract Farming and its Impact on Small Farmers in Less Developed Countries', Michigan State University, Department of Agricultural Economics, mimeo.

Mises, L. von (1949) *Human Action, A Treatise on Economics*, New Haven: Yale University Press.

Mokyr, J. (1984) 'Disparities, Gaps and Abysses', *Economic Development and Cultural Change* 33, 1: 173–8.

Monbeig, P. (1952) *Pionneurs et planteurs de São Paulo*, Paris.

Montiel, P. (1993) *Informal Financial Markets in Developing Countries*, Oxford: Blackwell.

Moore, B. (1991) *Social Origins of Dictatorship and Democracy*, Harmondsworth: Penguin.

Morse, R. (1951) 'São Paulo in the Nineteenth Century: Economic Roots of the Metropolis', *Inter-American Economic Affairs* 5: 14–16.

Mosley, P., Harrigan, J. and Toye, J. (1991) *Aid and Power*, 2 vols, London: Routledge.

Moursi, T.A. (1980) 'Agricultural Pricing Policy in Egypt: An Empirical Study 1965–1977', unpublished MA thesis, The American University in Cairo.

Moursi, T.A. (1986) 'Government Intervention and the Impact on Agriculture: The Case of Egypt', unpublished PhD thesis, University of California, Berkeley.

Mouzelis, N. (1978) *Modern Greece: Facets of Underdevelopment*, London: Macmillan.

Muir, R. (1986) 'Survey of Recent Developments', *Bulletin of Indonesian Economic Studies* 22, 2: 1–27.

Muramatsu, Y. (1966) 'A Documentary Study of Chinese Landlordism in late Ch'ing and early Republican Kiangnan', *Bulletin of the School of Oriental and African Studies* 29: 566–99.

Myers, R.H. (1980) *The Chinese Economy: Past and Present*, Belmont, CA: Wadsworth Inc.

Myers, R.H. (1991) 'How Did the Modern Chinese Economy Develop? A Review Article', *Journal of Asian Studies* 50: 604–28.

Myhrman, J. (1989) 'The New Institutional Economics and the Process of Economic Development', Working Papers in Political Science P-89-7, The Hoover Institution, Stanford University.

Myrdal, G. (1970) *The Challenge of World Poverty: A World Anti-Poverty Programme in Outline*, Harmondsworth: Penguin Books.

Nabli, M.K. and Nugent, J.B. (1989) 'The New Institutional Economics and Its Applicability to Development', *World Development*, 17, 9: 1333–47.

Nadkarni, M.V. (1980) *Marketable Surplus and Market Dependence in a Millet Region*, Bombay: Allied Press.

Nagaraj, K. (1985) in K.N. Raj, N. Bhattacharya, S. Guha and S. Padhi (eds) *Essays on the Commercialisation of Indian Agriculture*, Oxford University Press: Bombay.

Navin, Thomas R. and Sears, Marian V. (1955) 'The Rise of a Market for Industrial Securities, 1887–1902', *Business History Review* 29: 105–38.

Naya, S., Urrutia, M., Mark, S. and Fuentes, A. (eds) (1989) *Lessons in Development: A Comparative Study of Asia and Latin America*, San Francisco: International Centre for Economic Growth.

Nelson, R. and Winter, S.G. (1982) *An Evolutionary Theory of Economic Change*, Cambridge, MA: Harvard University Press.

Neuhaus, P. (1975) *História monetária do Brasil, 1900–45*, Rio de Janeiro.

Newbery, D. (1989) 'Agricultural Institutions for Insurance and Stabilization', in P. Bardhan (ed.) *The Economic Theory of Agrarian Institutions*, Oxford: Oxford University Press.

Newbery, D.M.G. and Stiglitz, J.E. (1981) *The Theory of Commodity Price Stabilization*, New York: Oxford University Press.

Neyman, J. (ed.) (1951) *Proceedings of the Second Berkeley Symposium on Mathematical Statistics and Probability*, Berkeley: University of California Press.

Nicholas, S.J. (1983) 'Agency Contracts, Institutional Modes and the Transition to Foreign Direct Investment by British Multinationals before 1939', *Journal of Economic History* 43.

Niskanen, W. (1971) *Bureaucracy and Representative Government*, Chicago: Aldine Atherton.

Njonjo, A. (1974) 'The Africanisation of the "White Highlands": A Study in Agrarian Class Struggle in Kenya, 1950–1974', unpublished PhD thesis, Princeton University.

Norbury, F. (1970) 'Venezuela', in W.A. Lewis (ed.) *Tropical Development, 1880–1913*, London: Allen & Unwin.

Normano, J.R. (1935) *Brazil: A Study of Economic Types*, Chapel Hill: University of North Carolina Press.

North, D.C. (1981) *Structure and Change in Economic History*, New York: W. W. Norton & Company.

North, D.C. (1989a) 'Transaction Cost Approach to the Historical Development of Polities and Economies', *Journal of Institutional and Theoretical Economics* 141, 4.

North, D.C. (1989b) 'Institutions and Economic Growth: An Historical Introduction', *World Development*, 17, 9.

North, D.C. (1990a) *Institutions, Institutional Change and Economic Performance*, Cambridge: Cambridge University Press.

North, D.C. (1990b) 'A Transaction Costs Theory of Politics', *Journal of Theoretical Politics* 2, 4: 355–67.

North, D.C. and Thomas, R.P. (1973) *The Rise of the Western World: A New Economic History*, Cambridge: Cambridge University Press.

North, D.C. and Wallis, J. (1987) 'Measuring the Transaction Sector in the American Economy 1870–1970', in S.L. Engerman and R.E. Gallman (eds) *Long-term Factors in American Economic Growth*, Chicago: Chicago University Press.

North, D.C. and Weingast, B. (1990) 'Constitutions and Commitment: The Evolution of Institutions Governing Public Choices in Seventeenth Century England', *Journal of Economic History* 49, 4: 803–31.

Nosti [Nava], J. (1948) *Agricultura de Guinea, promesa para España*, Madrid.

Olsen, W.K. (1991) 'Distress Sales and Exchange Relations in a Rural Area of Rayala-seema, Andhra Pradesh', unpublished DPhil thesis, University of Oxford.

Olson, M. (1965) *The Logic of Collective Action*, Cambridge MA: Harvard University Press.

Olson, M. (1982) *The Rise and Decline of Nations*, New Haven: Yale University Press.

Ostrom, E. (1990) *Governing the Commons: the Evolution of Institutions for Collective Action*, New York: Cambridge University Press.

Ostrom, E., Schroeder, L. and Wynne, S. (1993) *Institutional Incentives and Sustainable Development: Infrastructure Policies in Perspective*, Boulder, CO: West-view Press.

Othick, J. (1976) 'The Cocoa and Chocolate Industry in the Nineteenth Century', in D. Oddy and D. Miller (eds) *The Making of the Modern British Diet*, London: Croom Helm.

Owen, E.R.J. (1969) *Cotton and the Egyptian Economy 1820–1914*, Oxford: Oxford University Press.

Paauw, D. (1963) 'From Colonial to Guided Economy', in R. McVey (ed.) *Indonesia*, New Haven: HRAF.

Paauw, D. (1978) 'Exchange Rate Policy and Non-extractive Exports', *Ekonomi dan Keuangan Indonesia* 26, 2: 205–20.

Palaskas, T.B. and Harriss-White, B. (1993) 'Testing Market Integration: New Approaches with Case Material from the West Bengal Food Economy', *Journal of Development Studies* 30, 1: 1–57.

Pandelakis, N. (1991) *O Exilektrismos tis Elladas Apo tin Idiotiki Protovoulia sto Kratiko Monopolio (1889–1956)*, Athens.

Pandya, A. and Dholakia, N. (1992) 'An Institutional Theory of Exchange in Marketing', *European Journal of Marketing* 26, 12: 19–41.

Pangestu, M. and Boediono (1986) 'Indonesia: The Structure and Causes of Manufacturing Sector Protection', in C. Findlay and R. Garnaut (eds) *The Political Economy of Manufacturing Protection: Experiences of ASEAN and Australia*, Sydney: Allen & Unwin.

Panglaykim, J. and Arndt, H.W. (1966) 'Survey of Recent Developments', *Bulletin of Indonesian Economic Studies* 4: 1–35.

Papayiannakis, L. (1982) *I Elliniki Sidirodromi (1882–1910)*, Athens.

Papayiannopoulos, E. (1989) *I Dioriga tis Korinthou: Tehnikis Athlos ke Ikonomiko Tolmima*, Athens.

Parikh, K. (1993) 'Economic Reforms and Food and Agricultural Policy', Paper to the Conference on India's Economic Reforms, Queen Elizabeth House, Oxford.

Pastor, M. (1990) 'Capital Flight from Latin America', *World Development* 18, 1: 1–18.

Peláez, C.M. and Suzigan, W. (1976) *História monetária do Brasil: análise da política, comportamento e instituções monetárias*, Brasilia: Editora Universidade de Brasília.

Penders, C.L.M. (ed.) (1977) *Indonesia: Selected Documents on Colonialism and Nationalism, 1830–1942*, St Lucia: University of Queensland Press.

Penny, D. (1985) *Starvation*, Canberra: Australian National University Press.

Penrose, E.T. (1966) *The Theory of the Growth of the Firm*, Oxford: Basil Blackwell.

Pentzopoulos, D. (1962) *The Balkan Exchange of Minorities and its Impact upon Greece*, Paris.

Pepelasis, A.A. (1958) 'The Image of the Past and Economic Backwardness', *Human Organisation* 17, 4.

Pepelasis, A.A. (1959) 'The Legal System and Economic Development of Greece', *The Journal of Economic History* 19, 2.

Pepelasis, A.A. (1969) 'Venice and East Mediterranean Trade in the Eighteenth Century', Bureau of Business and Economic Research at Berkeley, unpublished mimeo.

Pepelasis Minoglou, I. (1984) 'To Xeno Kefaleo ke I Elliniki Viomihania ston Mesopolemo – i Periptosi tis Hellenic Trust', unpublished paper, presented at 50th meeting of the researchers of the National Bank of Greece Archive, 22 November.

Pepelasis Minoglou, I. (1993) 'The Greek State and the International Financial Community, 1922–1932: Demystifying the Foreign Factor', unpublished PhD thesis, University of London.

Pereira Filho, C. (1959) *Ilheus, terra do cacau*, Rio de Janeiro.

Pérez Hernández, J.M. (1862) *Estadística de la República Mexicana*, Guadalajara.

Perkins, D.H. (1975) 'Growth and Changing Structure of China's Twentieth-Century Economy', in D.H. Perkins (ed.) *China's Modern Economy in Historical Perspective*, Stanford: pp. 115–34.

Phillips, A. (1989) *The Enigma of Colonialism: British Policy in West Africa*, London: Currey.

Picavet, R. *et al.* (eds) (1990) *The New Institutional Economics: A Primrose Path or a Blind Alley?*, IVO Centre of Development Research, Tilburg University.

Pizanias, P. (1987)'Kentro ke Periferia: Theoria ke Istoria', *Mnimon* 11: 255–86.

Platteau, J.-P. (1990a) *Land Reform and Structural Adjustment in Sub-Saharan Africa: Controversies and Guidelines*, Namur, Report prepared for FAO.

Platteau, J.-P. (1990b) 'The Disappointing Performance of Rural Co-operative Organisations in the Third World: A Diagnosis Inferred from the New Institutional Economics', in R. Picavet *et al.* (eds) *The New Institutional Economics: A Primrose Path or a Blind Alley?* IVO Centre of Development Research, Tilburg University.

Platteau, J.-P. and Nugent, J. (1992) 'Share Contracts and their Rationale: Lessons from Marine Fishing', *Journal of Development Studies*, 28, 3.

Polanyi, K. (1966) *Dahomey and the Slave Trade: An Analysis of an Archaic Economy*, Seattle: University of Washington Press.

Polanyi, K. (1971) 'Aristotle Discovers the Economy', in K. Polanyi, C.M. Arensberg and H.W. Pearson (eds) *Trade and Market in the Early Empires*, Chicago: Regnery Co.

Pond, D. (1964) 'Investment in Indonesia, 1956–93', *Malayan Economic Review* 9, 2: 92–105.

Popkin, S.L. (1979) *The Rational Peasant*, Berkeley and Los Angeles: University of California Press.

Porter, E. M. (1990) *The Competitive Advantage of Nations*, London: Collier Macmillan.

Portes, A., Castells, M. and Benton, L.A. (eds) (1989) *The Informal Economy*, Baltimore: Johns Hopkins University Press.

Posner, R. (1975) 'The Social Costs of Monopoly and Regulation', *Journal of Political Economy* 83.

Posner, R. A. (1980) 'A Theory of Primitive Society with Special Reference to the Law', *Journal of Law and Economics* 23: 1–52.

Pratt, J.W. and Zeckhauser, R.J. (eds) (1985) *Principals and Agents: The Structure of Business*, Boston, MA: Harvard Business School Press.

Prebisch, R. (1921) 'Desde el primer Banco Nacional hasta la crisis de la Oficina de Cambios', *Revista de Ciencias Económicas* 9, 4: 283–307.

345

Preuss, P. (1901) [1987] *Cocoa, Its Cultivation and Preparation*, Brussels. (Chapter 13 of *Expedition nach Central- und Südamerika, 1899–1900*, Berlin, translated into English and published as Vol. 3 of *Archives of Cocoa Research*.)

Provincia de Buenos Aires (1882) *Memoria sobre la organisación de la Oficina del Crédito Público de la Provincia de Buenos Aires*, Buenos Aires.

Prowse, M. (1993) 'The "New" Frontier in Economics', *The Financial Times*, 24 December.

Przeworski, A. (1991) *Democracy and the Market*, Cambridge: Cambridge University Press.

Pujo, L. (1993) 'More Madness in my Method: On Searching for the Theoretical Bases of the Structure, Conduct Performance Methodology and its Applications to Under-developed Agricultural Markets', International Development Centre, Oxford, mimeo.

Pursell, G. and Gulati, A. (1993) 'Indian Agriculture: An Agenda for Reform', Paper for the Conference on India's Economic Reforms, Queen Elizabeth House, Oxford.

Putterman, L. (ed.) (1986) *The Economic Nature of the Firm*, Cambridge: Cambridge University Press.

Puttkamer, J. von (1912) *Gouverneursjahre in Kamerun*, Berlin.

Quarco, P. (1990) 'Structural Adjustment Programmes in Sub-Saharan Africa: Evolution of Approaches', *African Development Review* 2, 2.

Quijano, J.M. (ed.) (1983) *La banca, pasado y presente: problemas financieros mexicanos*, Mexico.

Quintero Ramos, A.R. (1965) *A History of Money and Banking in Argentina*, Rio Piedras: University of Rio Piedras Press.

Rangel, D.A. (1974) *Capital y desarrollo, la Venezuela agraria*, Caracas.

Rawski, T.G. (1989) *Economic Growth in Prewar China*, Berkeley: California University Press.

Ray, D. (1986) *Ghana: Politics Economics and Society*, Boulder, CO: Lynne Reinner.

Reber, V. B. (1979) *British Merchant Houses in Buenos Aires, 1810–1880*, Cambridge, MA: Harvard University Press.

Reinecke, F. (1902) *Samoa*, Berlin.

Republic of Indonesia, Department of Information (1969) *The Five-Year Development Plan, 1969–74*, Jakarta: Department of Information.

Republik Indonesia, Arsip Nasional, 43, 39, Residente Banda, 1863.

Republik Indonesia, Arsip Nasional, Jakarta, 30, 156, F. Schenk, Memorie van overgave, 10 July 1873.

Richards, A. (1991) 'Agricultural Employment, Wages and Government Policy in Egypt during and after the Oil Boom', in H. Handoussa and G. Potter (eds) *Employment and Structural Adjustment: Egypt in the 1990s*, Cairo: The American University in Cairo Press.

Ricklefs, M.C. (1993) *A History of Modern Indonesia since c.1300*, London: Macmillan.

Ridings, E.W. (1982) 'Business, Nationality and Dependency in Late Nineteenth-century Brazil', *Journal of Latin American Studies* 14: 63–8.

Ridings, E.W. (1989) 'Business Associationalism, the Legitimation of Enterprise and the Emergence of a Business Elite in Nineteenth-century Brazil', *Business History Review* 62: 757–96.

Riskin, C. (1975) 'Surplus and Stagnation in Modern China', in D.H. Perkins (ed.) *China's Modern Economy in Historical Perspective*, Stanford: pp. 49–84.

Riskin, C. (1978) 'The Symposium Papers: Discussion and Comments', *Modern China* 4: 359–75.

Roemer, J.E. (1982) *A General Theory of Exploitation and Class*, Cambridge, MA: Harvard University Press.

Roemer, J.E. (1988) *Free to Lose: An Introduction to Marxist Economic Philosophy*, London: Radius Hutchinson.

Roemer, M. (1984) 'Ghana: Missed Opportunities', in A.C. Harberger (ed.) *World Economic Growth: Case Studies of Developed and Developing Nations*, San Francisco: Institute for Contemporary Studies.

Roepke, W. (1922) *Cacao*, Haarlem. (Vol. 11 of *Onze Koloniale Landbouw*.)

Rogerson, W.P. (1982) 'The Social Costs of Monopoly and Regulation: A Game Theoretic Analysis', *Bell Journal of Economics* 13.

Romer, P.M. (1986) 'Increasing Returns and Long-run Growth', *Journal of Political Economy* 91, 51: 1002–37.

Root, H. (1989) 'Tying the King's Hands: Credible Commitment and Royal Fiscal Policy During the Old Regime', *Rationality and Society* 1: 240–58.

Rosa, J.M. (1909) *La reforma monetaria en la República Argentina*, Buenos Aires.

Rosenberg, N. and Birdzell, L.E. (1986) *How the West Grew Rich: The Economic Transformation of the Industrial World*, New York: Basic Books.

Rothchild, D. and Gyimah-Boadi, E. (1986) 'Ghana's Economic Decline and Development Strategies', in J. Ravenhill (ed.) *Africa in Economic Crisis*, London: Macmillan.

Rowe, J.W.F. (1932) *Studies in the Artificial Control of Raw Material Supplies*. No. 3: *Brazilian Coffee*, London.

Rowe, J.W.F. (1965) *Primary Commodities in International Trade*, Cambridge: Cambridge University Press.

Rudra, A. (1992) *The Political Economy of Indian Agriculture*, Calcutta: Bagchi & Company.

Ruf, F. (1991) 'Les crises cacaoyères: la malediction des ages d'or?', *Cahiers d'Etudes Africaines* 31, 121–2: 83–134.

Ruf, F. (1993) 'Indonesia's Position among Cocoa Producing Countries', *Indonesia Circle* 61: 21–37.

Ruger, A. (1960) 'Die Entstehung und Lage der Arbeiterklasse unter dem deutschen Kolonialregime in Kamerun, 1885–1905', in H. Stoecker (ed.) *Kamerun unter deutscher Kolonialherrschaft*, Berlin.

Rutherford, M. (1994) *Institutions in Economics: the Old and the New Institutionalism*, Cambridge: Cambridge University Press.

Ruttan, V. and Hayami, Y. (1984) 'Towards a Theory of Induced Institutional Innovation', *Journal of Development Studies* 20, 4: 203–23.

Sachs, J. (1984) *Theoretical Issues in International Borrowing*, Princeton Studies in International Finance, Princeton, NJ: International Finance Section, Princeton University.

Sachs, J. (1986) 'The Debt Overhang Problem of Developing Countries', in G. Calvo (ed.) *Debt Stabilization and Development: Essays in Memory of Carlos Díaz Alejandro*, Oxford: Basil Blackwell.

Sachs, J. (ed.) (1989) *Developing Country Debt and the World Economy*, Chicago: University of Chicago Press.

Saes, F.A.M. de (1986) *Crédito e bancos no desenvolvimento da economia paulista, 1850–1930*, São Paulo.

Sakellaropoulos, Th. D. (1991) *Thesmikos Metashimatismos ke Ikonomiki Anaptixi stin Ellada 1830–1922*, Athens.

Samaras, G. (1982) *Kratos ke Kefaleo stin Ellada*, Athens.

Samuel, P. (1990) 'Assessment of the Private Sector, A Case Study and its Methodological Implications', World Bank Discussion Paper, No. 93, Washington, DC.

Samuels, W. J. and Mercuro, N. (1984) 'A Critique of Rent-Seeking Theory', in D.C. Colander (ed.) *Neoclassical Political Economy: The Analysis of Rent-seeking and DUP Activities*, Cambridge, MA: Ballinger Publishing Company.

Sánchez Martínez, H. (1983) 'El sistema monetario y financiero mexicano bajo una perspectiva histórica: el porfiriato', in J.M. Quijano (ed.) *La banca, pasado y presente: problemas financieros mexicanos*, Mexico.

Sanghera, B.S. (1992) 'A Critique of Williamson's Transactions Costs Economics and it Relevance to Agricultural Economics', unpublished MSc thesis, International Development Centre, University of Oxford.

Sanz Casas, G. (1983) 'Política colonial y organisación del trabajo en la isla de Fernando Poo, 1880–1930', unpublished PhD thesis, University of Barcelona.

Sarkar, S. (1989) 'A Theory of Multistratum Competition for Primary Agricultural Markets of Less Developed Countries', in *Proceedings of The International Society for Agricultural Economics*, Athens.

Scherer, F.M. (1982) 'Inter-industry Technology Flows and Productivity Growth', *Review of Economics and Statistics* 64, 11: 627–34.

Scherer, F.M. (1986) *Innovation and Growth: Schumpeterian Perspectives*, Cambridge, MA: MIT Press.

Schmid, A. (1992) 'Legal Foundations of the Market: Implications for the Formerly Socialist Countries of Eastern Europe and Africa', *Journal of Economic Issues* 26, 3: 707–32.

Schotter, A. (1981) *The Economic Theory of Social Institutions*, New York: Cambridge University Press.

Scobie, J. R. (1954) 'Monetary Development in Argentina, 1852–1865', *Inter-American Economic Affairs* 8, 2: 54–83.

Scobie, J. R. (1964) *La lucha por la consolidación de la nacionalidad argentina (1852–62)*, Buenos Aires.

Scott, J.C. (1976) *The Moral Economy of the Peasant: Rebellion and Subsistence in Southeast Asia*, New Haven Yale University Press.

Scott M.M. (ed.) (1991) *The Corporation of the 1990s: Information Technology and Organisational Transformation*, Oxford: Oxford University Press.

Seabrook, J. (1990) *The Myth of the Market: Promises and Illusions*, Devon: Greenbooks.

Sebald, P. (1988) *Togo 1884–1914, eine Geschichte der deutschen 'Musterkolonie' auf der Grundlage amtlicher Quellen*, Berlin: Akademie-Verlag.

Secretaría de Fomento (México) (1890) *Boletín semestral de la República Mexicana 1889*, Mexico.

Secretaría de Fomento (México) (1894) *Anuario Estadístico de la República Mexicana, 1893–94*, Mexico.

Secretaría de Fomento (México) (1896) *Anuario Estadístico de la República Mexicana, 1895*, Mexico.

Secretaría de Hacienda (México) (1880) *Estadística de la República Mexicana*, Mexico.

Secretaría de Hacienda (México) (1896) *Memoria, 1895*, Mexico.

Secretaría de Hacienda y Crédito Público (México) (1977) *Documentos para el estudio de la industrialisación en México, 1837–1845*, Mexico.

Segers, W.A.I.M. (ed.) (1987) *Changing Economy in Indonesia:* Vol 8: *Manufacturing Industry 1870–1942*, Amsterdam: Royal Tropical Institute.

Sen, C. (1985) 'Commercialisation, Class Relations and Agricultural Performance in UP: A Note on Bhaduri's Hypothesis', in K.N. Raj, N. Bhattacharya, S. Guha and S. Padhi (eds) *Essays on the Commercialisation of Indian Agriculture*, Bombay: Oxford University Press.

Shaffer, J. D. (1979) 'Observations on the Political Economics of Regulation', *American Journal of Agricultural Economics* 11, 2: 723–31.

Shepherd, Jack (1941) *Industry in Southeast Asia*, New York: International Secretariat, Institute of Pacific Relations.

Sherrard, P. and Campbell, J. (1966/7) 'I Istoriki Anadisi tou Neoellinikou Kratous', *Synoro* 40.

Shillington, K. (1992) *Ghana and the Rawlings Factor*, London: Macmillan.

Shipton, P. (1987) 'The Kenyan Land Tenure Reform: Misunderstandings in the Public Creation of Private Property', Harvard Institute for International Development, Development Discussion Paper No. 239, New Haven.

Shklar, J. N. (1990) *The Faces of Injustice*, New Haven: Yale University Press.

Simon, H. (1986) 'Rationality in Psychology and Economics', in R.M. Hogarth and M.W. Reder (eds) *The Behavioral Foundations of Economic Theory, Journal of Business (supplement)*, 59: S209–S24.

Simopoulos, K. (1990) *Xenokratia ke Misellinismos ke Ipotelia*, Athens.

Sitsen, P.H.W. (c1943) 'Industrial Development of the Netherlands Indies', *Bulletins of the Netherlands and Netherlands Indies Council of the Institute of Pacific Relations*, no. 2.

Smith, G.D. and Sylla, R. (1993) 'The Transformation of Financial Capitalism: An Essay on the History of American Capital Markets', *Financial Markets, Institutions and Instruments* 2, 2.

Smith, R. (1988) 'Political Jurisprudence: the "New Institutionalism" and the Future of Public Law', *American Political Science Review* 82, 1: 84–108.

Smith, S.B. (1989) *Hegel's Critique of Liberalism: Rights in Context*, Chicago: University of Chicago Press.

Sociedade de Emigração para S. Thomé e Principe (1915) *Relatório da direcção, parecer do conselho fiscal, e lista dos accionistas; segundo anno, 1914*, Lisbon.

Solow, R.M. (1957) 'Technical Change and the Aggregate Production Function', *Review of Economics and Statistics* 39: 312–20.

Soskice, D., Bates, R.H. and Epstein, D. (1992) 'Ambition and Constraint', *Journal of Law, Economics, and Organisation* 3: 547–60.

Southall, R.J. (1975) 'Cadbury on the Gold Coast, 1907–1938', unpublished PhD thesis, Birmingham University.

Spulber, N. (1963) 'Changes in the Economic Structures of the Balkans, 1860–1960', in C. Jelavich and B. Jelavich (eds) *The Balkans in Transition*, Berkeley: University of California Press.

Stavrianos, L.S. (1958) *The Balkans Since 1453*, New York.

Stavrianos, L.S. (1963) 'The Influence of the West on the Balkans', in C. Jelavich and B. Jelavich (eds) *The Balkans in Transition*, Berkeley: University of California Press.

Stein, H. (1992) 'Deindustrialisation, Adjustment, the World Bank and the IMF in Africa', *World Development* 20, 1.

Stein, H. (1994) 'The World Bank and the Application of Asian Industrial Policy to Africa: Theoretical Considerations', *Journal of International Development*.

Stein, H. (ed.) (1995) *Asian Industrialisation and Africa: Case Studies in Policy Alternatives to Structural Adjustment*, London: Macmillan.

Stein, H. and Nafziger, W. (1991) 'Structural Adjustment, Human Needs and the World Bank Agenda', *Journal of Modern African Studies* 24, 1.

Stein, S. J. (1953) 'The Passing of a Coffee Plantation in the Paraíba Valley', *Hispanica-American Historical Review* 33: 331–64.

Stein, S. J. (1957a) *Vassouras: A Brazilian Coffee Country, 1850–1900*, Cambridge, MA: Harvard University Press.

Stein, S. J. (1957b) *The Brazilian Cotton Textile Manufacture: Textile Enterprise in an Underdeveloped Area*, Cambridge, MA: Harvard University Press.

Stephanides, D. ((1930) *I Isroi ton Xenon Kefaleon ke e Ikonomike ke Politike tis Sinepie*, Salonica.

Stern, N.H. and F.H.G. Ferreira (forthcoming) 'The World Bank as "Intellectual

Actor"', in J. Lewis and R. Webb (eds) *The Official History of the World Bank Vol. 12*, Washington, DC: Brookings.

Stiglitz, J.E. (1986) 'The New Development Economics', *World Development* 14, 2: 257–65.

Stiglitz, J.E. (1989) 'Rational Peasants, Efficient Institutions, and a Theory of Rural Organisation: Methodological Remarks for Development Economics', in P. Bardhan (ed.) *The Economic Theory of Agrarian Institutions*, Oxford: Clarendon Press.

Stiglitz, J. (1992a) 'Banks versus Markets as Mechanisms for Allocating and Coordinating Investment', in J. Roumasset and S. Barr (eds) *The Economics of Cooperation, East Asian Development and the Case for Pro-Market Intervention*, Boulder, CO: Westview Press.

Stiglitz, J. (1992b) 'The Design of Financial Systems for the Newly Emerging Democracies of Eastern Europe', in C. Clague and G. Raussere (eds) *The Emergence of Market Economies in Eastern Europe*, Oxford: Basil Blackwell.

Stinchcombe, A.L. (1968) *Constructing Social Theories*, New York: Harcourt, Brace & World.

Stokes, E. (1978) *The Peasant and the Raj: Studies in Agrarian Society and Peasant Rebellion in Colonial India*, Cambridge: Cambridge University Press.

Stollwerck, W. (1907) *Der Kakao and die Schokoladenindustrie, eine wirtschafts-statistische Untersuchung*, Jena.

Street, J.H. and James, D.D. (1982) 'Institutionalism, Structuralism and Dependency in Latin America', *Journal of Economic Issues* 16, 3: 673–89.

Streeton, H. and Orchard, L. (1994) *Public Goods, Public Enterprises and Public Choice: Theoretical Foundations of the Contemporary Attack on Government*, Basingstoke: Macmillan.

Subrahmanyam, S. and Stein, B. (eds) (1994) *Production Units in Micro and Macro Structural Perspective*, New Delhi: Oxford University Press.

Sumitro, Djojohadikusumo (1953) 'The Budget and its Implications', *Ekonomi dan Keuangan Indonesia* 6, 1: 3–30.

Sundiata, I.K. (1974) 'Prelude to Scandal: Liberia and Fernando Po, 1880–1930', *Journal of African History* 15, 1: 97–112.

Sundrum, R.M. (1973) 'Money Supply and Prices: A Reinterpretation', *Bulletin of Indonesian Economic Studies* 9, 3: 73–86.

Sutton, M. (1984) 'Indonesia, 1966–70', in T. Killick (ed.) *The IMF and Stabilisation: Developing Country Experience*, London: Heinemann.

Suzigan, W. (1986) *Indústria brasileira: origem e desenvolvimento*, São Paulo: Editora Brasiliense.

Svoronos, N.G. (1976) *Episkopisi tis Neoellinikis Istorias*, Athens.

Sylla, R. (1975) *The American Capital Market, 1846–1914: A Study of the Effects of Public Policy on Economic Development*, New York.

Sylla, R. and Toniolo, G. (eds) (1991) *Patterns of European Industrialisation*, London: Routledge.

Syrquin, M., Taylor, L. and Westphal, L. (eds) (1984) *Economic Structure and Performance: Essays in Honor of Hollis Chenery*, Orlando: Academic Press.

Taylor, A.J. (1972) *Laissez-faire and State Intervention in Nineteenth Century Britain*, London: Macmillan.

Teixeira, A. de Almeida (1934) *Angola intangivel*, Oporto.

Temporary National Economic Committee (1941) *Investigation of Concentration of Economic Power. Monograph 27: The Structure of Industry*, Washington, DC.

Thirlwall, A.P. (1993) 'The Renaissance of Keynesian Economics', *Banco Nazionale del Lavoro Quarterly* 186.

Thurow, L. (1992) *Head to Head*, New York: William Morrow & Company, Inc.

Tomlinson, B.R. (1988) 'The Historical Roots of Indian Poverty: Issues in the Economic and Social History of Modern South Asia 1880–1960', *Modern Asian Studies* 22: 123–40.

Tomlinson, B.R. (1993) *The Economy of Modern India, 1860–1970*, Cambridge: Cambridge University Press.

Topik, S. (1987) *The Political Economy of the Brazilian State, 1889–1930*, Austin: University of Texas Press.

Tosta Filho, I. (1957) *Cocoa Economy in Brazil*, Rio de Janeiro.

Toye, J. (1993) 'Is There a New Political Economy of Development?' in C. Colclough and J. Manor (eds) *States or Markets? Neo-Liberalism and the Development Policy Debate*, Oxford: Clarendon Press.

Triandaphyllopoulos, K. (1924) *To Ellinikon Idiotikon Dikeon kata ton Endecaton Ennaton Eona*, Athens.

Triner, G.D. (1990) 'Brazilian Banks and the Economy, 1906–1918', unpublished MA thesis, Columbia University.

Tsoukalas, C. (1977) *Exartisi ke Anaparagogi, O kinonikos Rolos ton Ekpedeftikon Mihanismon stin Ellada (1830–1922)*, Athens.

Tsoukalas, C. (1981) *Kinoniki Anaptixi ke Kratos: i Sygrotisi tou Dimosiou Horou stin Ellada*, Athens.

Tyson, L. D. (1992) *Who's Bashing Whom?* Washington: Institute for International Economics.

Unger, R. M. (1983) *The Critical Legal Studies Movement*, Cambridge, MA: Harvard University Press.

UNICEF (1986) *Ghana: Adjustment Policies and Programs to Protect Children and other Vulnerable Groups*, Accra: UNICEF.

UNICEF/Government of Ghana (1990) 'The Situation of Women and Children in Africa', mimeo.

United Nations Organisation, Food and Agricultural Organisation (1961) 'The World Coffee Economy', *Commodity Bulletin Series* 33. Rome.

Van Ark, B. (1986) *Indonesian Export Growth and Economic Development: 117 Years of Empirical Evidence, 1823–1940*, Research Memorandum no. 189, Groningen: Faculty of Economics, Institute of Economic Research.

Van Delden Laerne, C. F. (1885) *Brazil and Java: Report on Coffee-culture in America, Asia and Africa*, The Hague.

Van der Eng, P. (1992) 'The Real Domestic Product of Indonesia, 1880–1989', *Explorations in Economic History* 29: 343–73.

Van Gelderen, J. (1939) *The Recent Development of Economic Foreign Policy in the Netherlands East Indies*, London: Longmans Green.

Van Wijnbergen, S. (1991) 'The Mexican Debt Deal', *Economic Policy* 12: 13–56.

Varian, H. (1989) 'Measuring the Deadweight Costs of DUP and Rent-seeking Activities', *Economics and Politics* 1.

Vasco, C. (1905) 'A indústria do algodão', *Boletim do Centro Industrial do Brasil*, 30 Dec.

Veblen, T. (1919) *The Place of Science in Modern Civilisation and Other Essays*, New York: Huebsch.

Vermeer, E.B. (1988) *Economic Development in Provincial China: The Central Shaanxi since 1930*, Cambridge: Cambridge University Press.

Wade, R. (1988) *Village Republics: Economic Conditions for Collective Action in South India*, Cambridge: Cambridge University Press.

Wade, R. (1990) *Governing the Market: Economic Theory and the Role of Government in East Asian Industrialisation*, Princeton: Princeton University Press.

Wahba, M. (1986) 'The Role of the State in the Egyptian Economy: 1945–1981' upublished PhD thesis, University of Oxford.

Wallis, J. J. and North, D C. (1986) 'Measuring the Transaction Sector in the American

Economy, 1870–1970', in S.L. Engerman and R.E. Gallman (eds) *Long-term Factors in American Economic Growth*, Chicago: University of Chicago Press.

Walras, L. (1926/1954) *Elements of Pure Economics*, London: George Allen & Unwin.

Warr, P.G. (1984) 'Exchange Rate Protection in Indonesia', *Bulletin of Indonesian Economic Studies* 20, 2: 53–89.

Washbrook, D.A. (1988) 'Progress and Problems: South Asian Economic and Social History c. 1720–1860', *Modern Asian Studies* 22: 57–96.

Weber, M. (1979) *Economy and Society: an Outline of Interpretive Sociology*, Berkeley: University of California Press.

Whitley, R. (1992) *Business Systems in East Asia: Firms, Markets and Societies*, London: Sage.

Wigley J. and Lipman, C. (1992) *The Enterprise Economy*, London, Macmillan.

Williams, E. (1964) *History of the People of Trinidad and Tobago*, London.

Williamson, O.E. (1975) *Markets and Hierarchies*, New York: Free Press.

Williamson, O.E. (1985) *The Economic Institutions of Capitalism*, New York: Free Press.

Williamson, O.E. (1986) *Economic Organisation: Firms, Markets and Policy Control*, Brighton: Wheatsheaf Books.

Willner, Ann Ruth (1981) 'Repetition in Change: Cyclical Movement and Indonesian Development', *Economic Development and Cultural Change* 29, 2: 409–17.

Wood, G.A.R. and Lass, R.A. (1989) *Cocoa*, London.

World Bank (1981) *Accelerated Development in Sub-Saharan Africa*, Washington, DC: World Bank.

World Bank (1983) *Egypt: Issues of Trade Strategy and Investment Planning*, Report No. 4136–EGT, Washington, DC.

World Bank (1986) 'Experience with Structural Adjustment Lending', Operations Evaluation Department draft.

World Bank (1988, 1990) *World Debt Tables 1987–88, 1989–1990*, New York: Oxford University Press for the World Bank.

World Bank (1989) *Sub-Saharan Africa, from Crisis to Sustainable Growth*, Washington, DC: World Bank.

World Bank (1991a) *Egypt: Alleviating Poverty During Structural Adjustment*, Grey Cover Report No. 8515–EGT, A World Bank Country Study: Washington DC.

World Bank (1991b) *Report and Recommendation of the President of the IBRD to the Executive Directors on a Proposed Structural Adjustment Loan in an Amount Equivalent to US $300 Million to the Arab Republic of Egypt*, Washington DC.

World Bank (1992) *ARE: Public Sector Investment Review*, Report No. 10064–EGT, Washington, DC.

World Development Report WDR (1980, 1981, 1982, 1983, 1985, 1986, 1988, 1990, 1991, 1992). New York: Oxford University Press for the World Bank.

Wray, L. Randall (1990) *Money and Credit in Capitalist Economies, the Endogenous Money Approach*, Aldershot: Edward Elgar.

Wright, H. (1907) *Theobroma Cacao, or Cocoa, its Botany, Cultivation, Chemistry and Diseases*, Colombo.

Wright, T. (ed.)(1992) *The Chinese Economy in the Early Twentieth Century: Recent Chinese Studies*, London: Macmillan.

Xu, Xinwu (1992) 'The Process of the Disintegration of Modern China's Natural Economy', in T. Wright (ed.) *The Chinese Economy in the Early Twentieth Century: Recent Chinese Studies*, London: Macmillan.

Yeebo, Z. (1991) *Ghana: The Struggle for Popular Power, Rawlings: Saviour or Demagogue*, London: Beacon Press.

Yiannitsis, A.K. (1977) 'I Xenes Amesses Ependysis ke i Diamorfossi tis Neoellinikis Economias', *Epitheorisis Kinonikon Erevnon* 30/1, 2–3.

Zimmerman, S. (1969) *Theodor Wille, 1844–1969*, Hamburg.
Zolotas, X. (1928) *Nomismatika kai Sinallagmatika Phenomena stin Ellada: 1910–1927*, Athens.
Zolotas, X. (1964) *E Ellada is to Stadion tis Ekviomihanisseos*, Athens.
Zysman J. (1983) *Governments, Markets and Growth*, Ithaca and London: Cornell University Press.

INDEX